S0-BMV-581

STOP!

This is the back of the book.
You wouldn't want to spoil a great ending!

This book is printed "manga-style," in the authentic Japanese right-to-left format. Since none of the artwork has been flipped or altered, readers get to experience the story just as the creator intended. You've been asking for it, so TOKYOPOP® delivered: authentic, hot-off-the-press, and far more fun!

DIRECTIONS

If this is your first time reading manga-style, here's a quick guide to help you understand how it works.

It's easy... just start in the top right panel and follow the numbers. Have fun, and look for more 100% authentic manga from TOKYOPOP®!

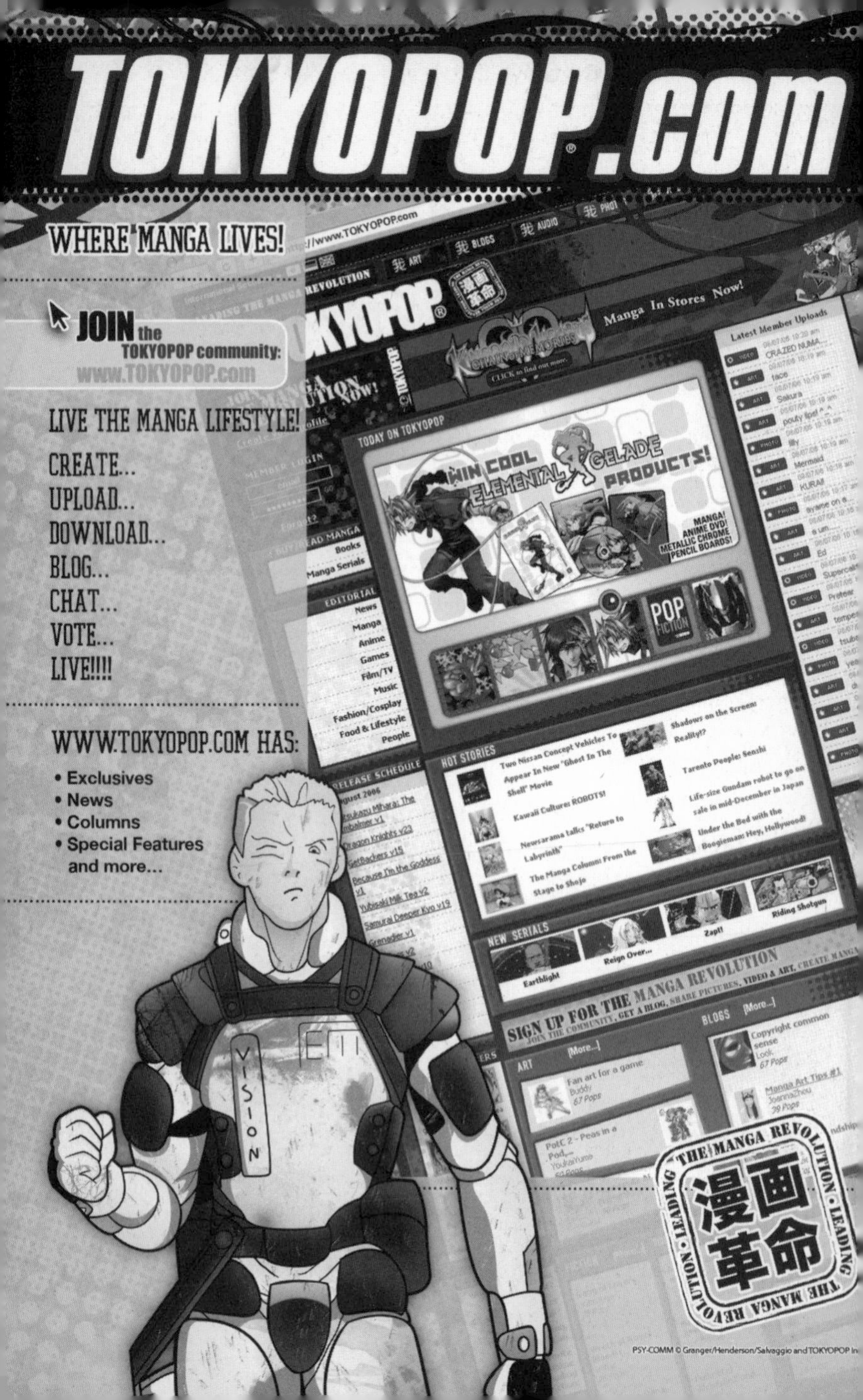
TOKYOPOP®.com
WHERE MANGA LIVES!
JOIN the TOKYOPOP community:
www.TOKYOPOP.com
LIVE THE MANGA LIFESTYLE!
CREATE...
UPLOAD...
DOWNLOAD...
BLOG...
CHAT...
VOTE...
LIVE!!!!
WWW.TOKYOPOP.COM HAS:
• Exclusives
• News
• Columns
• Special Features and more...
THE MANGA REVOLUTION • LEADING THE MANGA REVOLUTION • LEADING
漫画革命
PSY-COMM © Granger/Henderson/Salvaggio and TOKYOPOP Inc.

Doing high fashion **JUST FOR KICKS!**

GothicSports ™

Anya is a tenth grader adjusting to a brand new school. When she tries to join the sports teams she's rejected...so she forms her own, complete with cool, eye-catching uniforms. Thus begins the first Gothic-Lolita soccer team!

© Anike Hage / TOKYOPOP GmbH. All rights reserved

DRAMA

T
TEEN
AGE 13+

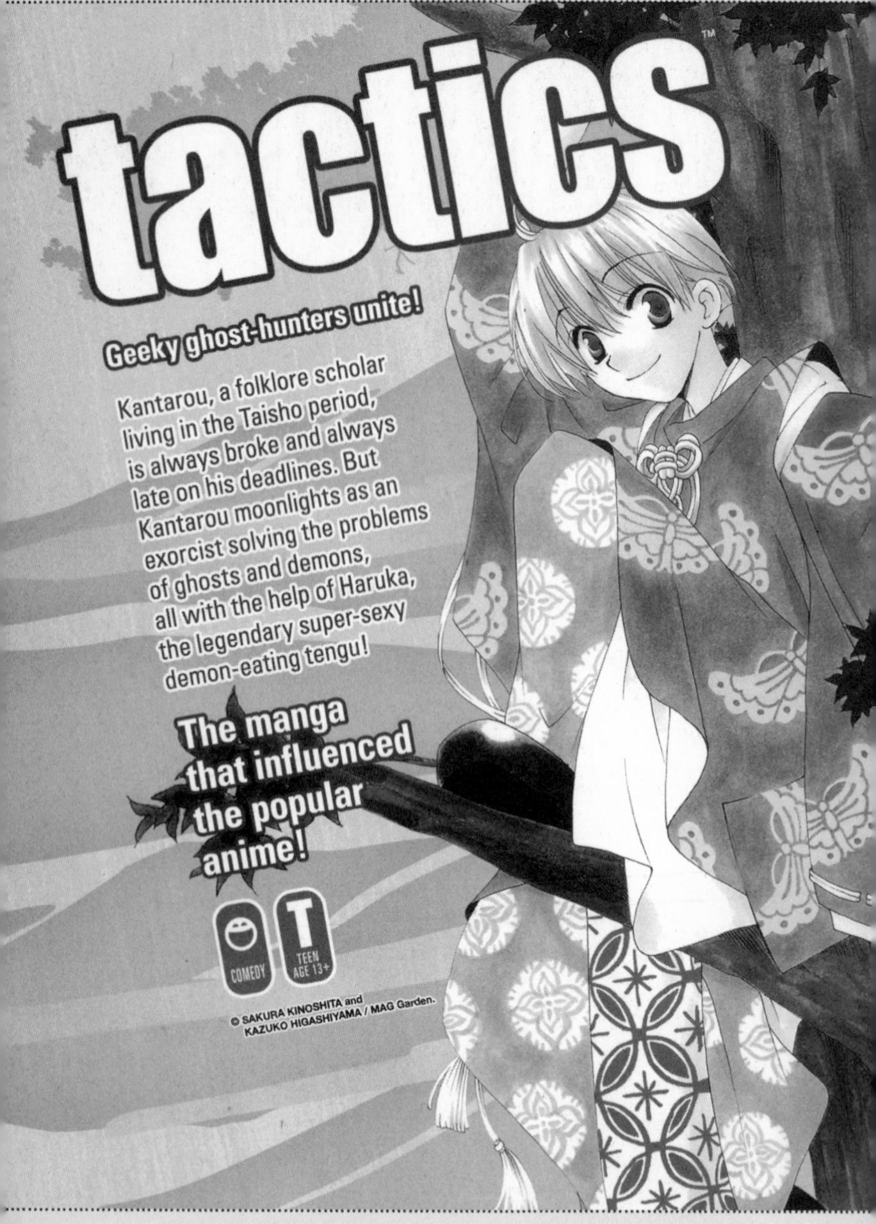
tactics™
Geeky ghost-hunters unite!
Kantarou, a folklore scholar
living in the Taisho period,
is always broke and always
late on his deadlines. But
Kantarou moonlights as an
exorcist solving the problems
of ghosts and demons,
all with the help of Haruka,
the legendary super-sexy
demon-eating tengu!
The manga
that influenced
the popular
anime!
COMEDY
T
TEEN
AGE 13+
© SAKURA KINOSHITA and
KAZUKO HIGASHIYAMA / MAG Garden.

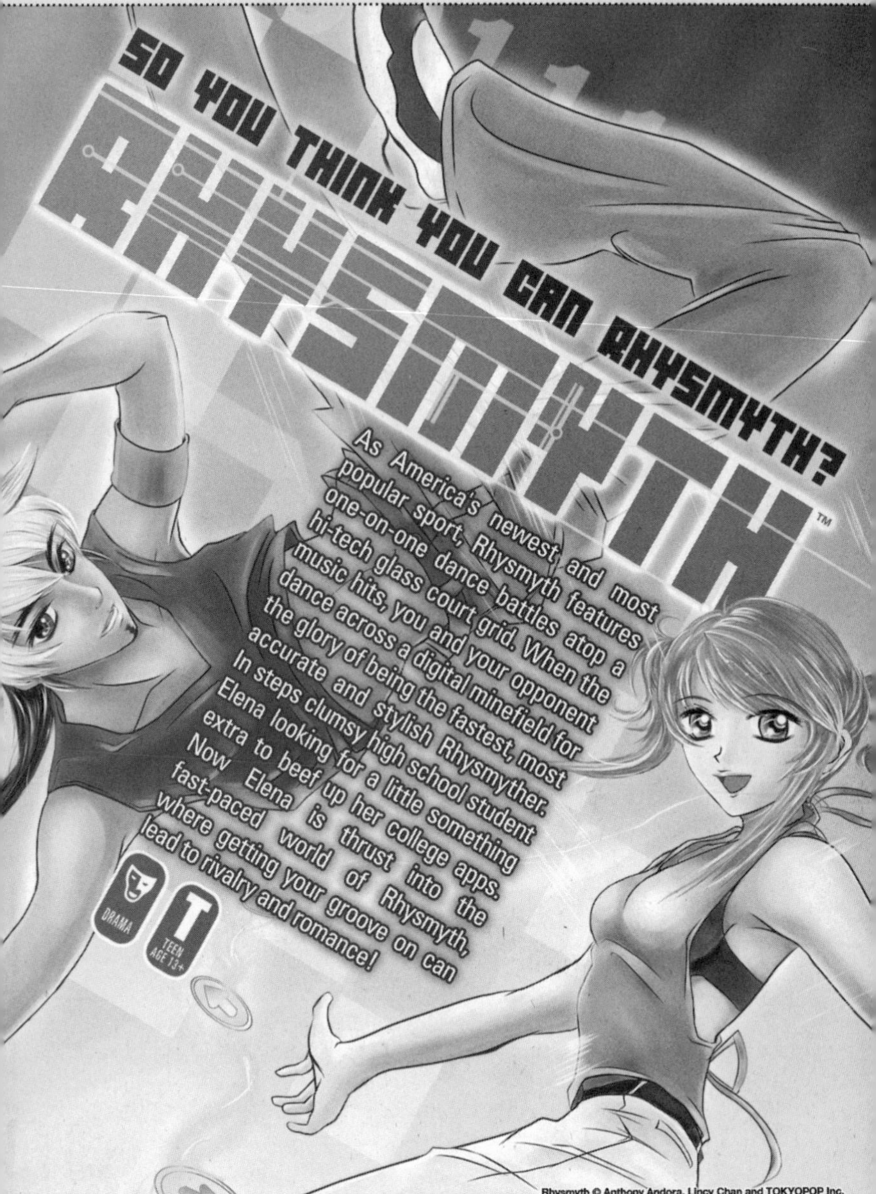
SO YOU THINK YOU CAN RHYSMYTH?
RHYSMYTH™
As America's newest and most popular sport, Rhysmyth features one-on-one dance battles atop a hi-tech glass court grid. When the music hits, you and your opponent dance across a digital minefield for the glory of being the fastest, most accurate and stylish Rhysmyther. In steps clumsy high school student Elena looking for a little something extra to beef up her college apps. Now Elena is thrust into the fast-paced world of Rhysmyth, where getting your groove on can lead to rivalry and romance!
DRAMA
T TEEN AGE 13+
Rhysmyth © Anthony Andora, Lincy Chan and TOKYOPOP Inc.

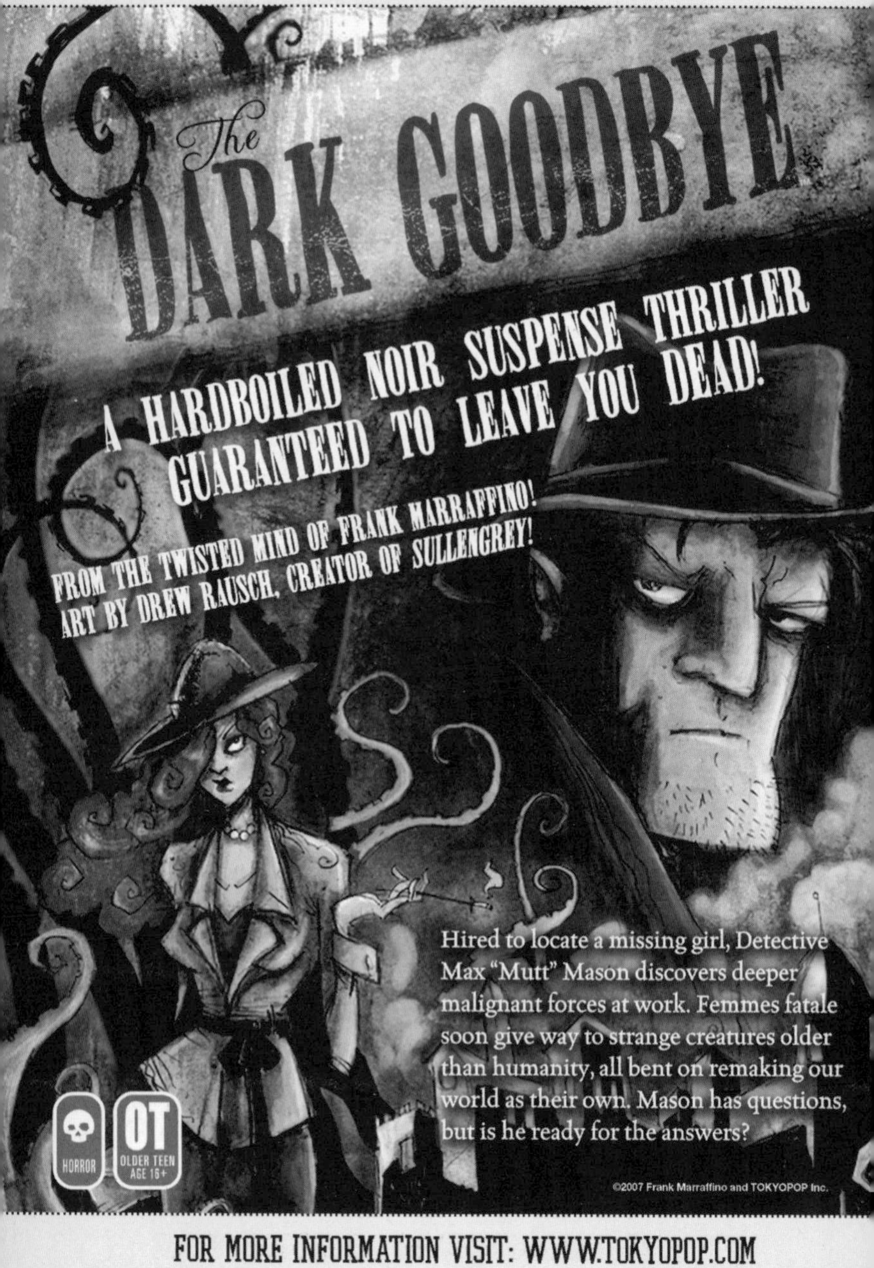
The DARK GOODBYE
A HARDBOILED NOIR SUSPENSE THRILLER GUARANTEED TO LEAVE YOU DEAD!
FROM THE TWISTED MIND OF FRANK MARRAFFINO!
ART BY DREW RAUSCH, CREATOR OF SULLENGREY!
Hired to locate a missing girl, Detective Max "Mutt" Mason discovers deeper malignant forces at work. Femmes fatale soon give way to strange creatures older than humanity, all bent on remaking our world as their own. Mason has questions, but is he ready for the answers?
HORROR
OT
OLDER TEEN AGE 16+
©2007 Frank Marraffino and TOKYOPOP Inc.

RG
聖
VEDA
伝

VOLUME 9

BY
CLAMP

HAMBURG // LONDON // LOS ANGELES // TOKYO

RG Veda Vol. 9
created by CLAMP

Translation - Haruko Furukawa
English Adaptation - Christine Schilling
Copy Editor - Stephanie Duchin
Retouch and Lettering - Star Print Brokers
Production Artist - Gavin Hignight
Cover Layout - James Lee

Editor - Hope Donovan
Digital Imaging Manager - Chris Buford
Pre-Production Supervisor - Erika Terriquez
Art Director - Anne Marie Horne
Production Manager - Elizabeth Brizzi
Managing Editor - Vy Nguyen
VP of Production - Ron Klamert
Editor-In-Chief - Rob Tokar
Publisher - Mike Kiley
President and C.O.O. - John Parker
C.E.O. and Chief Creative Officer - Stuart Levy

A  Manga

TOKYOPOP Inc.
5900 Wilshire Blvd. Suite 2000
Los Angeles, CA 90036

E-mail: info@TOKYOPOP.com
Come visit us online at www.TOKYOPOP.com

ISBN: 978-1-59532-492-4

First TOKYOPOP printing: April 2007
10 9 8 7 6 5 4 3 2 1
Printed in the USA

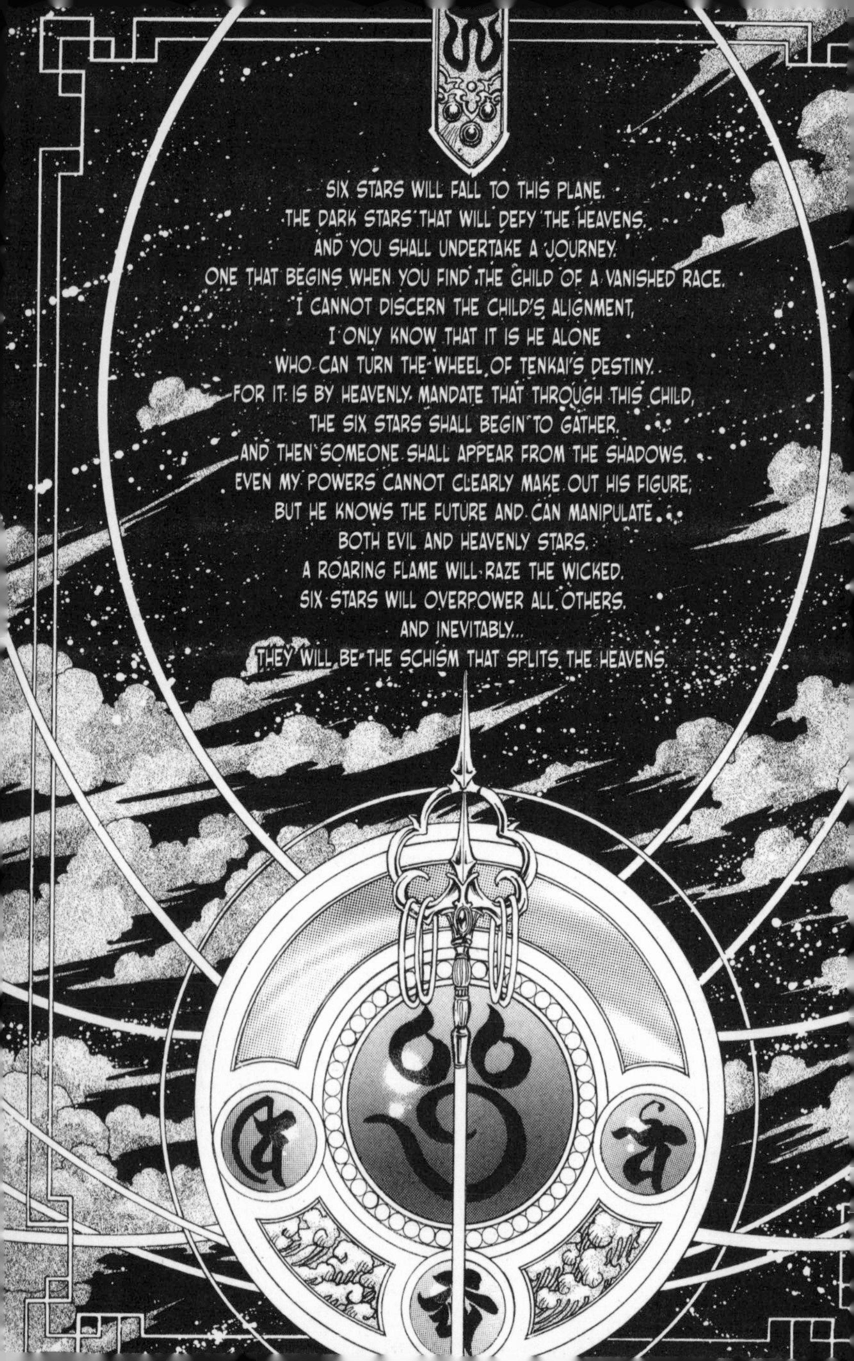
SIX STARS WILL FALL TO THIS PLANE.
THE DARK STARS THAT WILL DEFY THE HEAVENS.
AND YOU SHALL UNDERTAKE A JOURNEY.
ONE THAT BEGINS WHEN YOU FIND THE CHILD OF A VANISHED RACE.
I CANNOT DISCERN THE CHILD'S ALIGNMENT,
I ONLY KNOW THAT IT IS HE ALONE
WHO CAN TURN THE WHEEL OF TENKAI'S DESTINY.
FOR IT IS BY HEAVENLY MANDATE THAT THROUGH THIS CHILD,
THE SIX STARS SHALL BEGIN TO GATHER.
AND THEN SOMEONE SHALL APPEAR FROM THE SHADOWS.
EVEN MY POWERS CANNOT CLEARLY MAKE OUT HIS FIGURE;
BUT HE KNOWS THE FUTURE AND CAN MANIPULATE
BOTH EVIL AND HEAVENLY STARS.
A ROARING FLAME WILL RAZE THE WICKED.
SIX STARS WILL OVERPOWER ALL OTHERS.
AND INEVITABLY...
THEY WILL BE THE SCHISM THAT SPLITS THE HEAVENS.

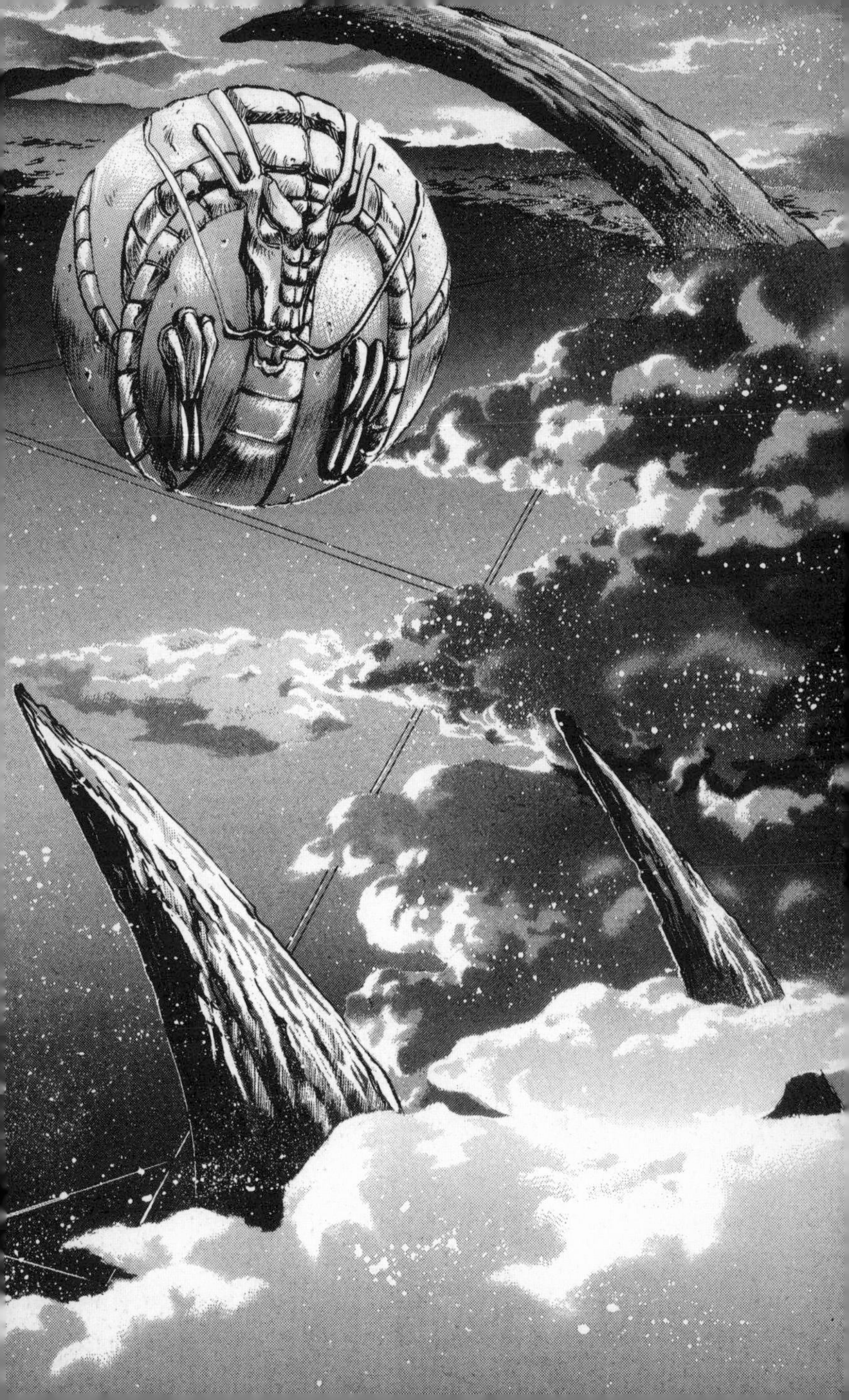

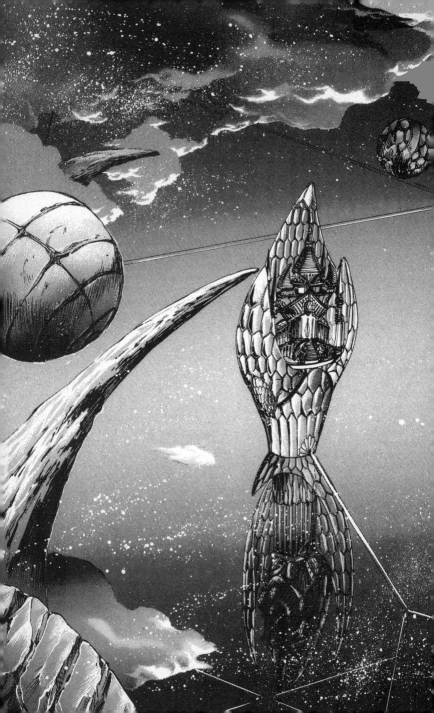

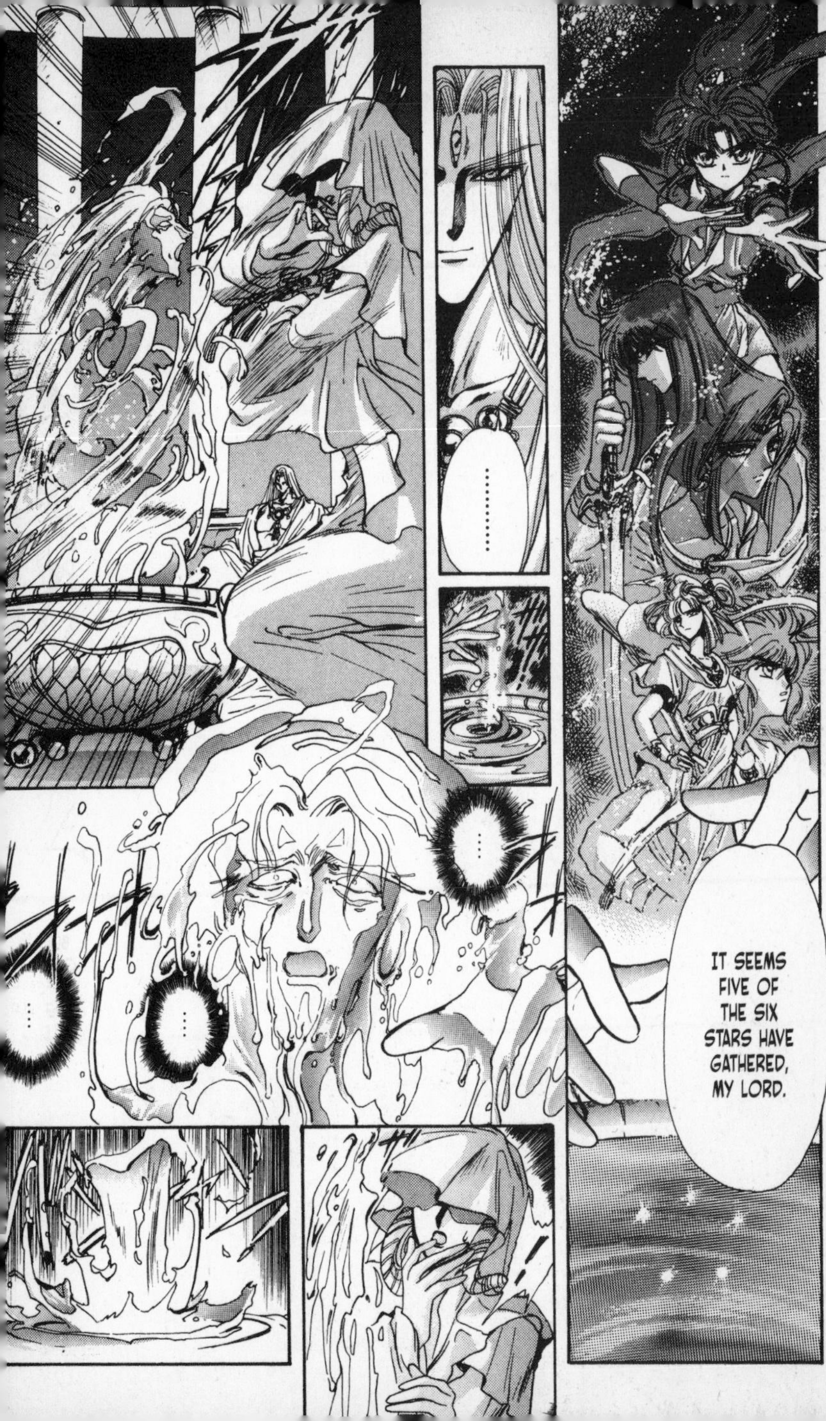
......
IT SEEMS FIVE OF THE SIX STARS HAVE GATHERED, MY LORD.
...
...
...

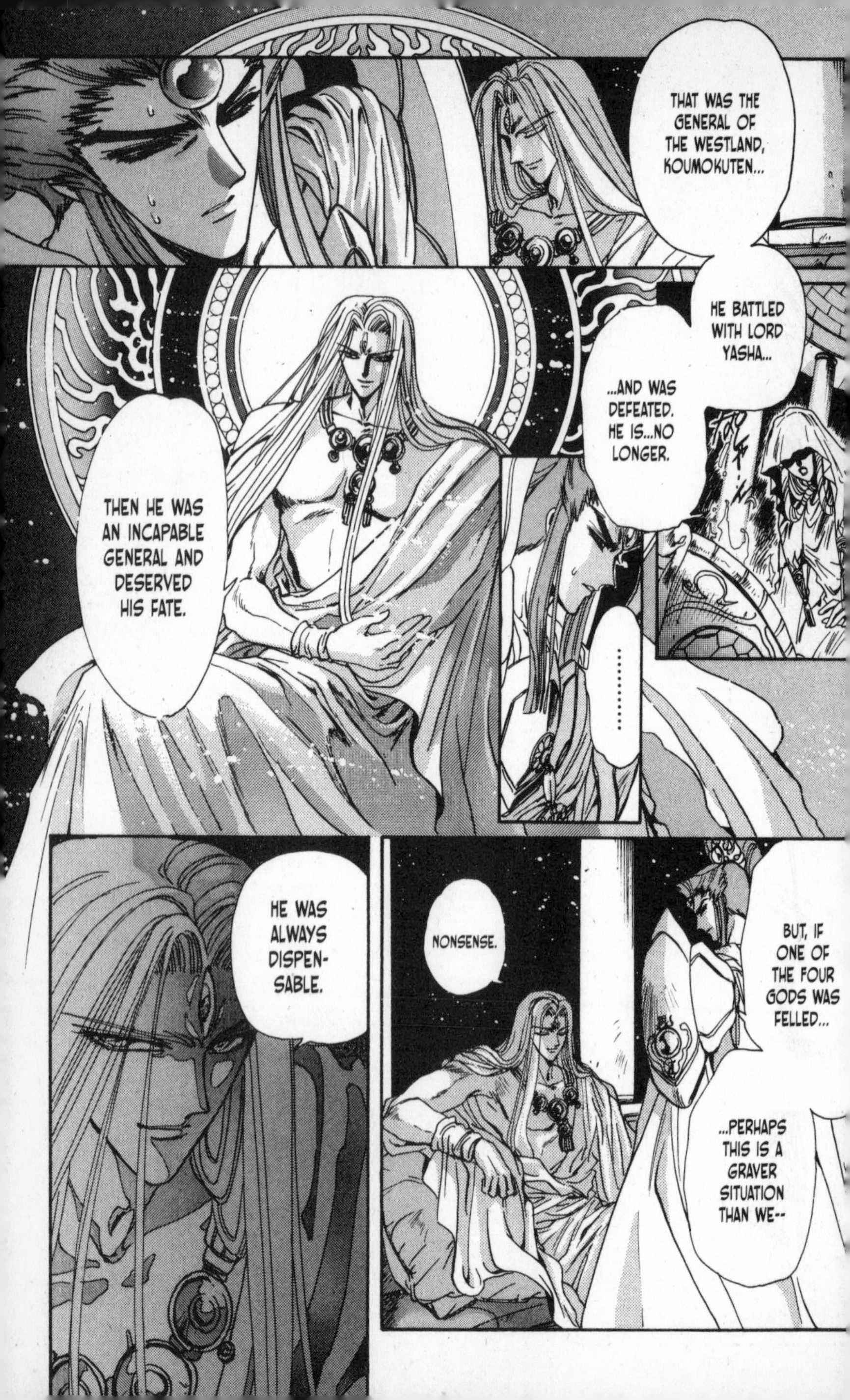
THAT WAS THE GENERAL OF THE WESTLAND, KOUMOKUTEN...
HE BATTLED WITH LORD YASHA...
...AND WAS DEFEATED. HE IS...NO LONGER.
THEN HE WAS AN INCAPABLE GENERAL AND DESERVED HIS FATE.
......
BUT, IF ONE OF THE FOUR GODS WAS FELLED...
...PERHAPS THIS IS A GRAVER SITUATION THAN WE--
NONSENSE.
HE WAS ALWAYS DISPENSABLE.

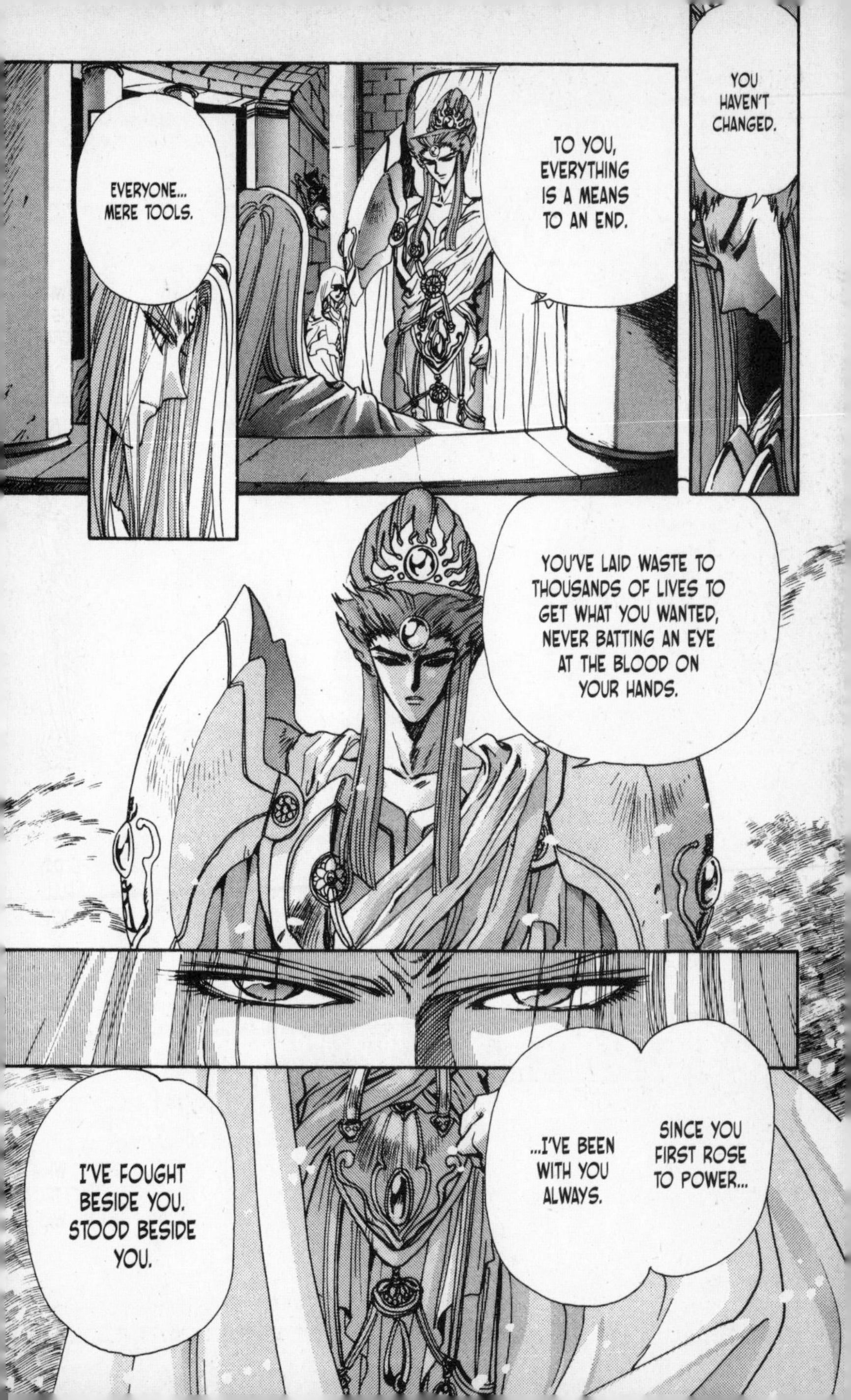
YOU HAVEN'T CHANGED.
TO YOU, EVERYTHING IS A MEANS TO AN END.
EVERYONE... MERE TOOLS.
YOU'VE LAID WASTE TO THOUSANDS OF LIVES TO GET WHAT YOU WANTED, NEVER BATTING AN EYE AT THE BLOOD ON YOUR HANDS.
SINCE YOU FIRST ROSE TO POWER...
...I'VE BEEN WITH YOU ALWAYS.
I'VE FOUGHT BESIDE YOU. STOOD BESIDE YOU.

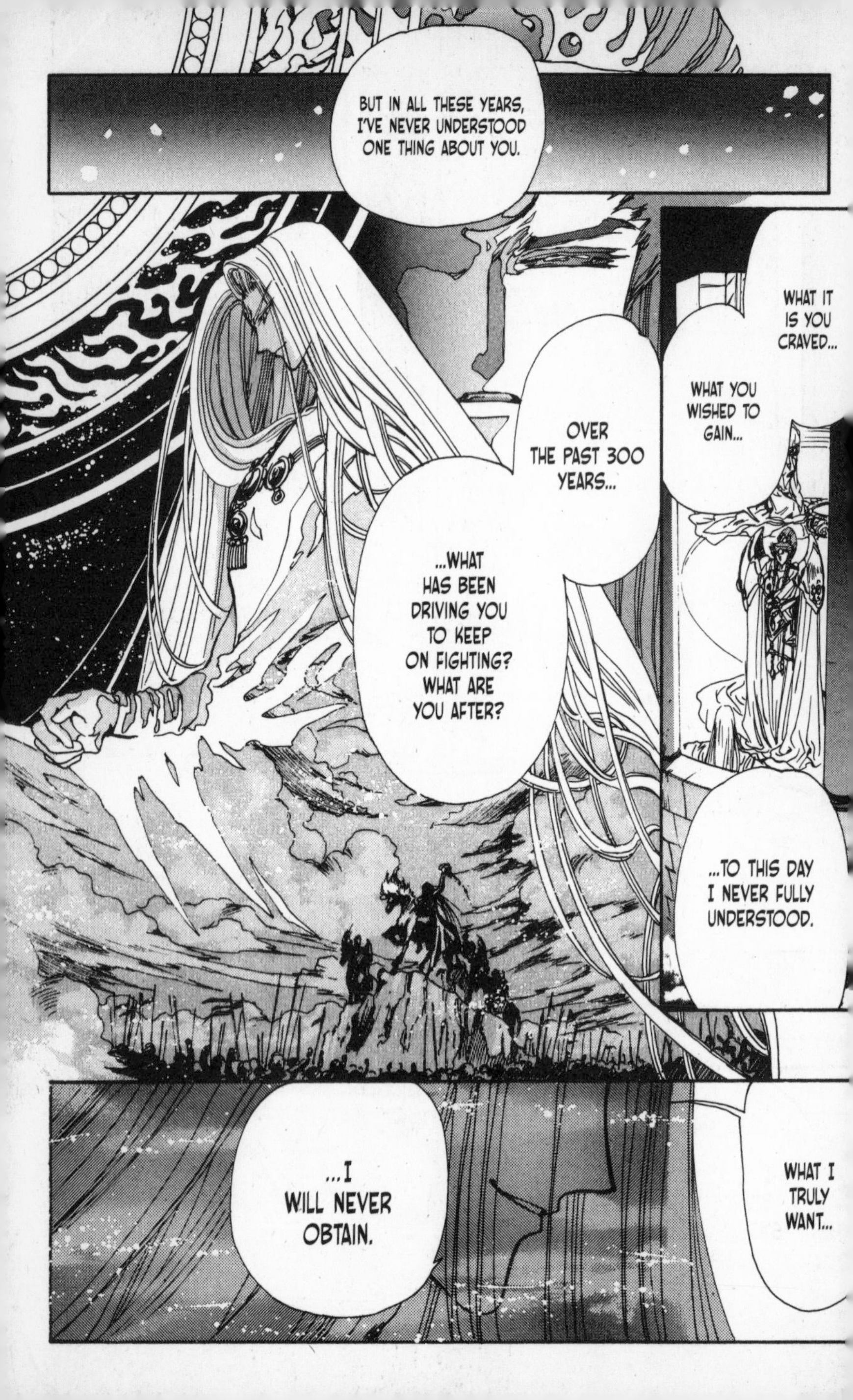
BUT IN ALL THESE YEARS, I'VE NEVER UNDERSTOOD ONE THING ABOUT YOU.
WHAT IT IS YOU CRAVED...
WHAT YOU WISHED TO GAIN...
...TO THIS DAY I NEVER FULLY UNDERSTOOD.
OVER THE PAST 300 YEARS...
...WHAT HAS BEEN DRIVING YOU TO KEEP ON FIGHTING? WHAT ARE YOU AFTER?
WHAT I TRULY WANT...
...I WILL NEVER OBTAIN.

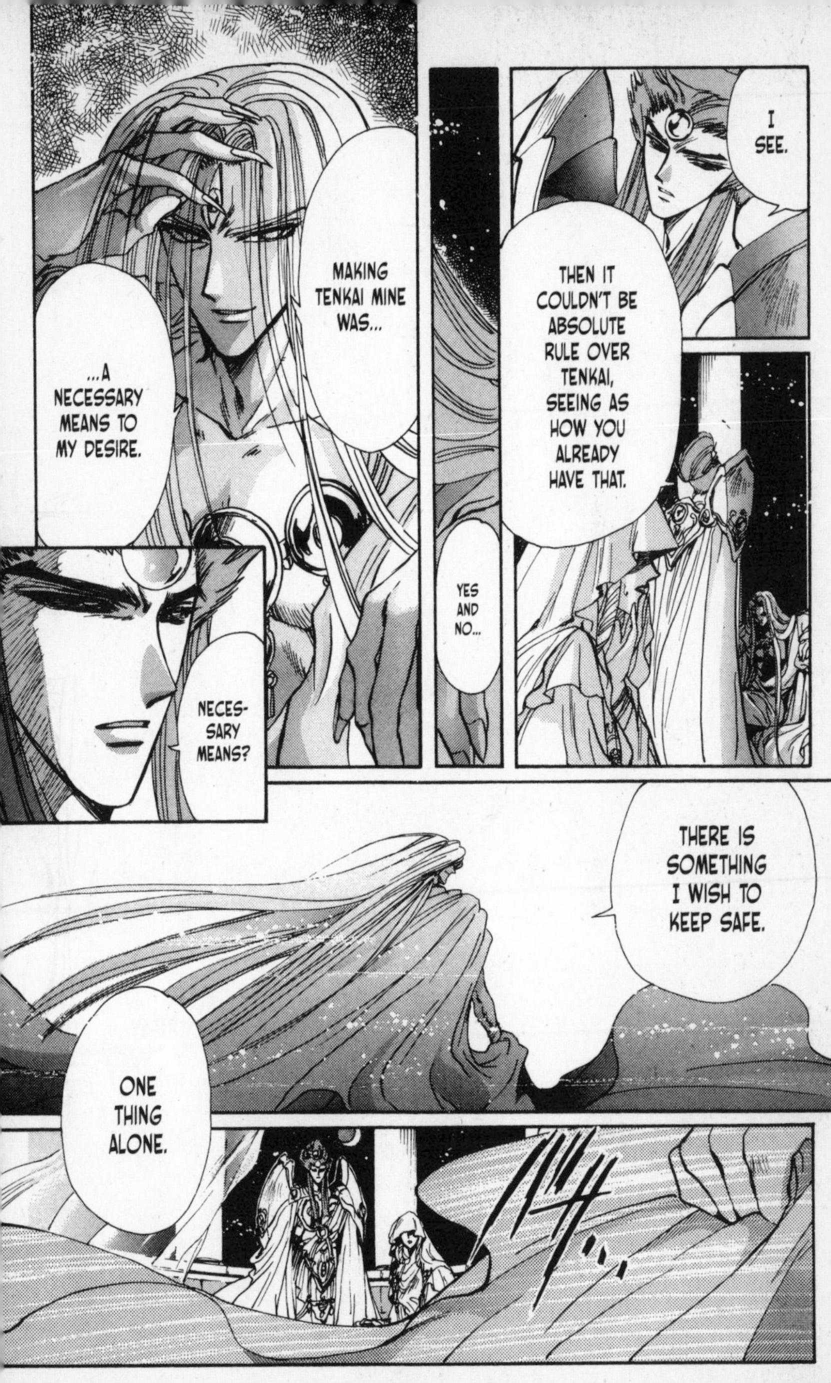
I SEE.
THEN IT COULDN'T BE ABSOLUTE RULE OVER TENKAI, SEEING AS HOW YOU ALREADY HAVE THAT.
YES AND NO...
MAKING TENKAI MINE WAS...
...A NECESSARY MEANS TO MY DESIRE.
NECES-SARY MEANS?
THERE IS SOMETHING I WISH TO KEEP SAFE.
ONE THING ALONE.

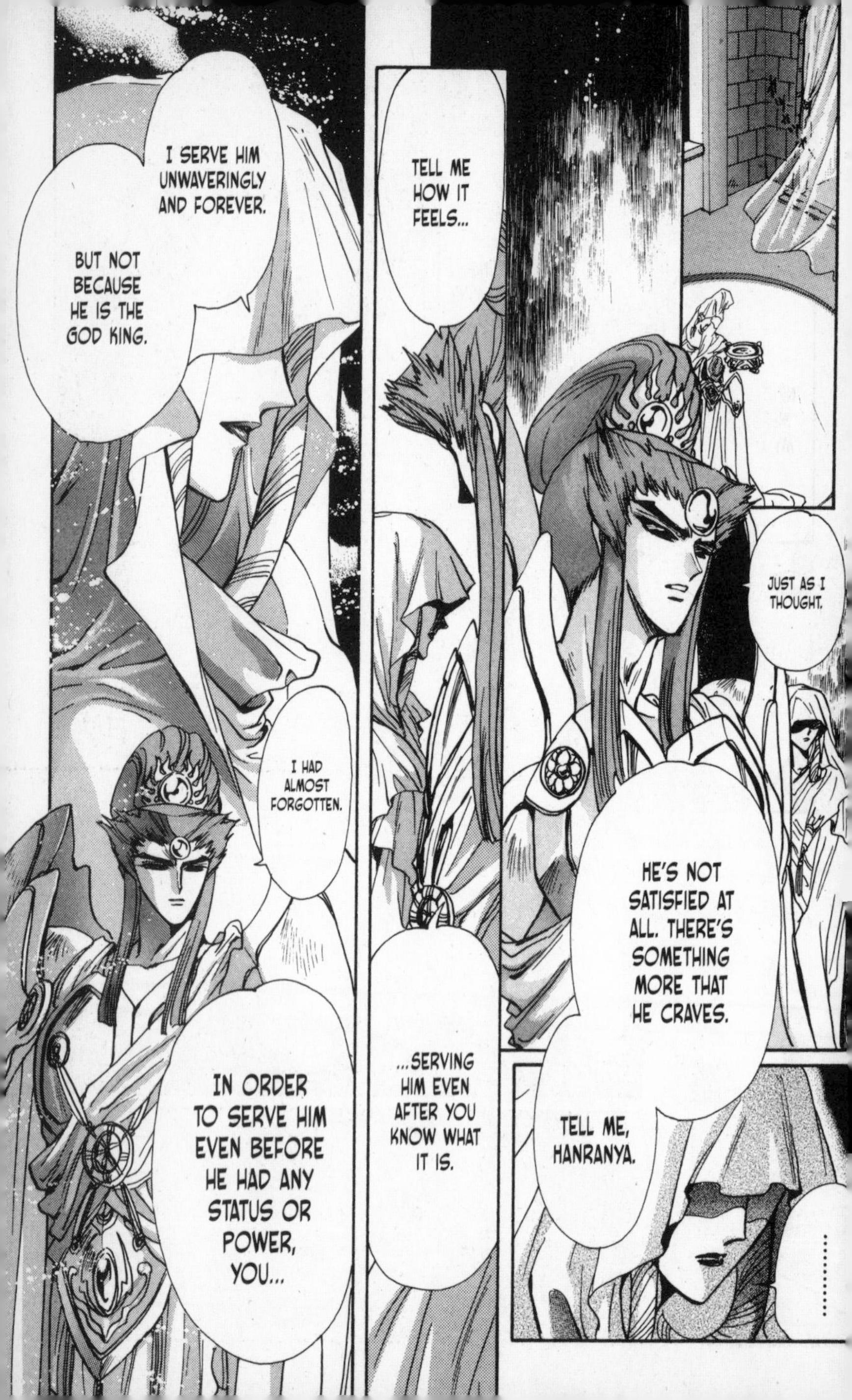
JUST AS I THOUGHT.
HE'S NOT SATISFIED AT ALL. THERE'S SOMETHING MORE THAT HE CRAVES.
TELL ME, HANRANYA.
......
TELL ME HOW IT FEELS...
...SERVING HIM EVEN AFTER YOU KNOW WHAT IT IS.
I SERVE HIM UNWAVERINGLY AND FOREVER.
BUT NOT BECAUSE HE IS THE GOD KING.
I HAD ALMOST FORGOTTEN.
IN ORDER TO SERVE HIM EVEN BEFORE HE HAD ANY STATUS OR POWER, YOU...

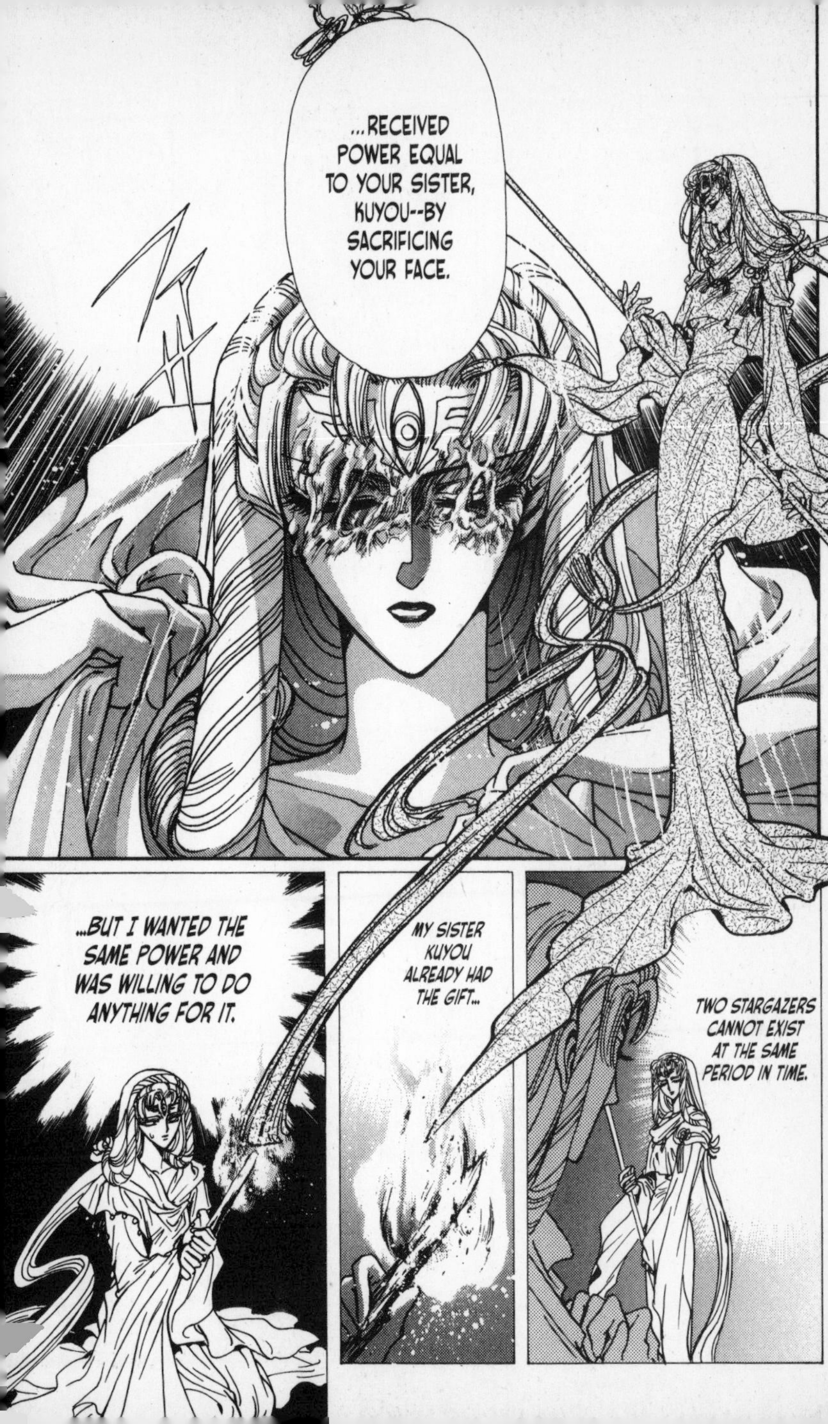
...RECEIVED POWER EQUAL TO YOUR SISTER, KUYOU--BY SACRIFICING YOUR FACE.
TWO STARGAZERS CANNOT EXIST AT THE SAME PERIOD IN TIME.
MY SISTER KUYOU ALREADY HAD THE GIFT...
...BUT I WANTED THE SAME POWER AND WAS WILLING TO DO ANYTHING FOR IT.

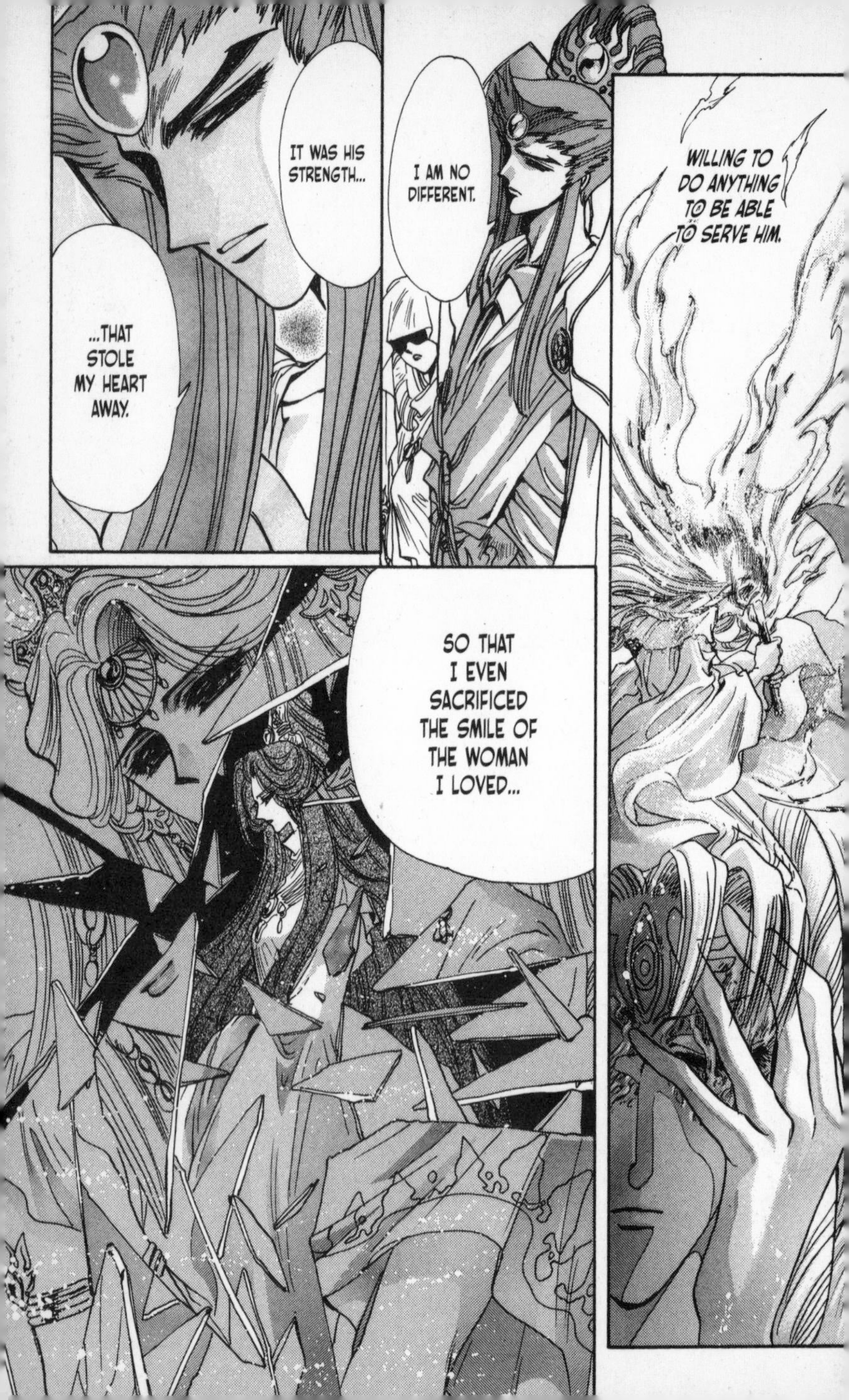
WILLING TO DO ANYTHING TO BE ABLE TO SERVE HIM.
I AM NO DIFFERENT.
IT WAS HIS STRENGTH...
...THAT STOLE MY HEART AWAY.
SO THAT I EVEN SACRIFICED THE SMILE OF THE WOMAN I LOVED...

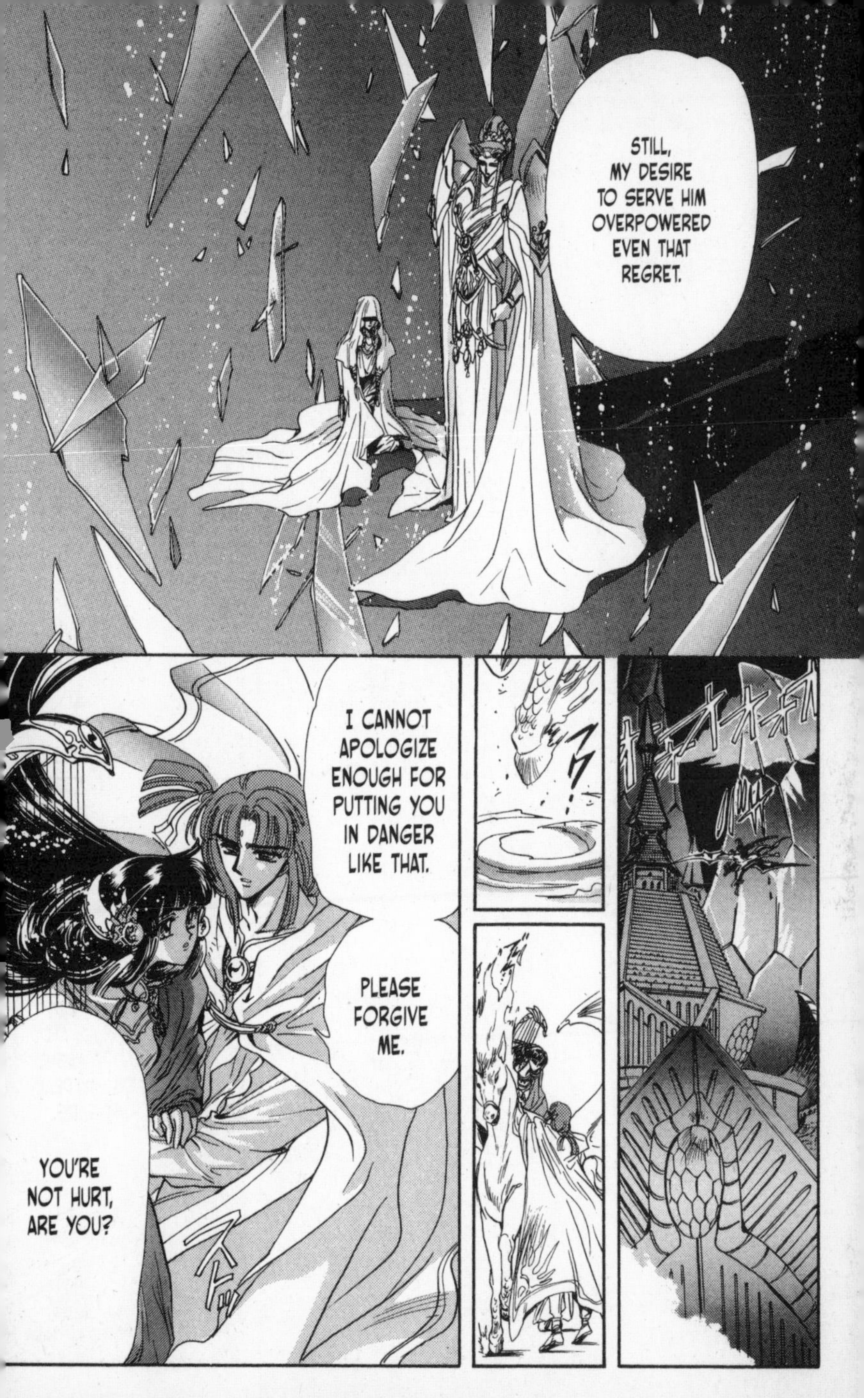
STILL, MY DESIRE TO SERVE HIM OVERPOWERED EVEN THAT REGRET.
I CANNOT APOLOGIZE ENOUGH FOR PUTTING YOU IN DANGER LIKE THAT.
PLEASE FORGIVE ME.
YOU'RE NOT HURT, ARE YOU?

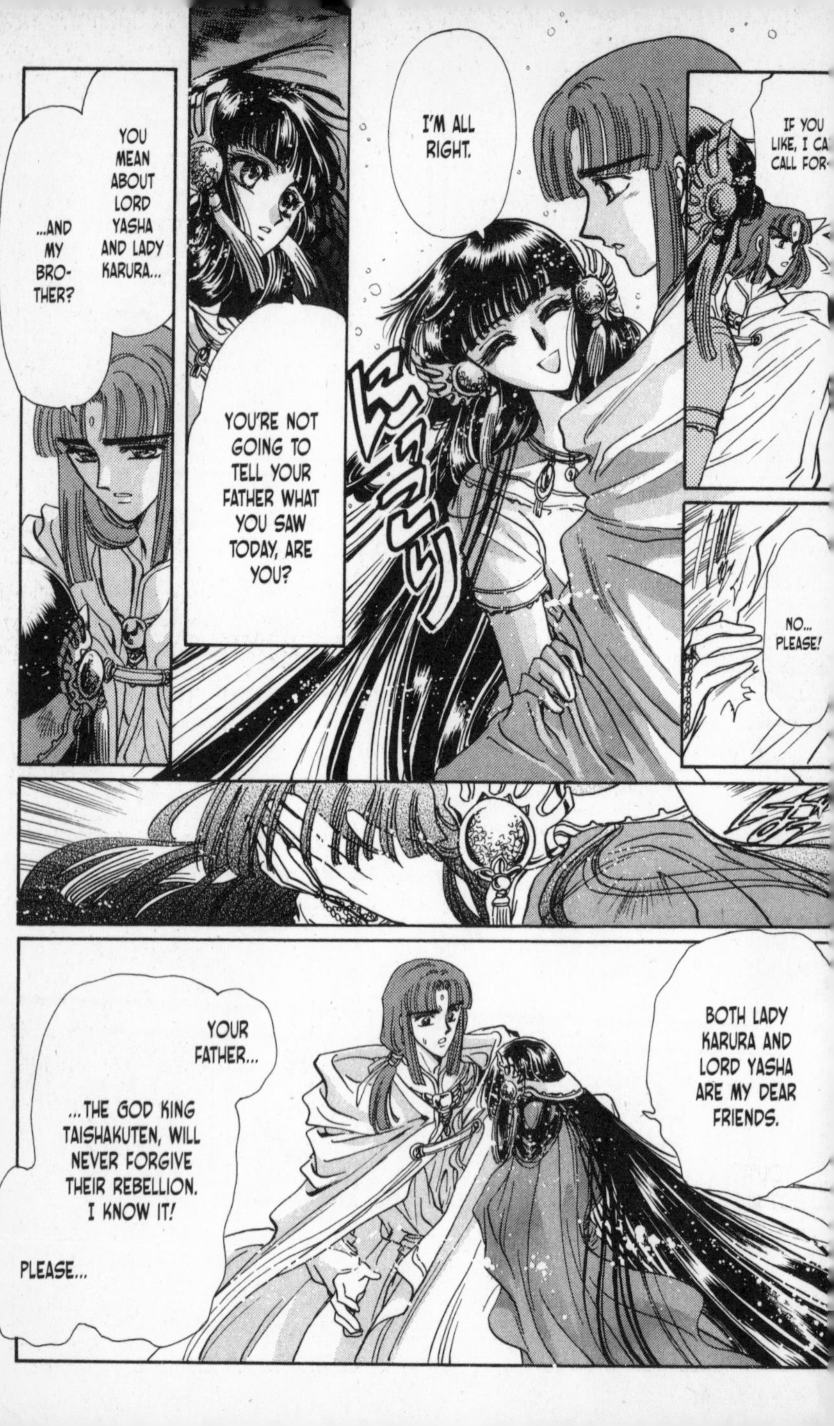
IF YOU LIKE, I CA CALL FOR-
NO... PLEASE!
I'M ALL RIGHT.
YOU'RE NOT GOING TO TELL YOUR FATHER WHAT YOU SAW TODAY, ARE YOU?
YOU MEAN ABOUT LORD YASHA AND LADY KARURA...
...AND MY BROTHER?
BOTH LADY KARURA AND LORD YASHA ARE MY DEAR FRIENDS.
YOUR FATHER...
...THE GOD KING TAISHAKUTEN, WILL NEVER FORGIVE THEIR REBELLION. I KNOW IT!
PLEASE...

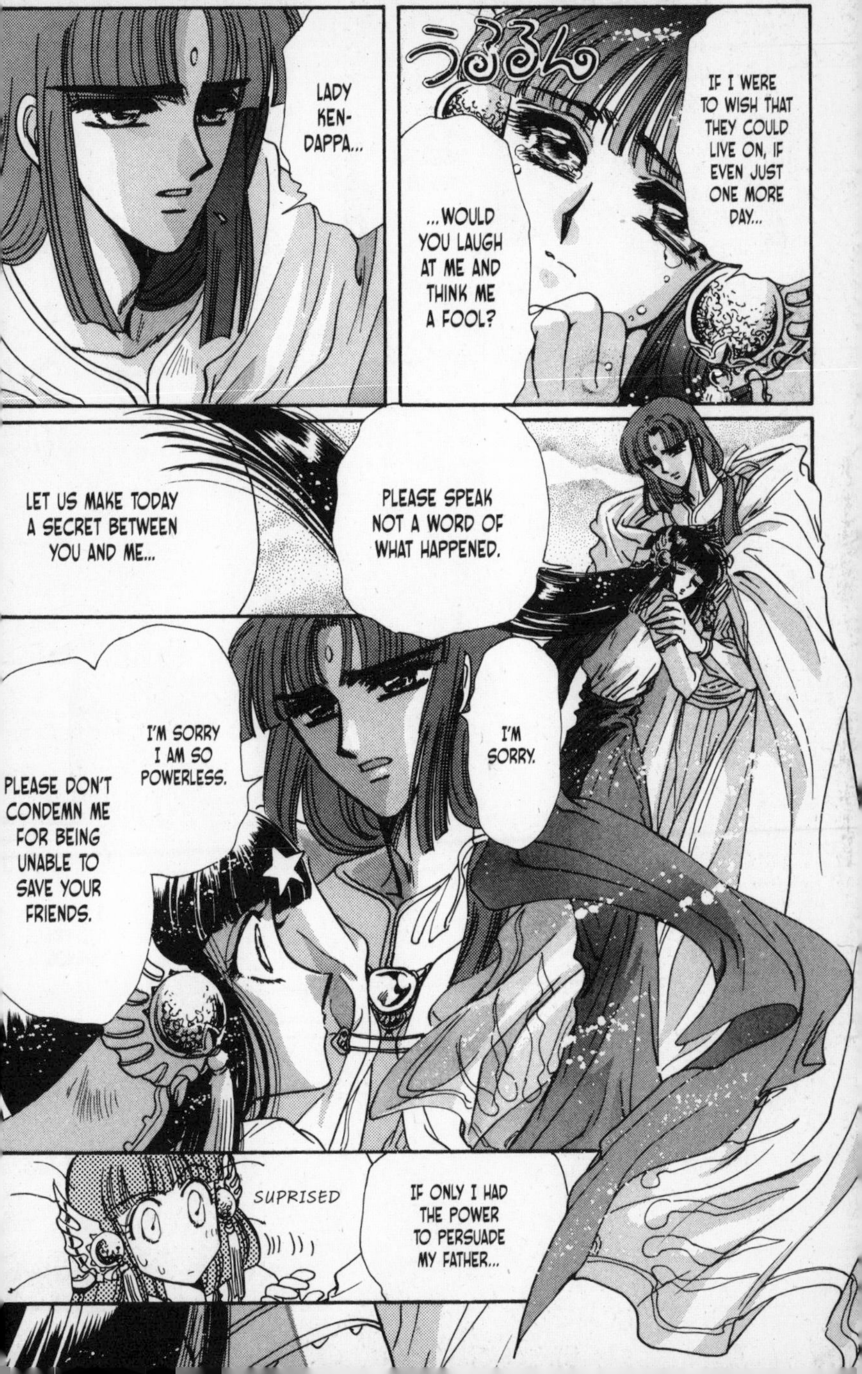
うるるん
IF I WERE TO WISH THAT THEY COULD LIVE ON, IF EVEN JUST ONE MORE DAY...
...WOULD YOU LAUGH AT ME AND THINK ME A FOOL?
LADY KEN-DAPPA...
PLEASE SPEAK NOT A WORD OF WHAT HAPPENED.
LET US MAKE TODAY A SECRET BETWEEN YOU AND ME...
I'M SORRY.
I'M SORRY I AM SO POWERLESS.
PLEASE DON'T CONDEMN ME FOR BEING UNABLE TO SAVE YOUR FRIENDS.
IF ONLY I HAD THE POWER TO PERSUADE MY FATHER...
SUPRISED

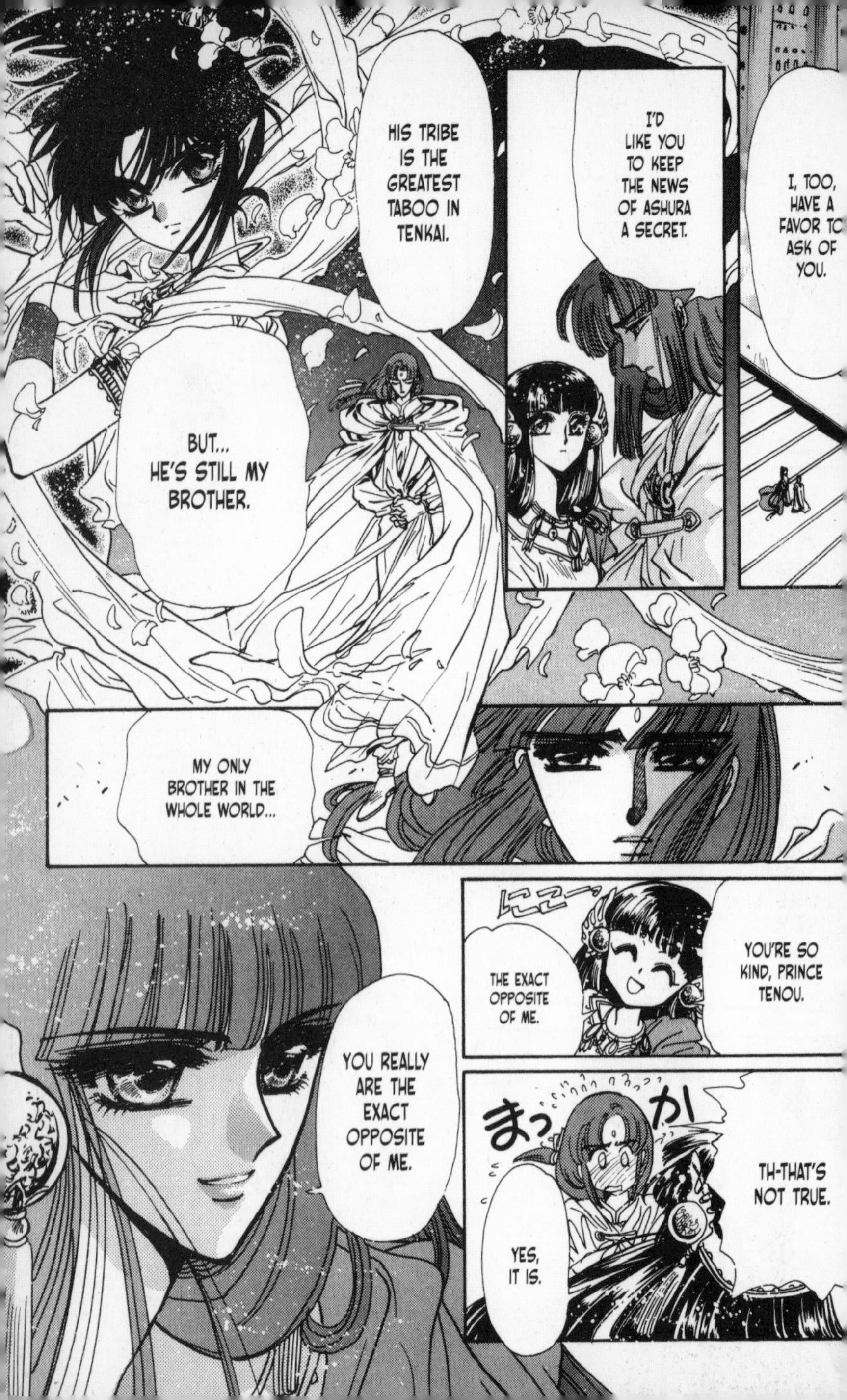
I, TOO, HAVE A FAVOR TO ASK OF YOU.
I'D LIKE YOU TO KEEP THE NEWS OF ASHURA A SECRET.
HIS TRIBE IS THE GREATEST TABOO IN TENKAI.
BUT... HE'S STILL MY BROTHER.
MY ONLY BROTHER IN THE WHOLE WORLD...
YOU'RE SO KIND, PRINCE TENOU.
THE EXACT OPPOSITE OF ME.
まっか
TH-THAT'S NOT TRUE.
YES, IT IS.
YOU REALLY ARE THE EXACT OPPOSITE OF ME.

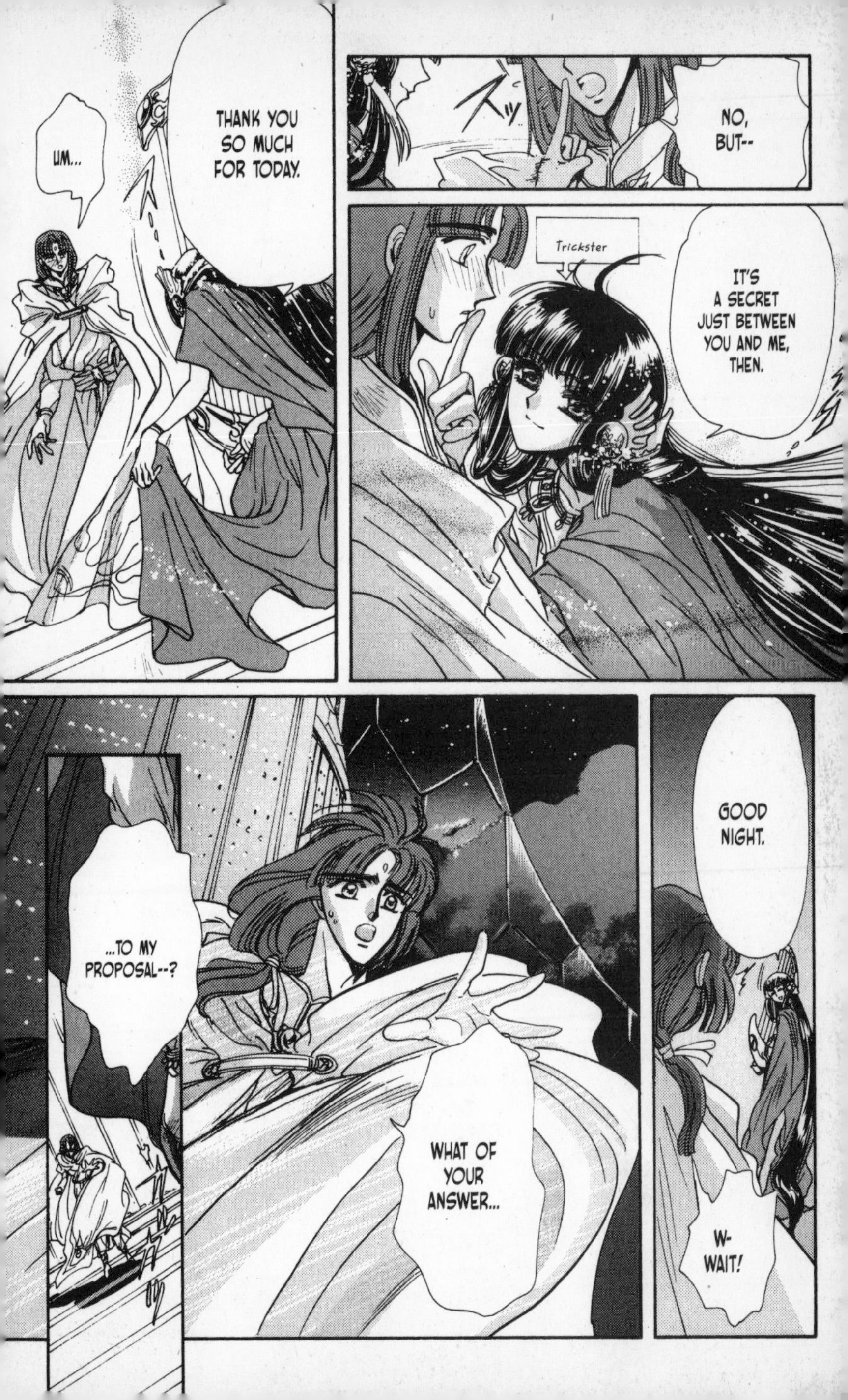
NO, BUT--
スッ..
Trickster
IT'S A SECRET JUST BETWEEN YOU AND ME, THEN.
THANK YOU SO MUCH FOR TODAY.
UM...
GOOD NIGHT.
W-WAIT!
WHAT OF YOUR ANSWER...
...TO MY PROPOSAL--?

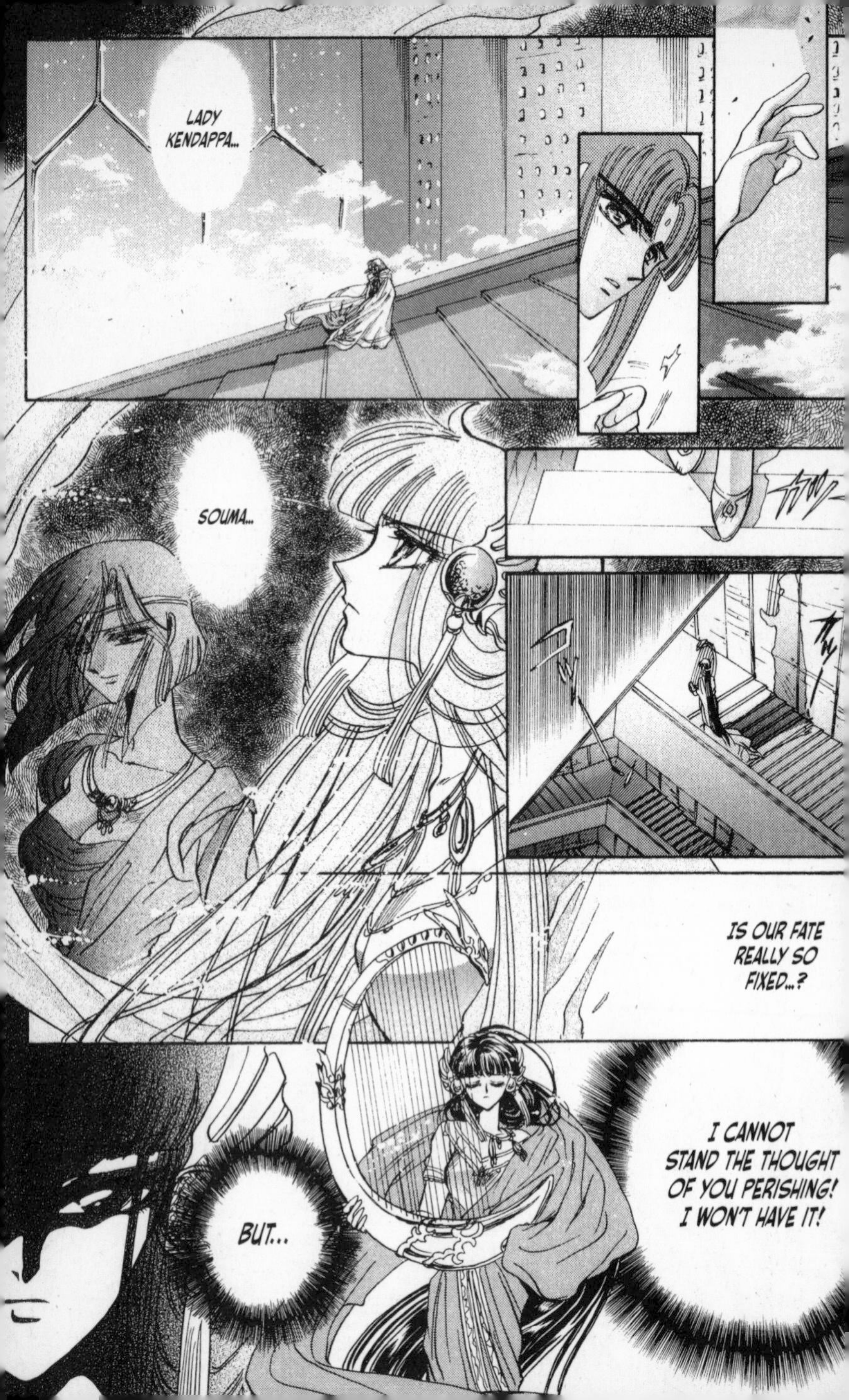
LADY KENDAPPA...
SOUMA...
IS OUR FATE REALLY SO FIXED...?
I CANNOT STAND THE THOUGHT OF YOU PERISHING! I WON'T HAVE IT!
BUT...

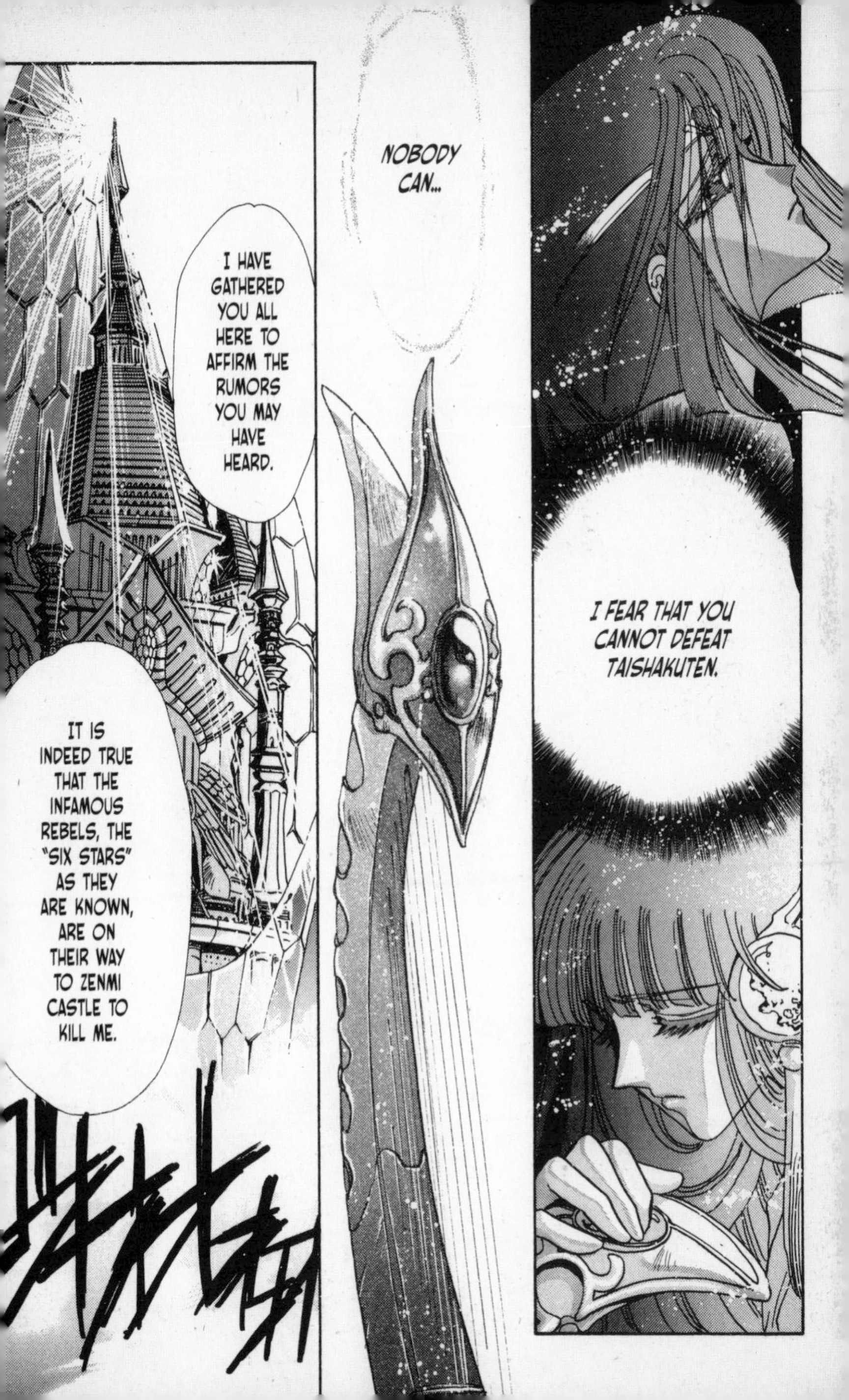
I FEAR THAT YOU CANNOT DEFEAT TAISHAKUTEN.
NOBODY CAN...
I HAVE GATHERED YOU ALL HERE TO AFFIRM THE RUMORS YOU MAY HAVE HEARD.
IT IS INDEED TRUE THAT THE INFAMOUS REBELS, THE "SIX STARS" AS THEY ARE KNOWN, ARE ON THEIR WAY TO ZENMI CASTLE TO KILL ME.

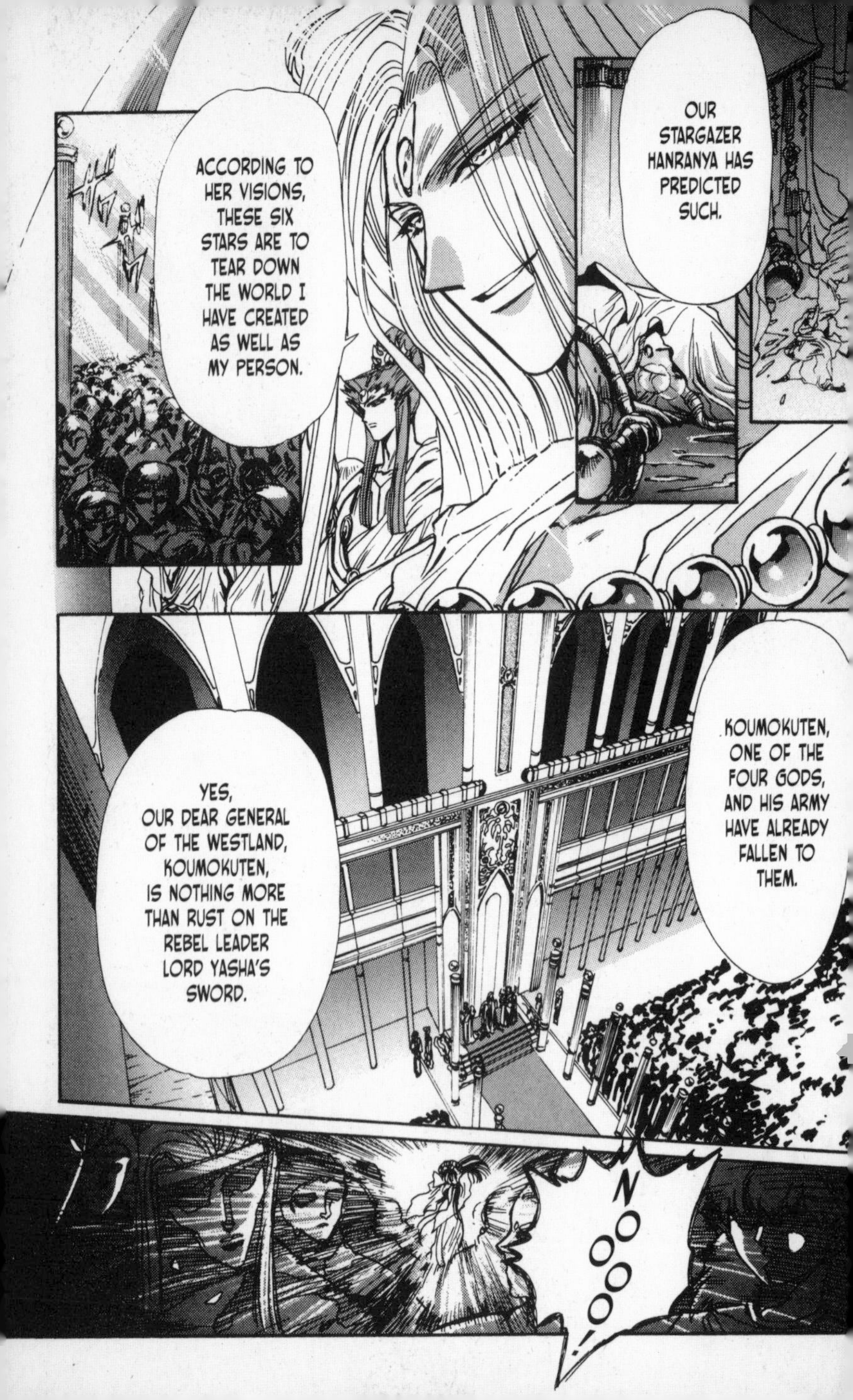
OUR STARGAZER HANRANYA HAS PREDICTED SUCH.
ACCORDING TO HER VISIONS, THESE SIX STARS ARE TO TEAR DOWN THE WORLD I HAVE CREATED AS WELL AS MY PERSON.
KOUMOKUTEN, ONE OF THE FOUR GODS, AND HIS ARMY HAVE ALREADY FALLEN TO THEM.
YES, OUR DEAR GENERAL OF THE WESTLAND, KOUMOKUTEN, IS NOTHING MORE THAN RUST ON THE REBEL LEADER LORD YASHA'S SWORD.
NOOOO!

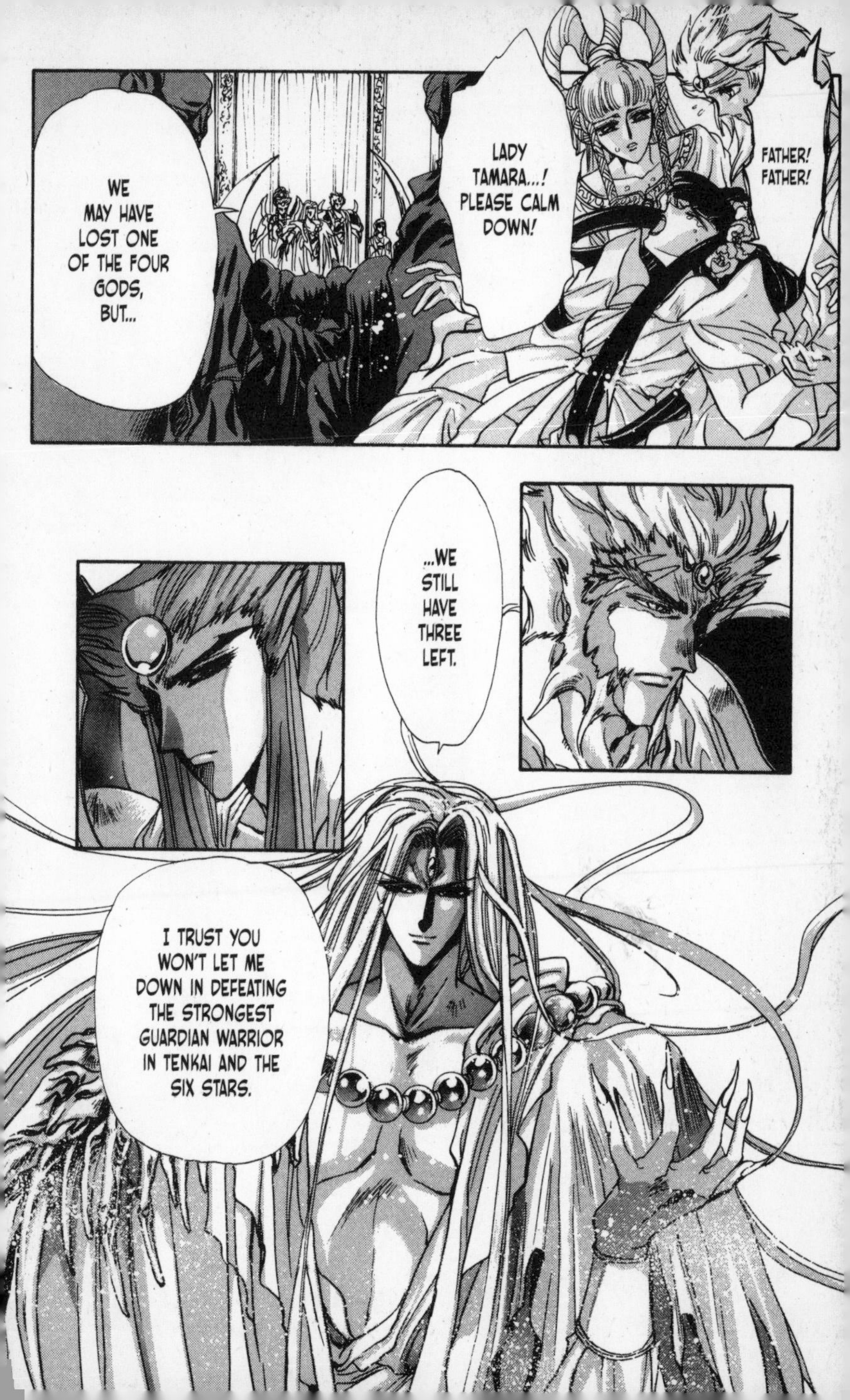
FATHER! FATHER!
LADY TAMARA...! PLEASE CALM DOWN!
WE MAY HAVE LOST ONE OF THE FOUR GODS, BUT...
...WE STILL HAVE THREE LEFT.
I TRUST YOU WON'T LET ME DOWN IN DEFEATING THE STRONGEST GUARDIAN WARRIOR IN TENKAI AND THE SIX STARS.

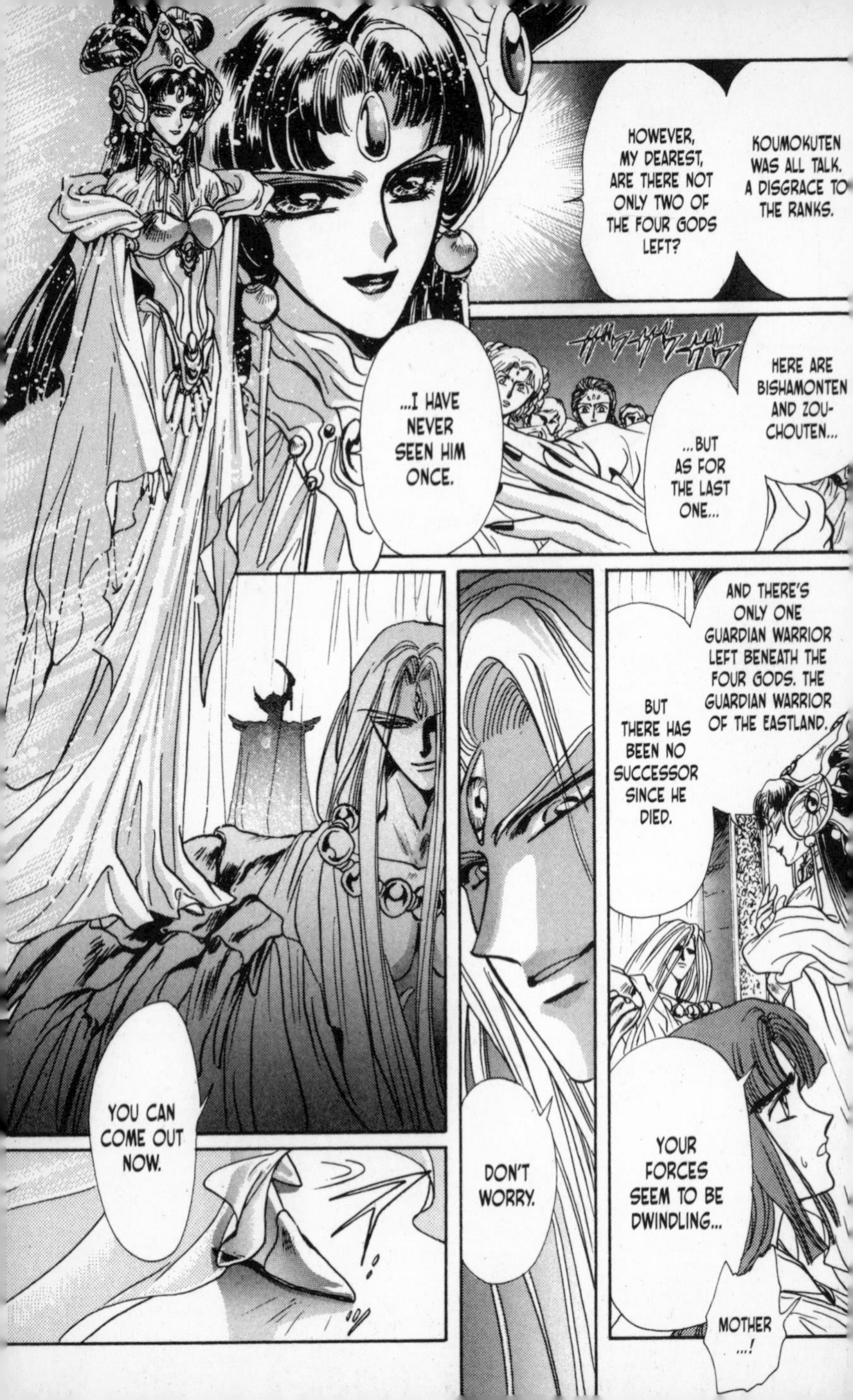
KOUMOKUTEN WAS ALL TALK. A DISGRACE TO THE RANKS.
HOWEVER, MY DEAREST, ARE THERE NOT ONLY TWO OF THE FOUR GODS LEFT?
ザワザワザワ
HERE ARE BISHAMONTEN AND ZOU-CHOUTEN...
...BUT AS FOR THE LAST ONE...
...I HAVE NEVER SEEN HIM ONCE.
AND THERE'S ONLY ONE GUARDIAN WARRIOR LEFT BENEATH THE FOUR GODS. THE GUARDIAN WARRIOR OF THE EASTLAND.
BUT THERE HAS BEEN NO SUCCESSOR SINCE HE DIED.
YOUR FORCES SEEM TO BE DWINDLING...
MOTHER ...!
DON'T WORRY.
YOU CAN COME OUT NOW.

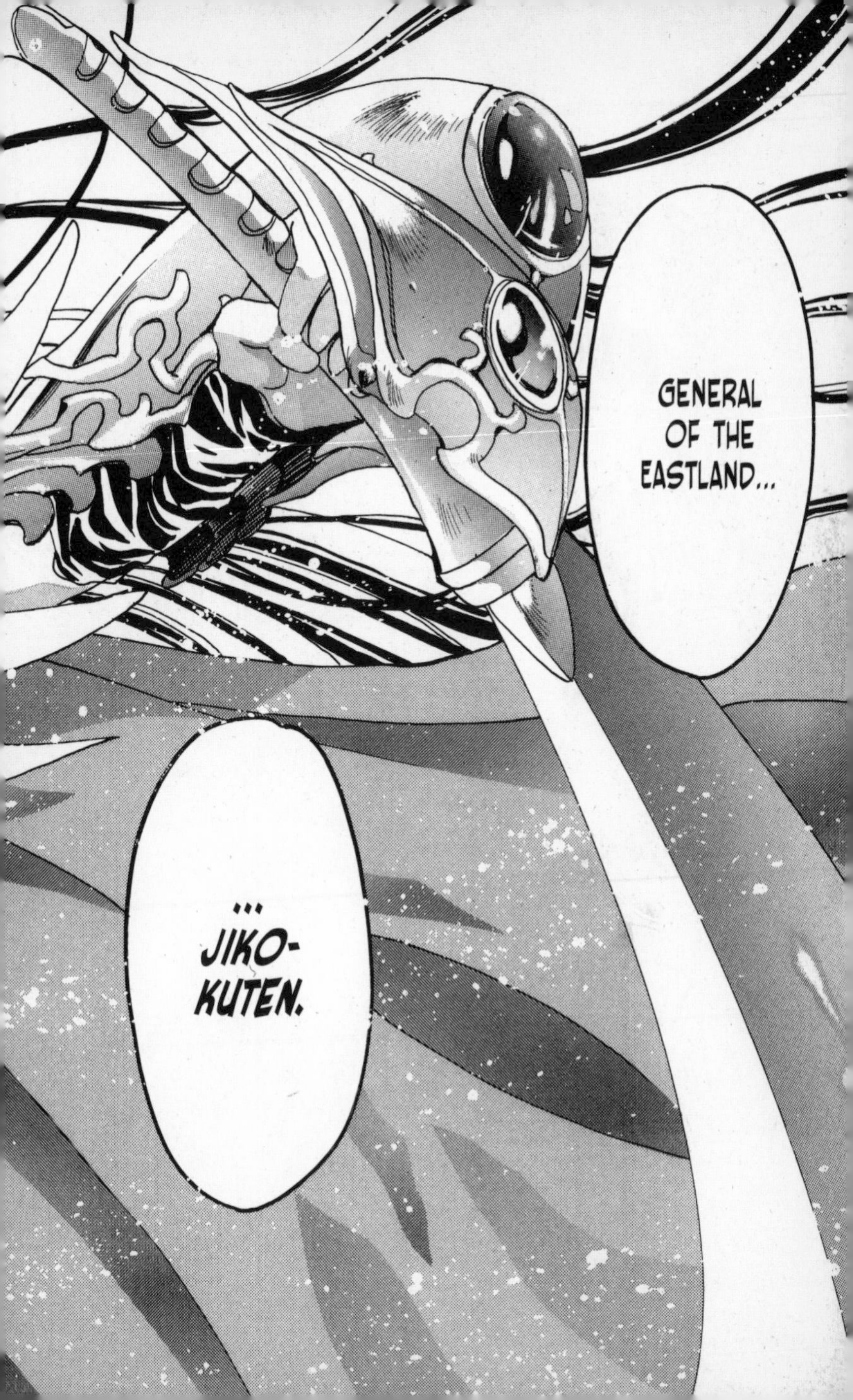
GENERAL OF THE EASTLAND...
...JIKO-KUTEN.

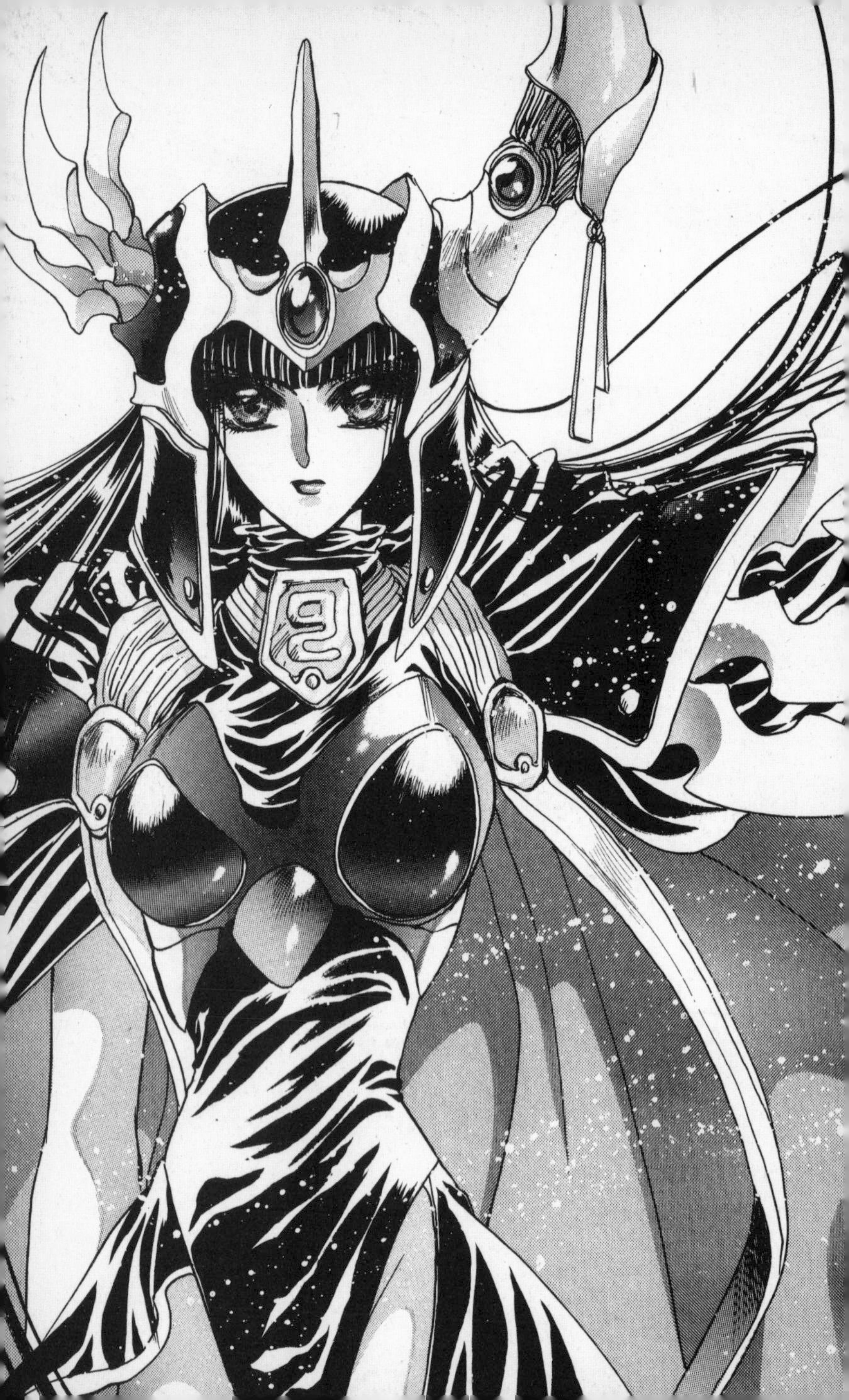

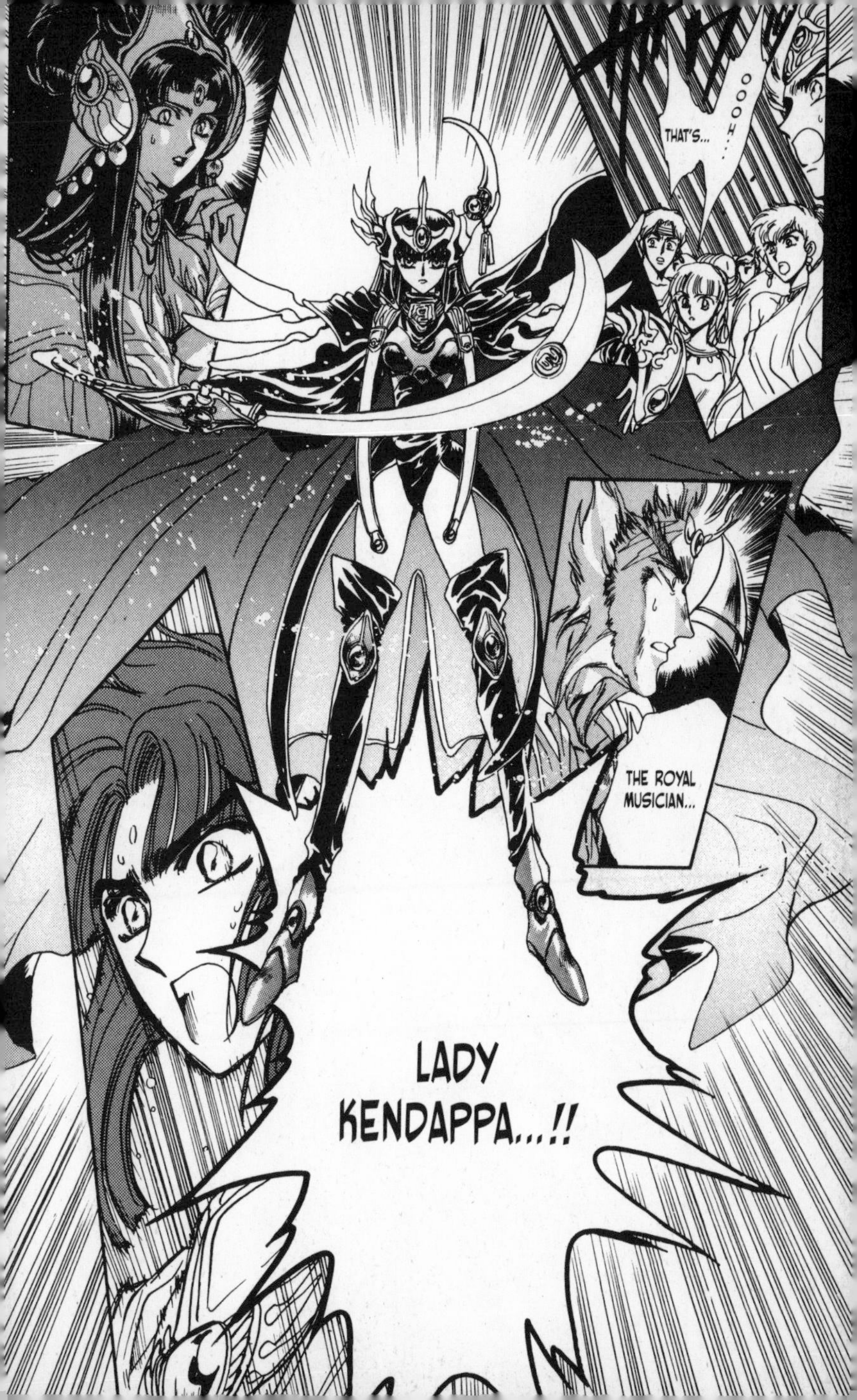
OOOH...
THAT'S...
THE ROYAL MUSICIAN...
LADY KENDAPPA...!!

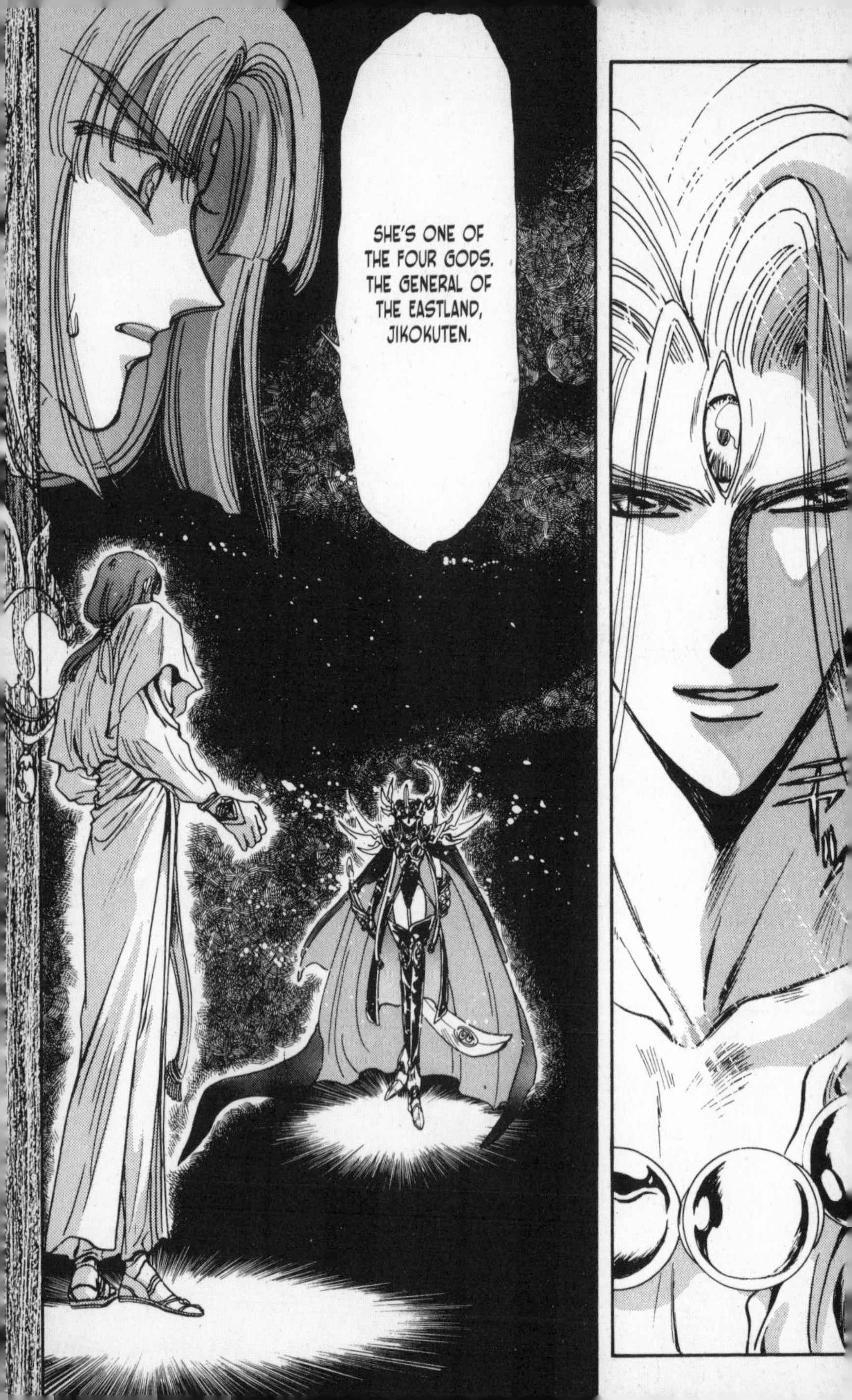
SHE'S ONE OF THE FOUR GODS. THE GENERAL OF THE EASTLAND, JIKOKUTEN.

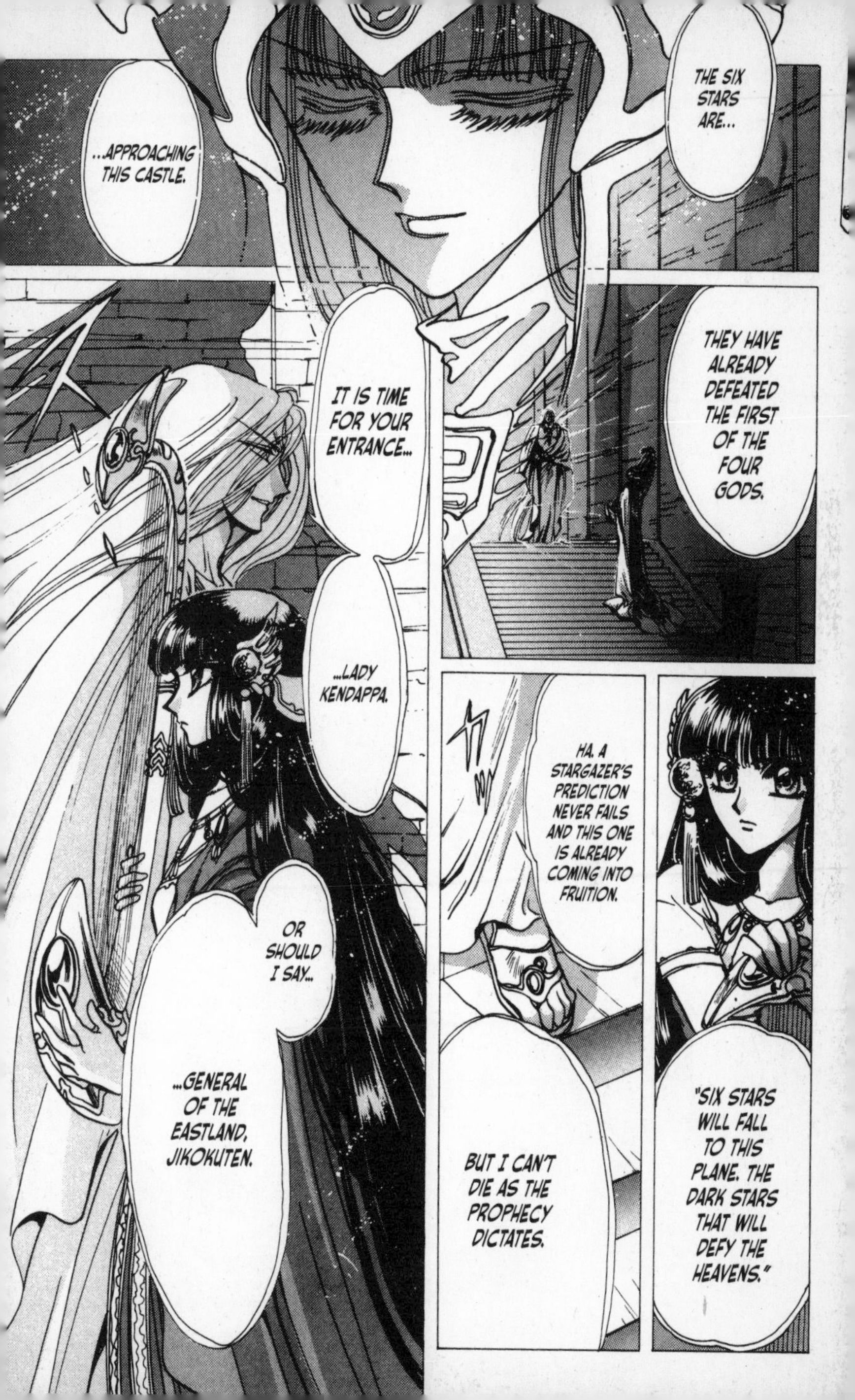
THE SIX STARS ARE...
...APPROACHING THIS CASTLE.
THEY HAVE ALREADY DEFEATED THE FIRST OF THE FOUR GODS.
"SIX STARS WILL FALL TO THIS PLANE. THE DARK STARS THAT WILL DEFY THE HEAVENS."
HA. A STARGAZER'S PREDICTION NEVER FAILS AND THIS ONE IS ALREADY COMING INTO FRUITION.
BUT I CAN'T DIE AS THE PROPHECY DICTATES.
IT IS TIME FOR YOUR ENTRANCE...
...LADY KENDAPPA.
OR SHOULD I SAY...
...GENERAL OF THE EASTLAND, JIKOKUTEN.

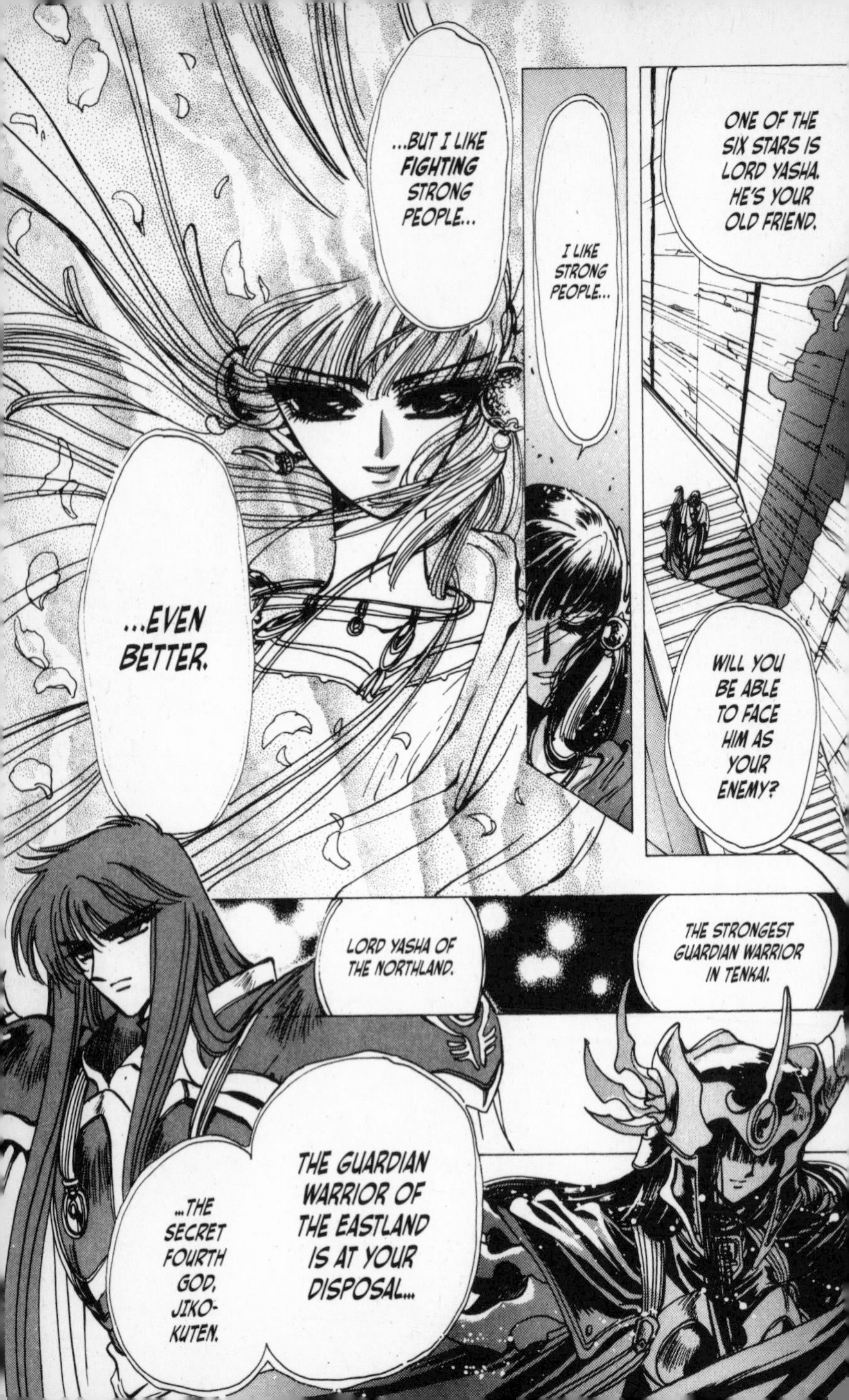
ONE OF THE SIX STARS IS LORD YASHA. HE'S YOUR OLD FRIEND.
WILL YOU BE ABLE TO FACE HIM AS YOUR ENEMY?
I LIKE STRONG PEOPLE...
...BUT I LIKE FIGHTING STRONG PEOPLE...
...EVEN BETTER.
THE STRONGEST GUARDIAN WARRIOR IN TENKAI.
LORD YASHA OF THE NORTHLAND.
THE GUARDIAN WARRIOR OF THE EASTLAND IS AT YOUR DISPOSAL...
...THE SECRET FOURTH GOD, JIKO-KUTEN.

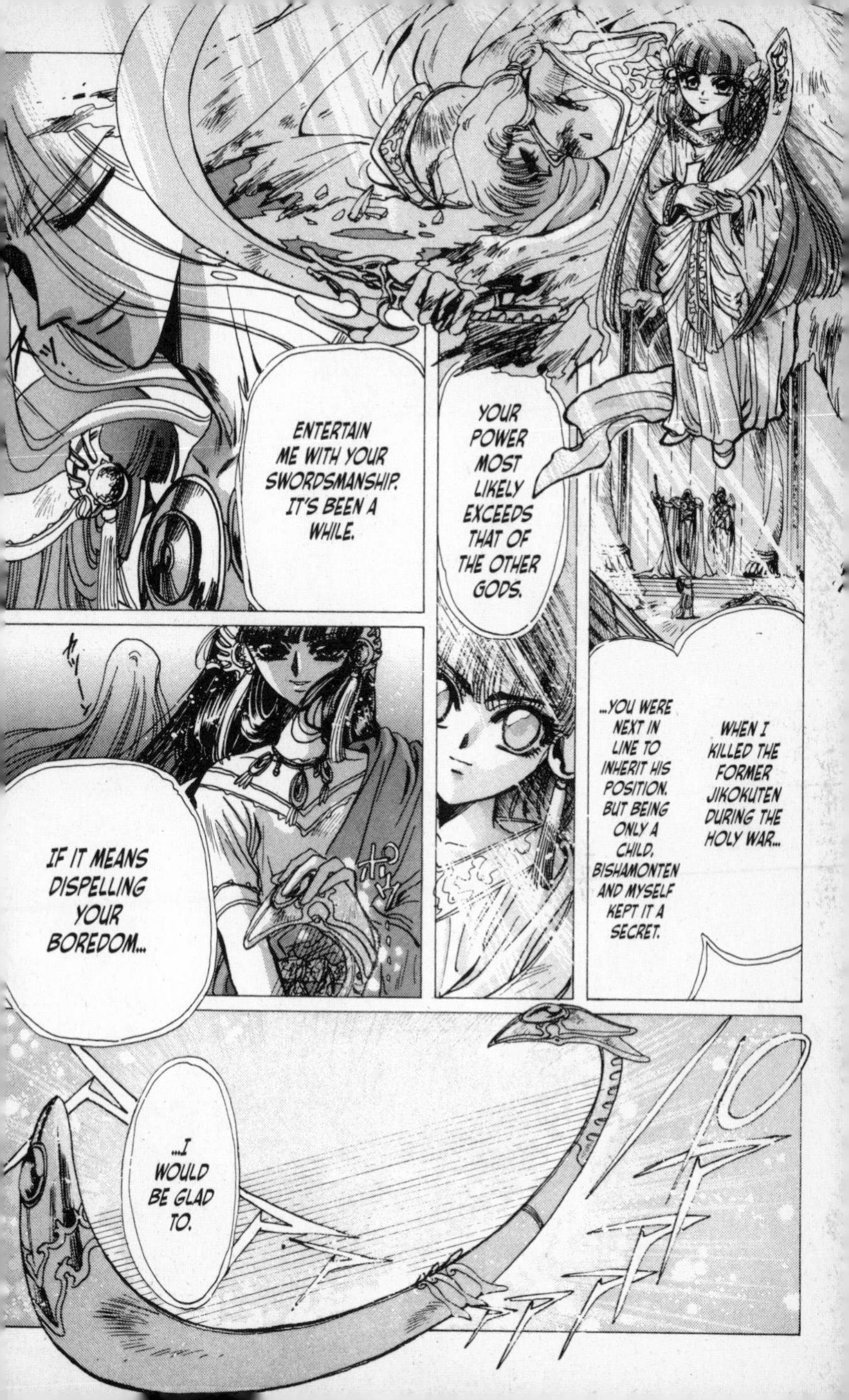
WHEN I KILLED THE FORMER JIKOKUTEN DURING THE HOLY WAR...
...YOU WERE NEXT IN LINE TO INHERIT HIS POSITION. BUT BEING ONLY A CHILD, BISHAMONTEN AND MYSELF KEPT IT A SECRET.
YOUR POWER MOST LIKELY EXCEEDS THAT OF THE OTHER GODS.
ENTERTAIN ME WITH YOUR SWORDSMANSHIP. IT'S BEEN A WHILE.
IF IT MEANS DISPELLING YOUR BOREDOM...
...I WOULD BE GLAD TO.

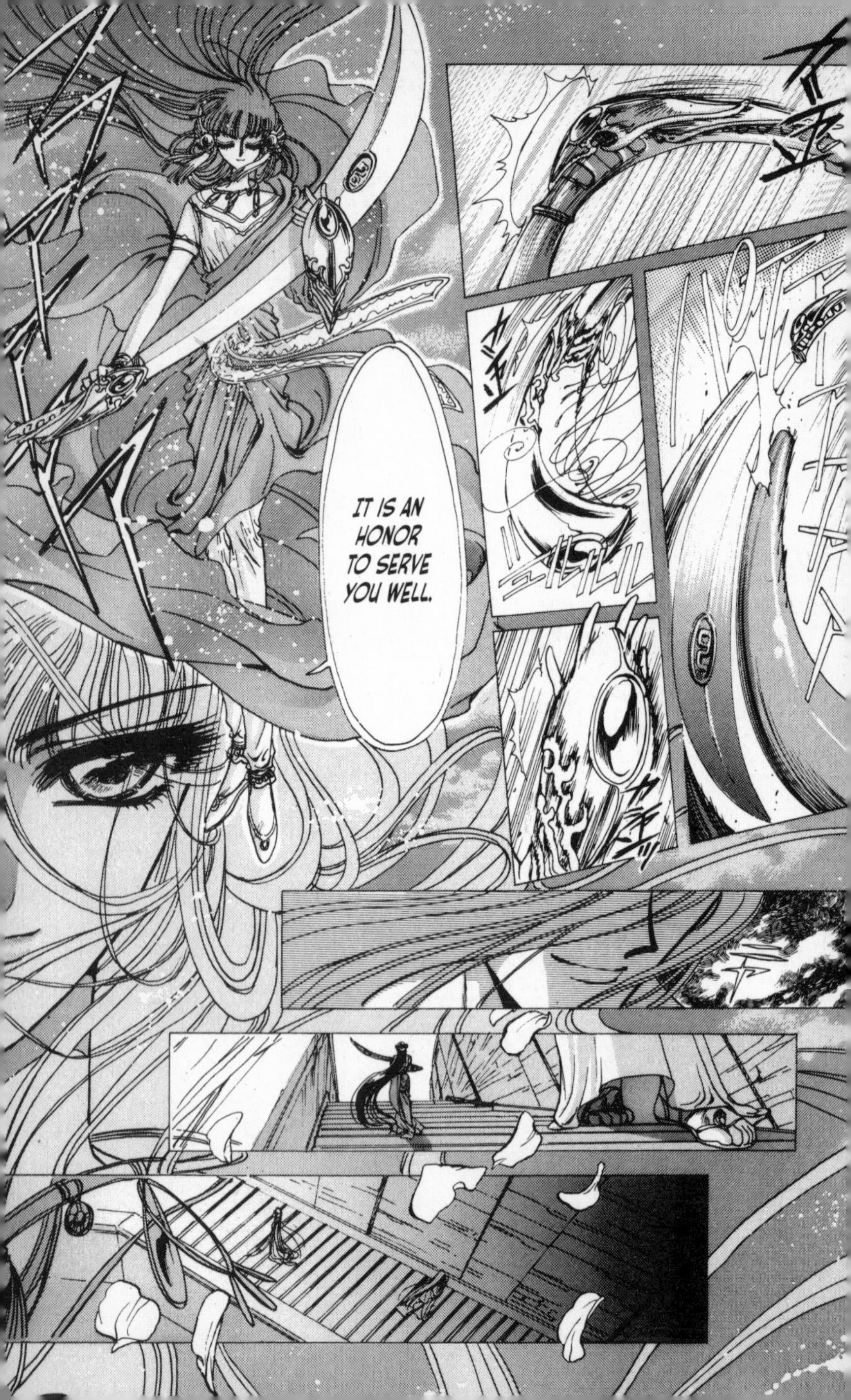
IT IS AN HONOR TO SERVE YOU WELL.

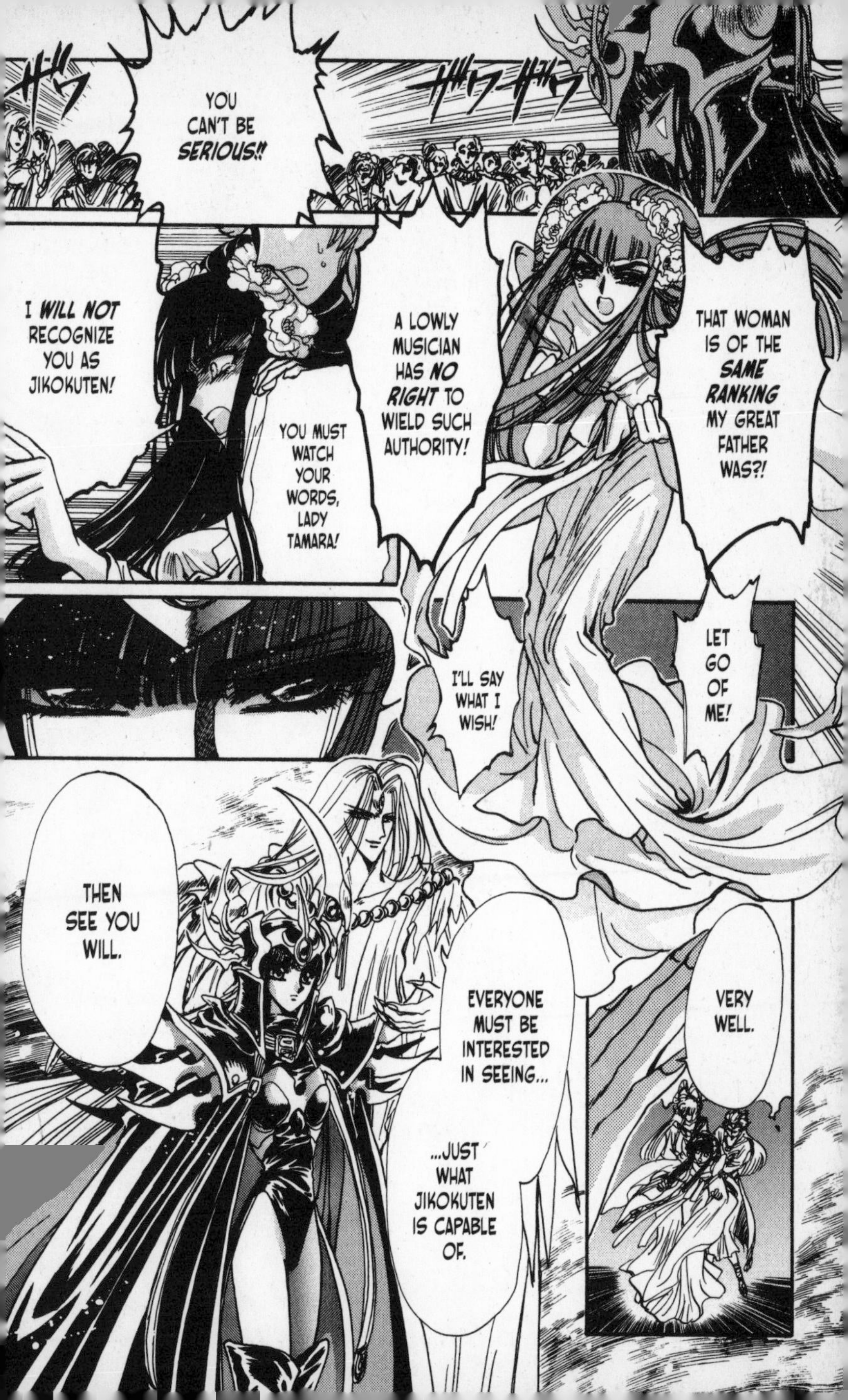
ザワ ザワ
ザワ
YOU CAN'T BE *SERIOUS!!*
THAT WOMAN IS OF THE *SAME RANKING* MY GREAT FATHER WAS?!
A LOWLY MUSICIAN HAS *NO RIGHT* TO WIELD SUCH AUTHORITY!
I *WILL NOT* RECOGNIZE YOU AS JIKOKUTEN!
YOU MUST WATCH YOUR WORDS, LADY TAMARA!
LET GO OF ME!
I'LL SAY WHAT I WISH!
VERY WELL.
EVERYONE MUST BE INTERESTED IN SEEING...
...JUST WHAT JIKOKUTEN IS CAPABLE OF.
THEN SEE YOU WILL.

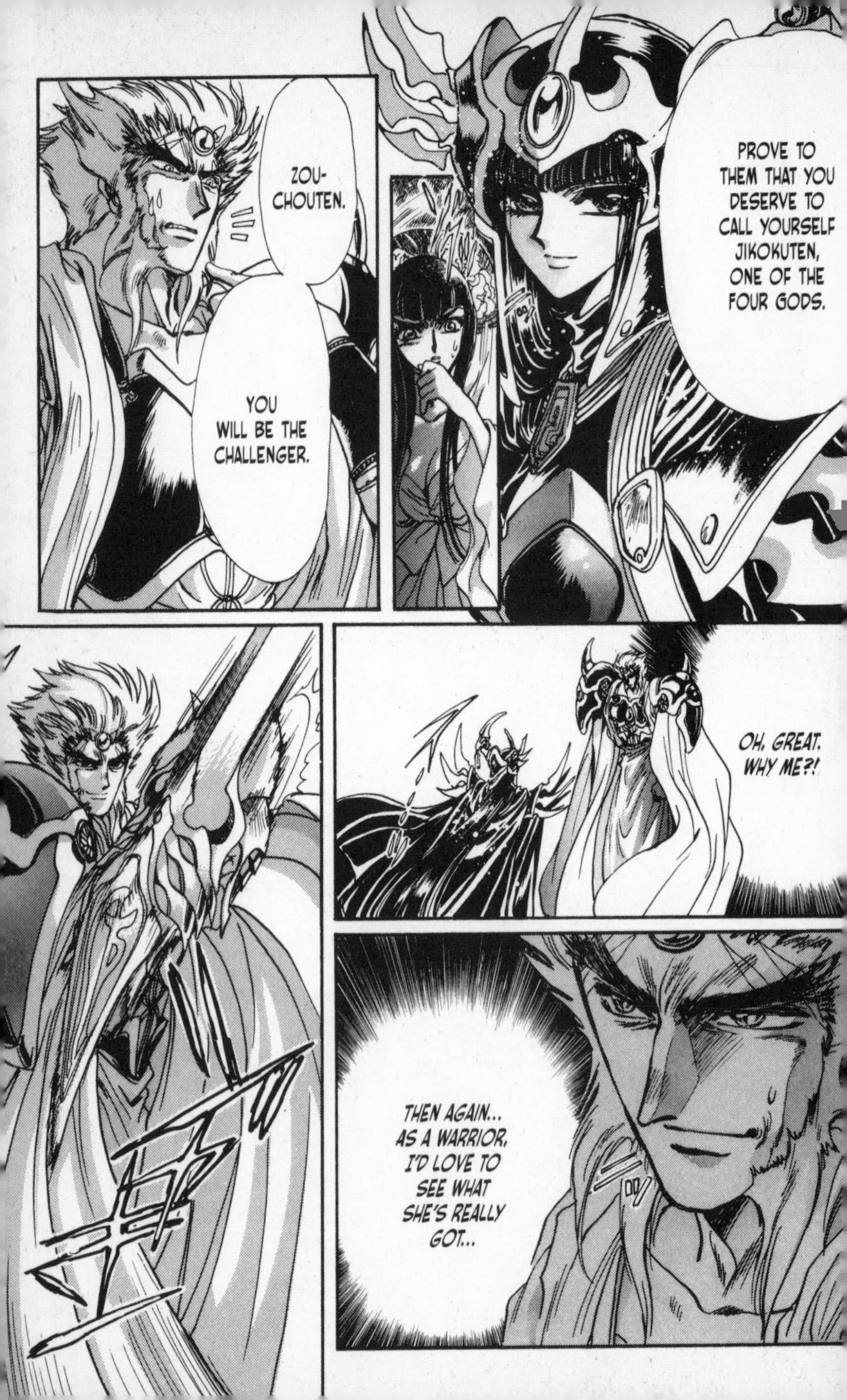
PROVE TO THEM THAT YOU DESERVE TO CALL YOURSELF JIKOKUTEN, ONE OF THE FOUR GODS.
ZOU-CHOUTEN.
YOU WILL BE THE CHALLENGER.
OH, GREAT. WHY ME?!
THEN AGAIN... AS A WARRIOR, I'D LOVE TO SEE WHAT SHE'S REALLY GOT...

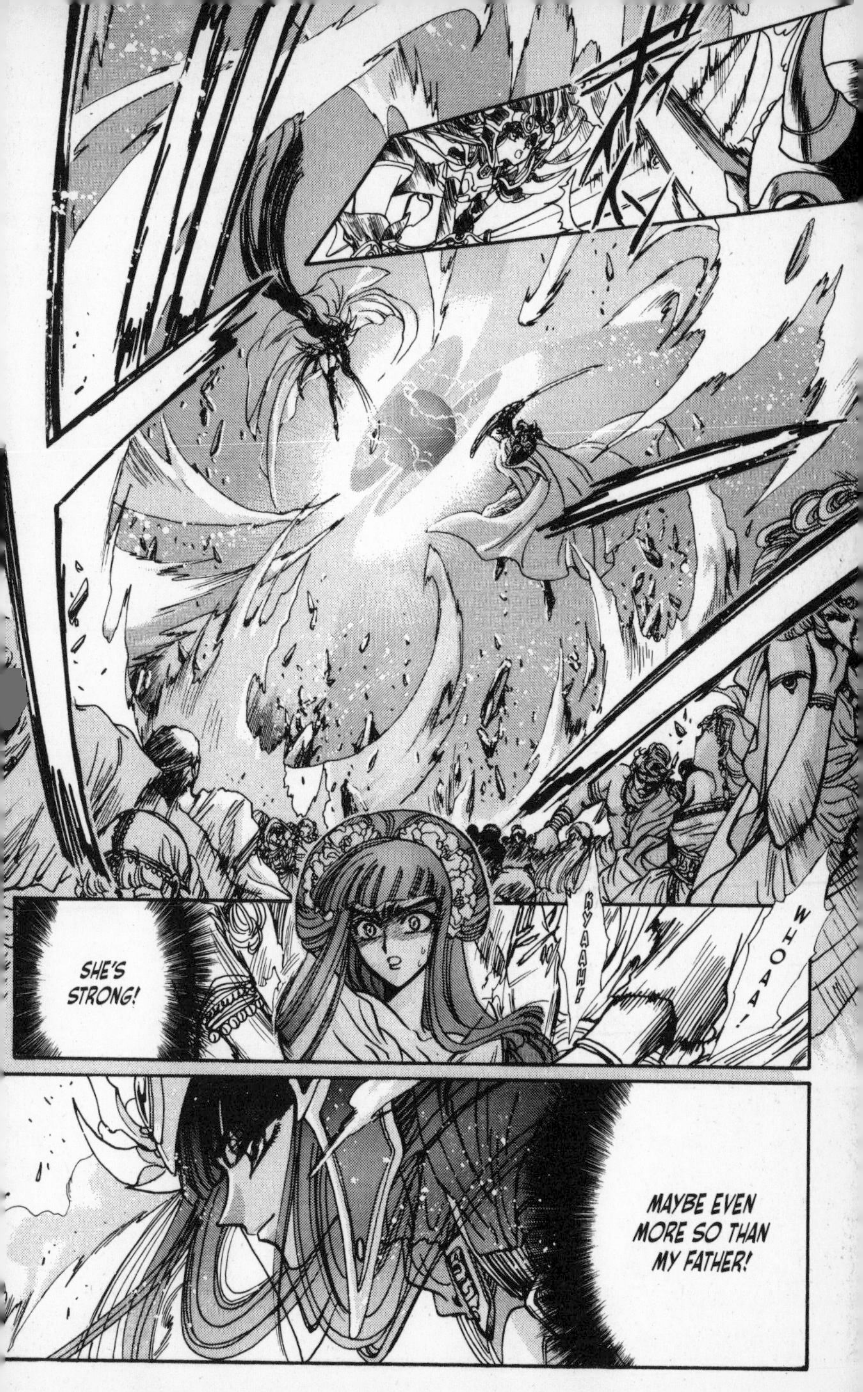
WHOAAA!
KYAAAH!
SHE'S STRONG!
MAYBE EVEN MORE SO THAN MY FATHER!

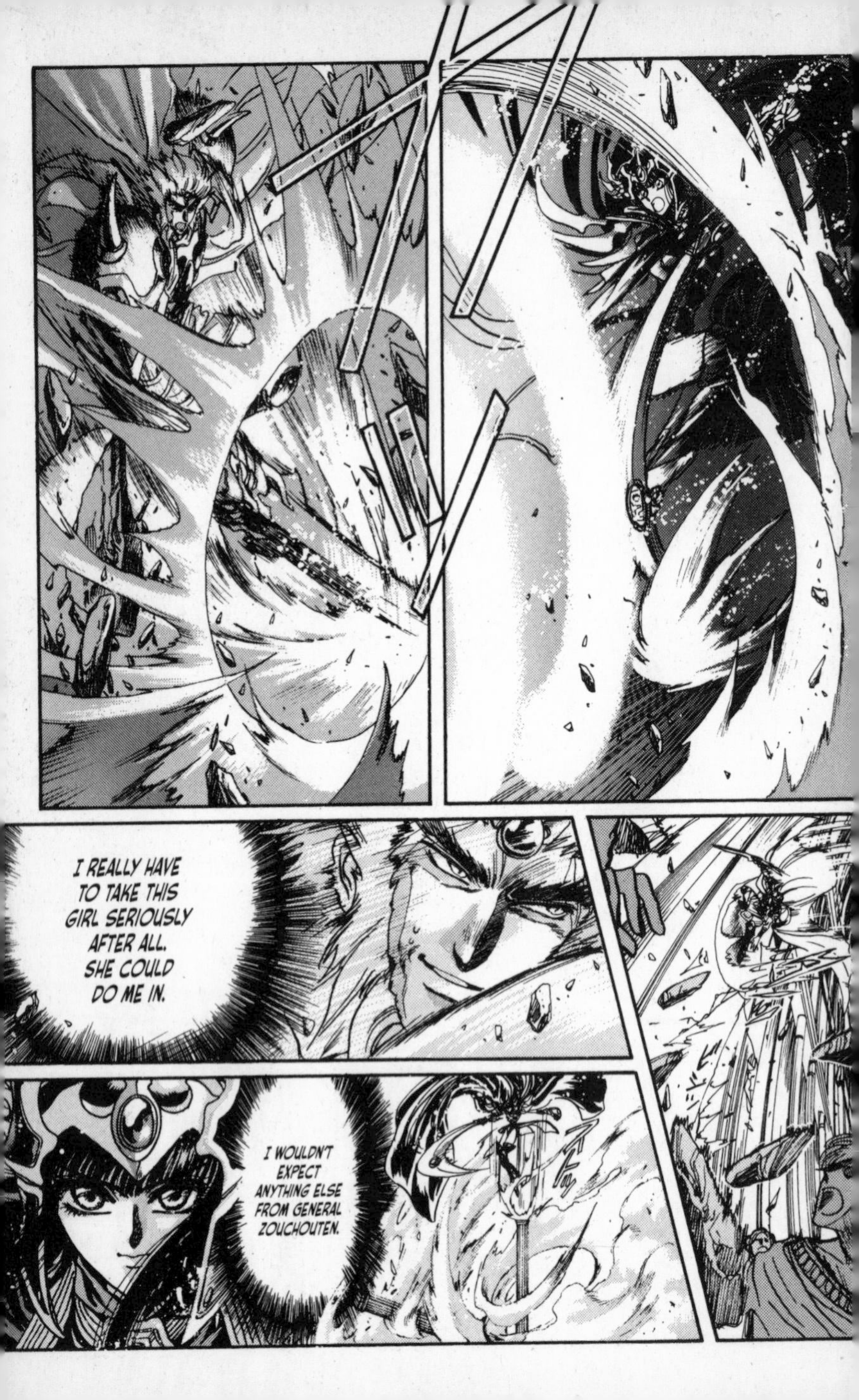
I REALLY HAVE TO TAKE THIS GIRL SERIOUSLY AFTER ALL. SHE COULD DO ME IN.
I WOULDN'T EXPECT ANYTHING ELSE FROM GENERAL ZOUCHOUTEN.

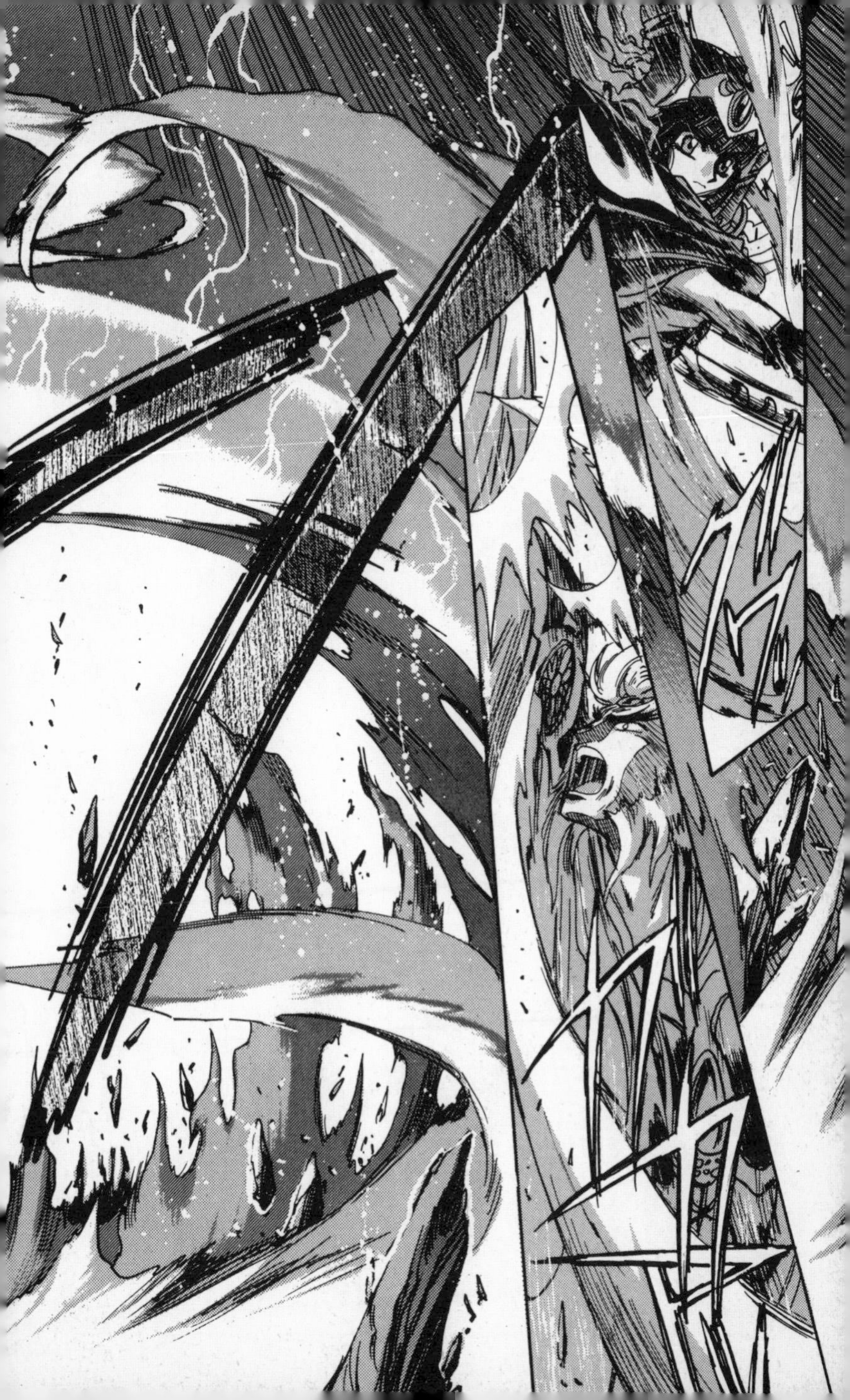

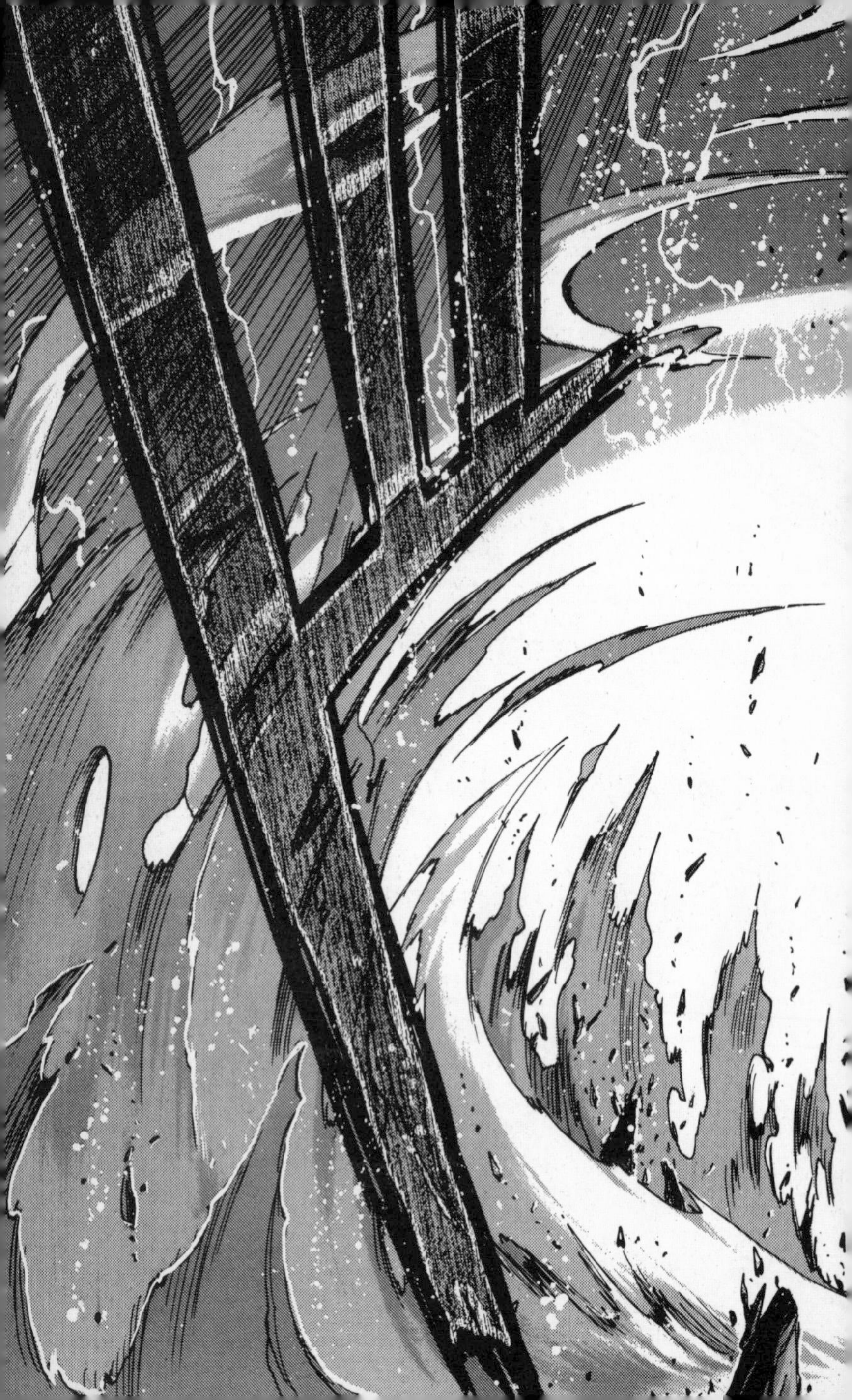

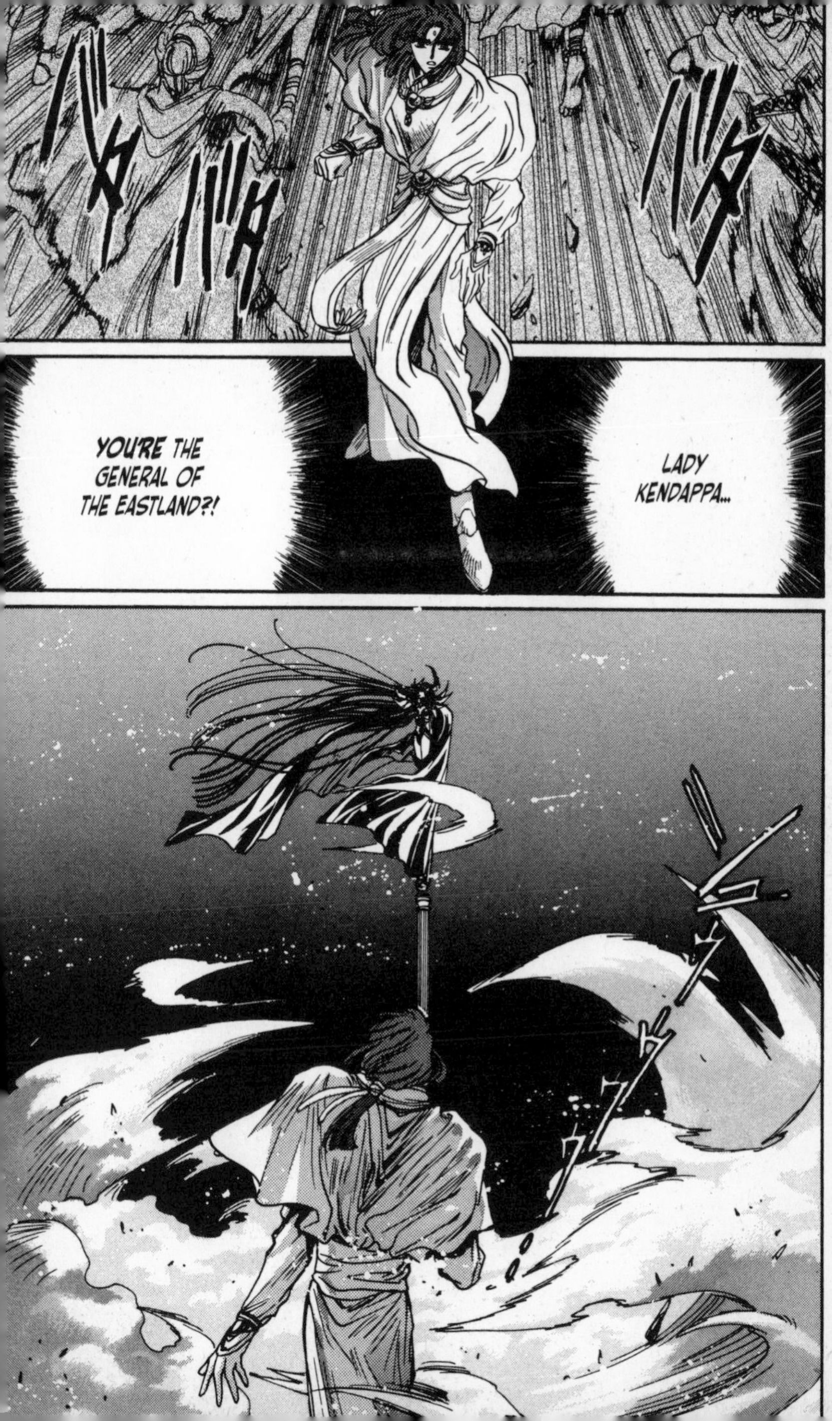
バタ
バタ バタ
LADY KENDAPPA...
YOU'RE THE GENERAL OF THE EASTLAND?!

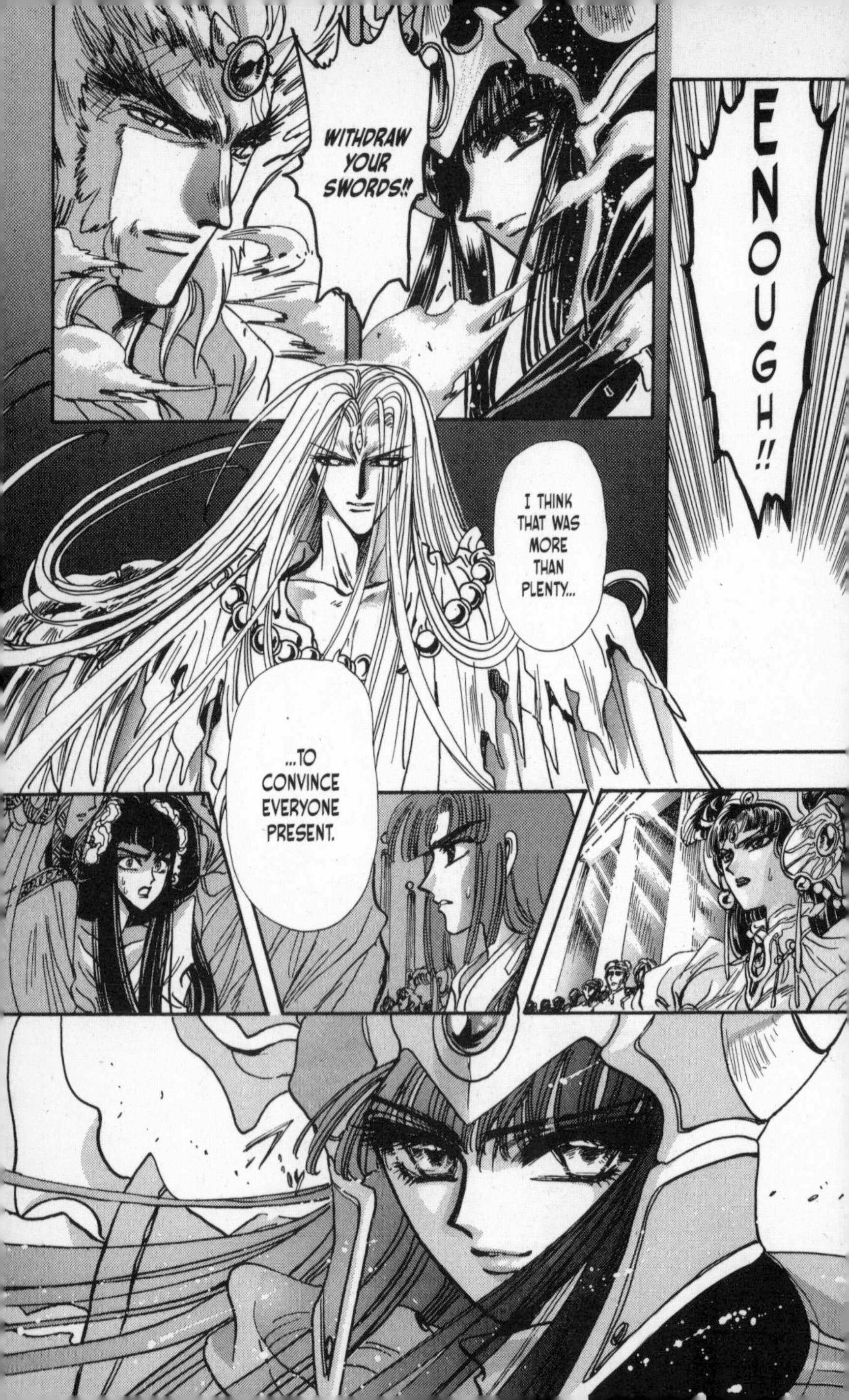
ENOUGH!!
WITHDRAW YOUR SWORDS!!
I THINK THAT WAS MORE THAN PLENTY...
...TO CONVINCE EVERYONE PRESENT.

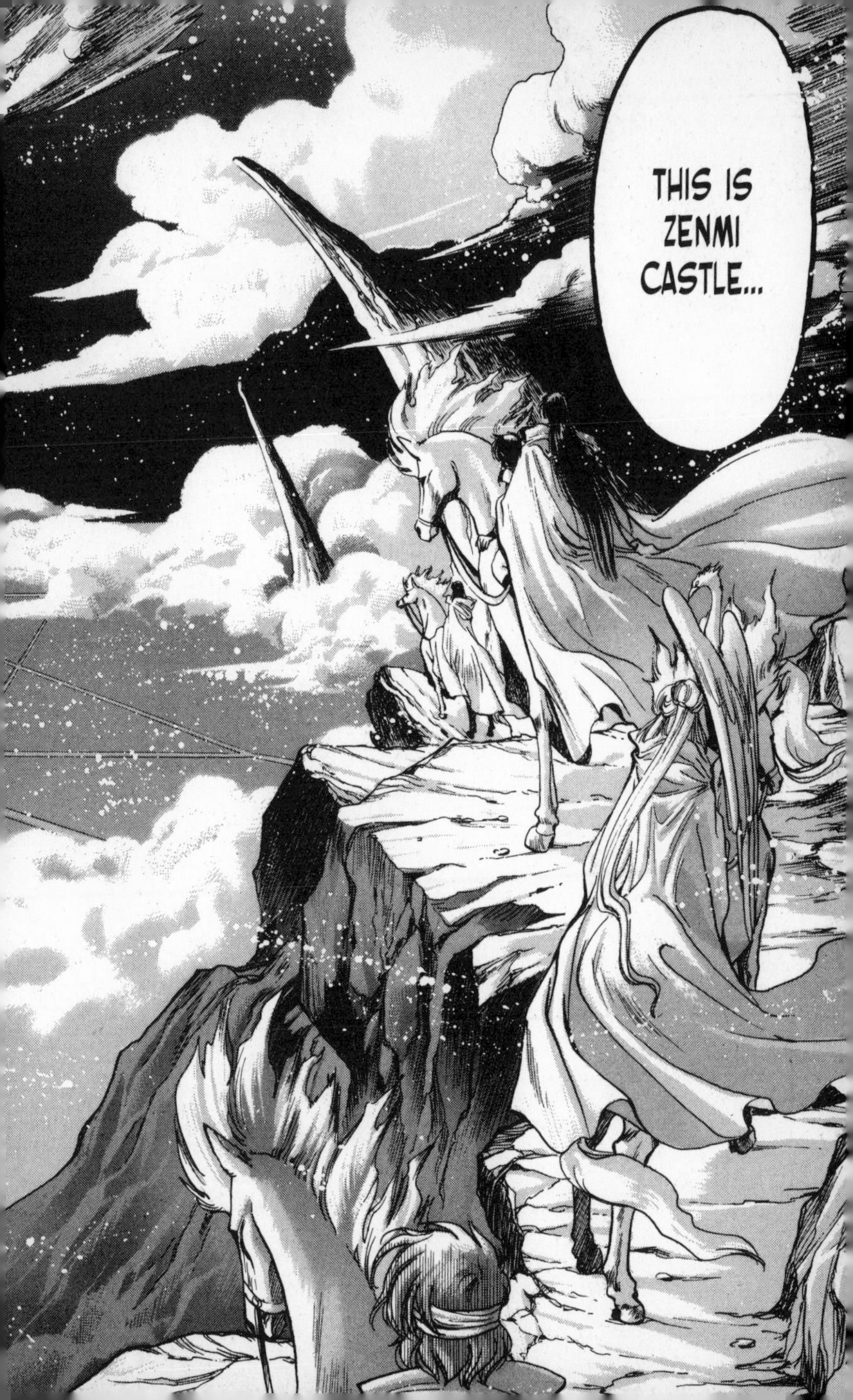
THIS IS ZENMI CASTLE...

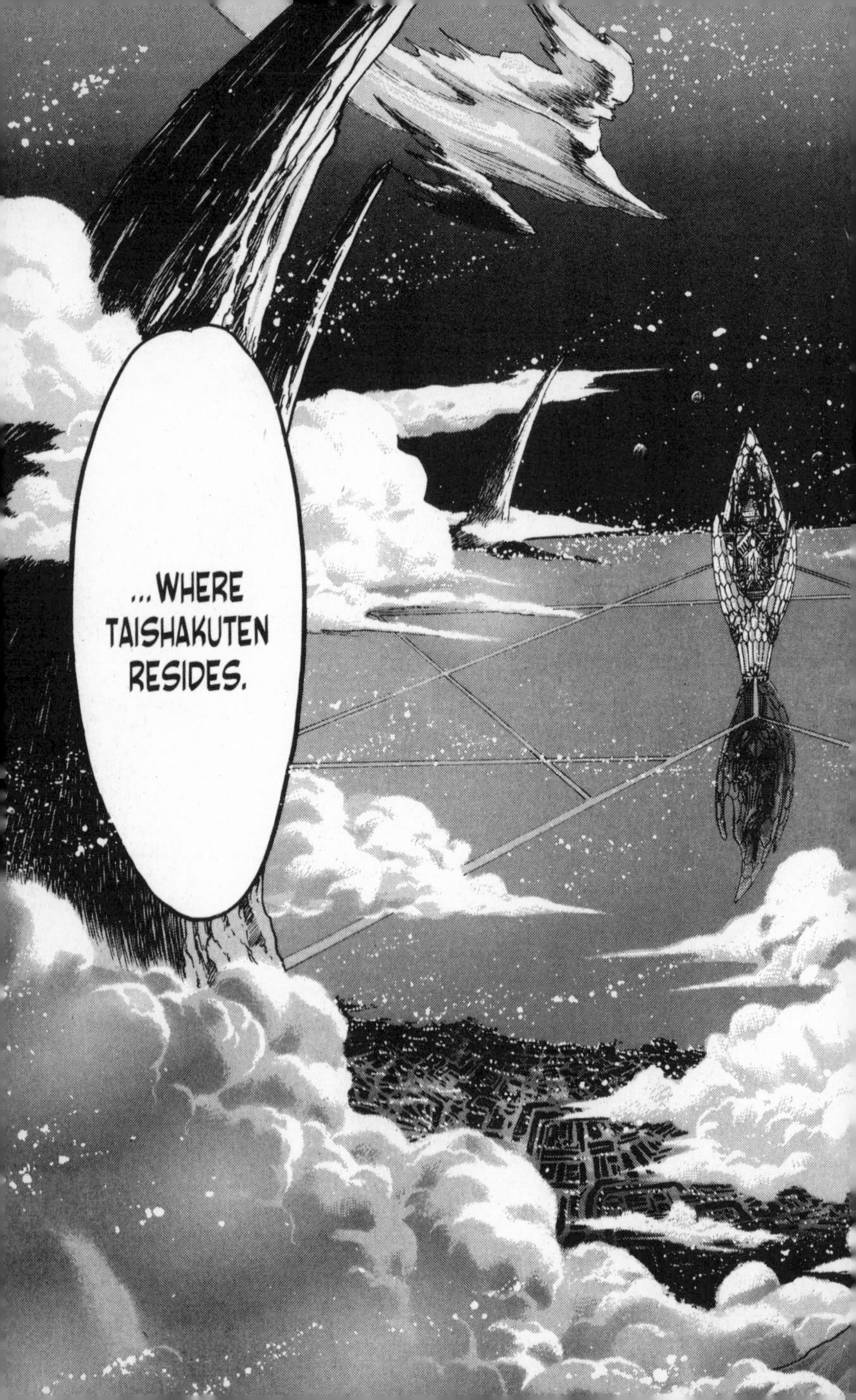
...WHERE TAISHAKUTEN RESIDES.

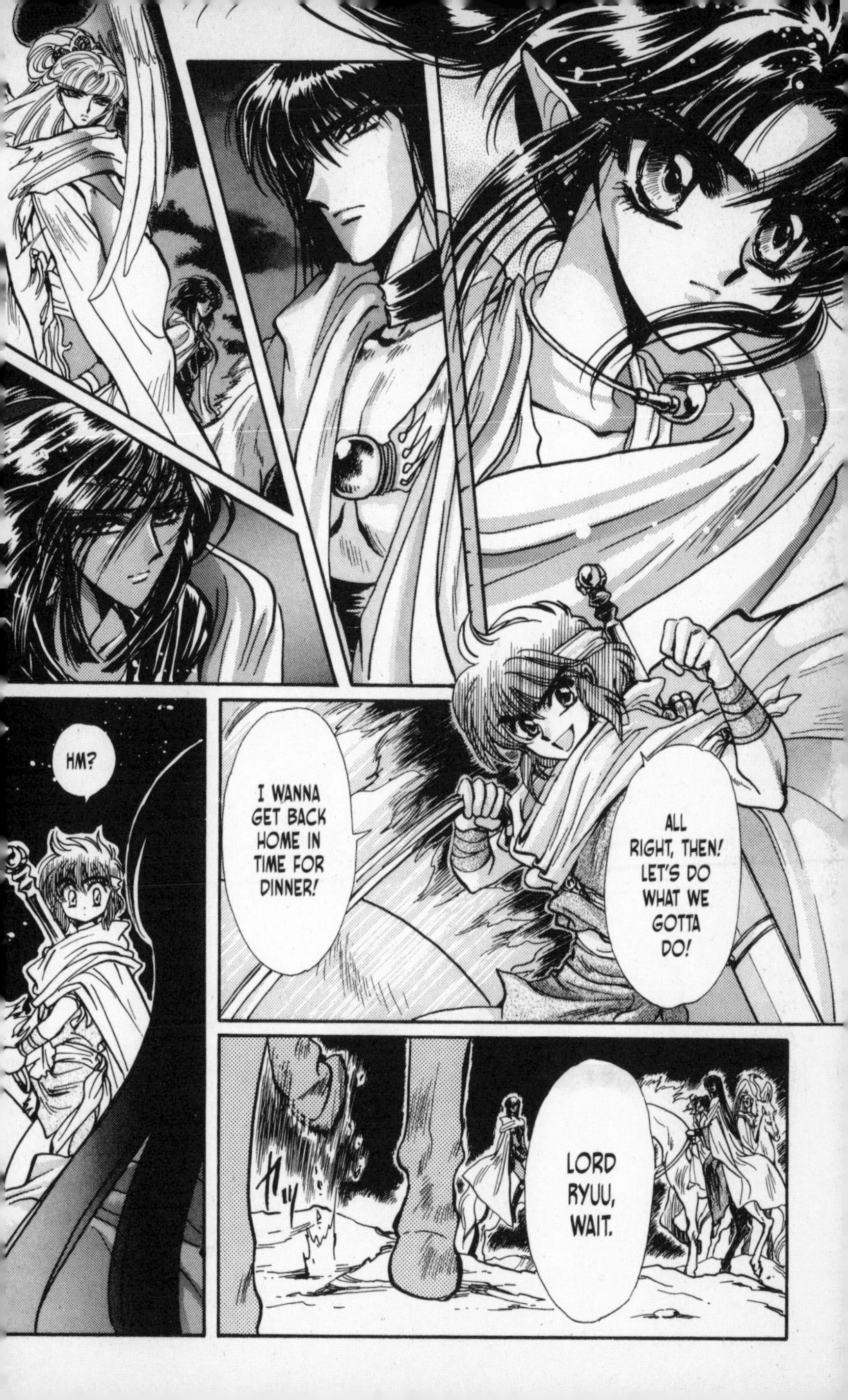
ALL RIGHT, THEN! LET'S DO WHAT WE GOTTA DO!
I WANNA GET BACK HOME IN TIME FOR DINNER!
LORD RYUU, WAIT.
HM?

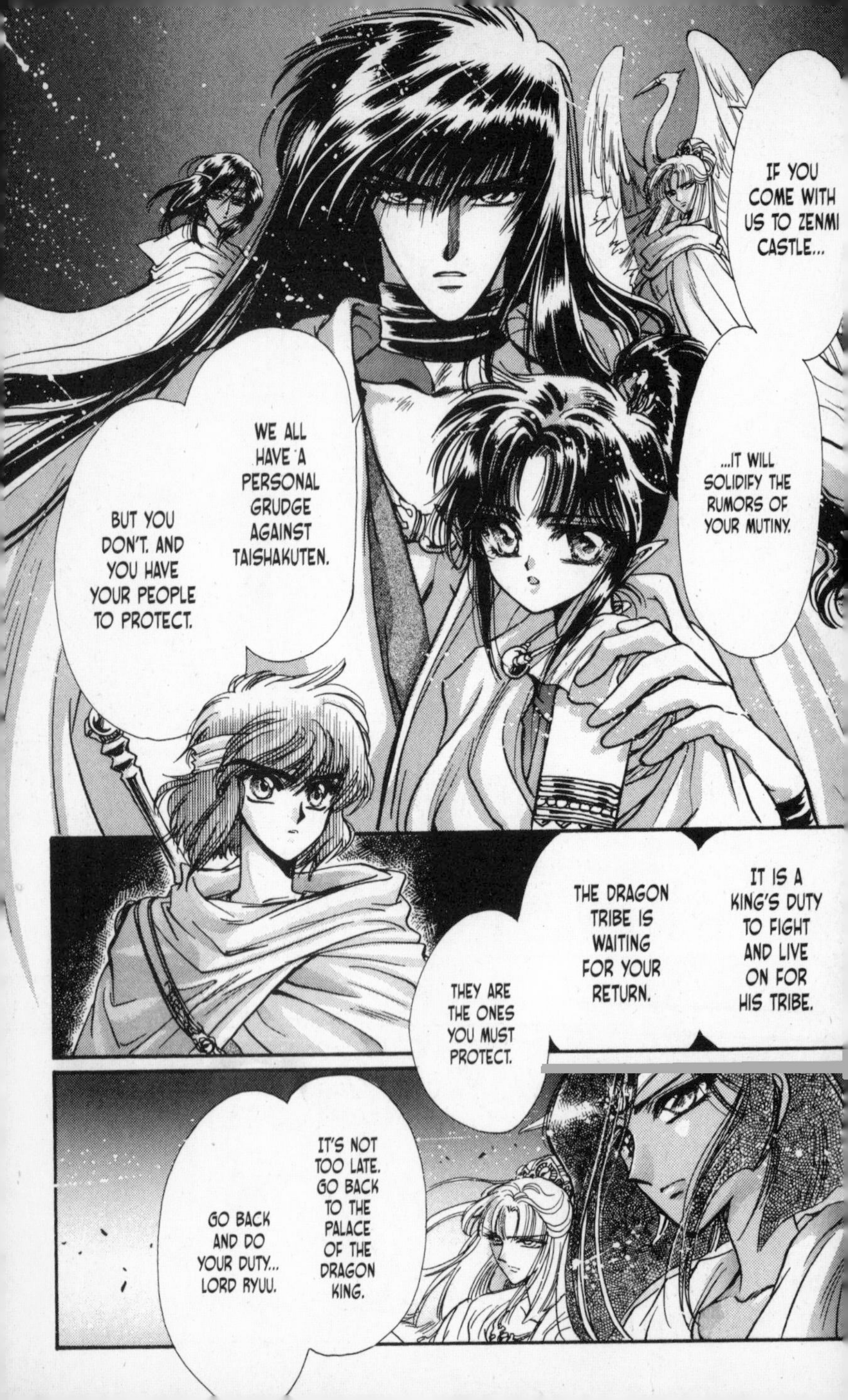
IF YOU COME WITH US TO ZENMI CASTLE...
...IT WILL SOLIDIFY THE RUMORS OF YOUR MUTINY.
WE ALL HAVE A PERSONAL GRUDGE AGAINST TAISHAKUTEN.
BUT YOU DON'T. AND YOU HAVE YOUR PEOPLE TO PROTECT.
IT IS A KING'S DUTY TO FIGHT AND LIVE ON FOR HIS TRIBE.
THE DRAGON TRIBE IS WAITING FOR YOUR RETURN.
THEY ARE THE ONES YOU MUST PROTECT.
IT'S NOT TOO LATE. GO BACK TO THE PALACE OF THE DRAGON KING.
GO BACK AND DO YOUR DUTY... LORD RYUU.

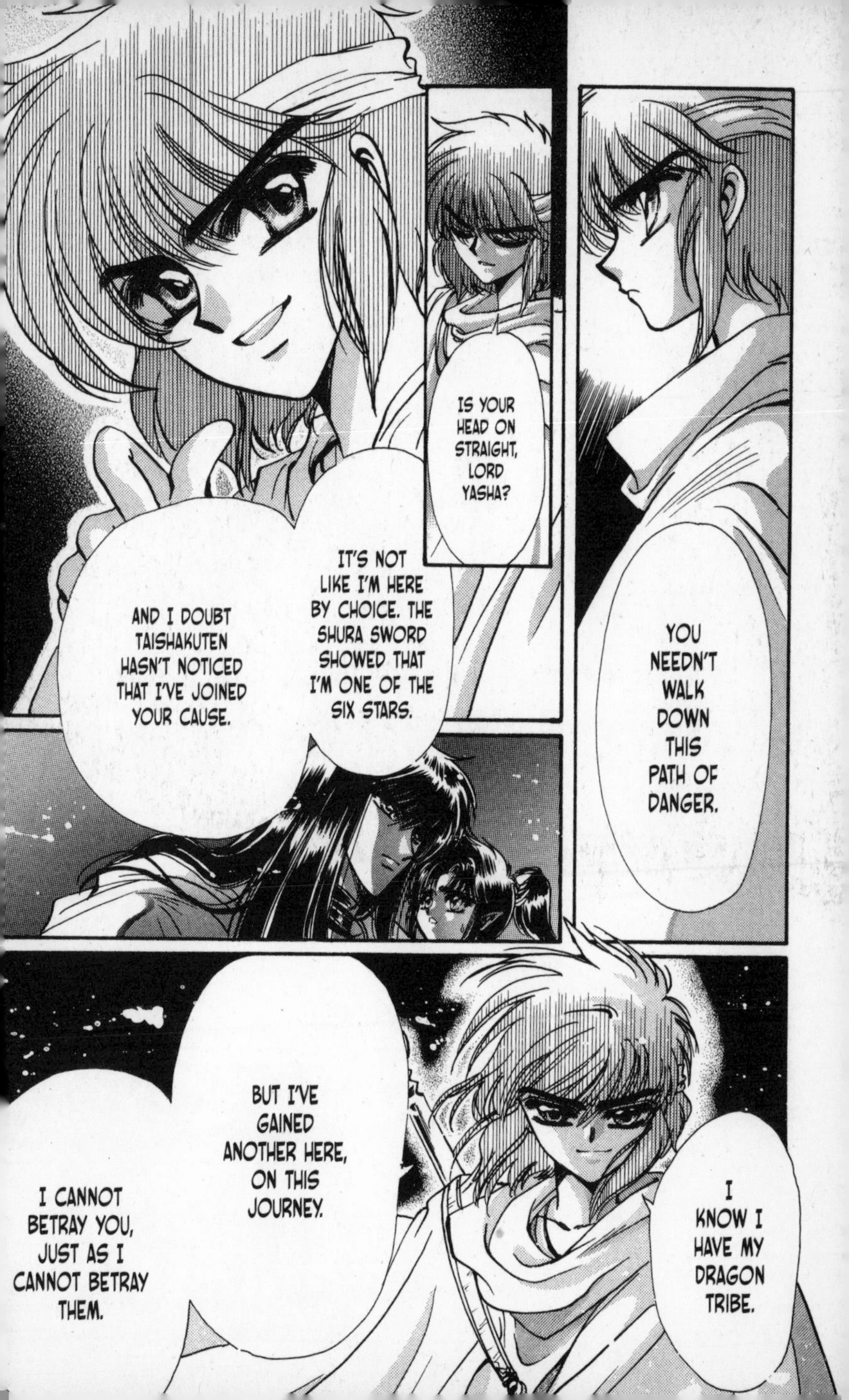
YOU NEEDN'T WALK DOWN THIS PATH OF DANGER.
IS YOUR HEAD ON STRAIGHT, LORD YASHA?
IT'S NOT LIKE I'M HERE BY CHOICE. THE SHURA SWORD SHOWED THAT I'M ONE OF THE SIX STARS.
AND I DOUBT TAISHAKUTEN HASN'T NOTICED THAT I'VE JOINED YOUR CAUSE.
I KNOW I HAVE MY DRAGON TRIBE.
BUT I'VE GAINED ANOTHER HERE, ON THIS JOURNEY.
I CANNOT BETRAY YOU, JUST AS I CANNOT BETRAY THEM.

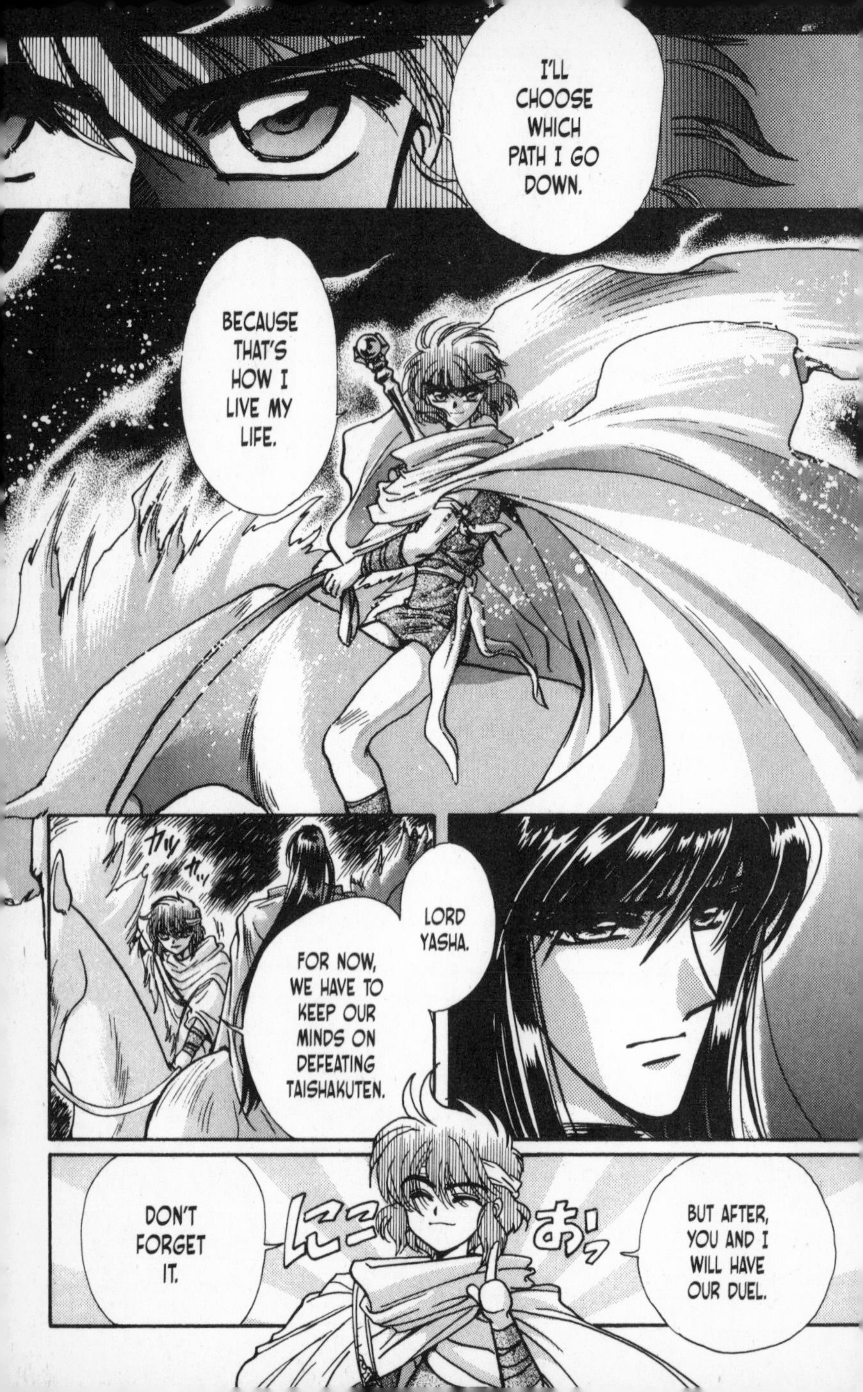
I'LL CHOOSE WHICH PATH I GO DOWN.
BECAUSE THAT'S HOW I LIVE MY LIFE.
LORD YASHA.
カッ
カッ
FOR NOW, WE HAVE TO KEEP OUR MINDS ON DEFEATING TAISHAKUTEN.
BUT AFTER, YOU AND I WILL HAVE OUR DUEL.
おっ
にこ
DON'T FORGET IT.

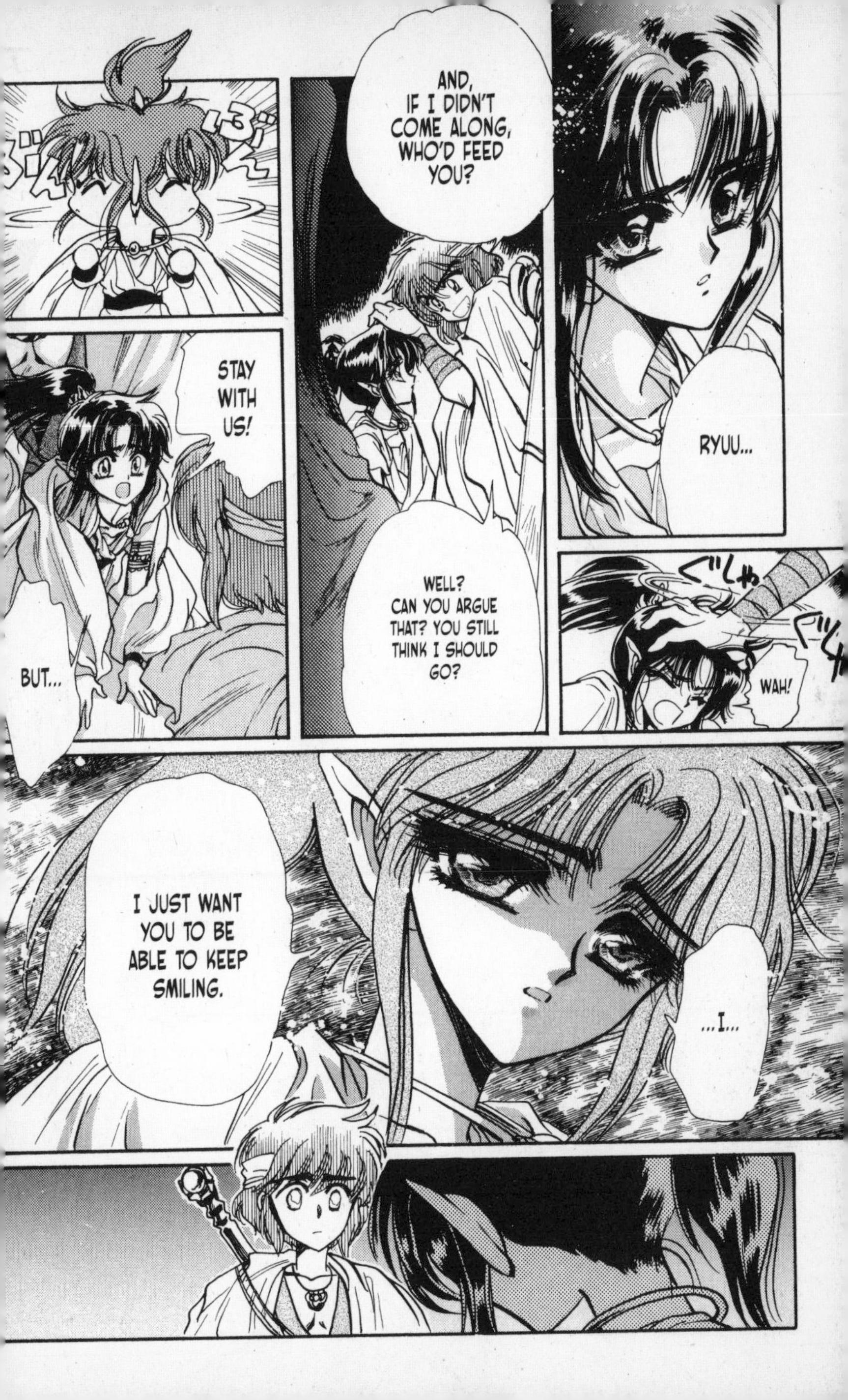
RYUU...
ぐしゃ
ぐしゃ
WAH!
AND, IF I DIDN'T COME ALONG, WHO'D FEED YOU?
WELL? CAN YOU ARGUE THAT? YOU STILL THINK I SHOULD GO?
STAY WITH US!
BUT...
...I...
I JUST WANT YOU TO BE ABLE TO KEEP SMILING.

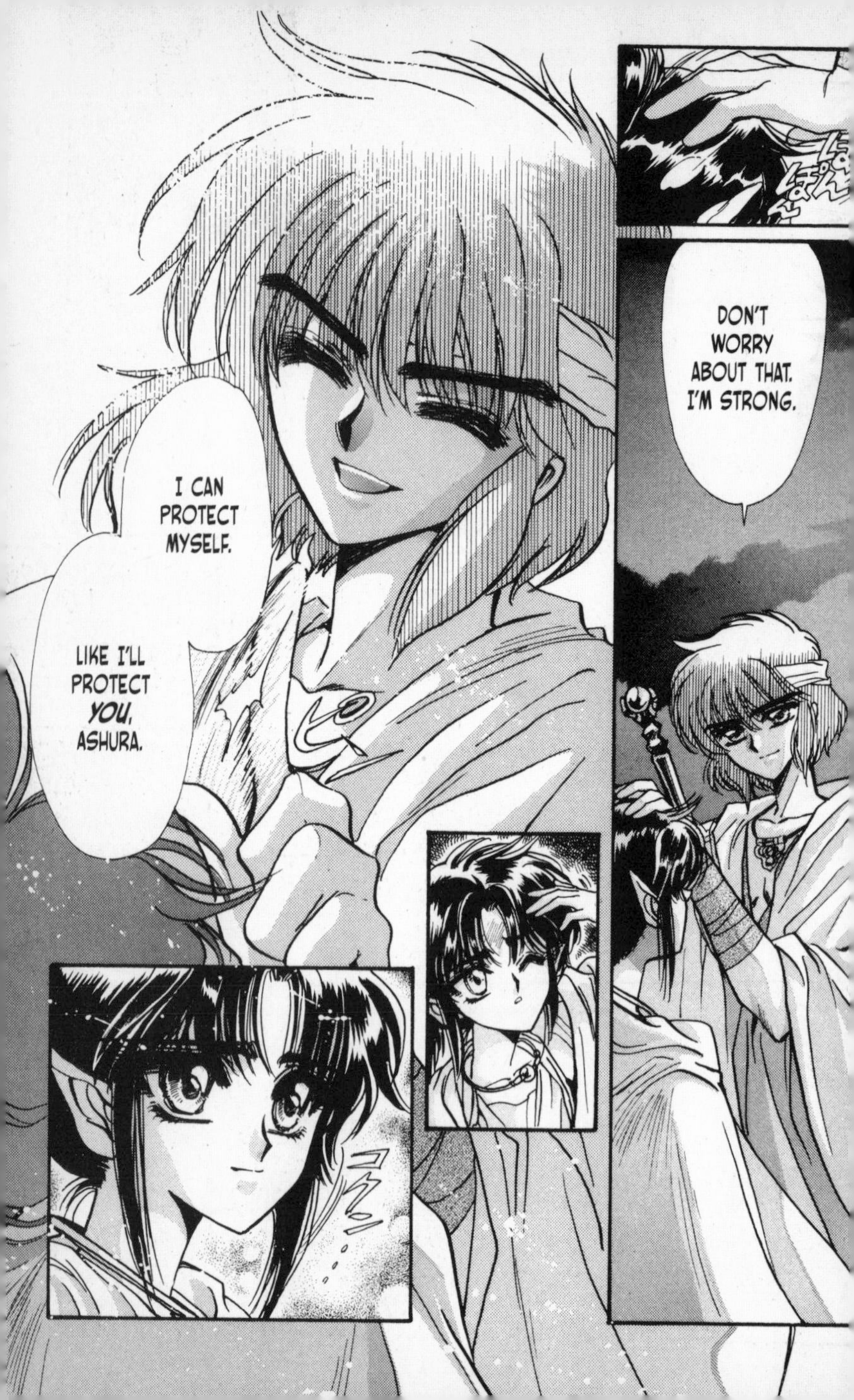
DON'T WORRY ABOUT THAT. I'M STRONG.
I CAN PROTECT MYSELF.
LIKE I'LL PROTECT *YOU*, ASHURA.

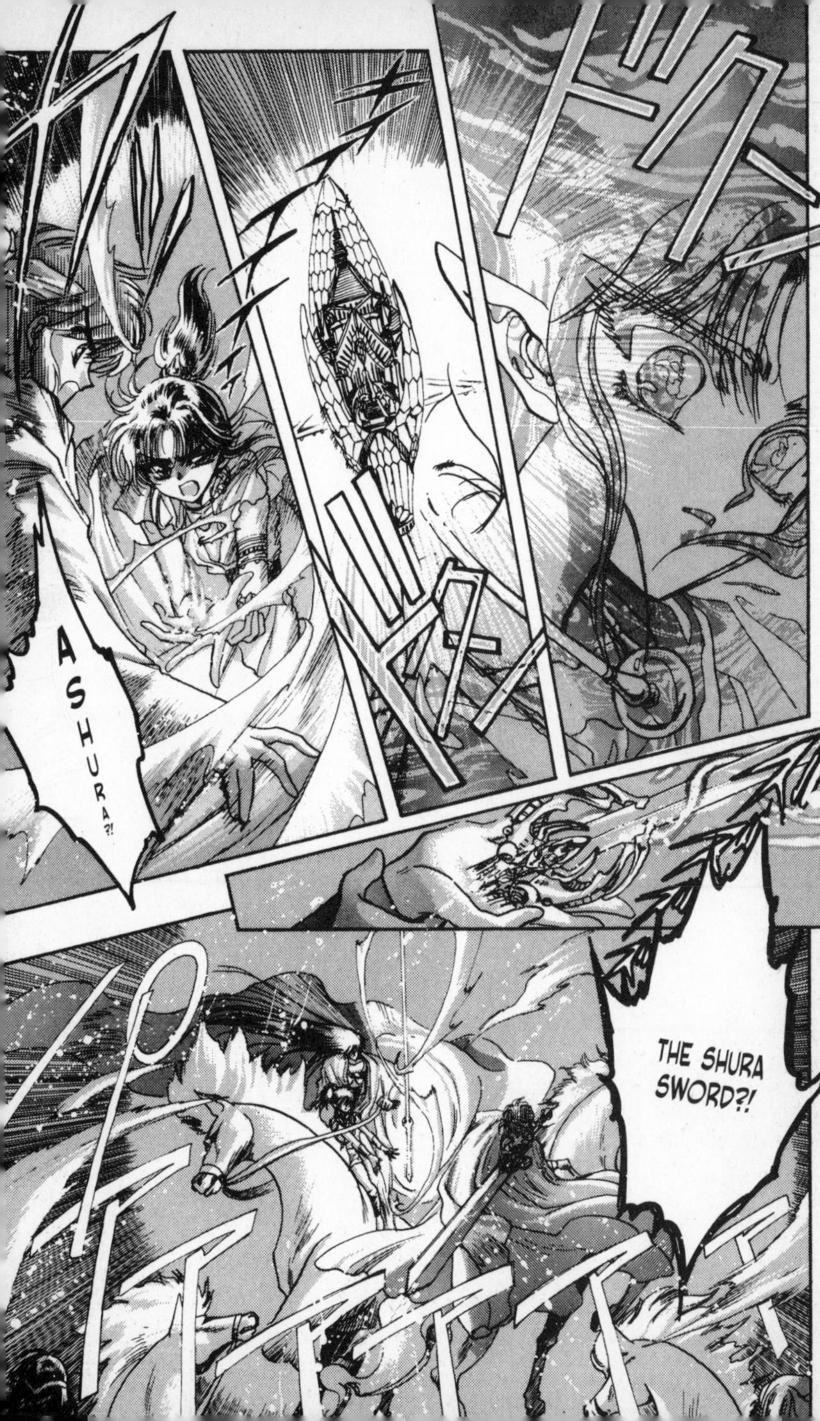
ASHURA?!
THE SHURA SWORD?!

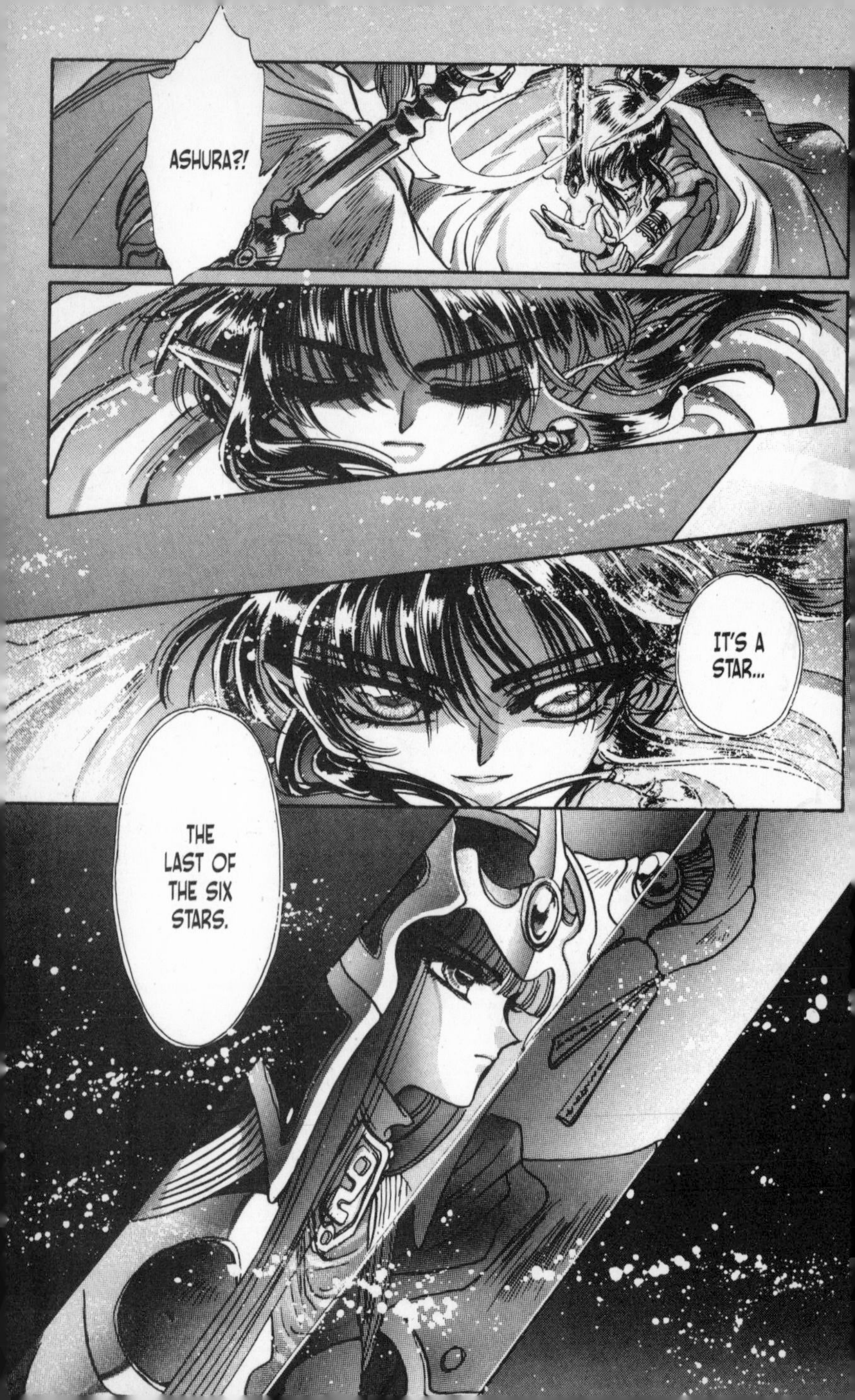
ASHURA?!
IT'S A STAR...
THE LAST OF THE SIX STARS.

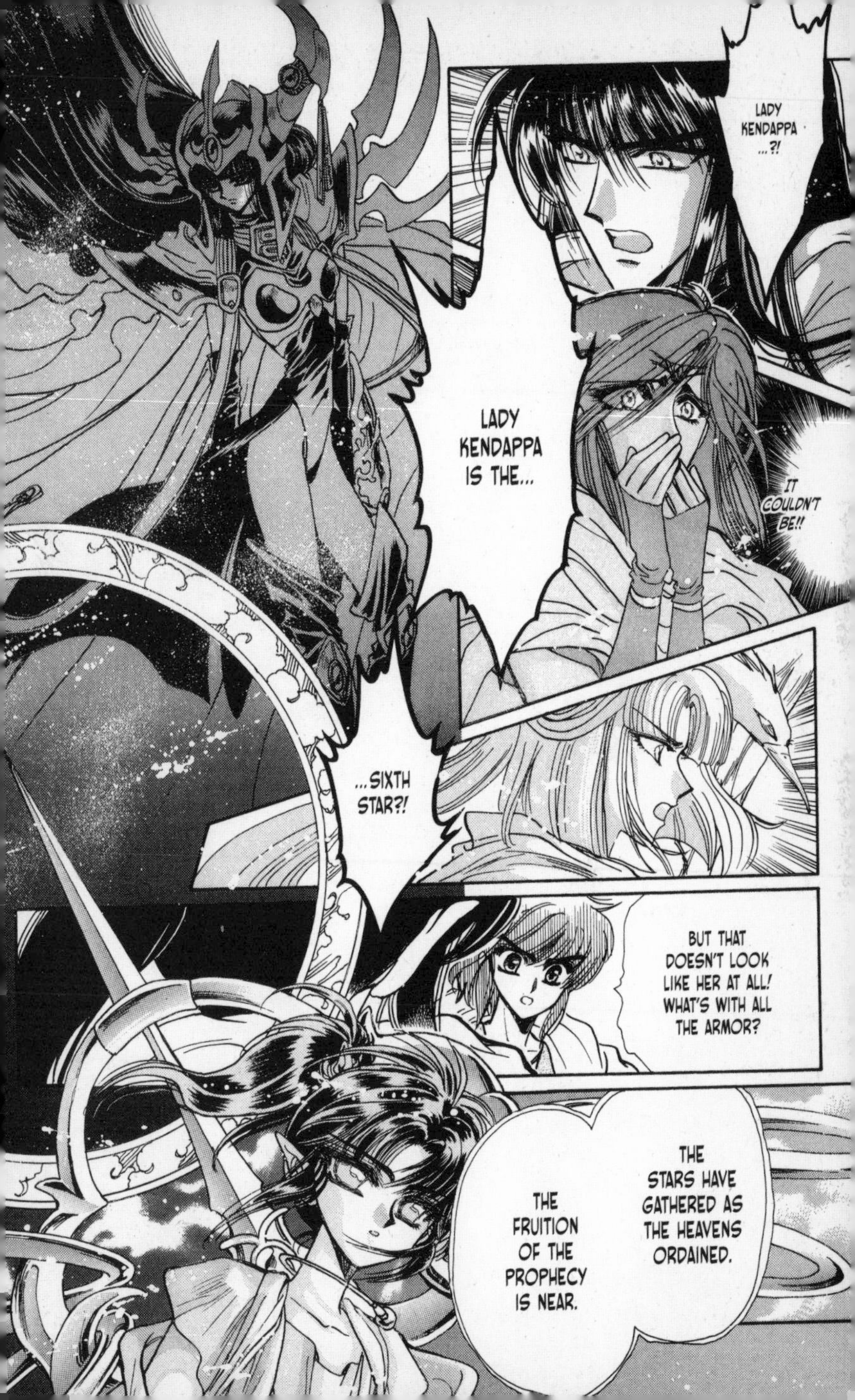
LADY KENDAPPA ...?!
IT COULDN'T BE!!
LADY KENDAPPA IS THE...
...SIXTH STAR?!
BUT THAT DOESN'T LOOK LIKE HER AT ALL! WHAT'S WITH ALL THE ARMOR?
THE STARS HAVE GATHERED AS THE HEAVENS ORDAINED.
THE FRUITION OF THE PROPHECY IS NEAR.

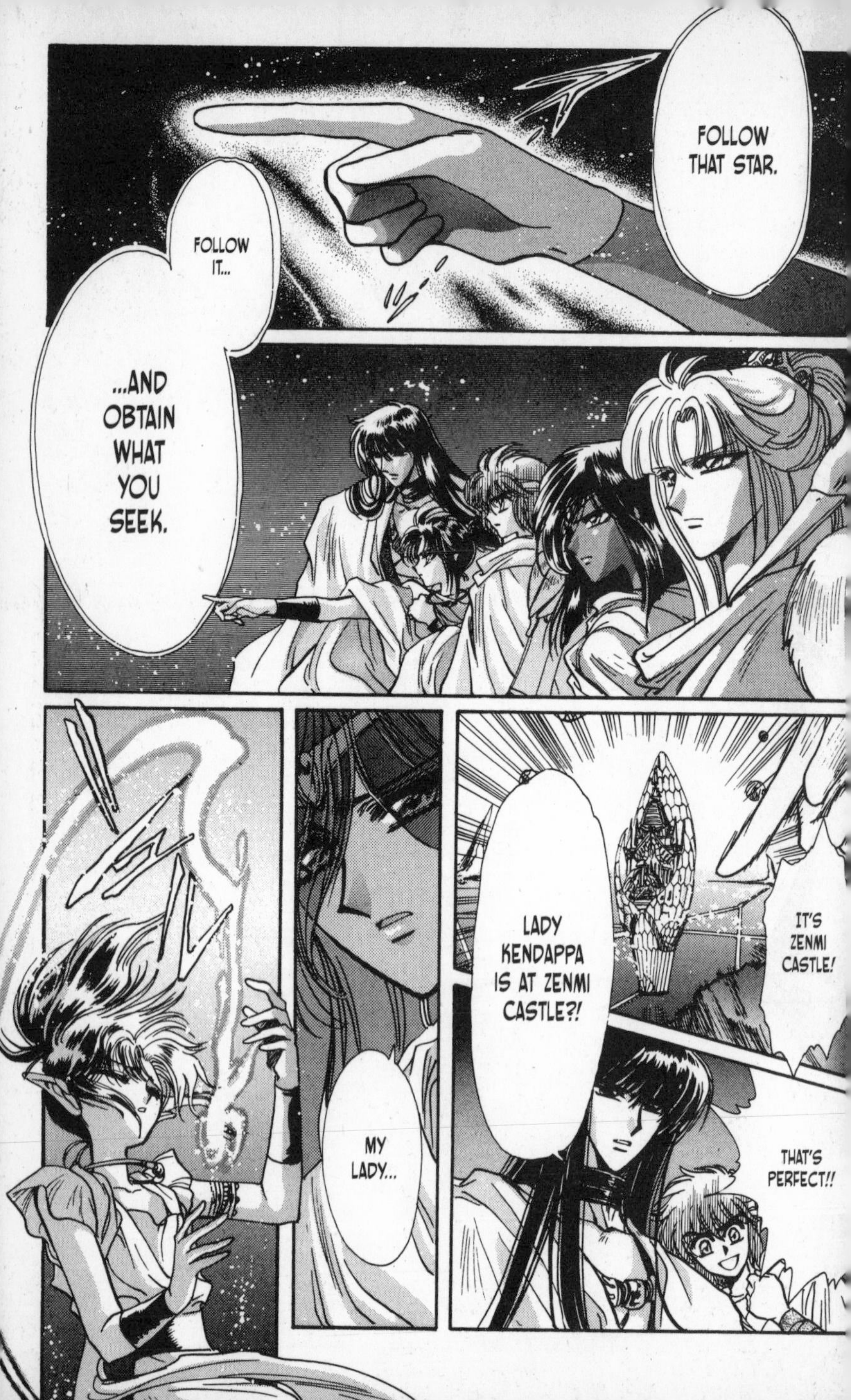
FOLLOW THAT STAR.
FOLLOW IT...
...AND OBTAIN WHAT YOU SEEK.
IT'S ZENMI CASTLE!
LADY KENDAPPA IS AT ZENMI CASTLE?!
THAT'S PERFECT!!
MY LADY...

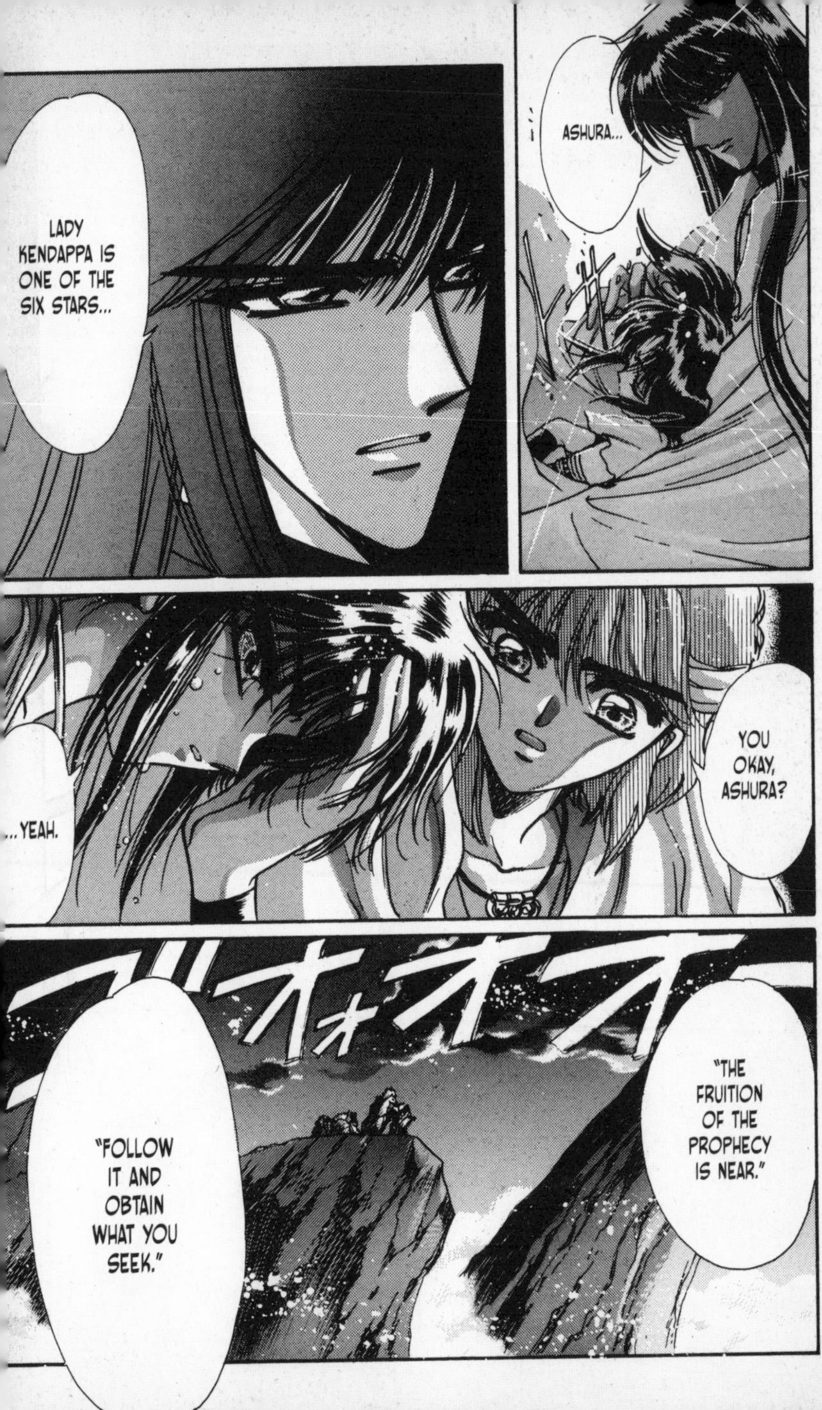
ASHURA...
LADY KENDAPPA IS ONE OF THE SIX STARS...
YOU OKAY, ASHURA?
...YEAH.
"THE FRUITION OF THE PROPHECY IS NEAR."
"FOLLOW IT AND OBTAIN WHAT YOU SEEK."

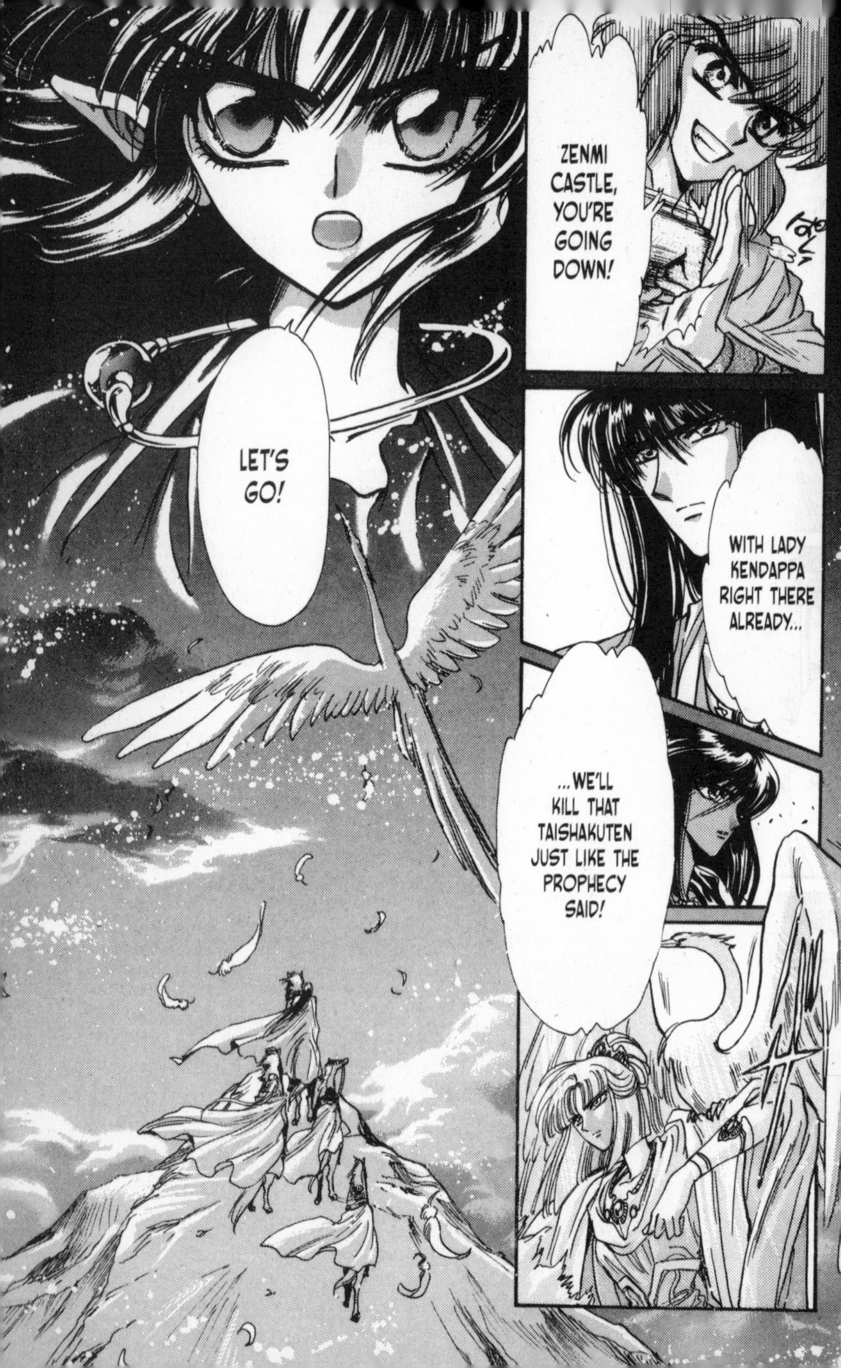

ZENMI CASTLE, YOU'RE GOING DOWN!
WITH LADY KENDAPPA RIGHT THERE ALREADY...
...WE'LL KILL THAT TAISHAKUTEN JUST LIKE THE PROPHECY SAID!
LET'S GO!

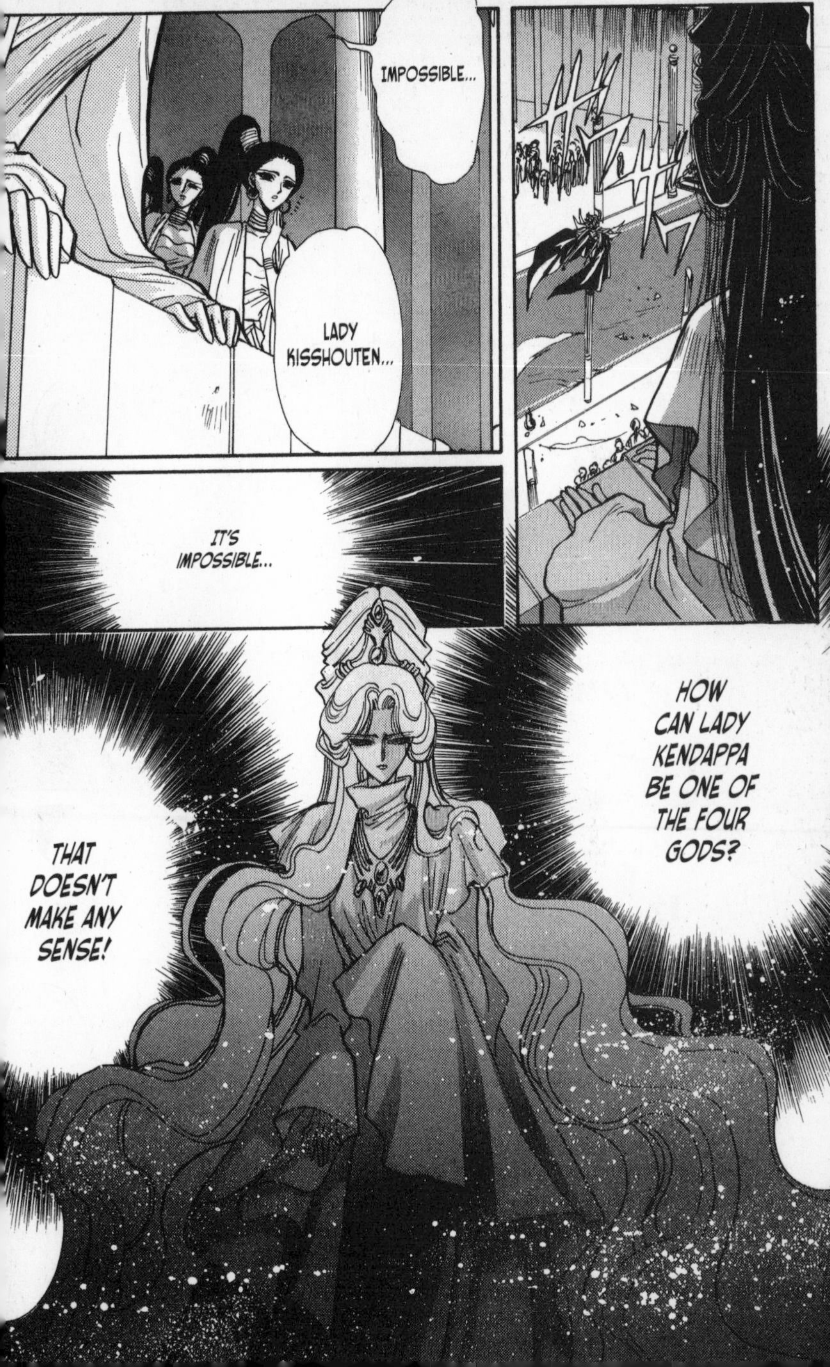
IMPOSSIBLE...
LADY KISSHOUTEN...
IT'S IMPOSSIBLE...
HOW CAN LADY KENDAPPA BE ONE OF THE FOUR GODS?
THAT DOESN'T MAKE ANY SENSE!

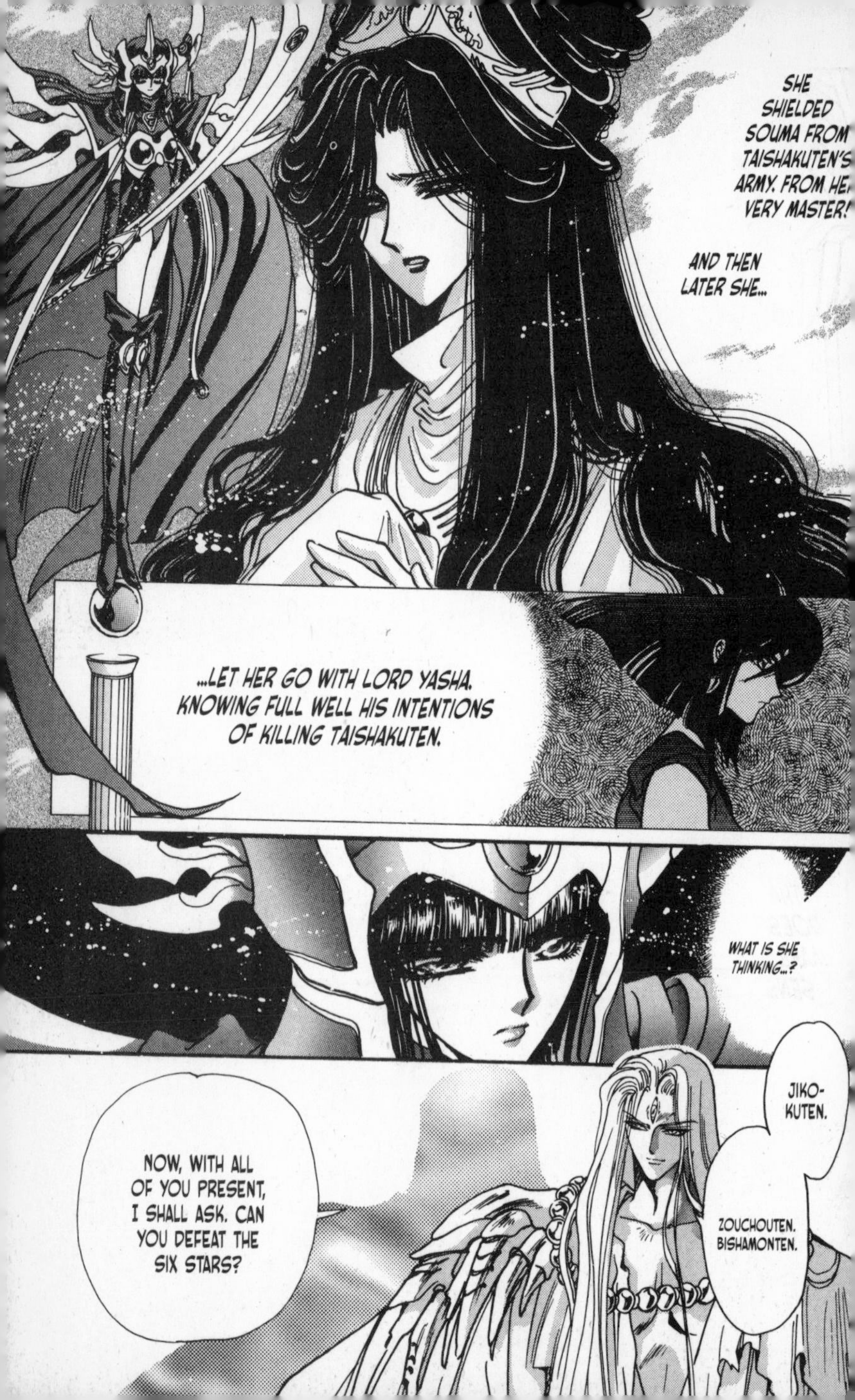
SHE SHIELDED SOUMA FROM TAISHAKUTEN'S ARMY. FROM HER VERY MASTER!
AND THEN LATER SHE...
...LET HER GO WITH LORD YASHA. KNOWING FULL WELL HIS INTENTIONS OF KILLING TAISHAKUTEN.
WHAT IS SHE THINKING...?
JIKO-KUTEN.
ZOUCHOUTEN. BISHAMONTEN.
NOW, WITH ALL OF YOU PRESENT, I SHALL ASK. CAN YOU DEFEAT THE SIX STARS?

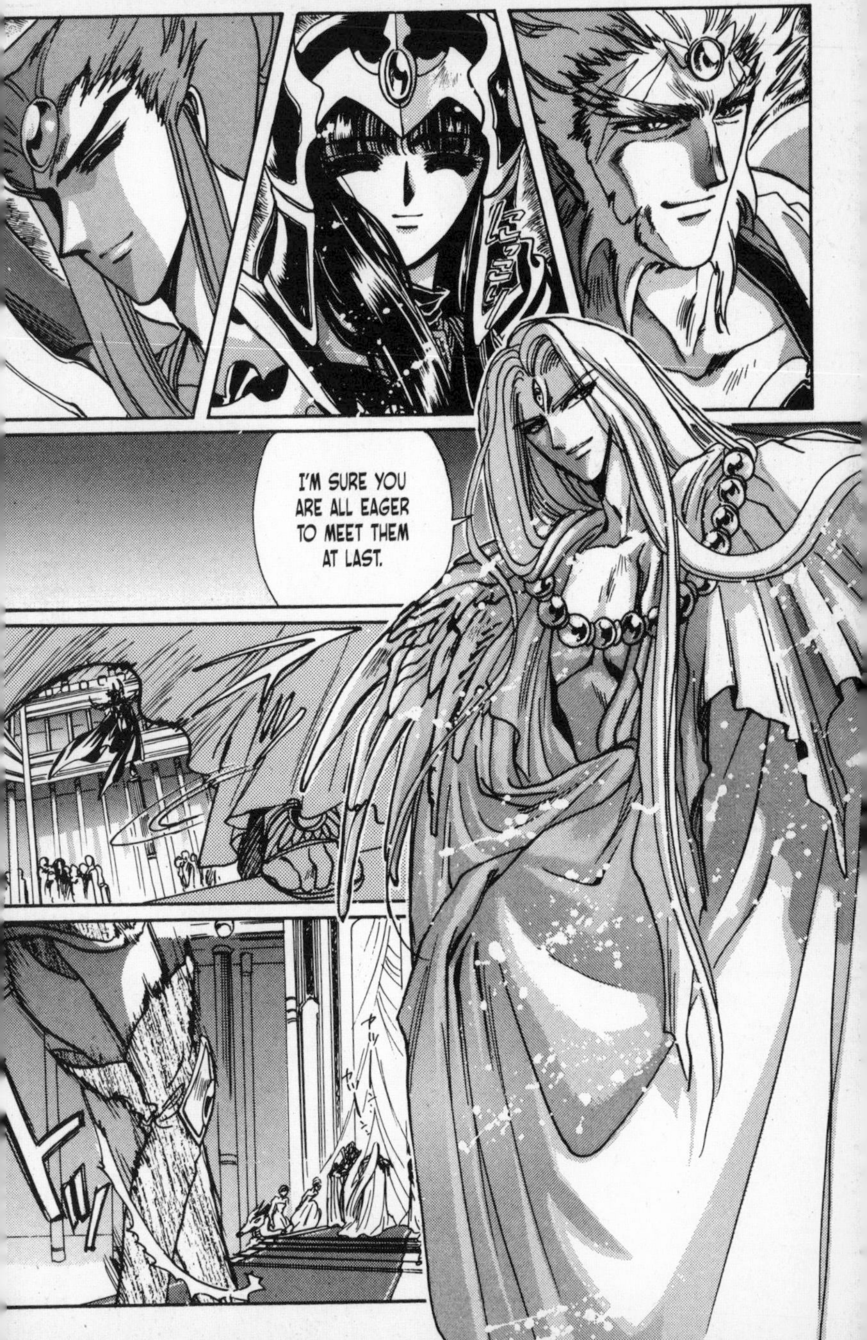
I'M SURE YOU ARE ALL EAGER TO MEET THEM AT LAST.

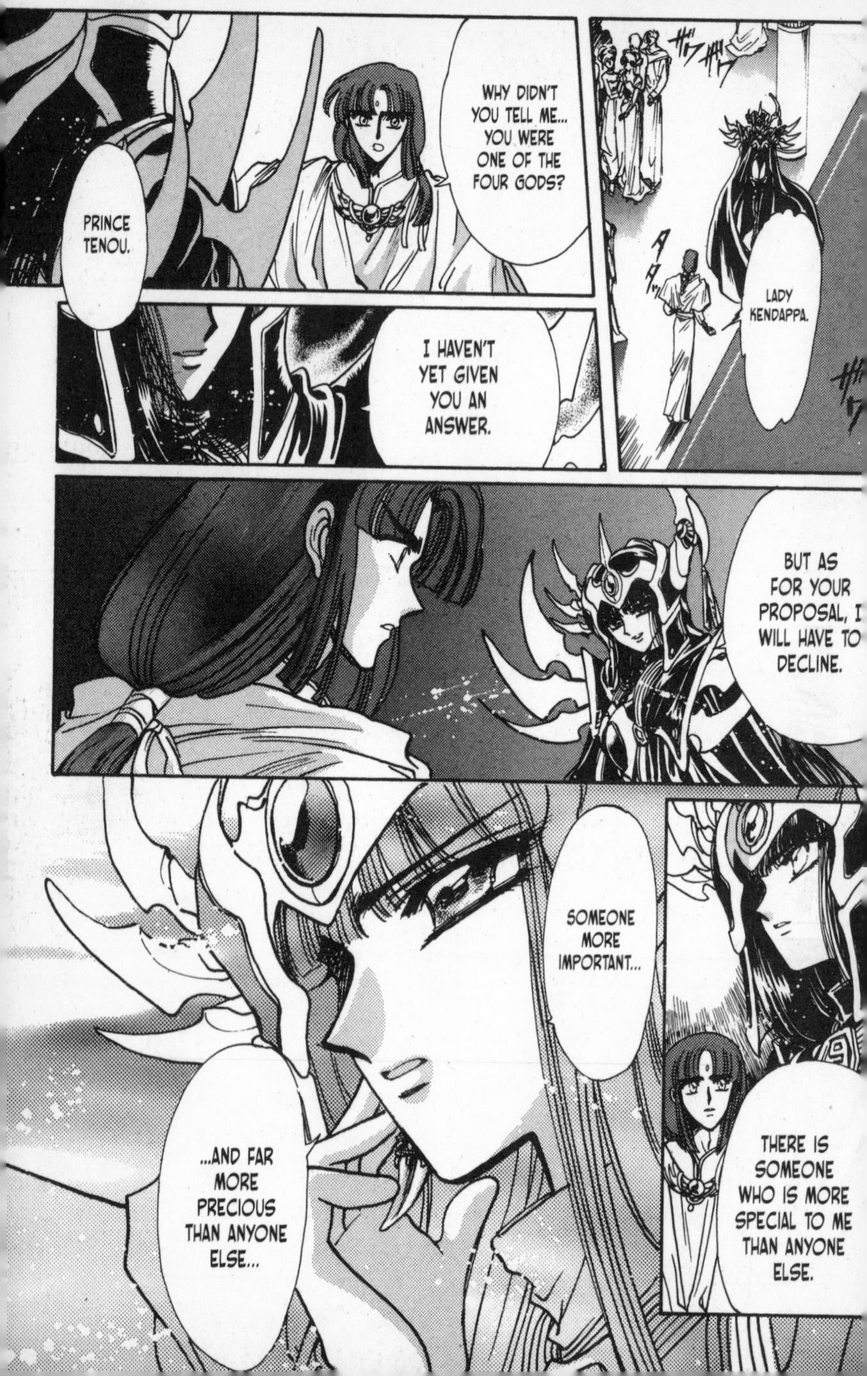
LADY KENDAPPA.
WHY DIDN'T YOU TELL ME... YOU WERE ONE OF THE FOUR GODS?
PRINCE TENOU.
I HAVEN'T YET GIVEN YOU AN ANSWER.
BUT AS FOR YOUR PROPOSAL, I WILL HAVE TO DECLINE.
THERE IS SOMEONE WHO IS MORE SPECIAL TO ME THAN ANYONE ELSE.
SOMEONE MORE IMPORTANT...
...AND FAR MORE PRECIOUS THAN ANYONE ELSE...

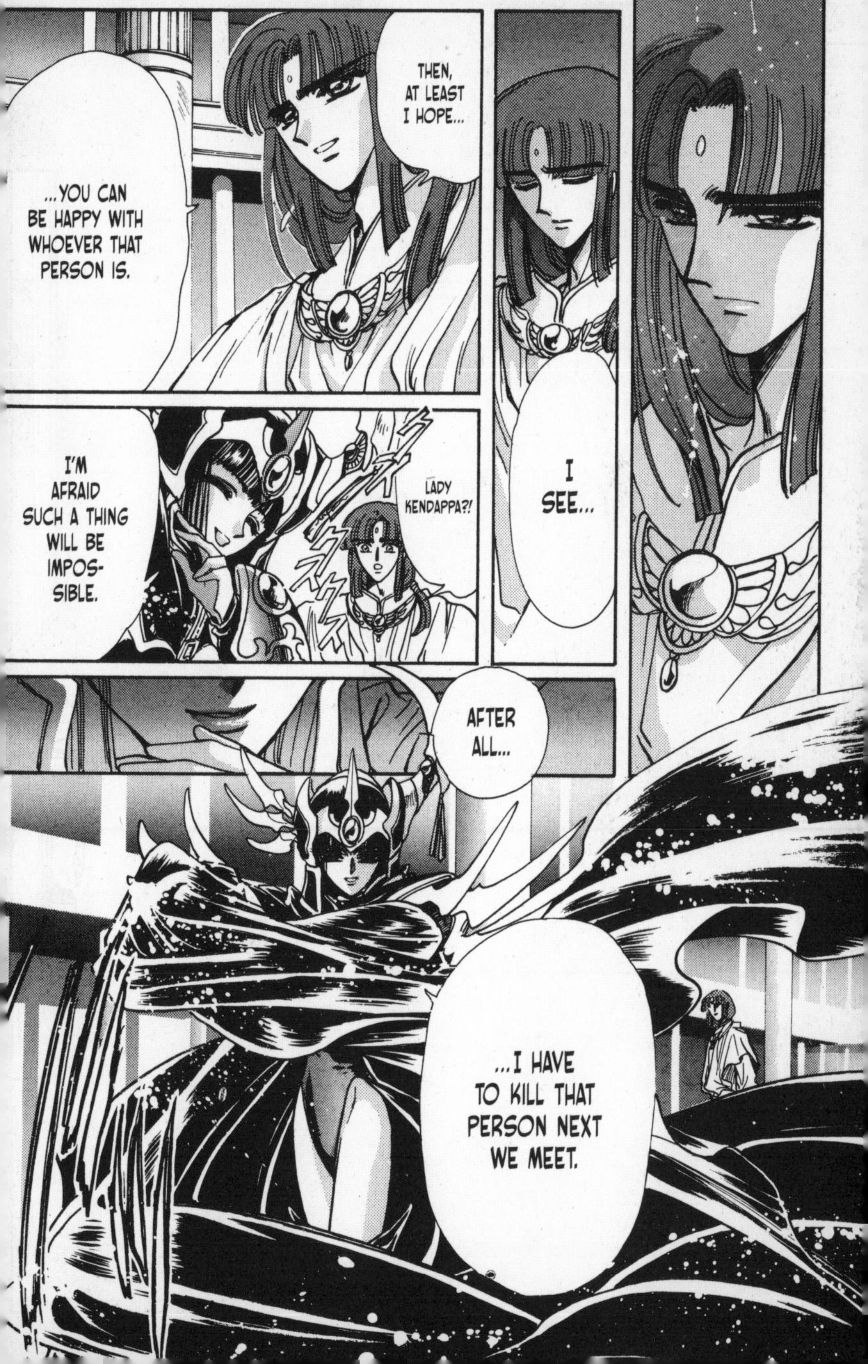
I SEE...
THEN, AT LEAST I HOPE...
...YOU CAN BE HAPPY WITH WHOEVER THAT PERSON IS.
LADY KENDAPPA?!
I'M AFRAID SUCH A THING WILL BE IMPOSSIBLE.
AFTER ALL...
...I HAVE TO KILL THAT PERSON NEXT WE MEET.

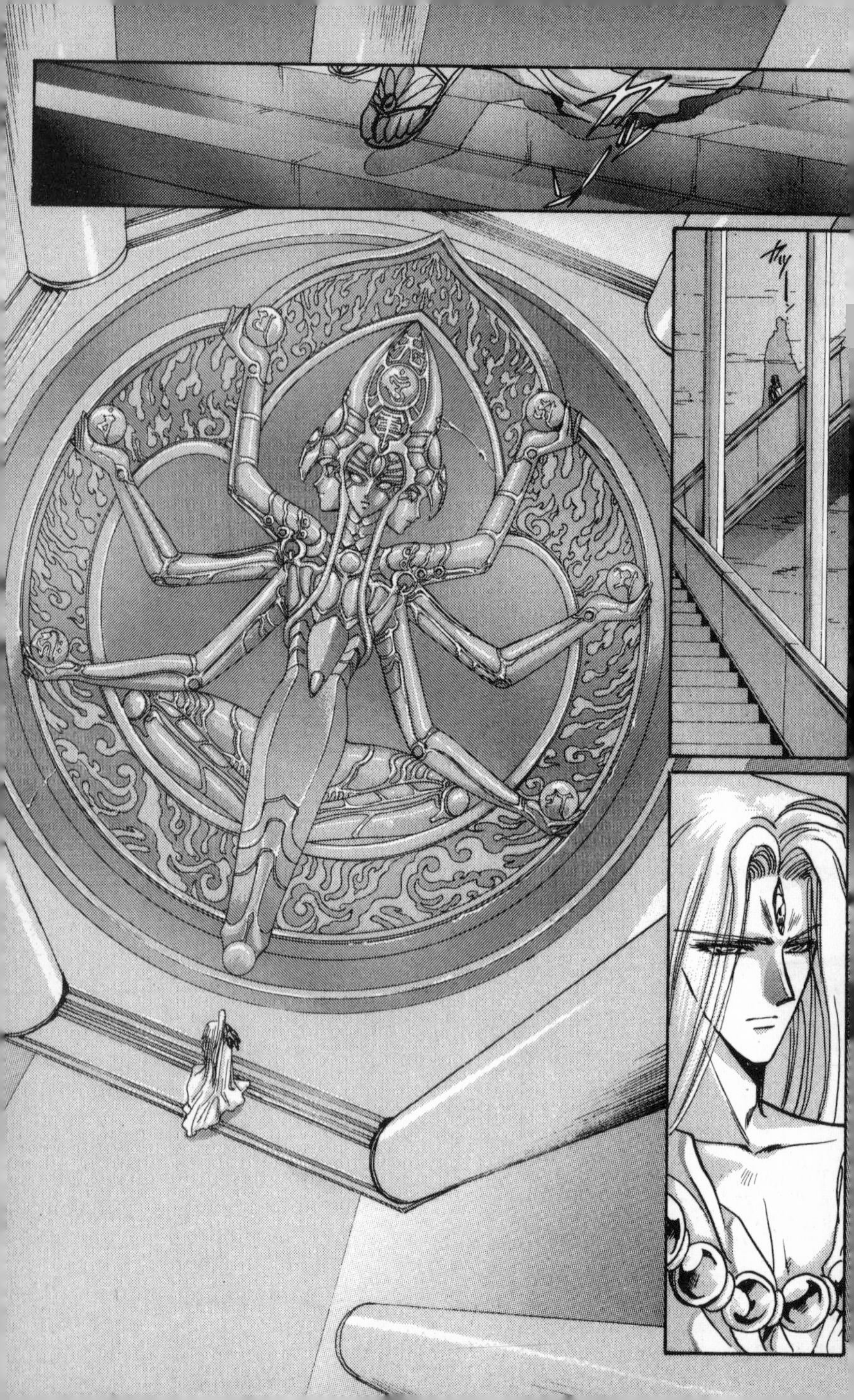
ガッーン

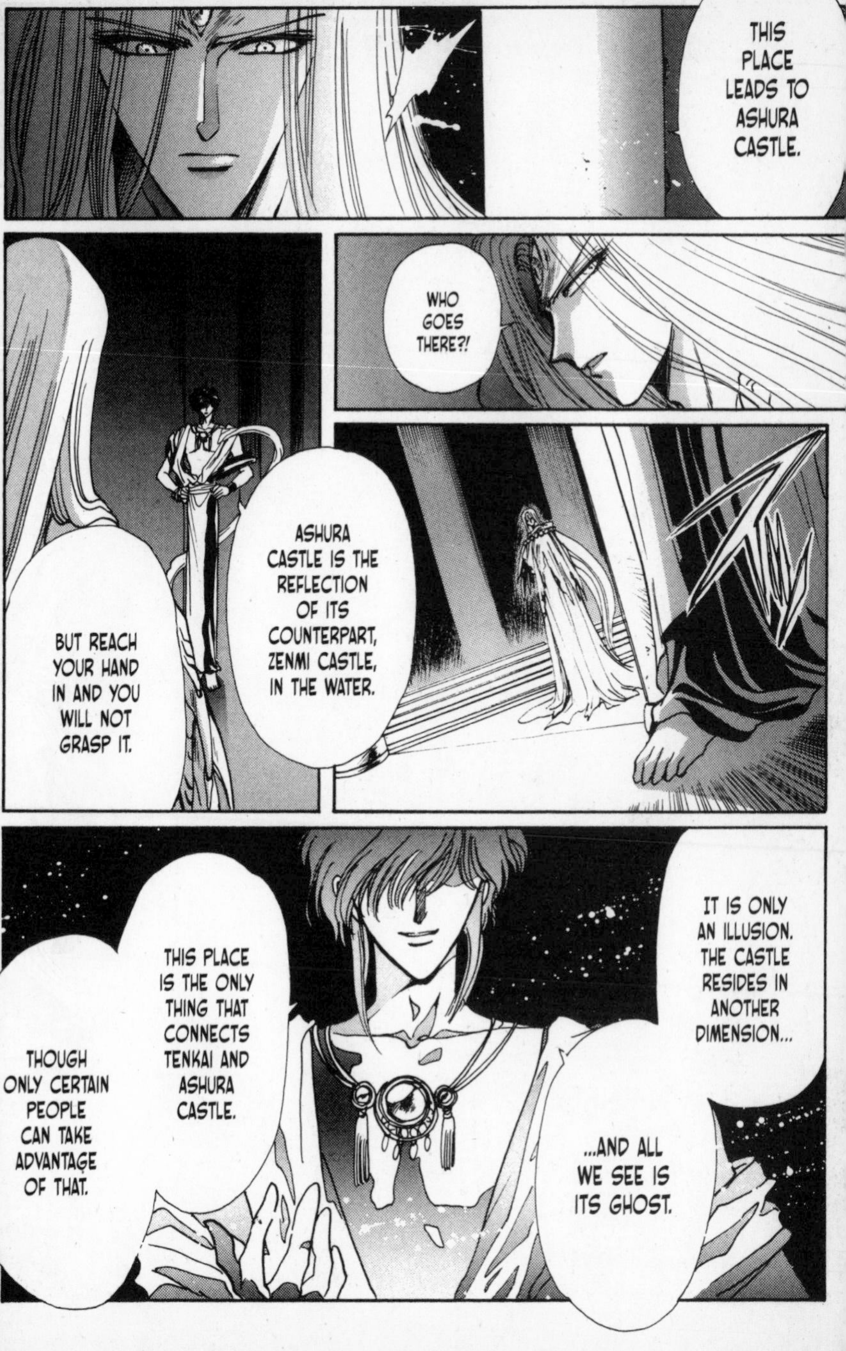
THIS PLACE LEADS TO ASHURA CASTLE.
WHO GOES THERE?!
ASHURA CASTLE IS THE REFLECTION OF ITS COUNTERPART, ZENMI CASTLE, IN THE WATER.
BUT REACH YOUR HAND IN AND YOU WILL NOT GRASP IT.
IT IS ONLY AN ILLUSION. THE CASTLE RESIDES IN ANOTHER DIMENSION...
...AND ALL WE SEE IS ITS GHOST.
THIS PLACE IS THE ONLY THING THAT CONNECTS TENKAI AND ASHURA CASTLE.
THOUGH ONLY CERTAIN PEOPLE CAN TAKE ADVANTAGE OF THAT.

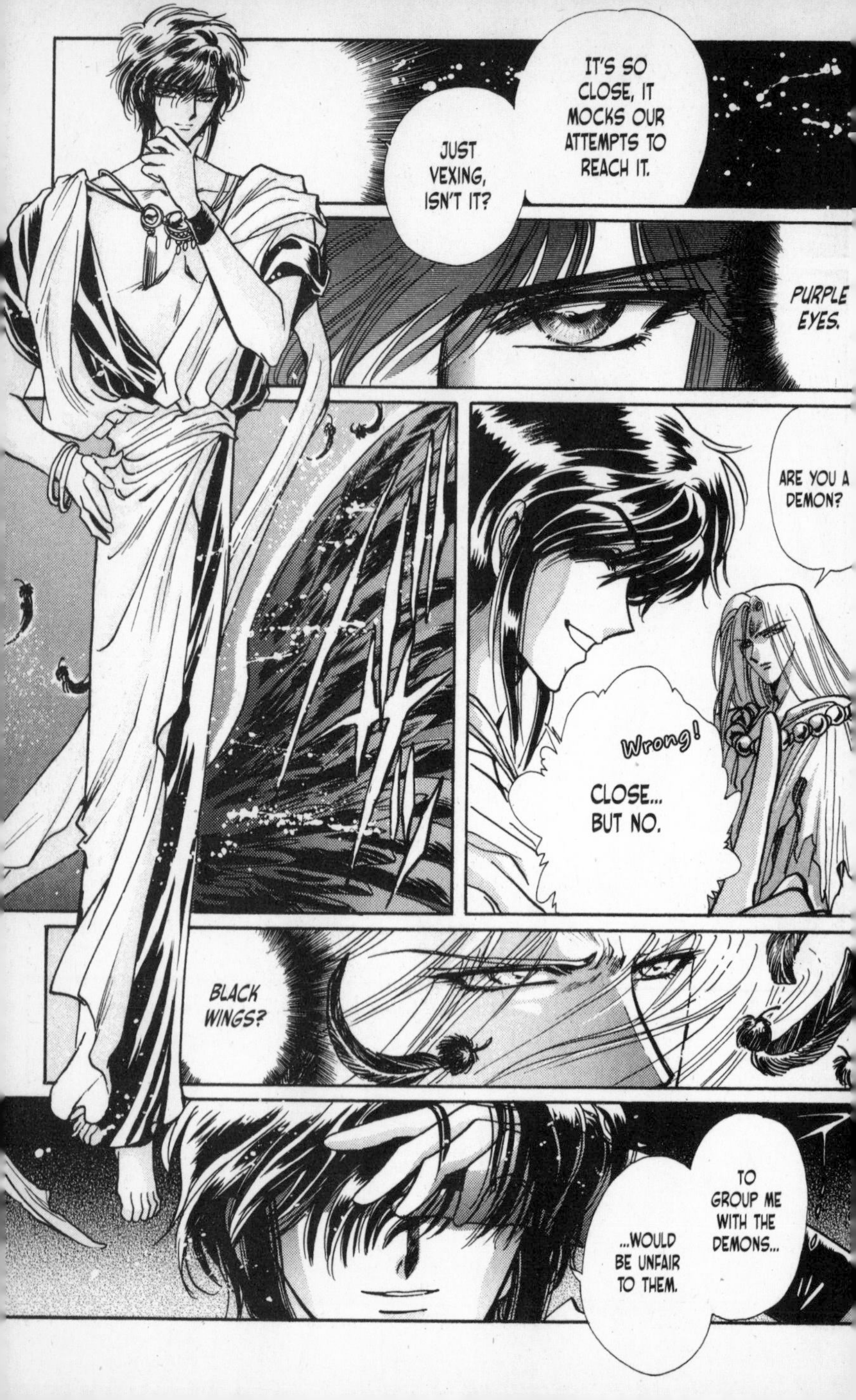
IT'S SO CLOSE, IT MOCKS OUR ATTEMPTS TO REACH IT.
JUST VEXING, ISN'T IT?
PURPLE EYES.
ARE YOU A DEMON?
Wrong!
CLOSE... BUT NO.
BLACK WINGS?
TO GROUP ME WITH THE DEMONS...
...WOULD BE UNFAIR TO THEM.

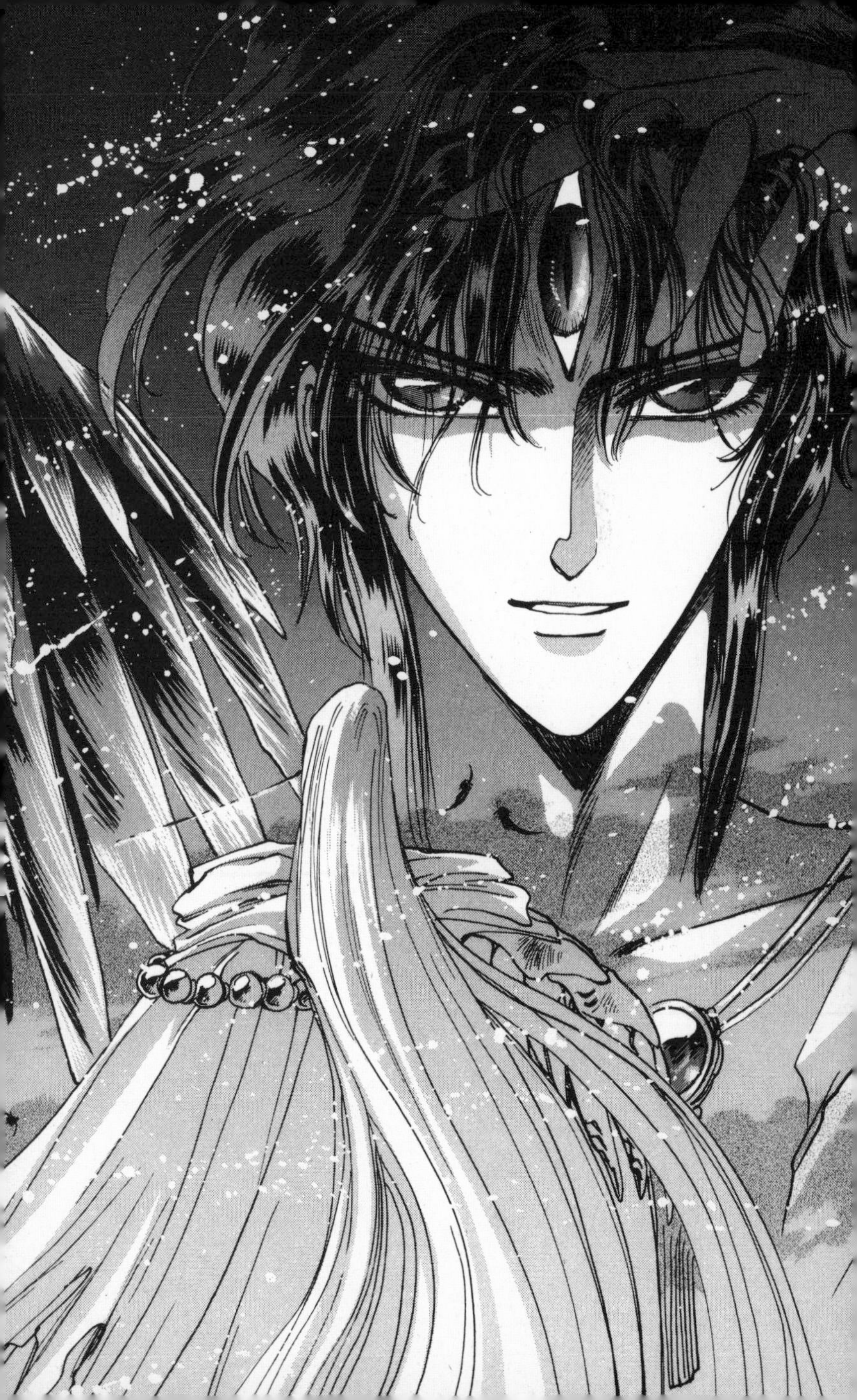

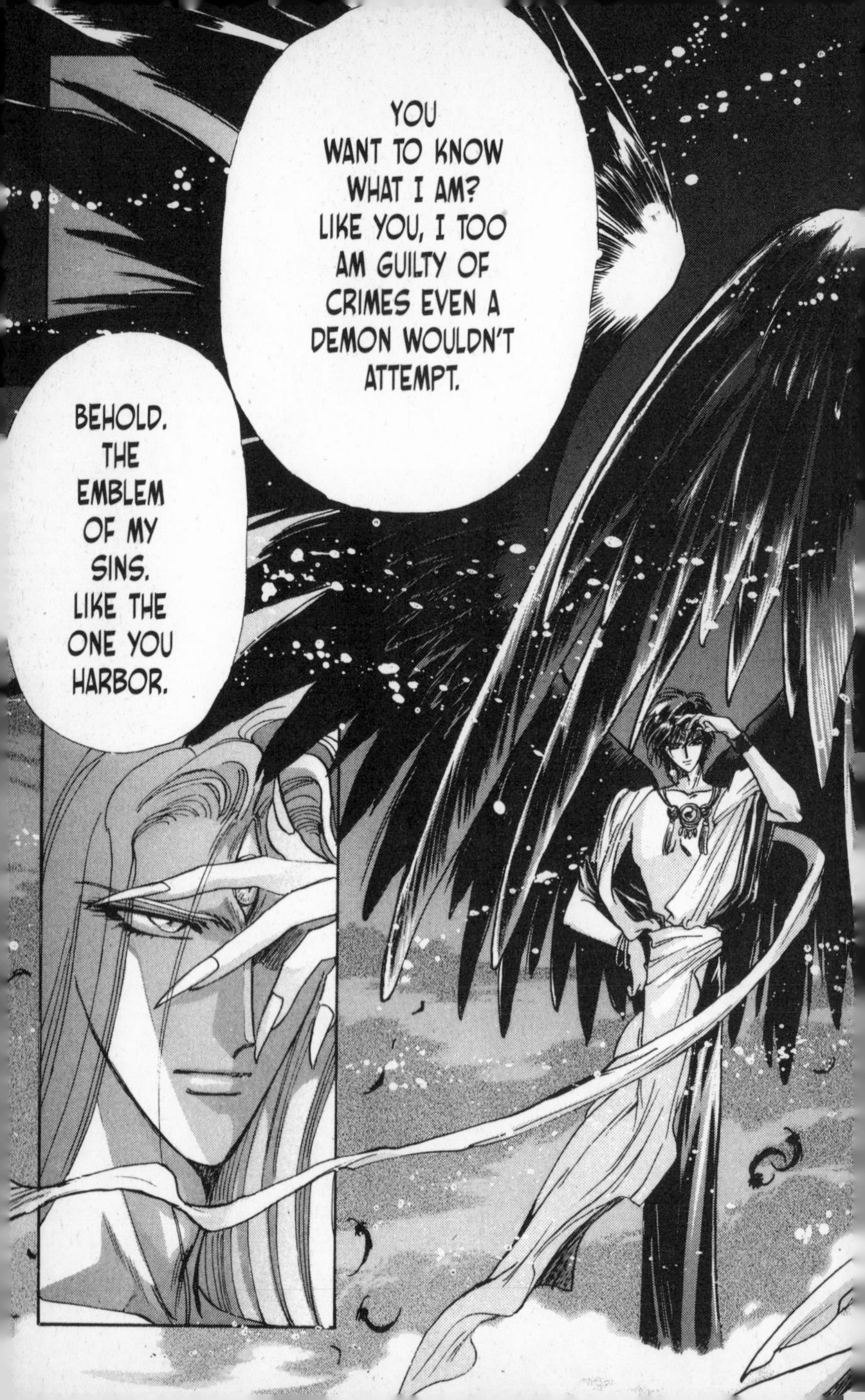
YOU WANT TO KNOW WHAT I AM? LIKE YOU, I TOO AM GUILTY OF CRIMES EVEN A DEMON WOULDN'T ATTEMPT.
BEHOLD. THE EMBLEM OF MY SINS. LIKE THE ONE YOU HARBOR.

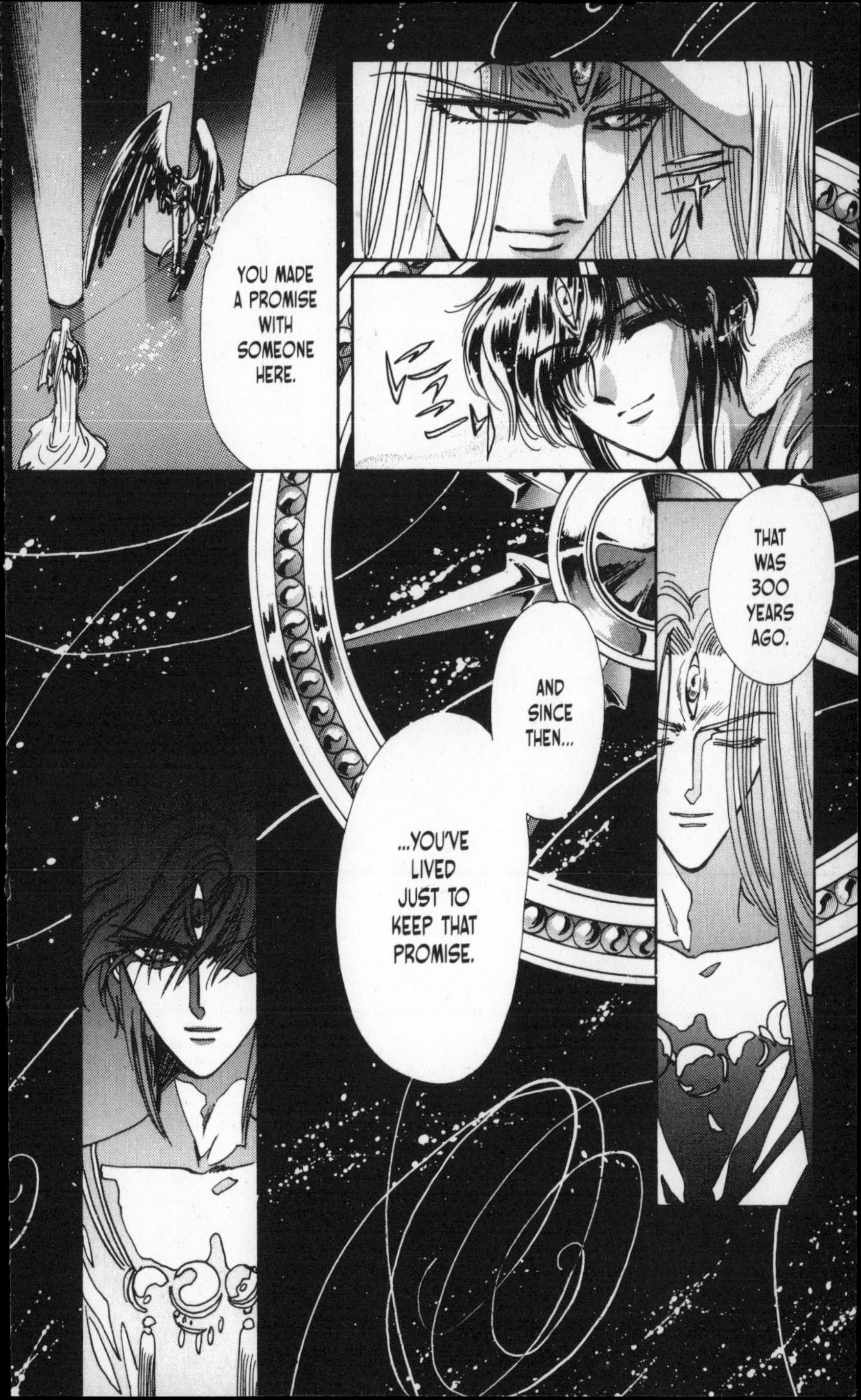
YOU MADE A PROMISE WITH SOMEONE HERE.
THAT WAS 300 YEARS AGO.
AND SINCE THEN...
...YOU'VE LIVED JUST TO KEEP THAT PROMISE.

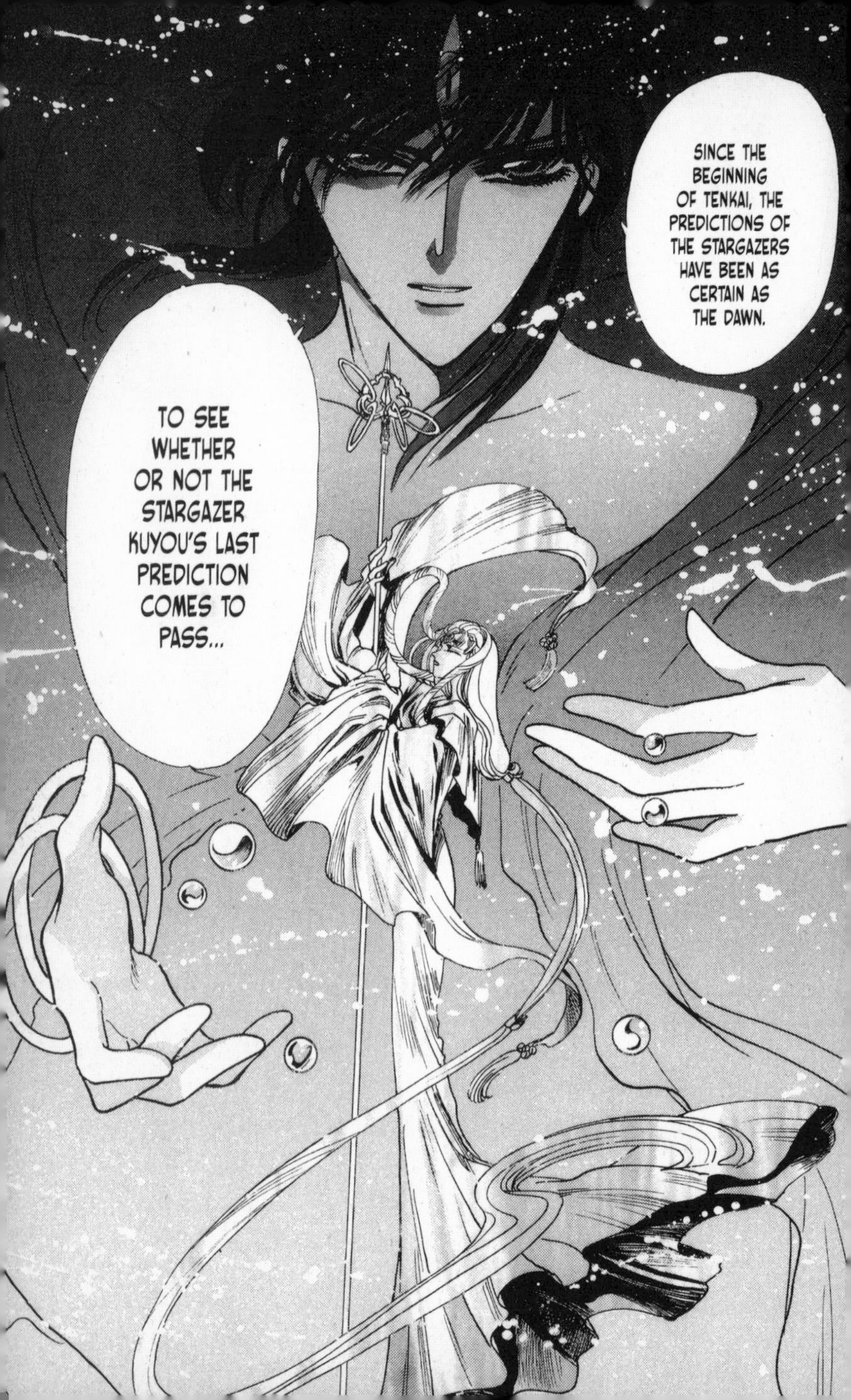
SINCE THE BEGINNING OF TENKAI, THE PREDICTIONS OF THE STARGAZERS HAVE BEEN AS CERTAIN AS THE DAWN.
TO SEE WHETHER OR NOT THE STARGAZER KUYOU'S LAST PREDICTION COMES TO PASS...

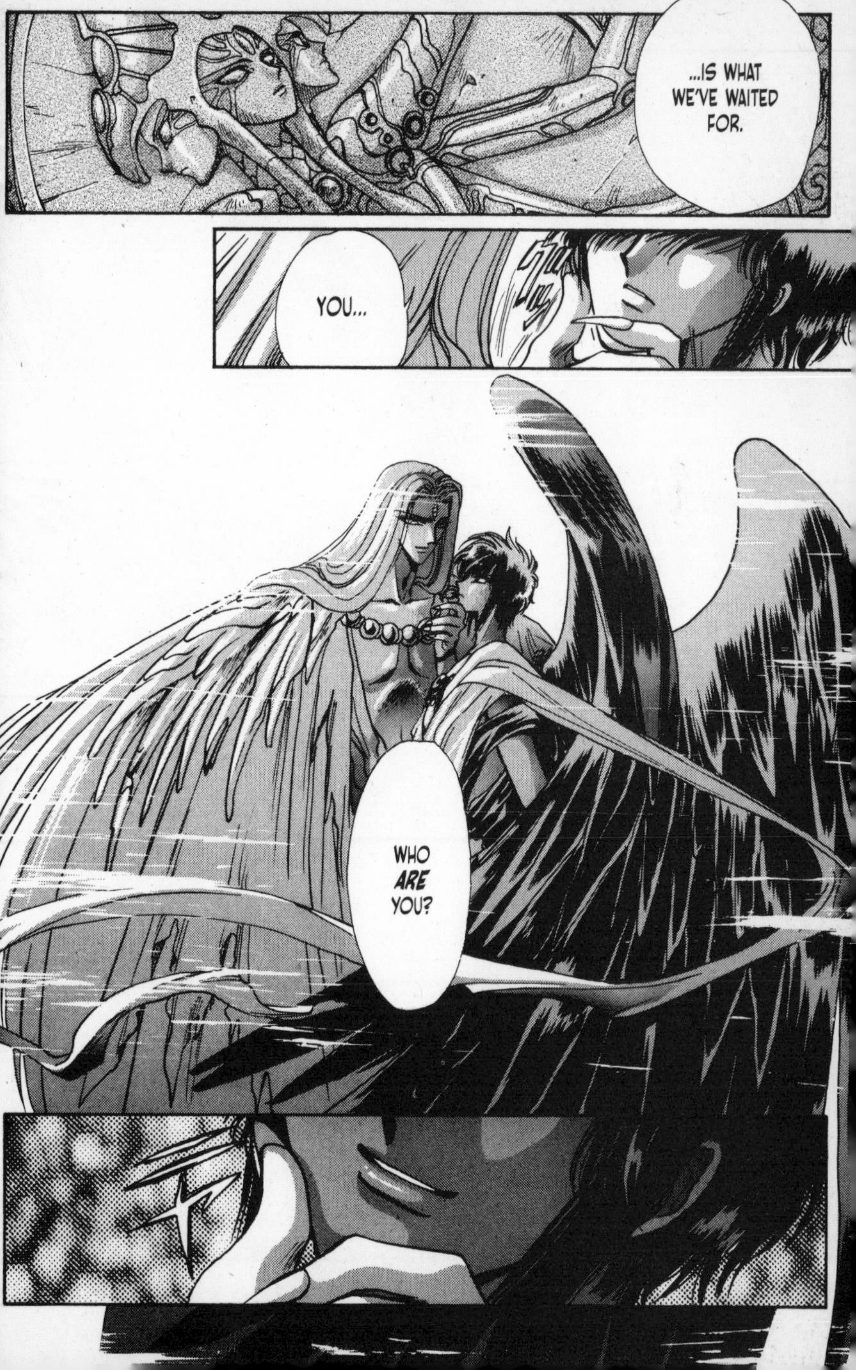
...IS WHAT WE'VE WAITED FOR.
YOU...
WHO *ARE* YOU?

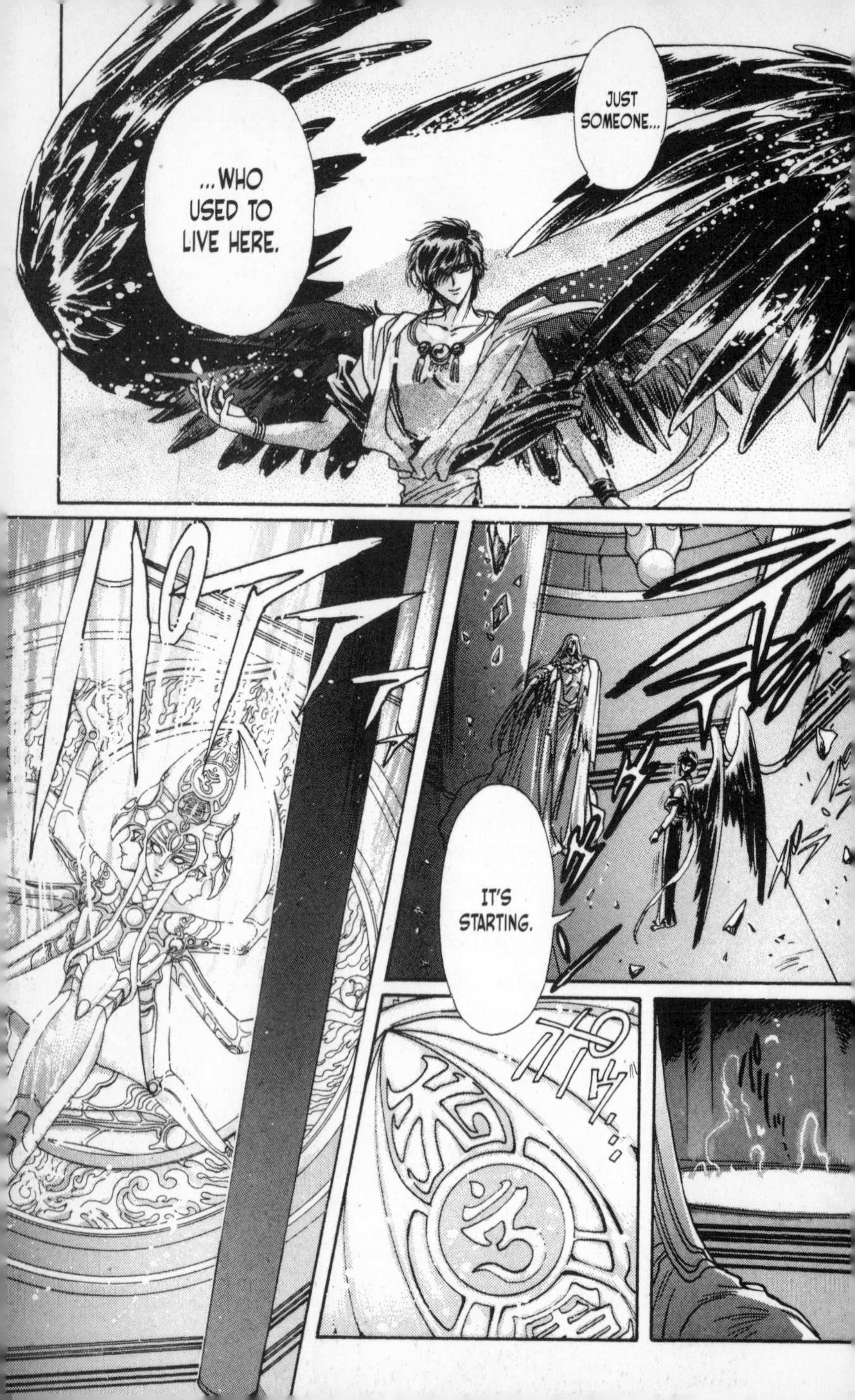
JUST SOMEONE...
...WHO USED TO LIVE HERE.
IT'S STARTING.

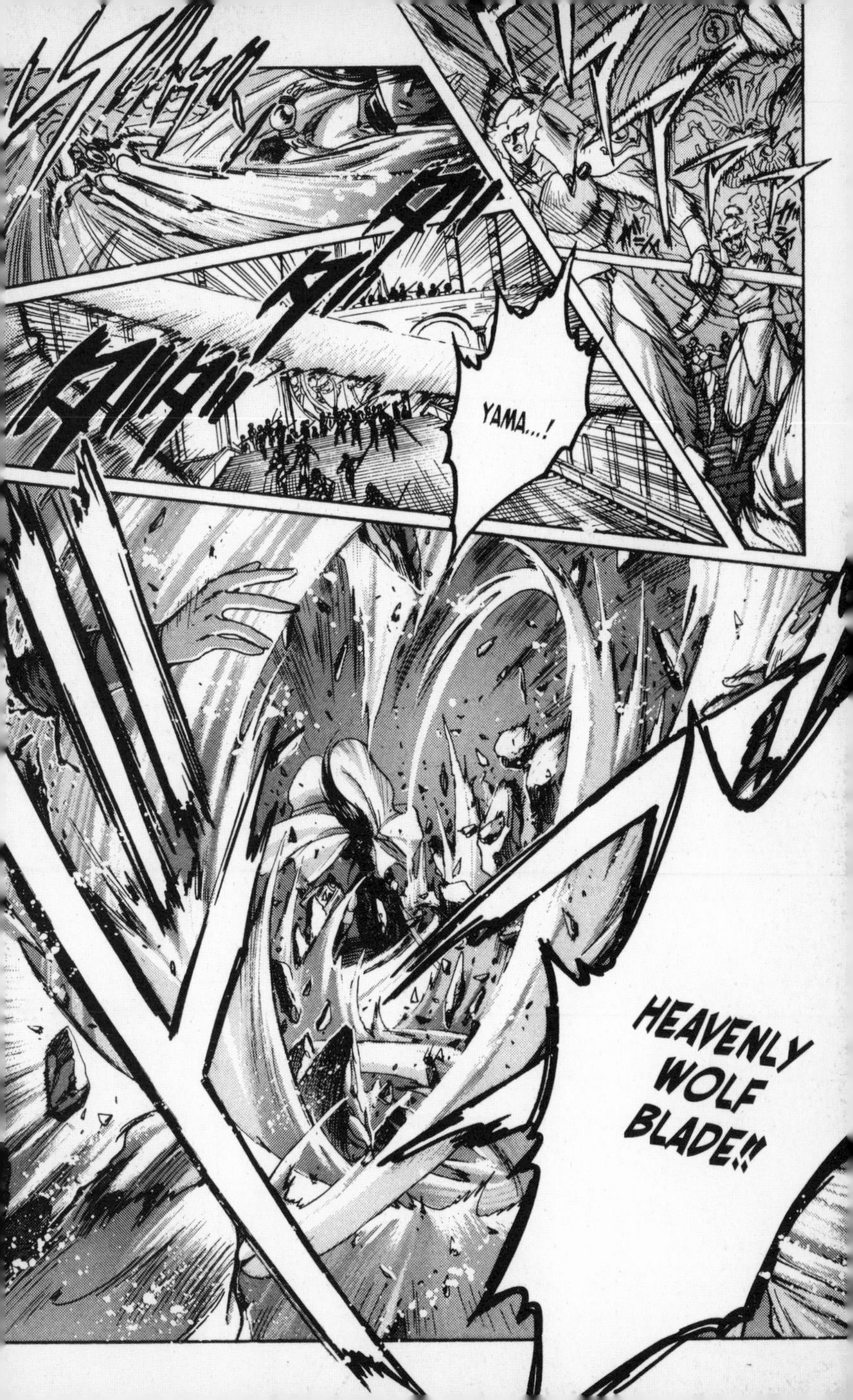
YAMA...!
HEAVENLY WOLF BLADE!!

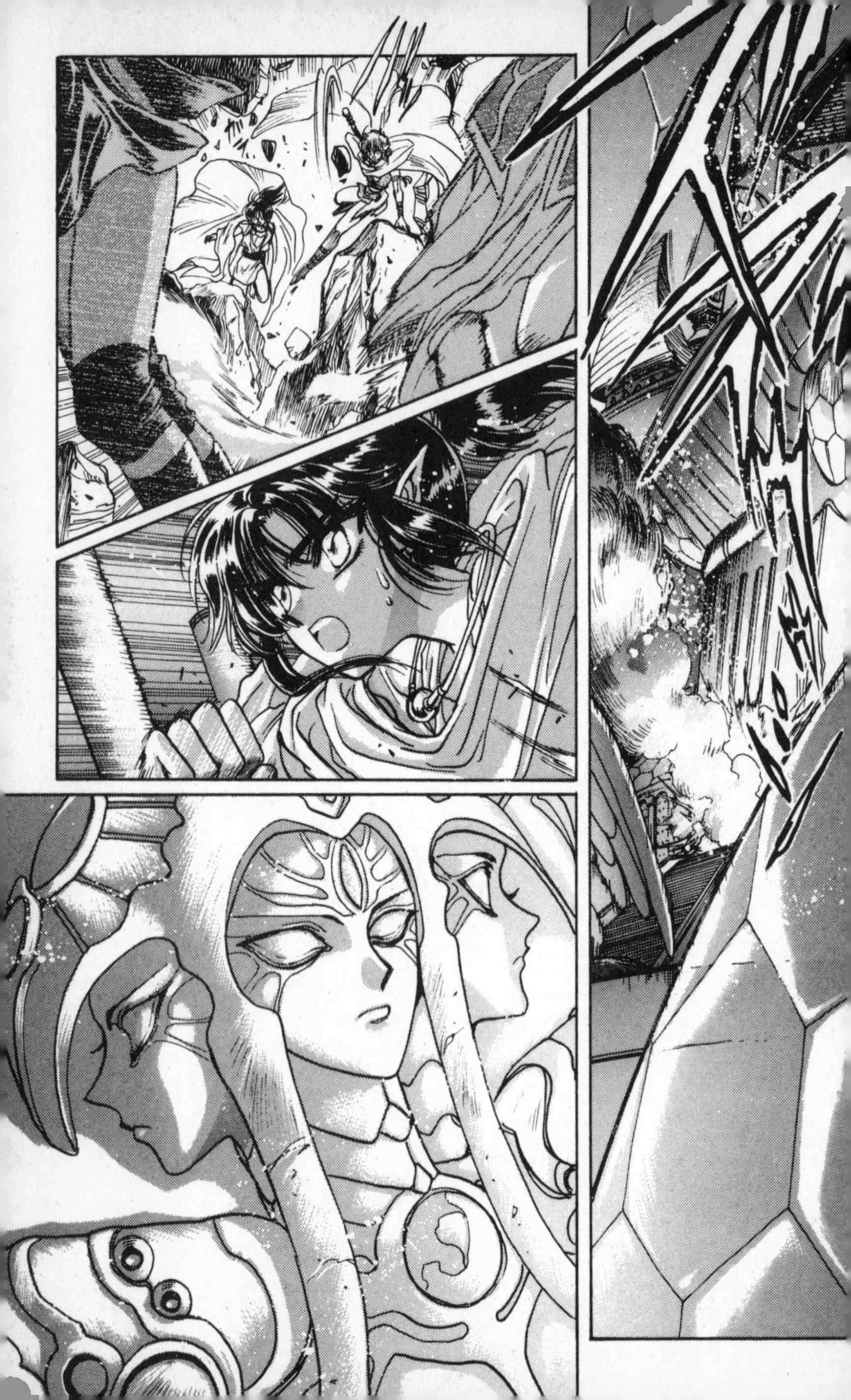

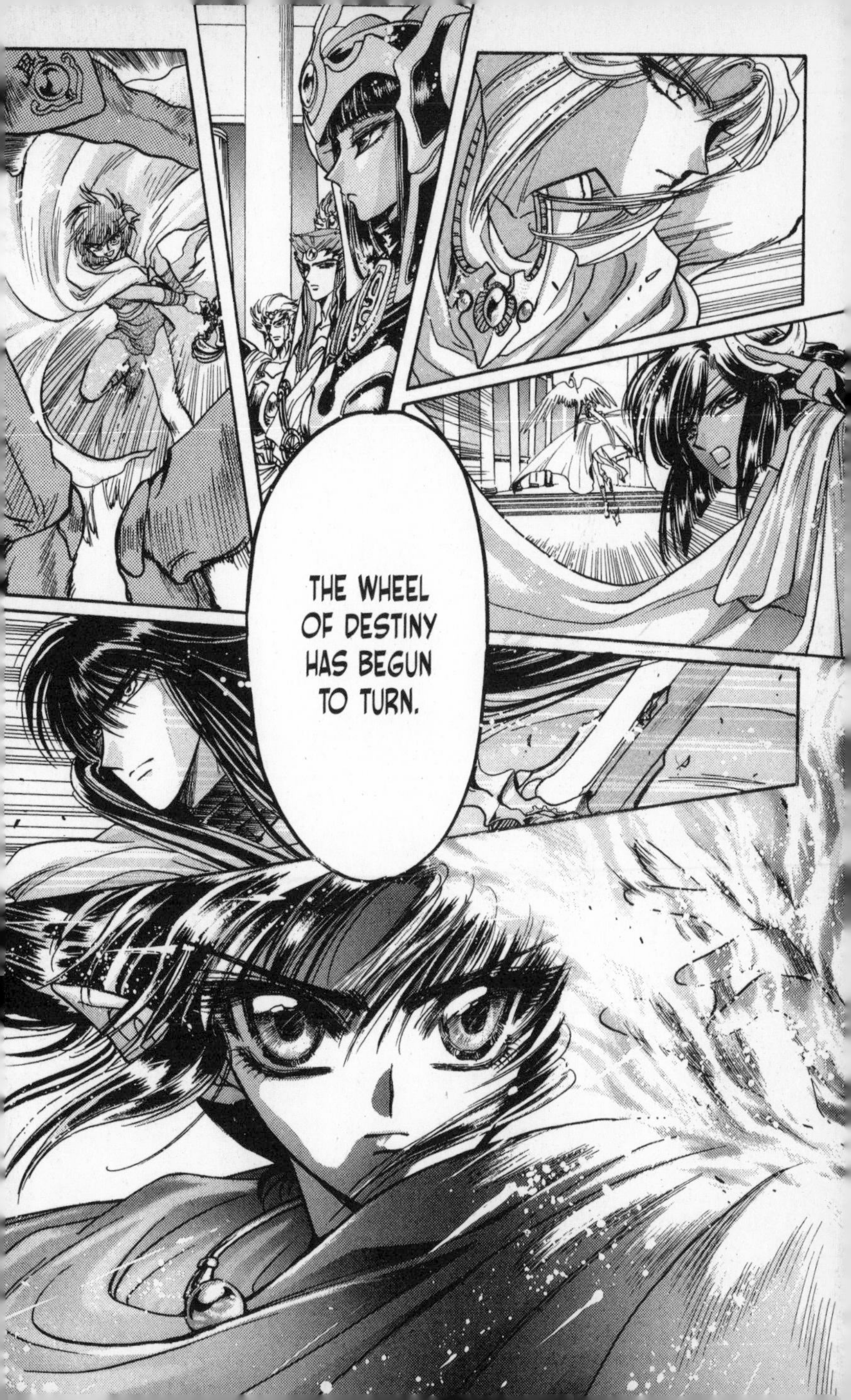
THE WHEEL OF DESTINY HAS BEGUN TO TURN.

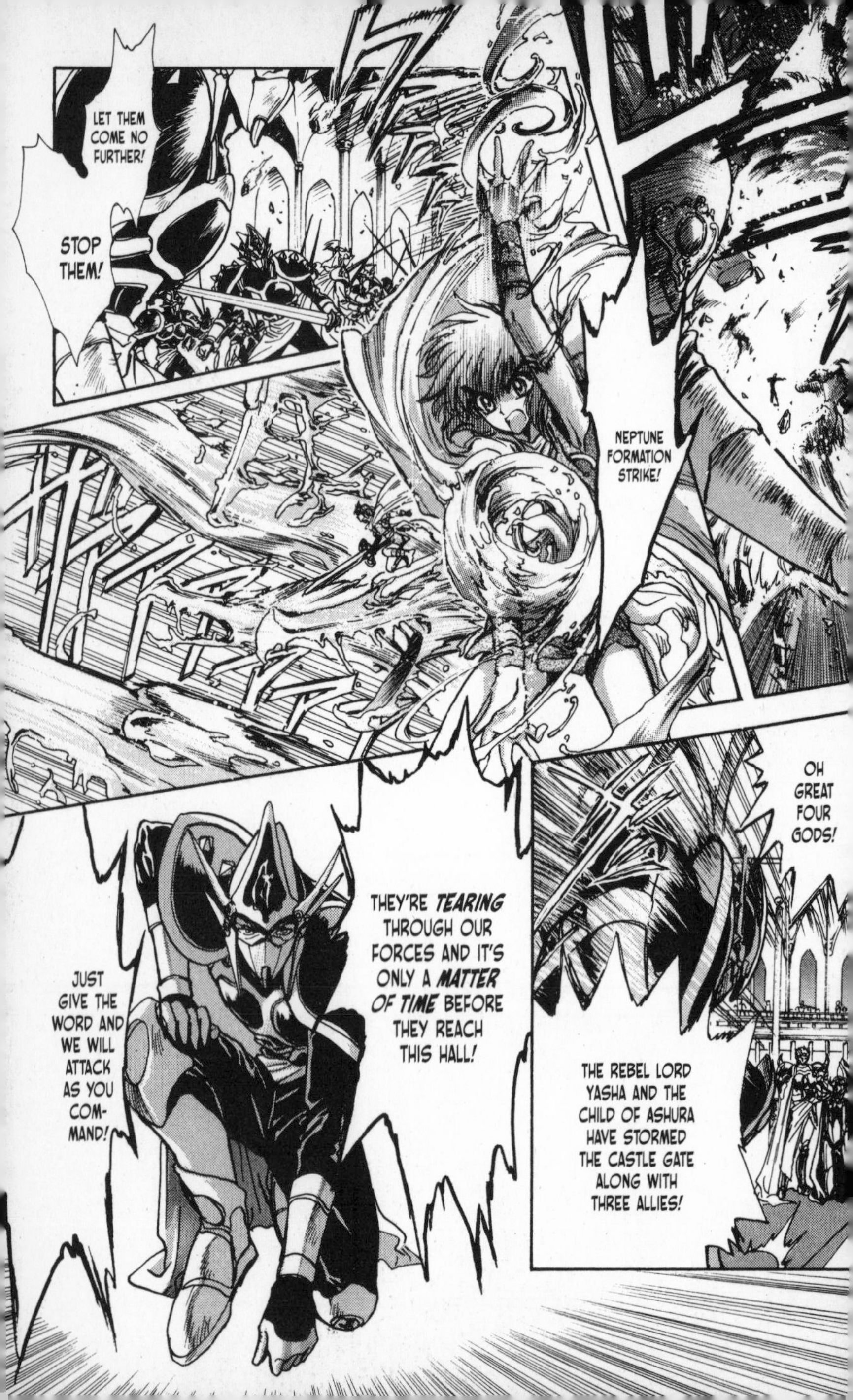
NEPTUNE FORMATION STRIKE!
LET THEM COME NO FURTHER!
STOP THEM!
OH GREAT FOUR GODS!
THE REBEL LORD YASHA AND THE CHILD OF ASHURA HAVE STORMED THE CASTLE GATE ALONG WITH THREE ALLIES!
THEY'RE *TEARING* THROUGH OUR FORCES AND IT'S ONLY A *MATTER OF TIME* BEFORE THEY REACH THIS HALL!
JUST GIVE THE WORD AND WE WILL ATTACK AS YOU COM-MAND!

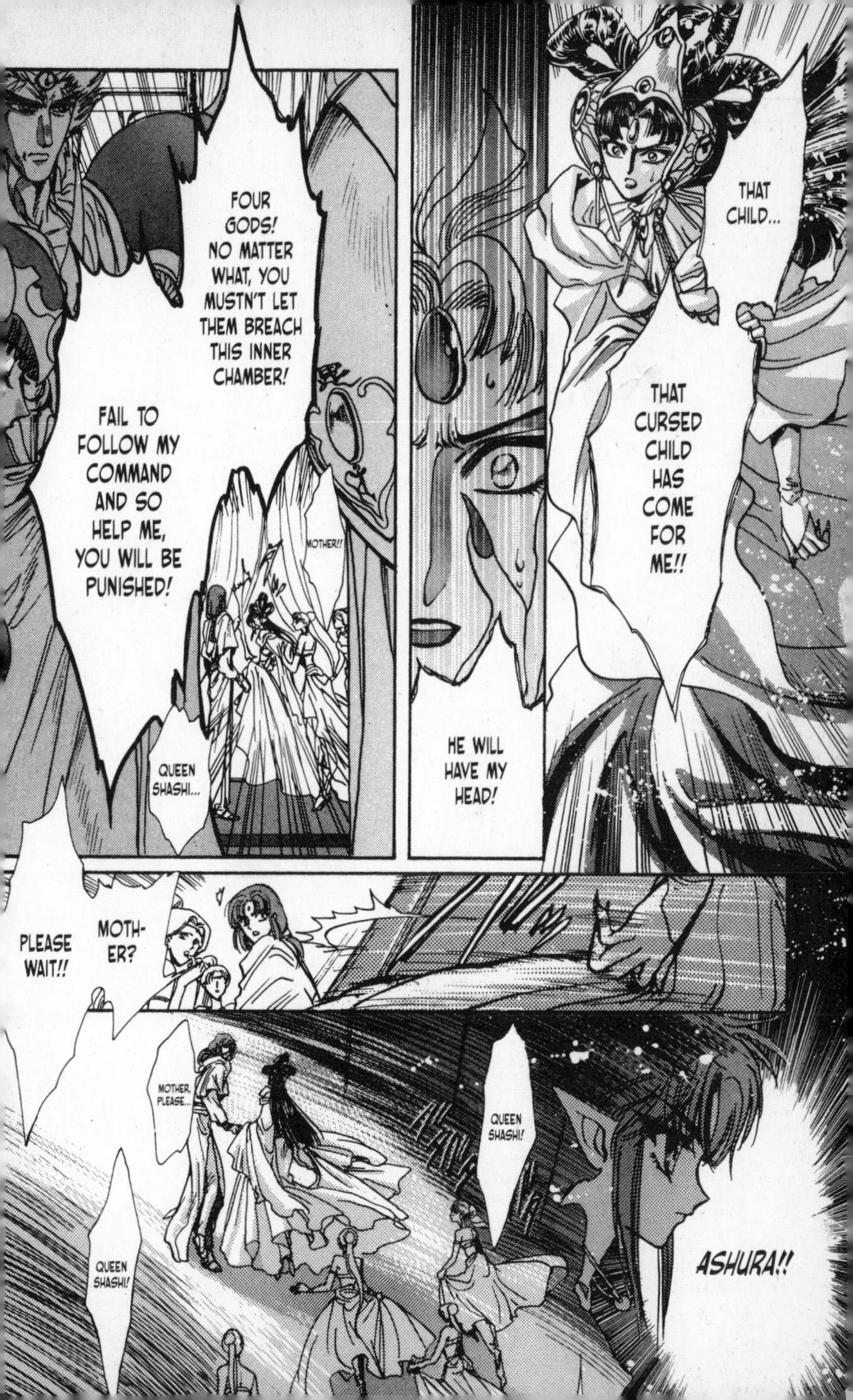

THAT CHILD...
THAT CURSED CHILD HAS COME FOR ME!!
HE WILL HAVE MY HEAD!
FOUR GODS! NO MATTER WHAT, YOU MUSTN'T LET THEM BREACH THIS INNER CHAMBER!
FAIL TO FOLLOW MY COMMAND AND SO HELP ME, YOU WILL BE PUNISHED!
MOTHER!!
QUEEN SHASHI...
MOTH-ER?
PLEASE WAIT!!
ASHURA!!
QUEEN SHASHI!
MOTHER, PLEASE...
QUEEN SHASHI!

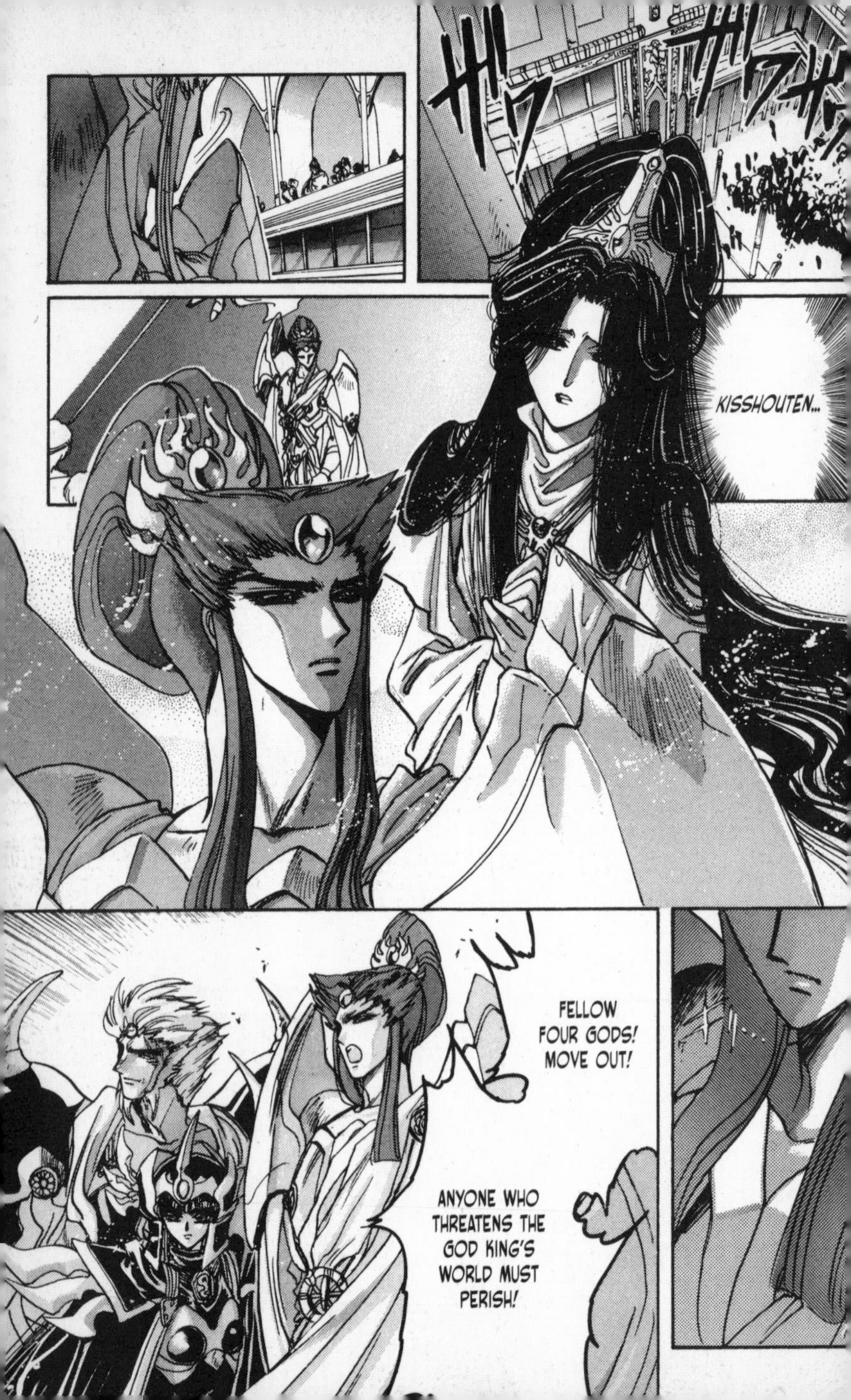
ザワ
ザワザ
KISSHOUTEN...
FELLOW FOUR GODS! MOVE OUT!
ANYONE WHO THREATENS THE GOD KING'S WORLD MUST PERISH!

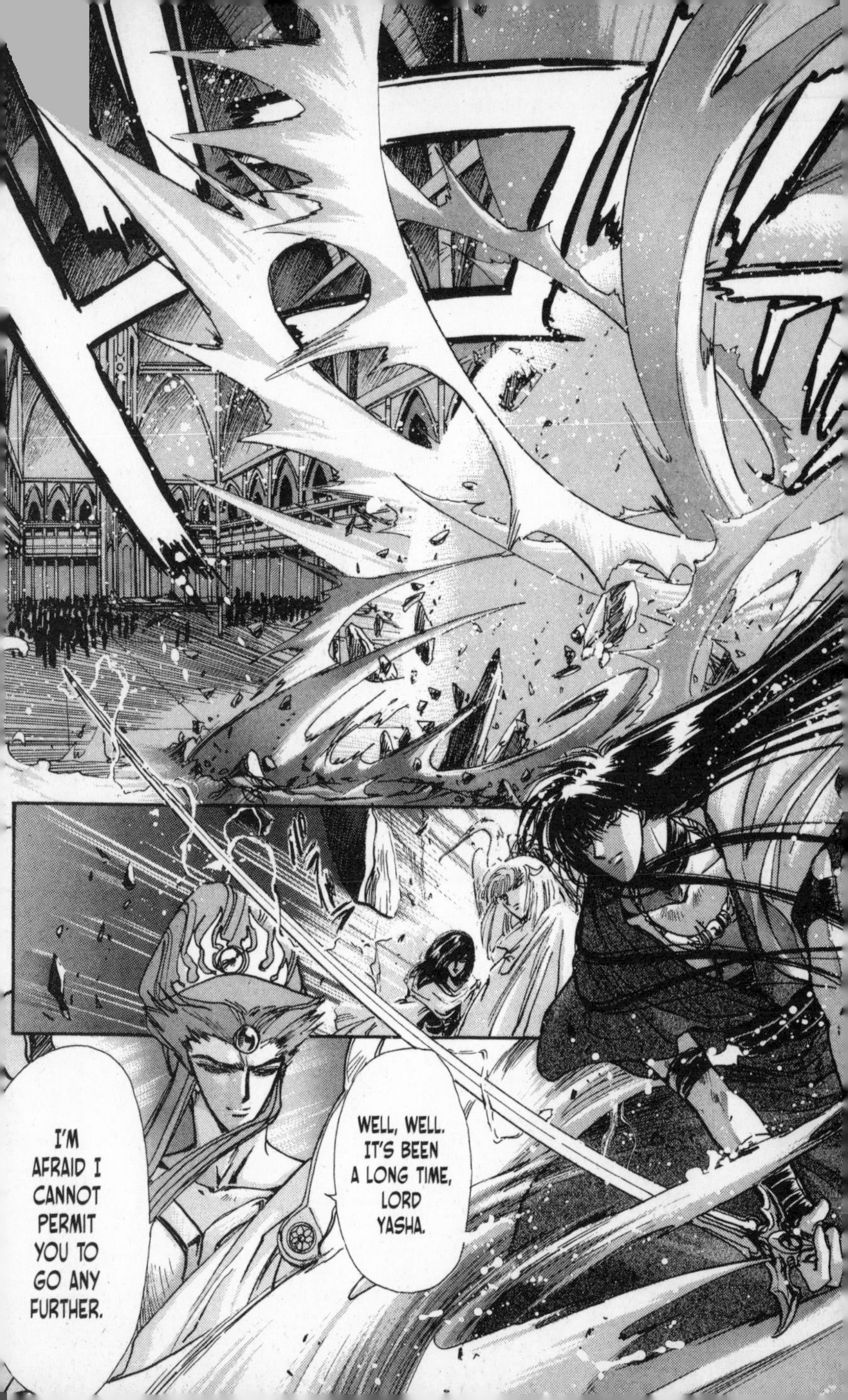
WELL, WELL. IT'S BEEN A LONG TIME, LORD YASHA.
I'M AFRAID I CANNOT PERMIT YOU TO GO ANY FURTHER.

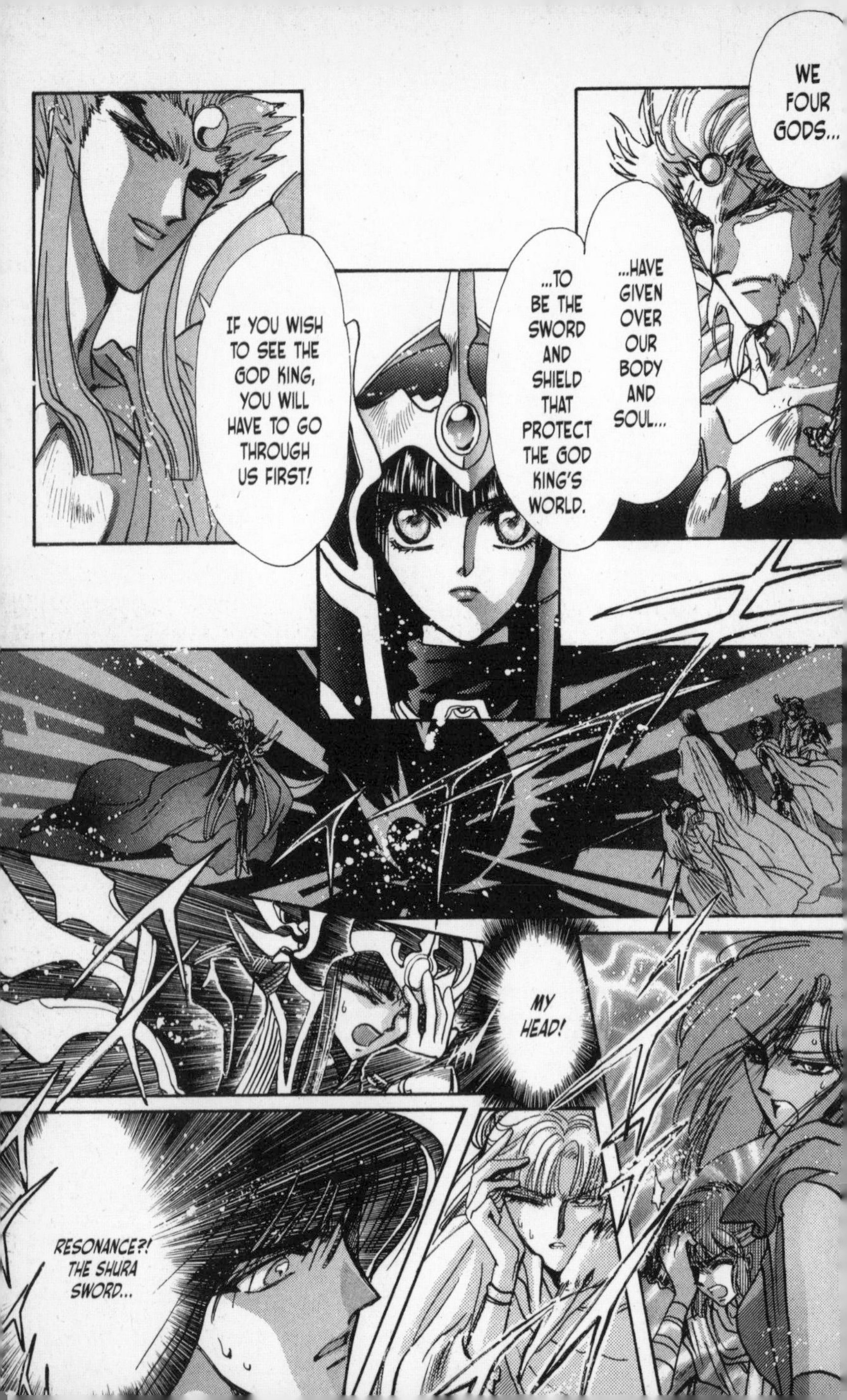
WE FOUR GODS...
...HAVE GIVEN OVER OUR BODY AND SOUL...
...TO BE THE SWORD AND SHIELD THAT PROTECT THE GOD KING'S WORLD.
IF YOU WISH TO SEE THE GOD KING, YOU WILL HAVE TO GO THROUGH US FIRST!
MY HEAD!
RESONANCE?! THE SHURA SWORD...

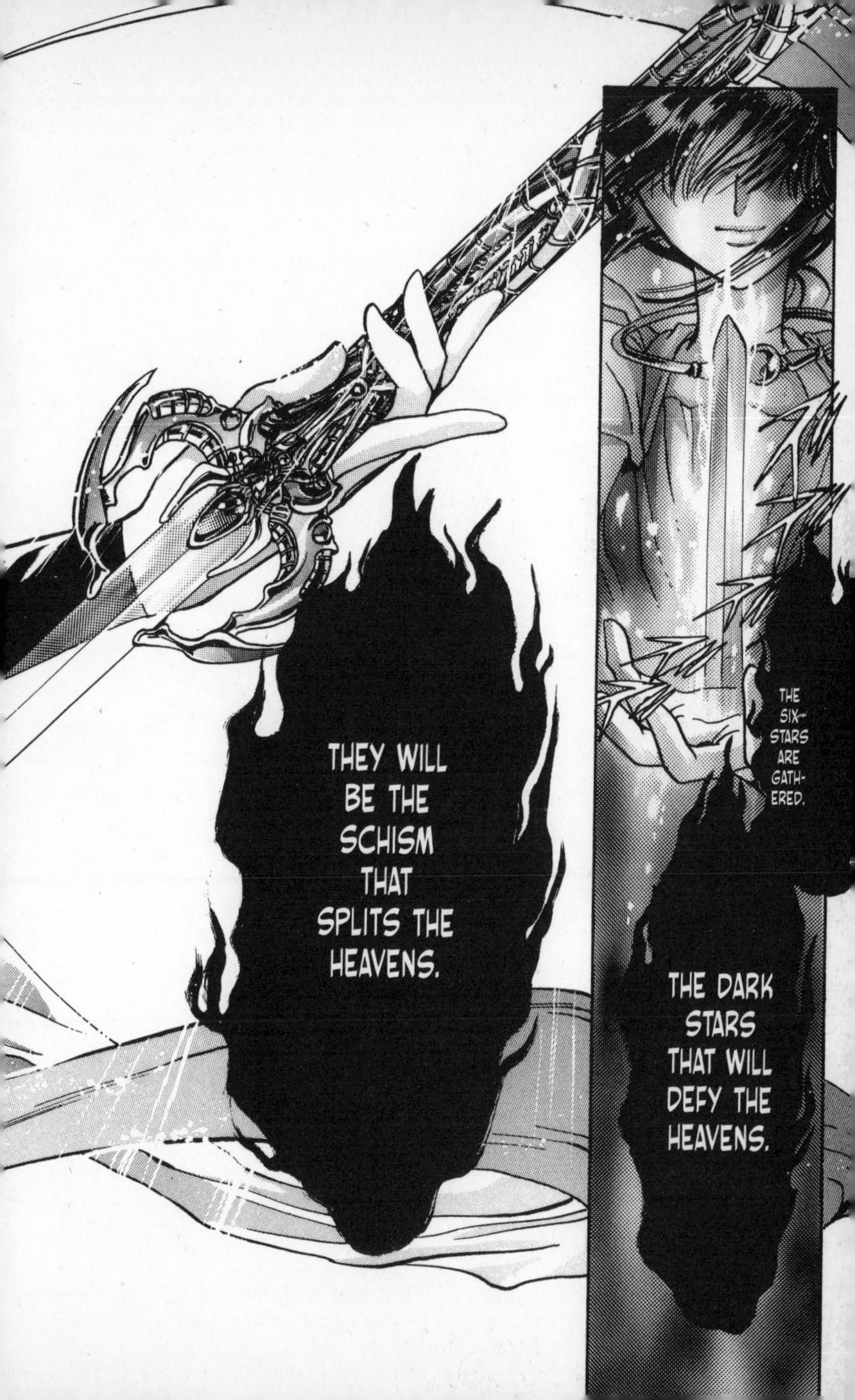
THE SIX-STARS ARE GATHERED.
THE DARK STARS THAT WILL DEFY THE HEAVENS.
THEY WILL BE THE SCHISM THAT SPLITS THE HEAVENS.

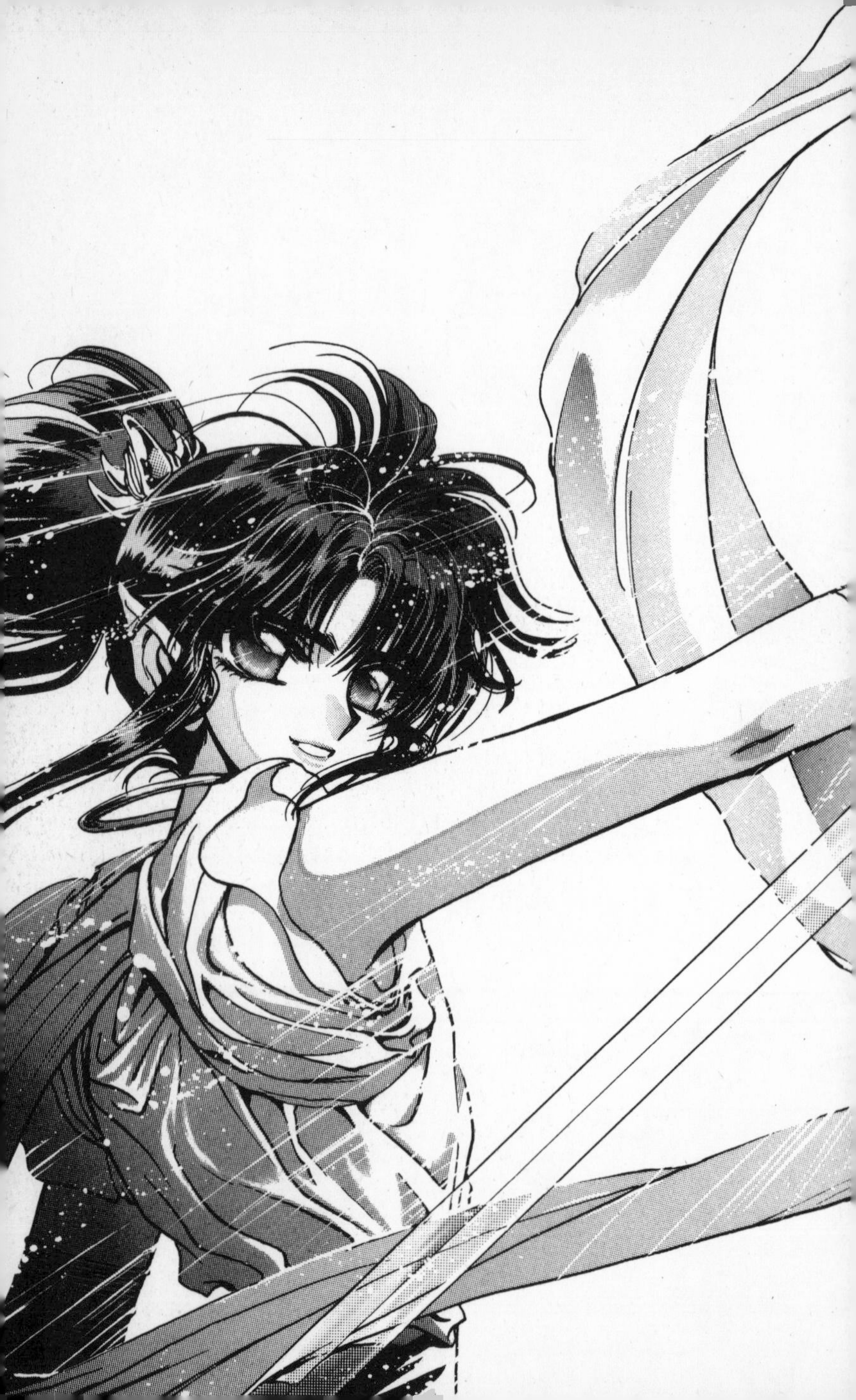

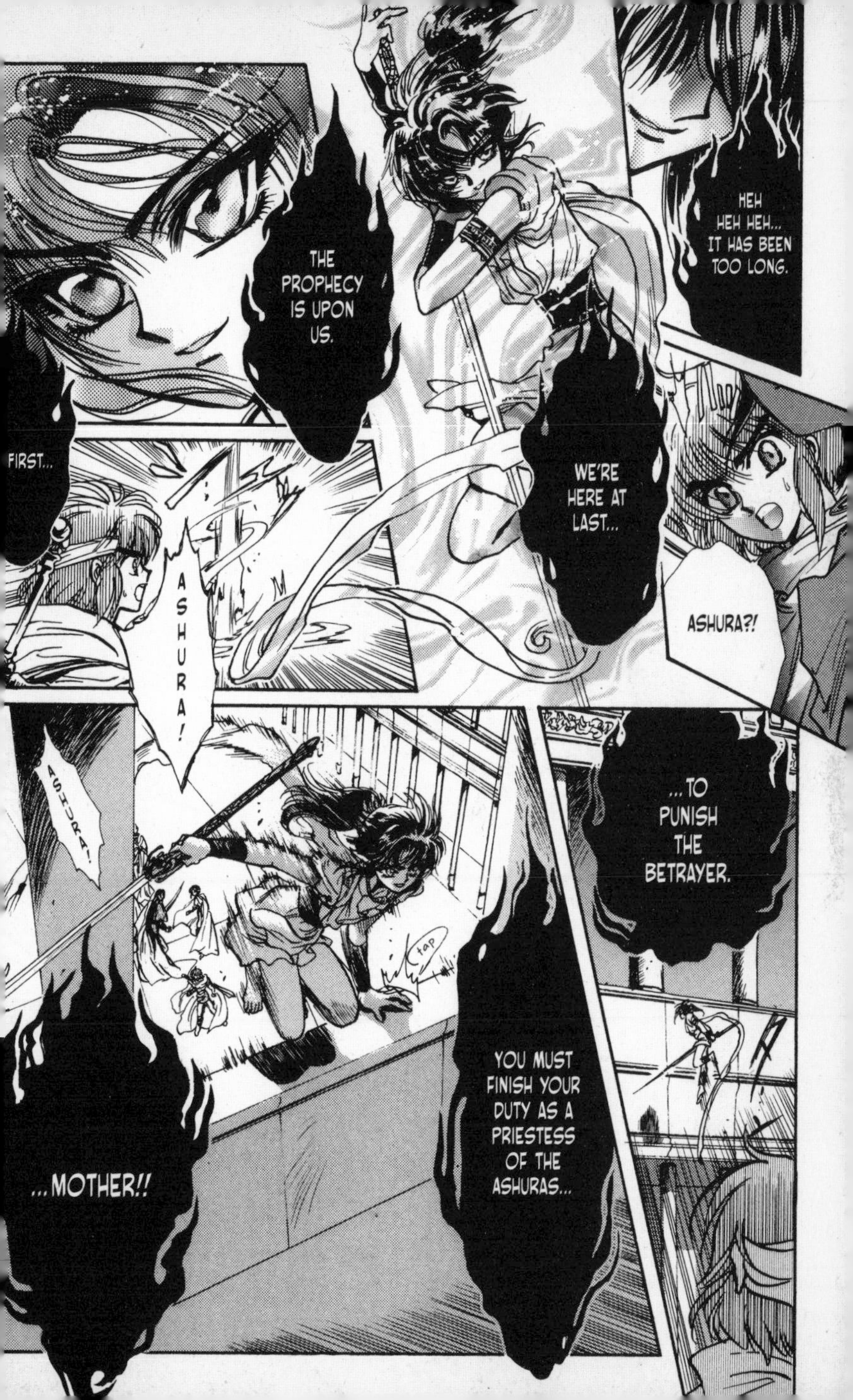
HEH HEH HEH... IT HAS BEEN TOO LONG.
THE PROPHECY IS UPON US.
ASHURA?!
WE'RE HERE AT LAST...
FIRST...
ASHURA!
...TO PUNISH THE BETRAYER.
YOU MUST FINISH YOUR DUTY AS A PRIESTESS OF THE ASHURAS...
ASHURA!
tap
...MOTHER!!

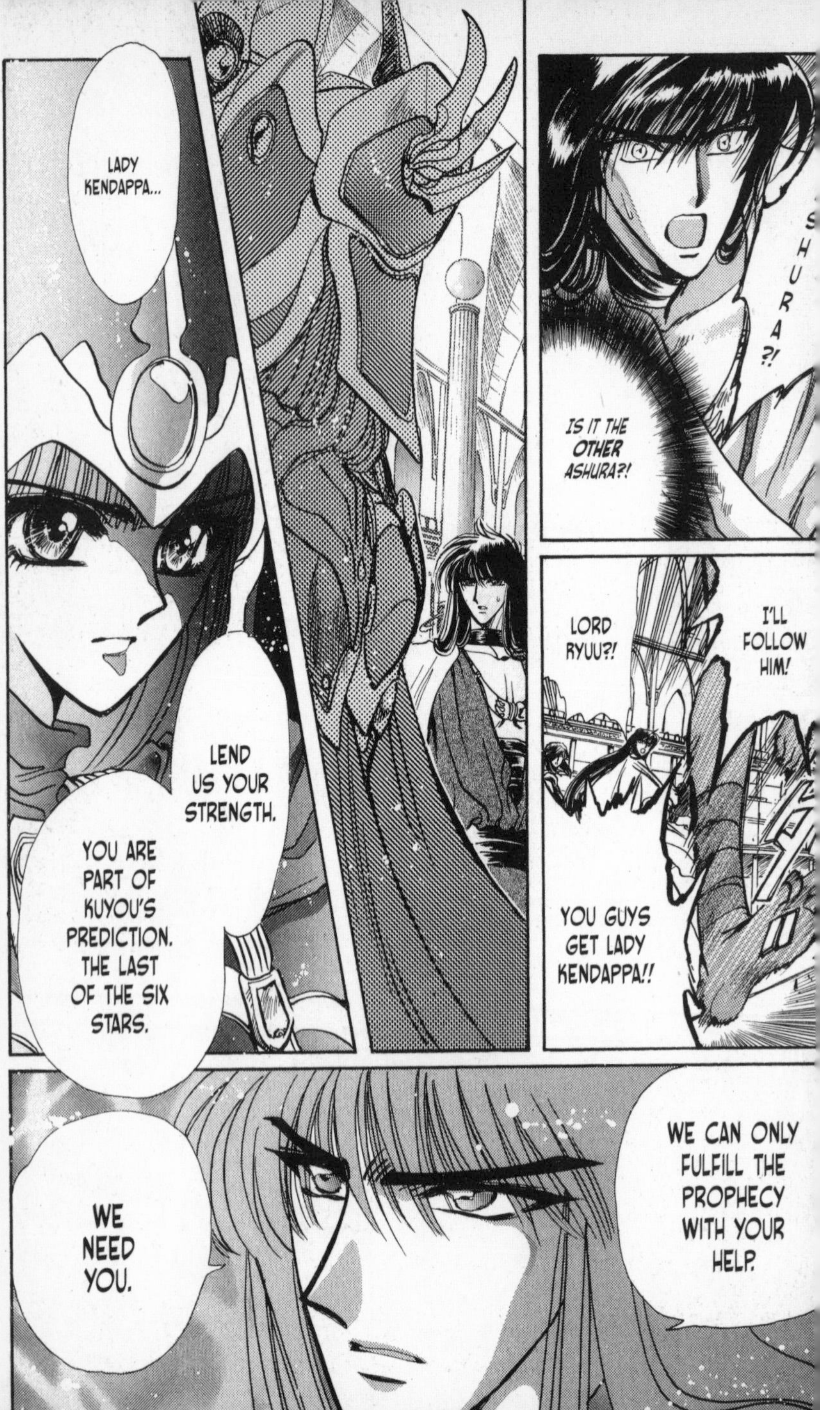
SHURA?!
IS IT THE OTHER ASHURA?!
I'LL FOLLOW HIM!
LORD RYUU?!
YOU GUYS GET LADY KENDAPPA!!
LADY KENDAPPA...
LEND US YOUR STRENGTH.
YOU ARE PART OF KUYOU'S PREDICTION. THE LAST OF THE SIX STARS.
WE CAN ONLY FULFILL THE PROPHECY WITH YOUR HELP.
WE NEED YOU.

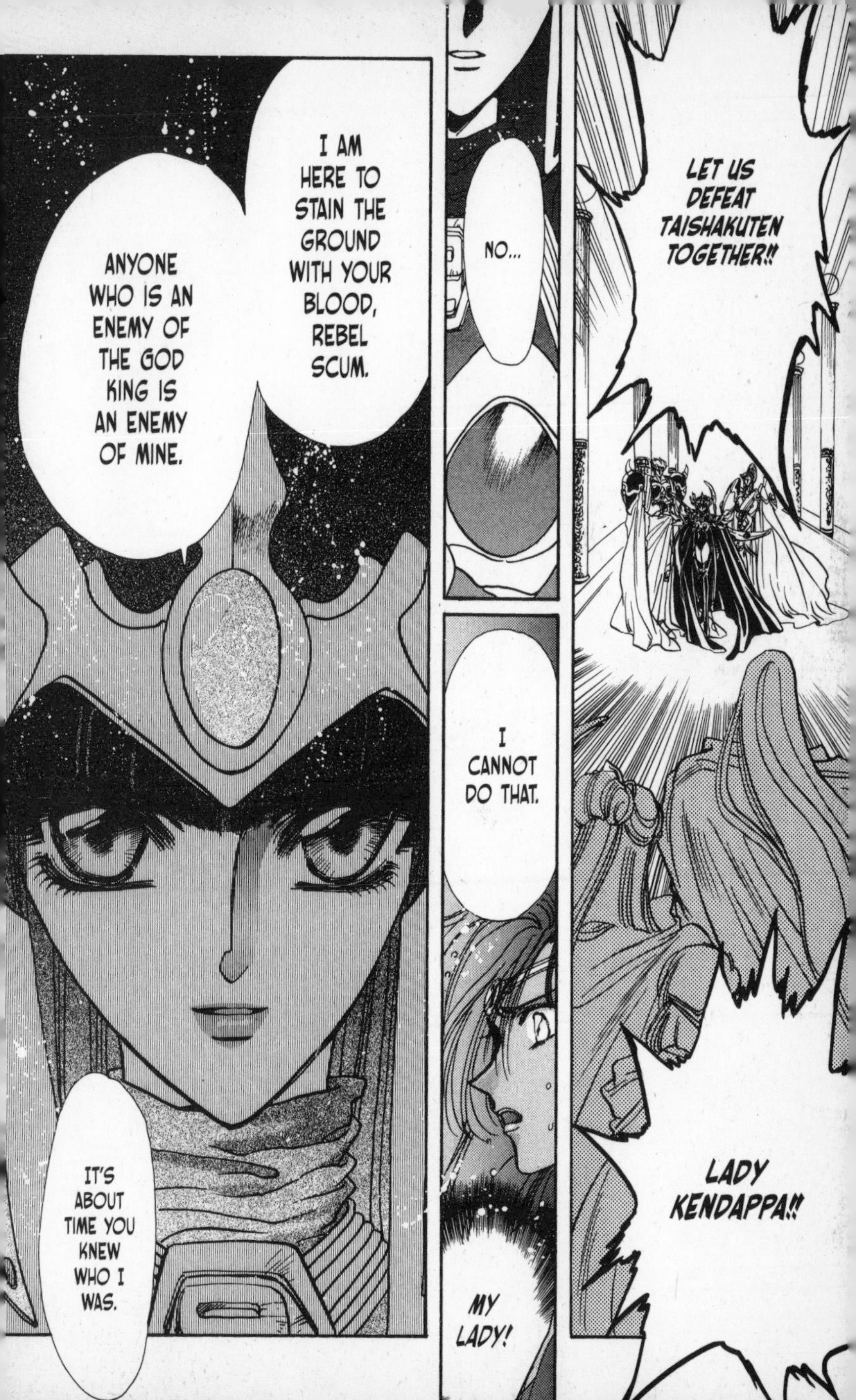
LET US DEFEAT TAISHAKUTEN TOGETHER!!
LADY KENDAPPA!!
NO...
I CANNOT DO THAT.
MY LADY!
I AM HERE TO STAIN THE GROUND WITH YOUR BLOOD, REBEL SCUM.
ANYONE WHO IS AN ENEMY OF THE GOD KING IS AN ENEMY OF MINE.
IT'S ABOUT TIME YOU KNEW WHO I WAS.

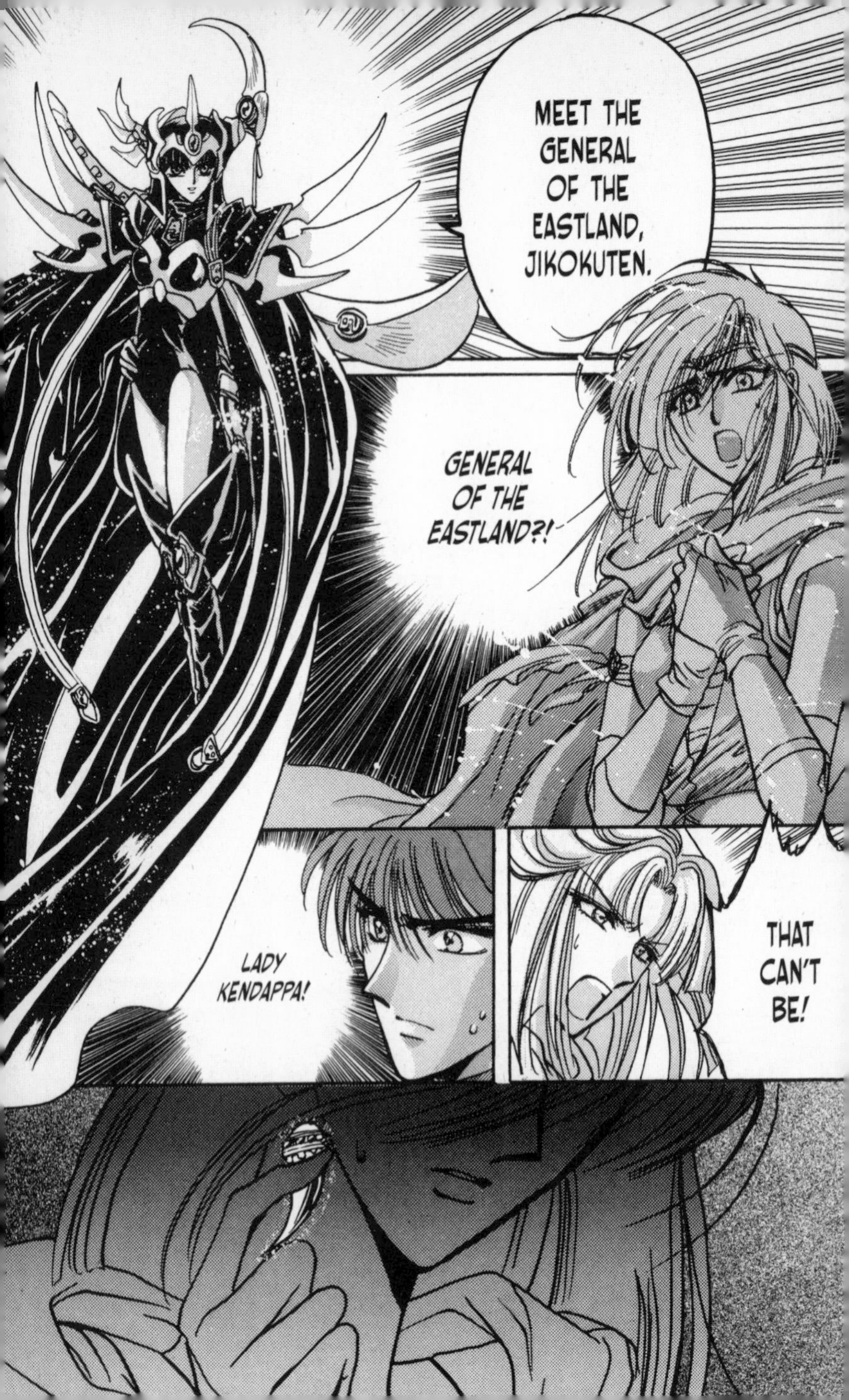
MEET THE GENERAL OF THE EASTLAND, JIKOKUTEN.
GENERAL OF THE EASTLAND?!
THAT CAN'T BE!
LADY KENDAPPA!

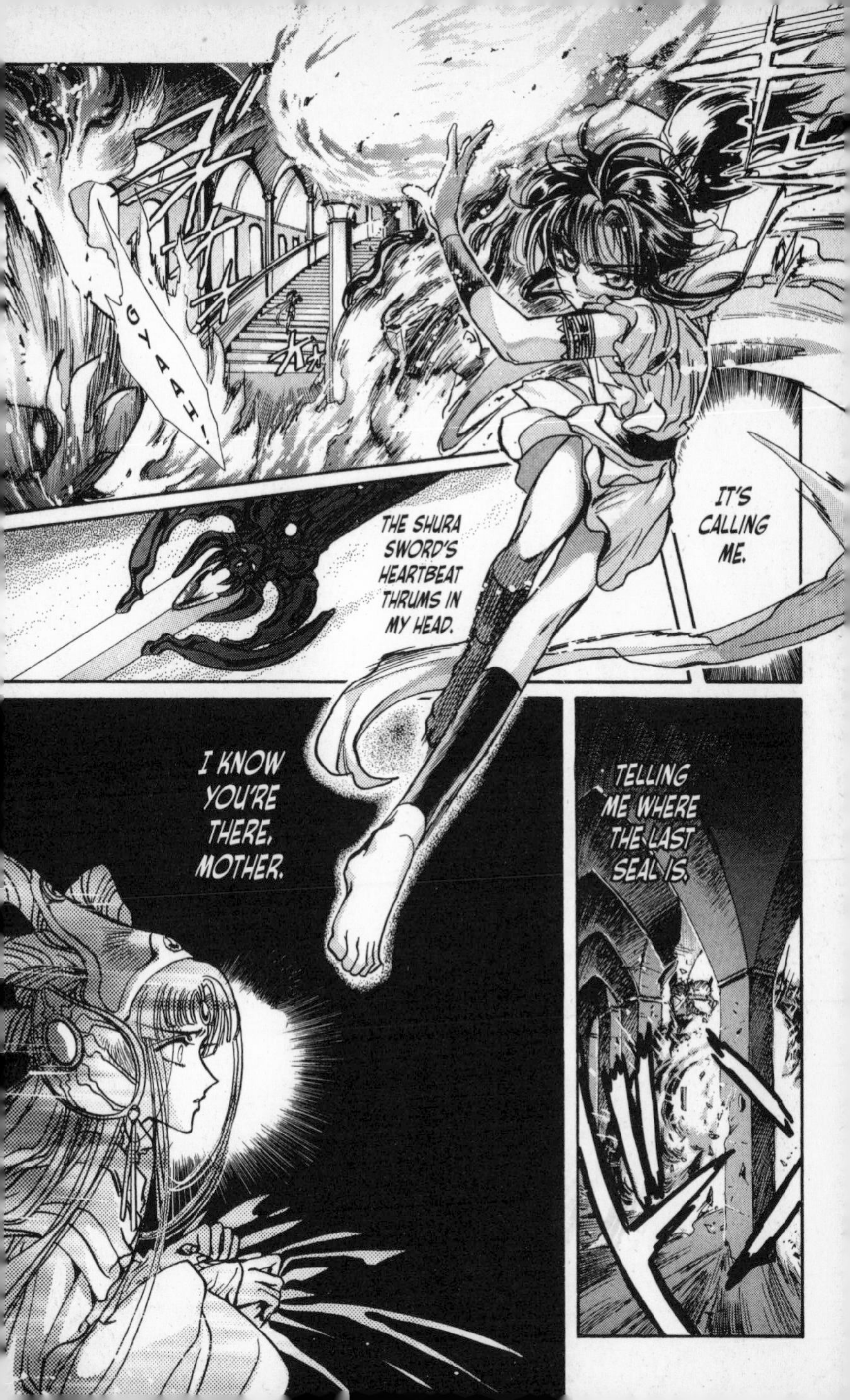
GYAAH!
IT'S CALLING ME.
THE SHURA SWORD'S HEARTBEAT THRUMS IN MY HEAD.
TELLING ME WHERE THE LAST SEAL IS.
I KNOW YOU'RE THERE, MOTHER.

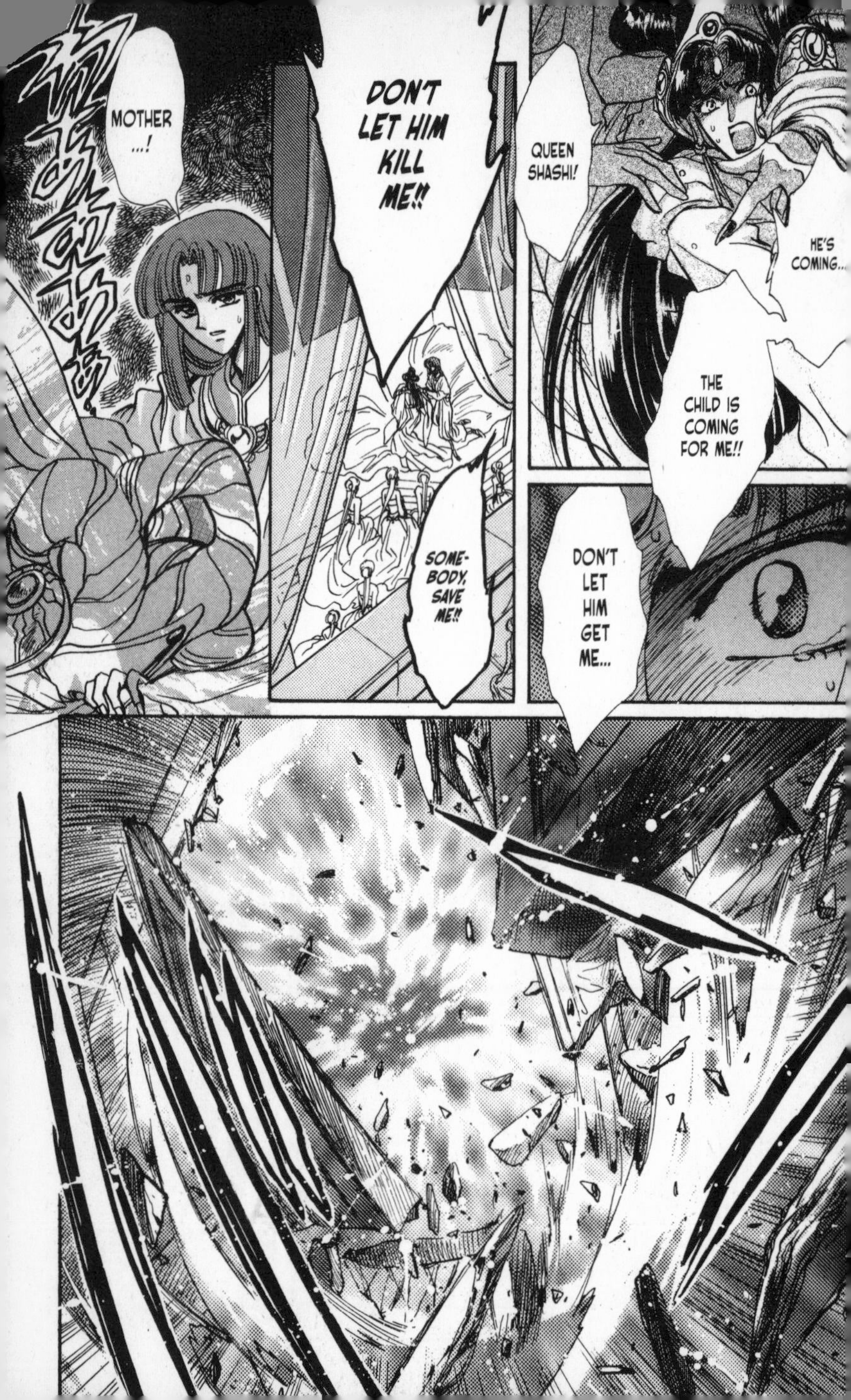
QUEEN SHASHI!
HE'S COMING...
THE CHILD IS COMING FOR ME!!
DON'T LET HIM GET ME...
DON'T LET HIM KILL ME!!
SOME-BODY, SAVE ME!!
MOTHER ...!

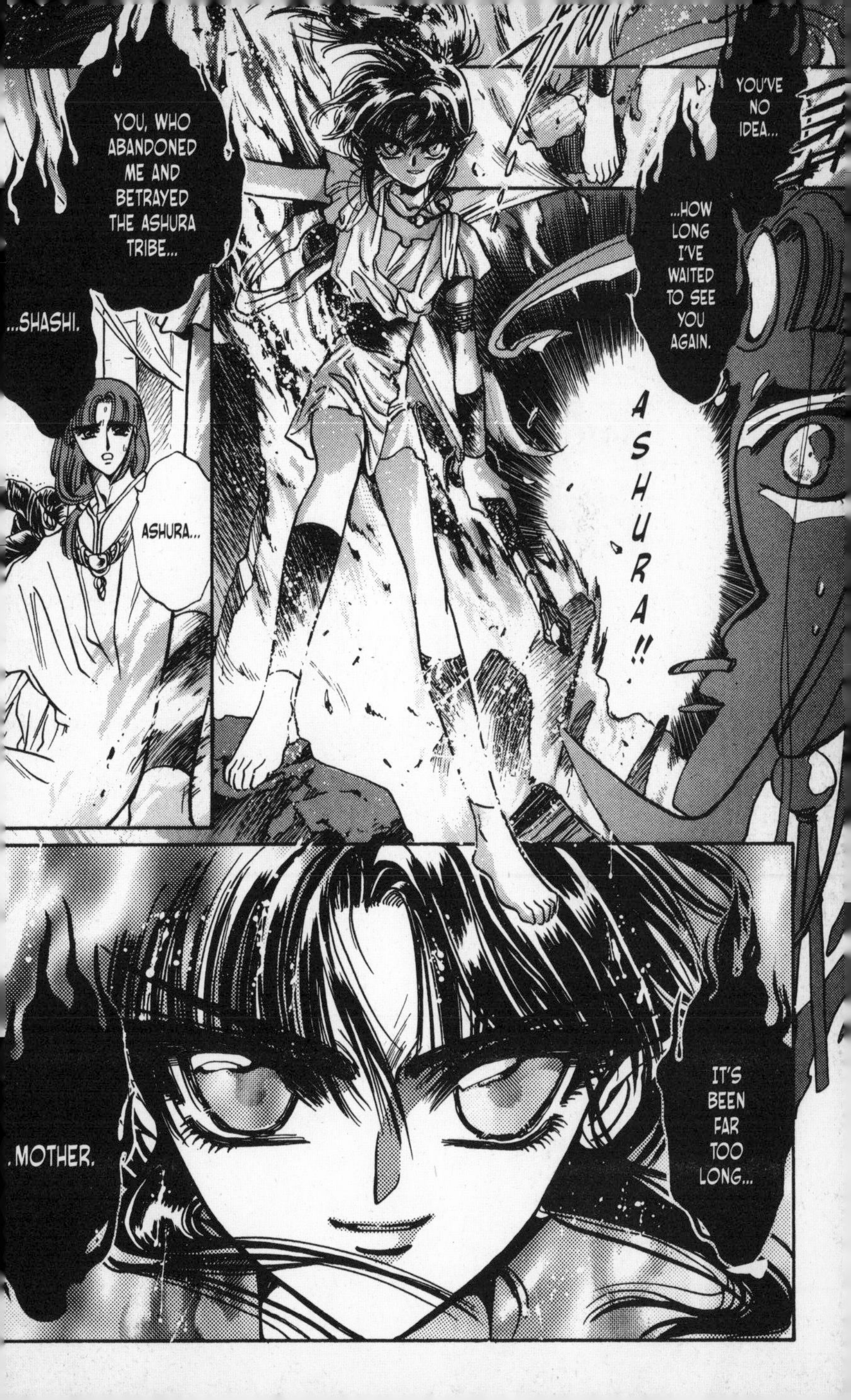
YOU'VE NO IDEA...
...HOW LONG I'VE WAITED TO SEE YOU AGAIN.
ASHURA!!
YOU, WHO ABANDONED ME AND BETRAYED THE ASHURA TRIBE...
...SHASHI.
ASHURA...
IT'S BEEN FAR TOO LONG...
.MOTHER.

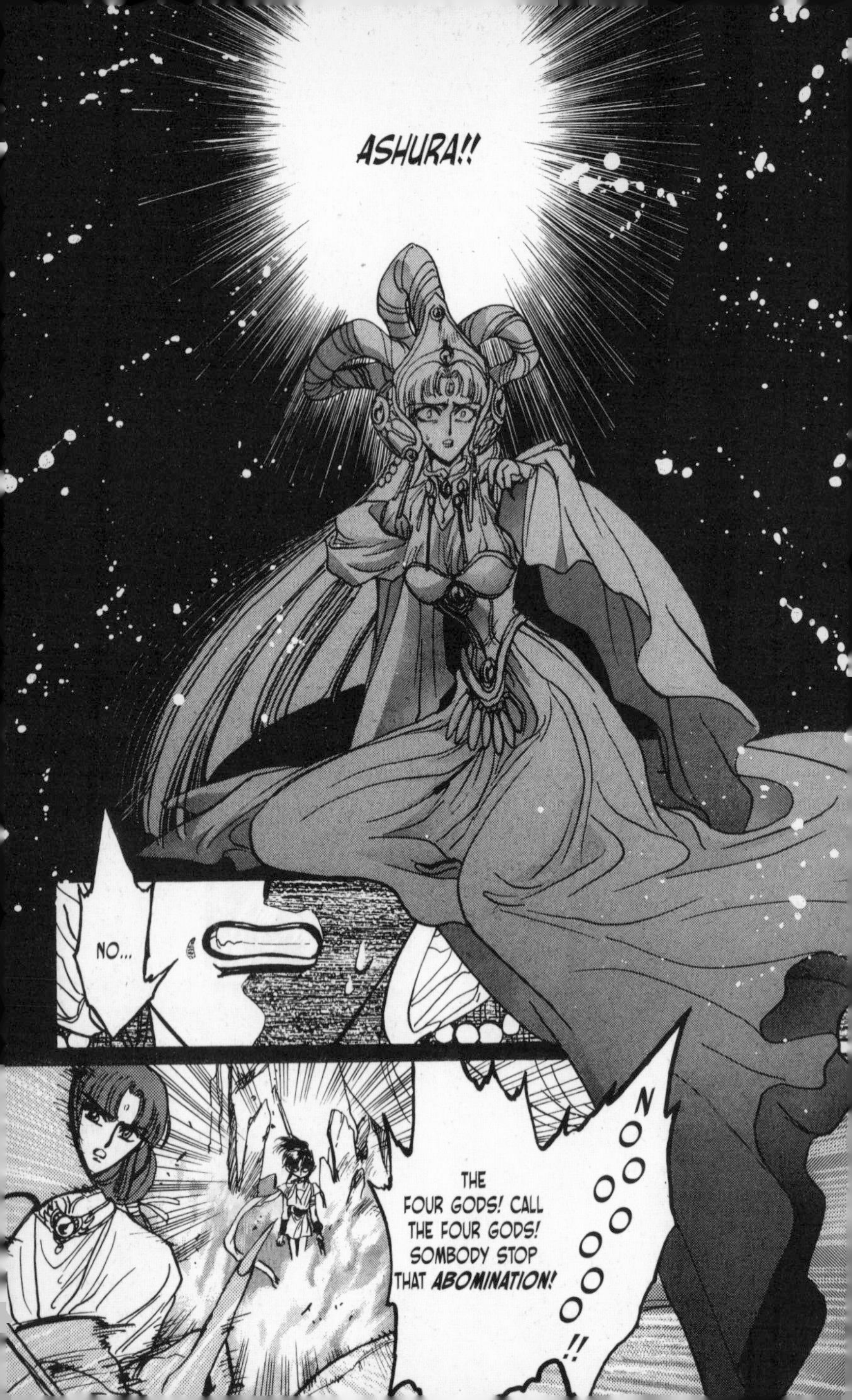
ASHURA!!
NO...
NOOOOOOOOO!!
THE FOUR GODS! CALL THE FOUR GODS! SOMBODY STOP THAT ABOMINATION!

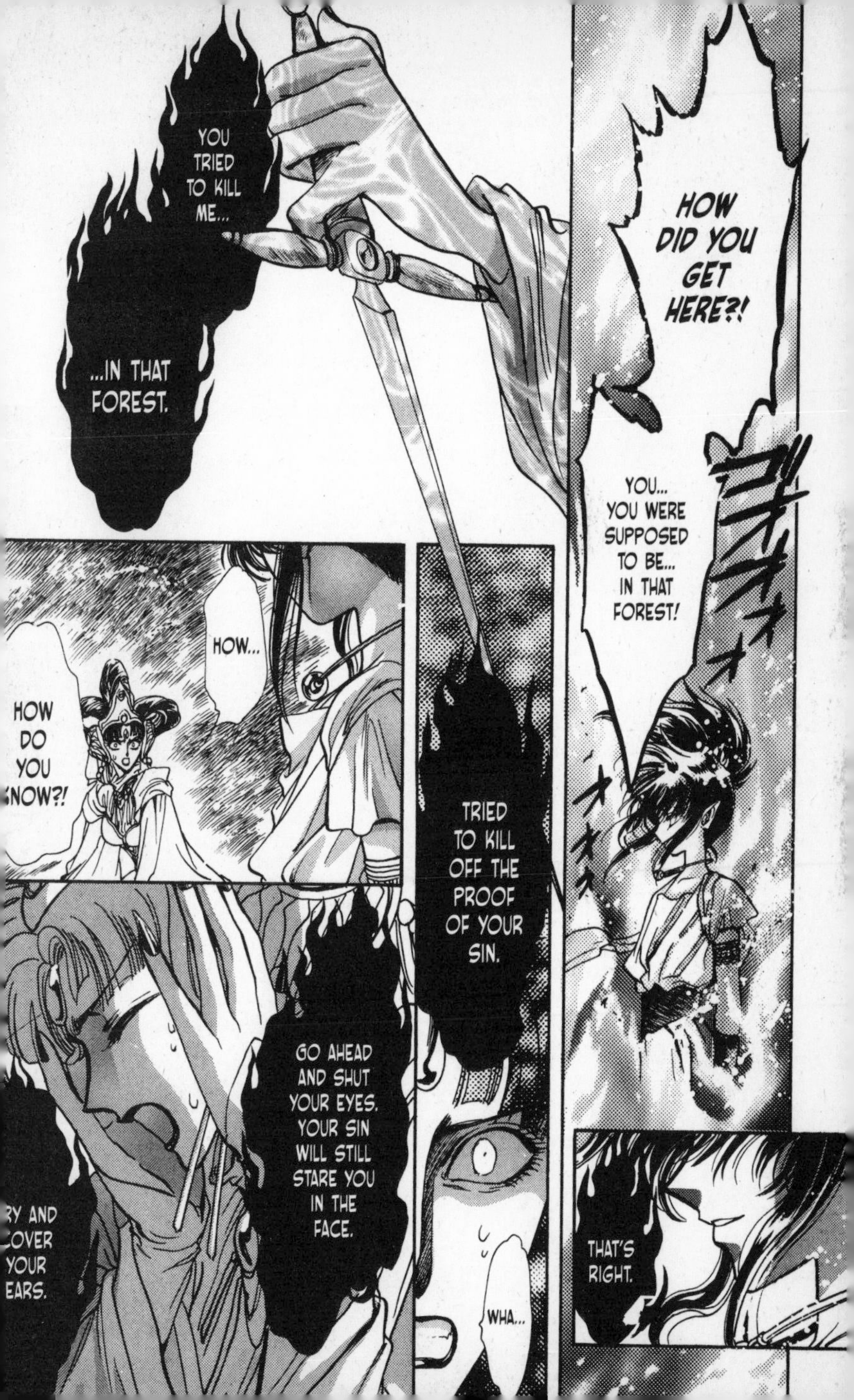

HOW DID YOU GET HERE?!
YOU... YOU WERE SUPPOSED TO BE... IN THAT FOREST!
THAT'S RIGHT.
YOU TRIED TO KILL ME...
...IN THAT FOREST.
TRIED TO KILL OFF THE PROOF OF YOUR SIN.
HOW...
HOW DO YOU NOW?!
WHA...
GO AHEAD AND SHUT YOUR EYES. YOUR SIN WILL STILL STARE YOU IN THE FACE.
RY AND COVER YOUR EARS.

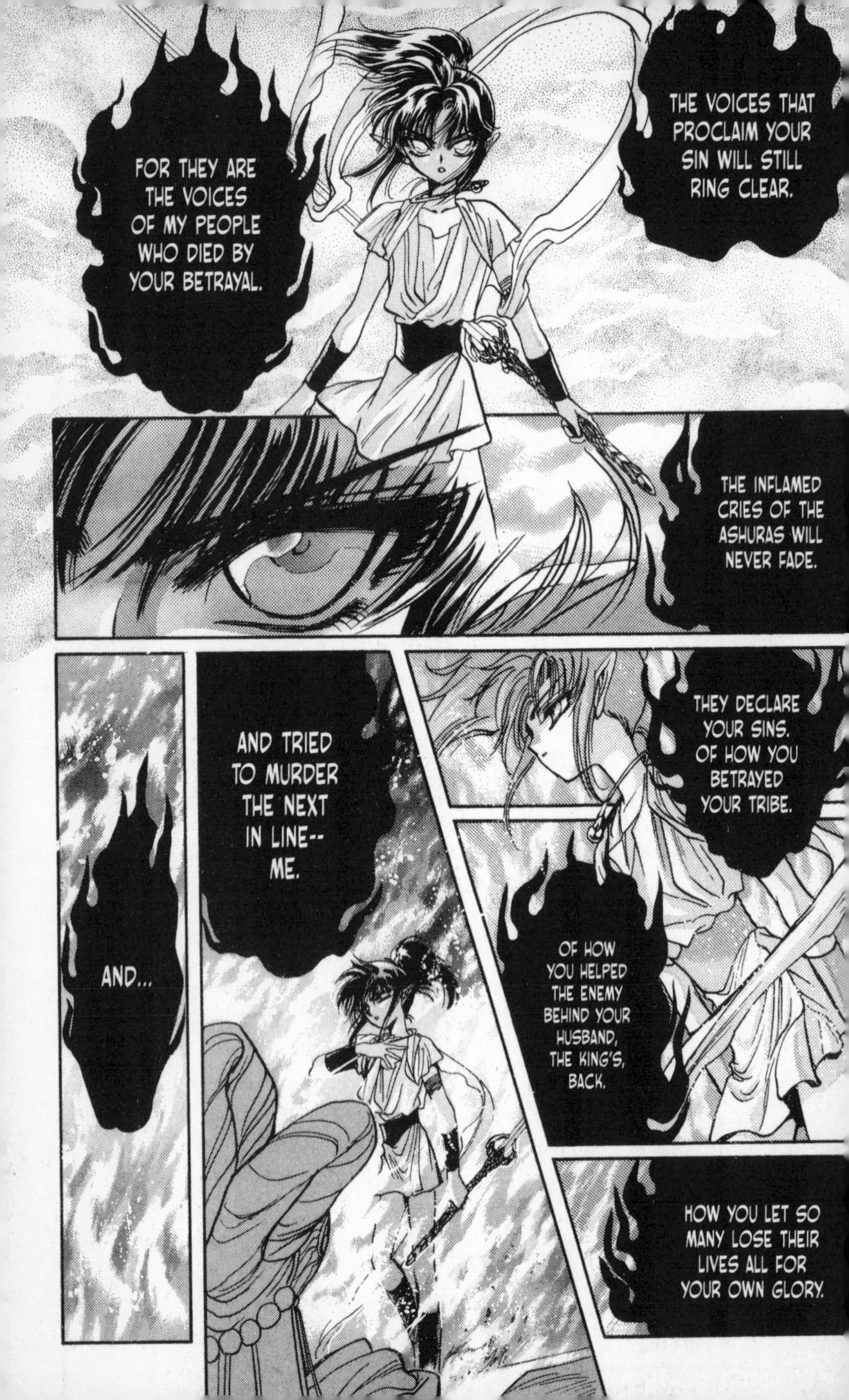
THE VOICES THAT PROCLAIM YOUR SIN WILL STILL RING CLEAR.
FOR THEY ARE THE VOICES OF MY PEOPLE WHO DIED BY YOUR BETRAYAL.
THE INFLAMED CRIES OF THE ASHURAS WILL NEVER FADE.
THEY DECLARE YOUR SINS. OF HOW YOU BETRAYED YOUR TRIBE.
OF HOW YOU HELPED THE ENEMY BEHIND YOUR HUSBAND, THE KING'S, BACK.
HOW YOU LET SO MANY LOSE THEIR LIVES ALL FOR YOUR OWN GLORY.
AND TRIED TO MURDER THE NEXT IN LINE-- ME.
AND...

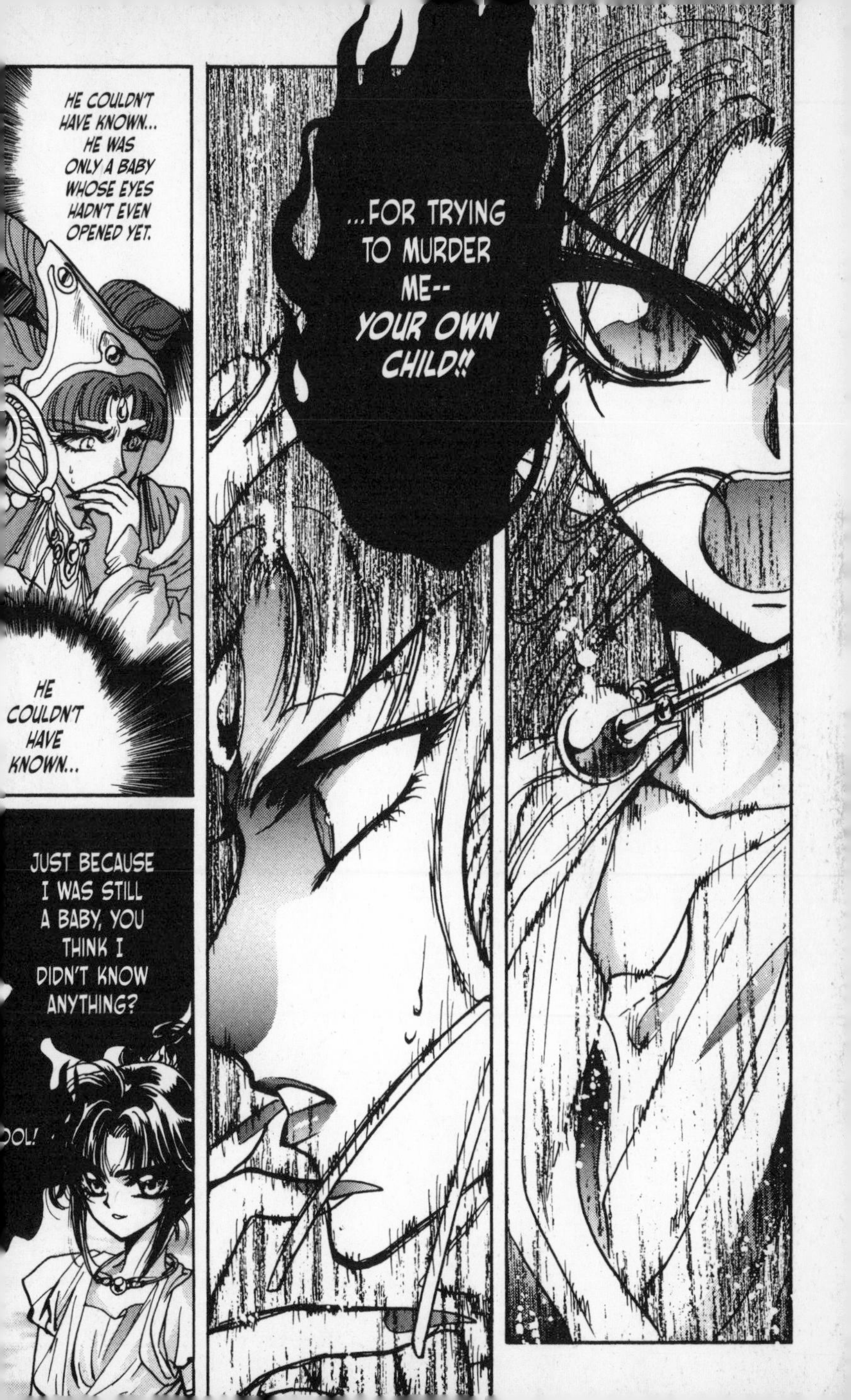
...FOR TRYING TO MURDER ME-- YOUR OWN CHILD!!
HE COULDN'T HAVE KNOWN... HE WAS ONLY A BABY WHOSE EYES HADN'T EVEN OPENED YET.
HE COULDN'T HAVE KNOWN...
JUST BECAUSE I WAS STILL A BABY, YOU THINK I DIDN'T KNOW ANYTHING?

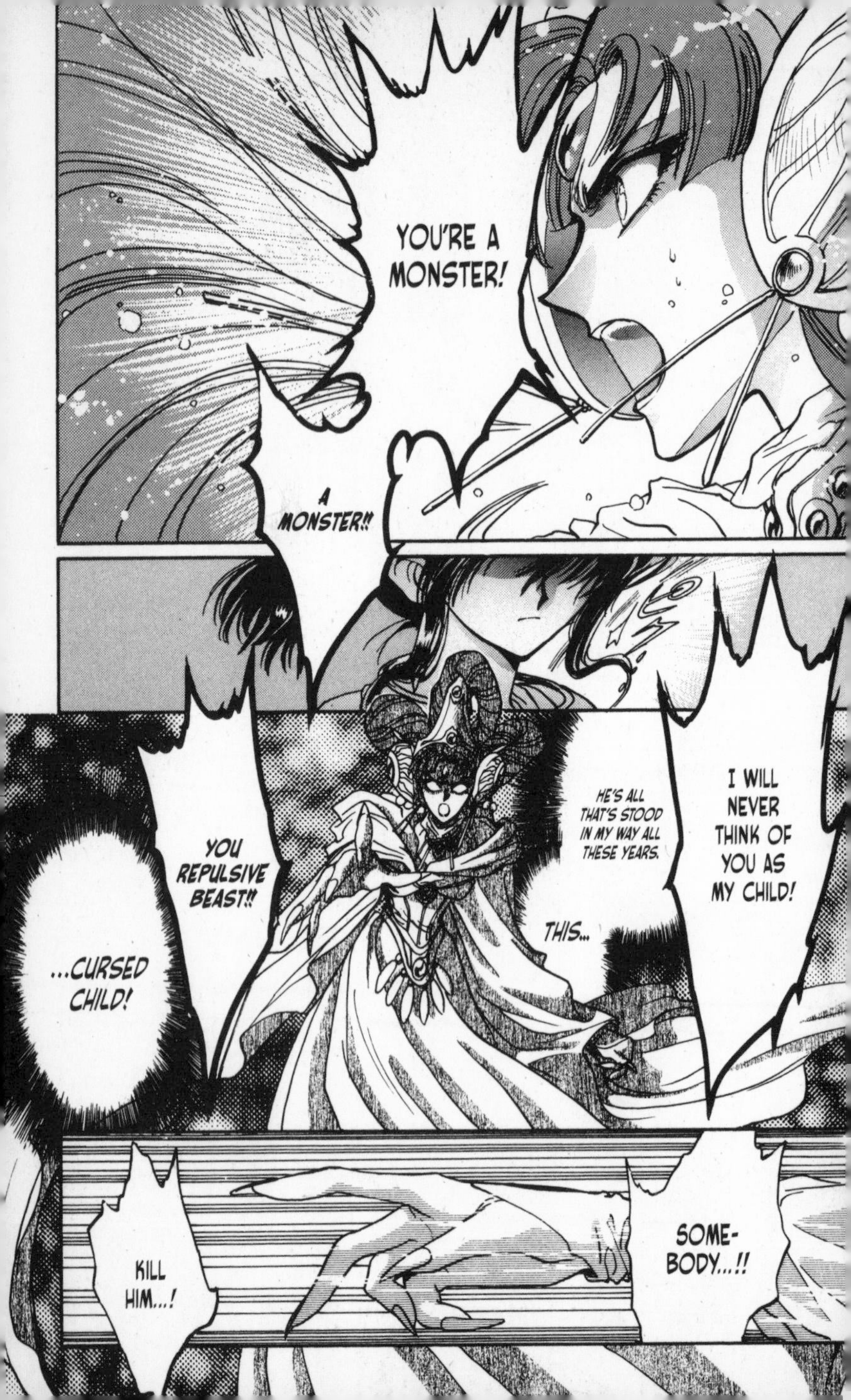
YOU'RE A MONSTER!
A MONSTER!!
I WILL NEVER THINK OF YOU AS MY CHILD!
HE'S ALL THAT'S STOOD IN MY WAY ALL THESE YEARS.
THIS...
YOU REPULSIVE BEAST!!
...CURSED CHILD!
SOME-BODY...!!
KILL HIM...!

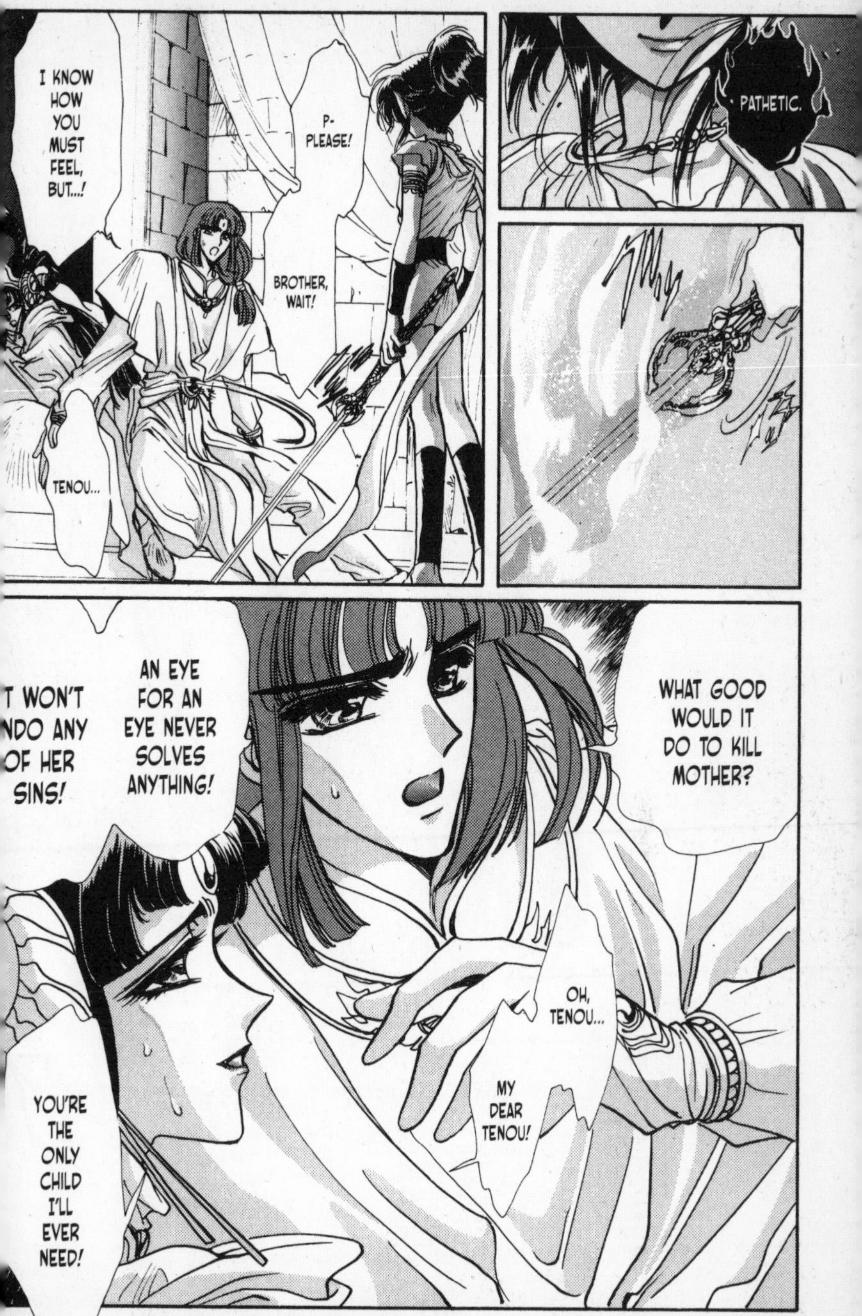

PATHETIC.
P-PLEASE!
BROTHER, WAIT!
I KNOW HOW YOU MUST FEEL, BUT...!
TENOU...
WHAT GOOD WOULD IT DO TO KILL MOTHER?
AN EYE FOR AN EYE NEVER SOLVES ANYTHING!
T WON'T NDO ANY OF HER SINS!
OH, TENOU...
MY DEAR TENOU!
YOU'RE THE ONLY CHILD I'LL EVER NEED!

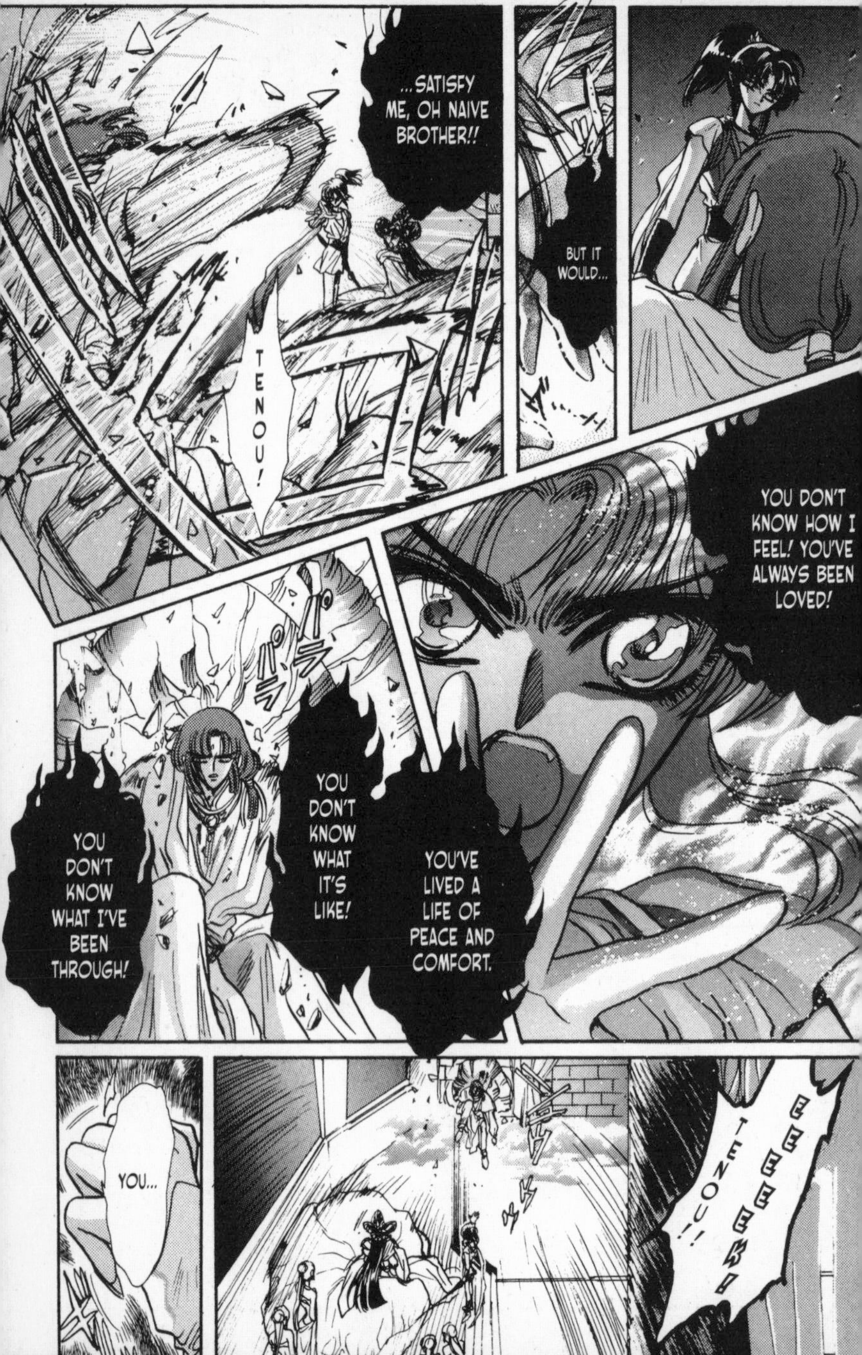
BUT IT WOULD...
...SATISFY ME, OH NAIVE BROTHER!!
TENOU!
YOU DON'T KNOW HOW I FEEL! YOU'VE ALWAYS BEEN LOVED!
YOU'VE LIVED A LIFE OF PEACE AND COMFORT.
YOU DON'T KNOW WHAT IT'S LIKE!
YOU DON'T KNOW WHAT I'VE BEEN THROUGH!
EEEEEEK!
TENOU!!
YOU...

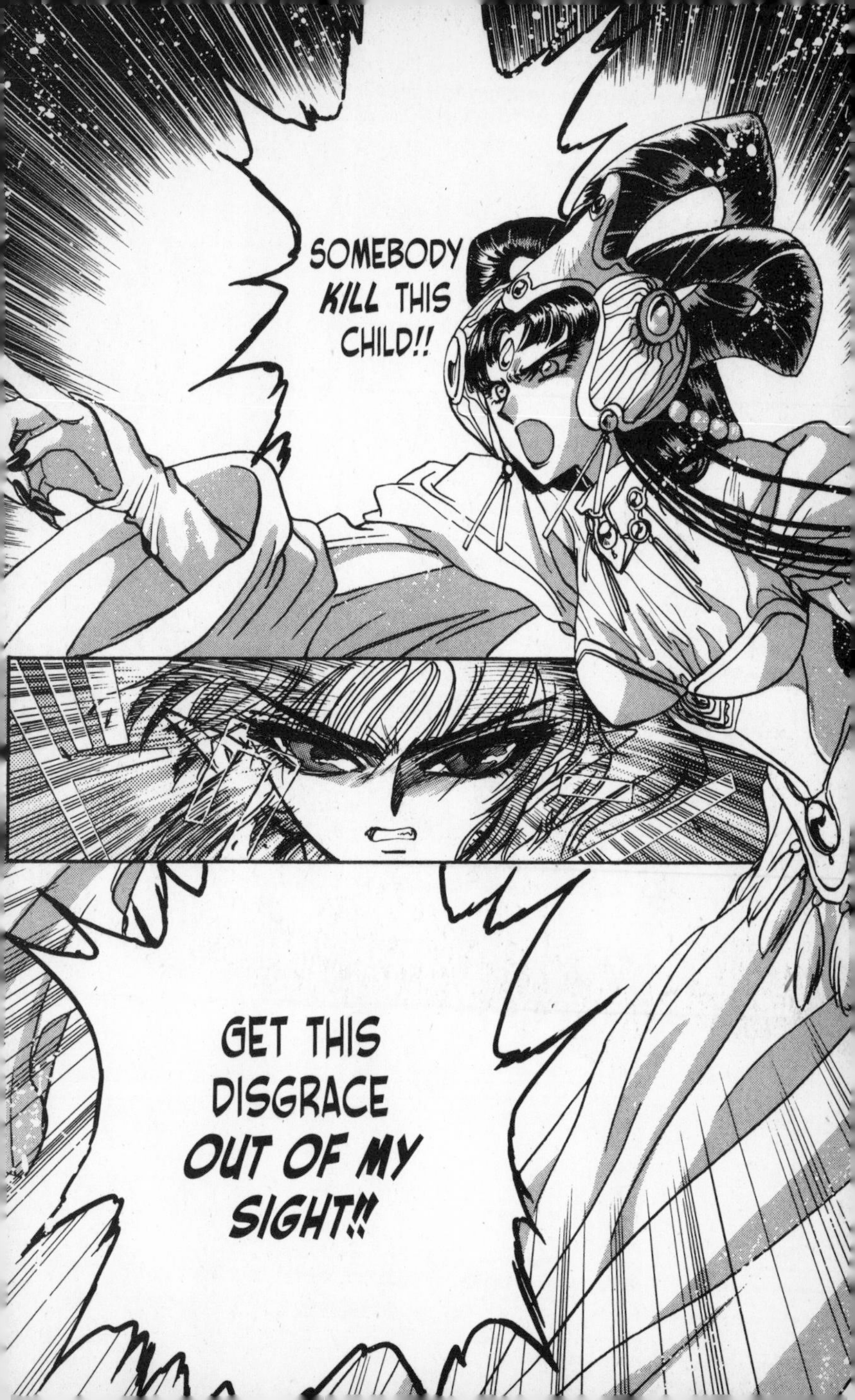
SOMEBODY KILL THIS CHILD!!
GET THIS DISGRACE OUT OF MY SIGHT!!

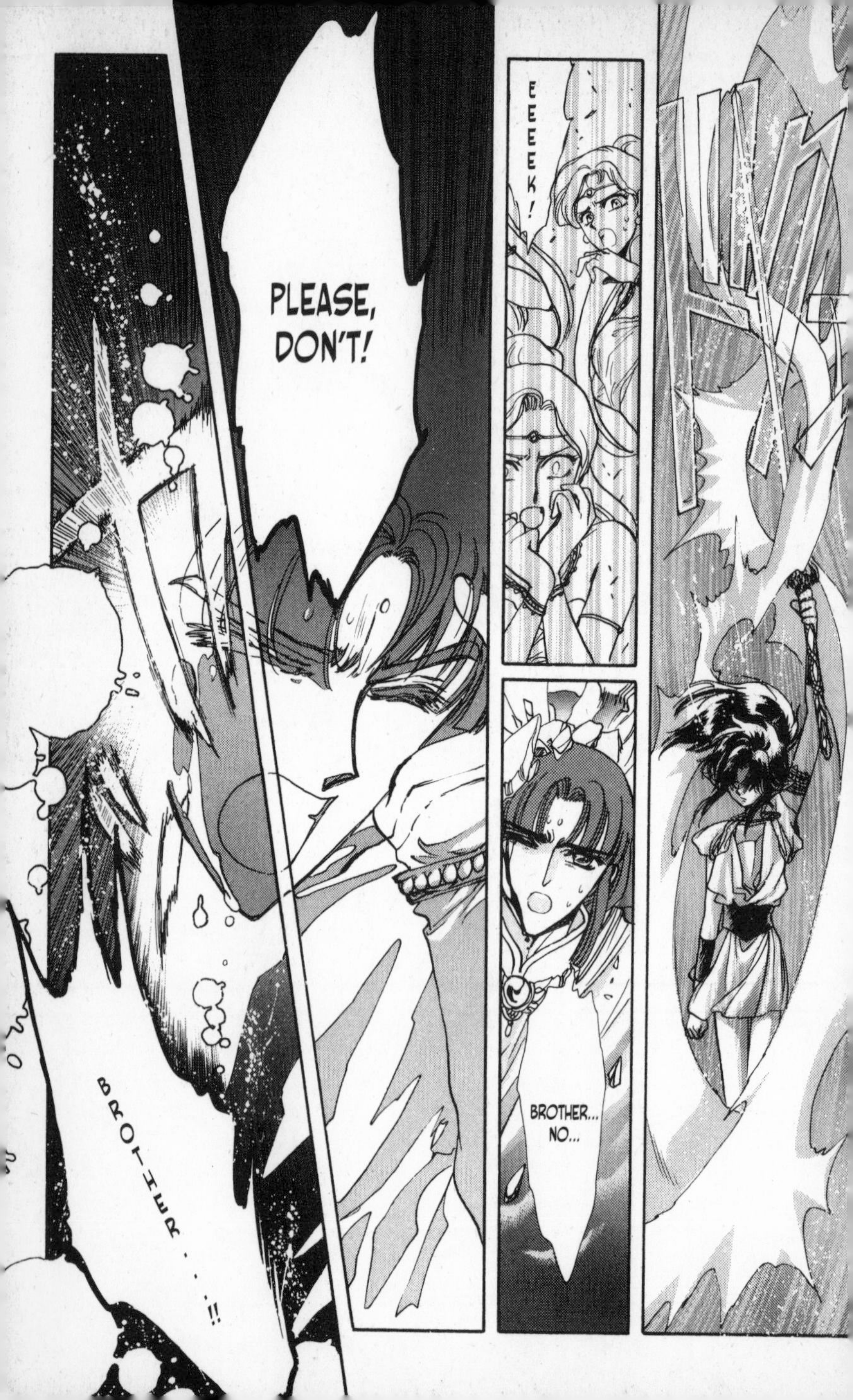
EEEEK!
BROTHER... NO...
PLEASE, DON'T!
BROTHER . . . !!

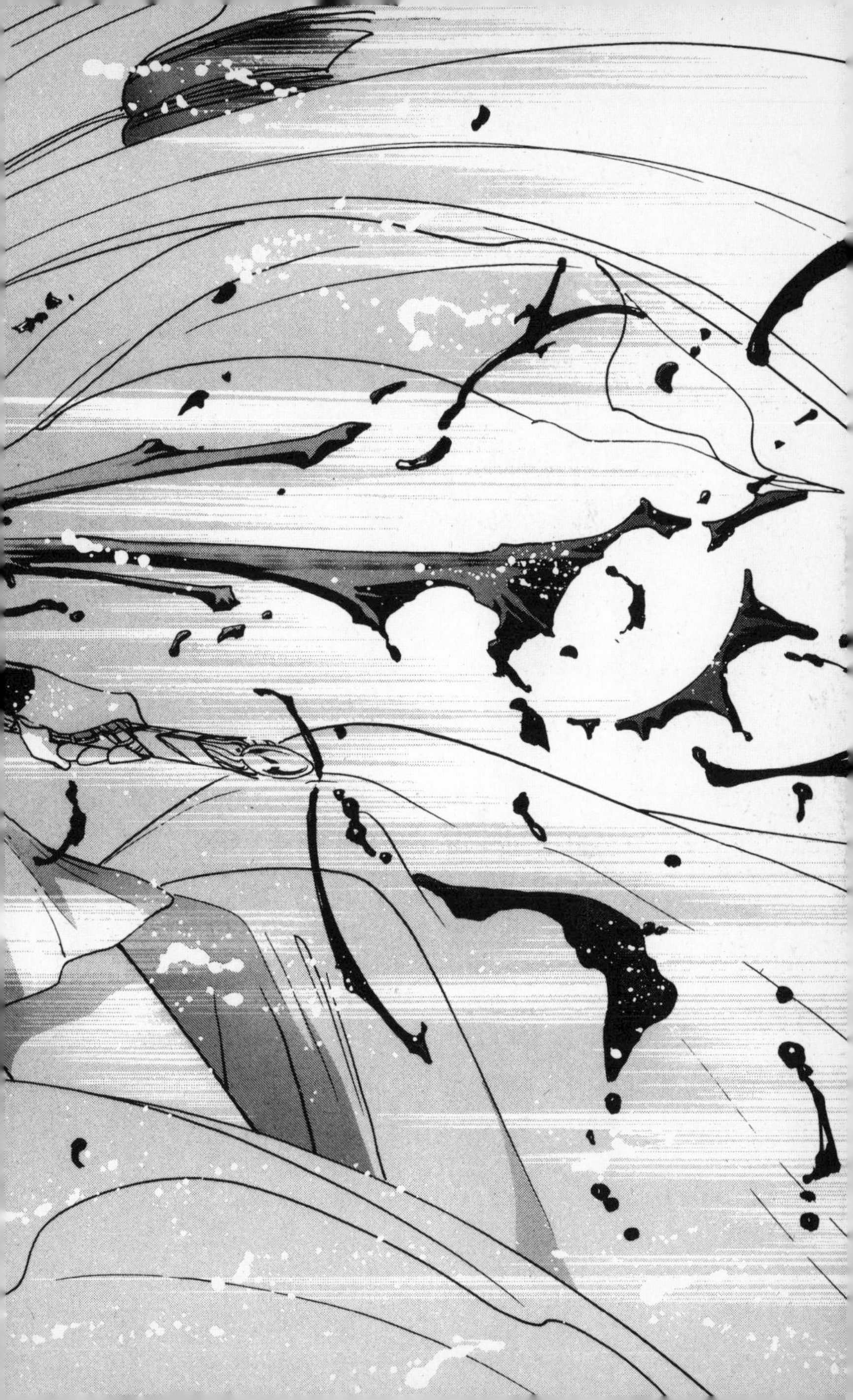

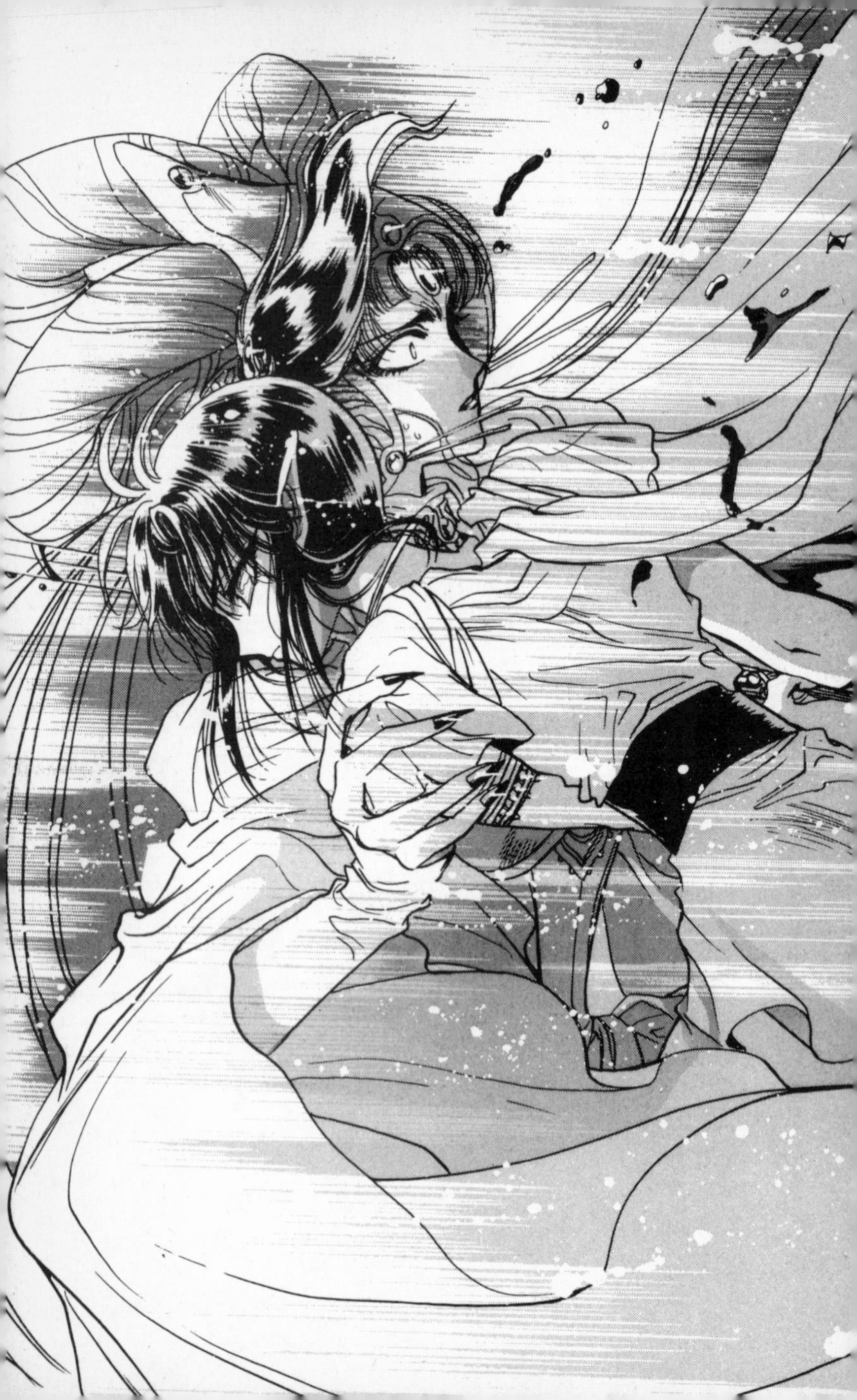

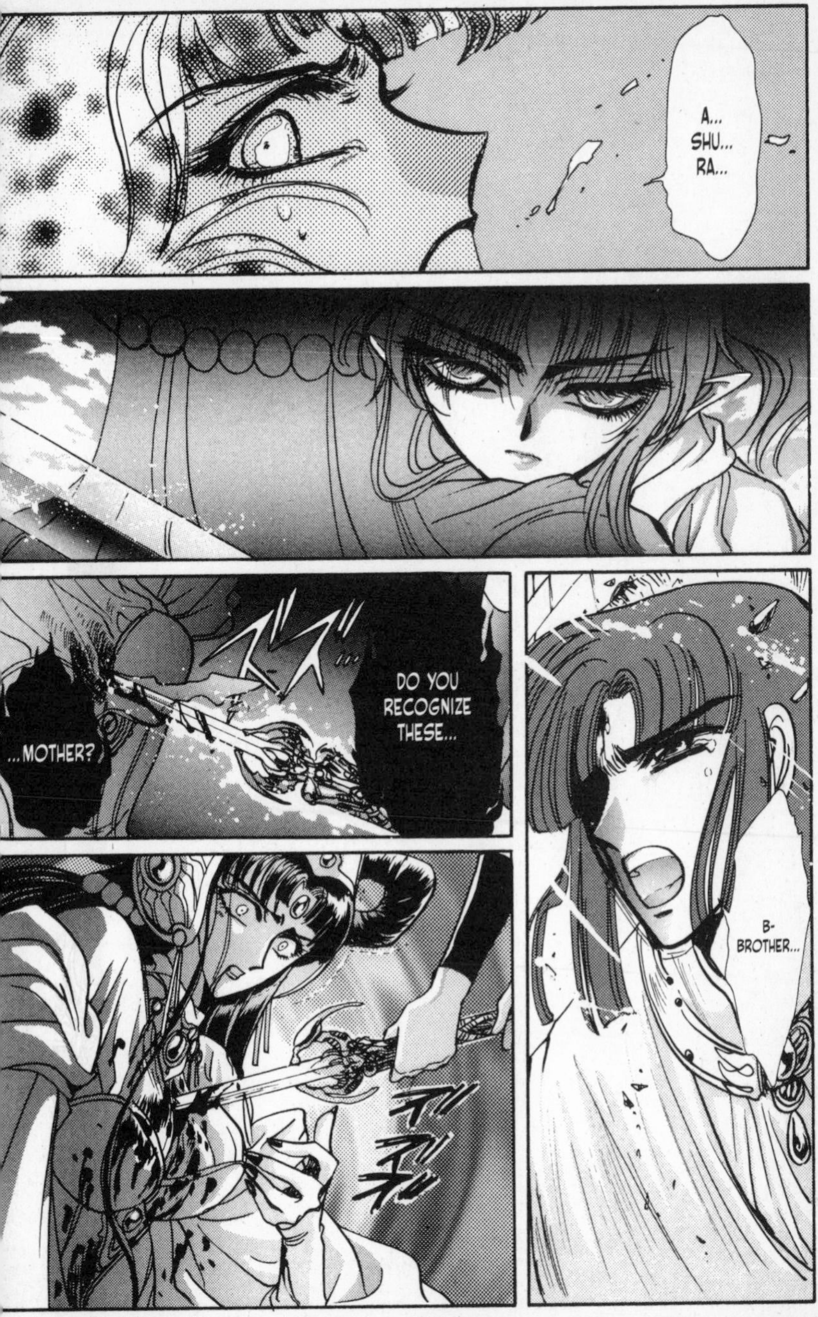
A... SHU... RA...
B- BROTHER...
DO YOU RECOGNIZE THESE...
...MOTHER?

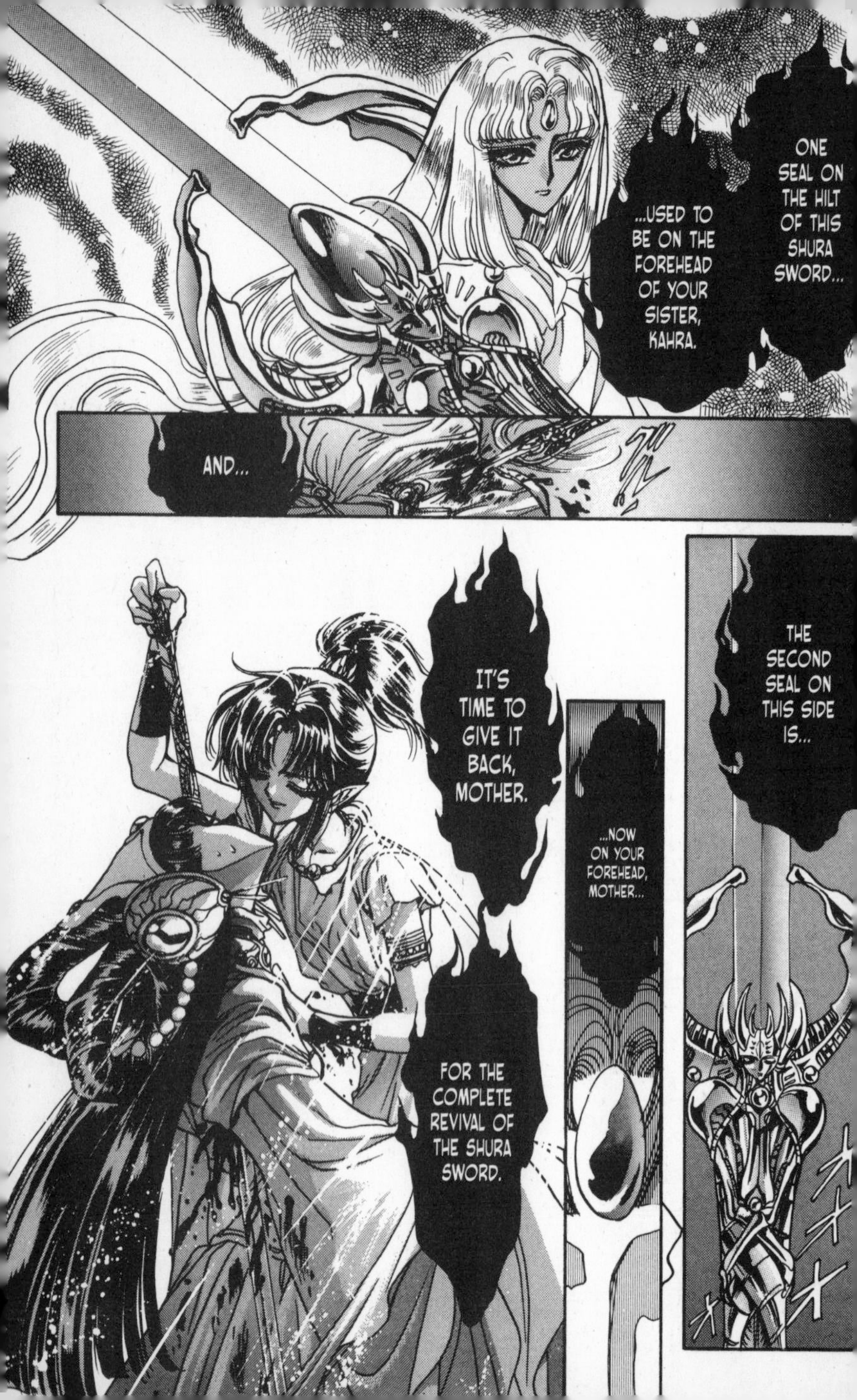
ONE SEAL ON THE HILT OF THIS SHURA SWORD...
...USED TO BE ON THE FOREHEAD OF YOUR SISTER, KAHRA.
AND...
THE SECOND SEAL ON THIS SIDE IS...
...NOW ON YOUR FOREHEAD, MOTHER...
IT'S TIME TO GIVE IT BACK, MOTHER.
FOR THE COMPLETE REVIVAL OF THE SHURA SWORD.

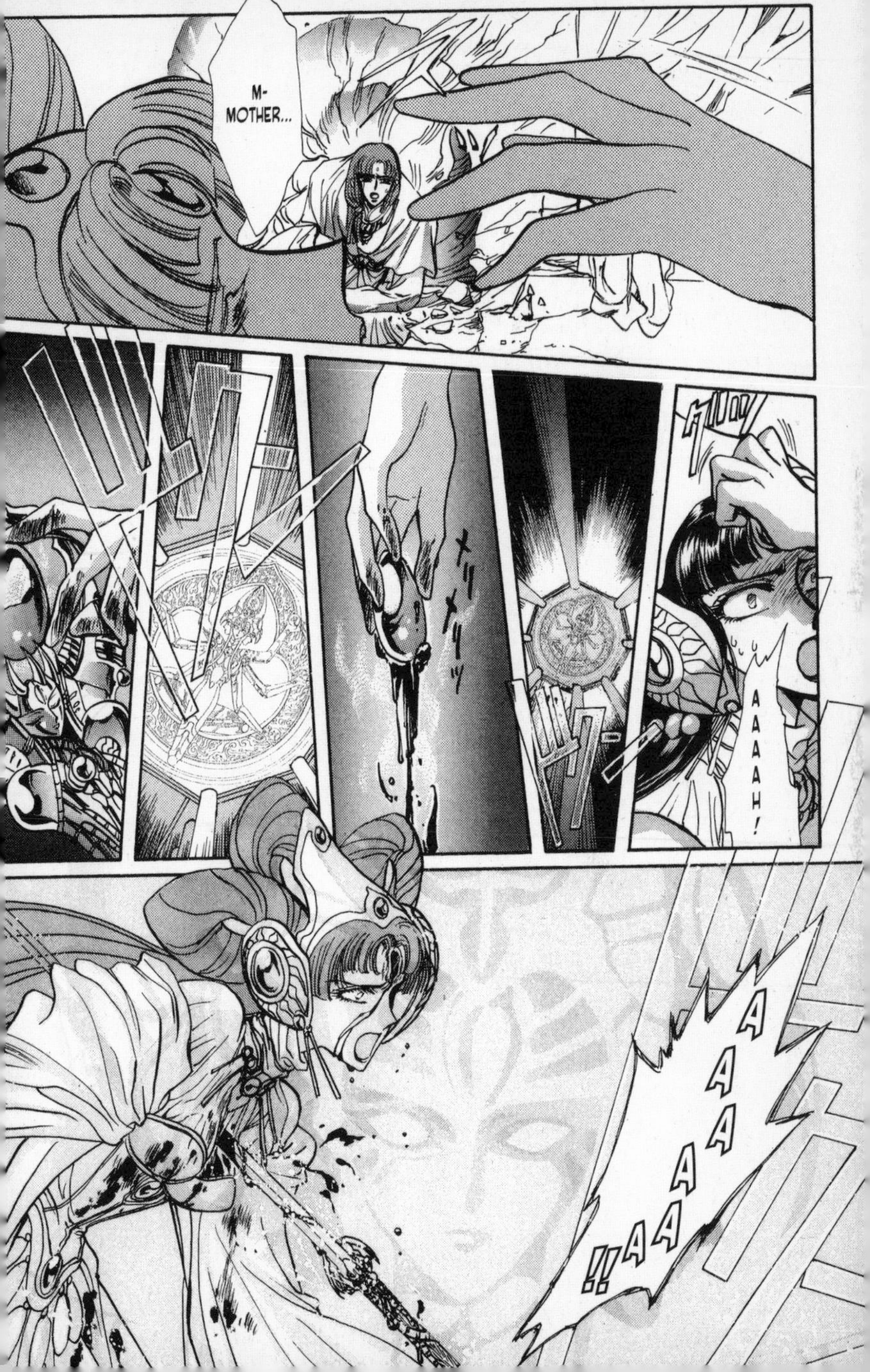
M-
MOTHER...
AAAAAH!
AAAAAAAA!!

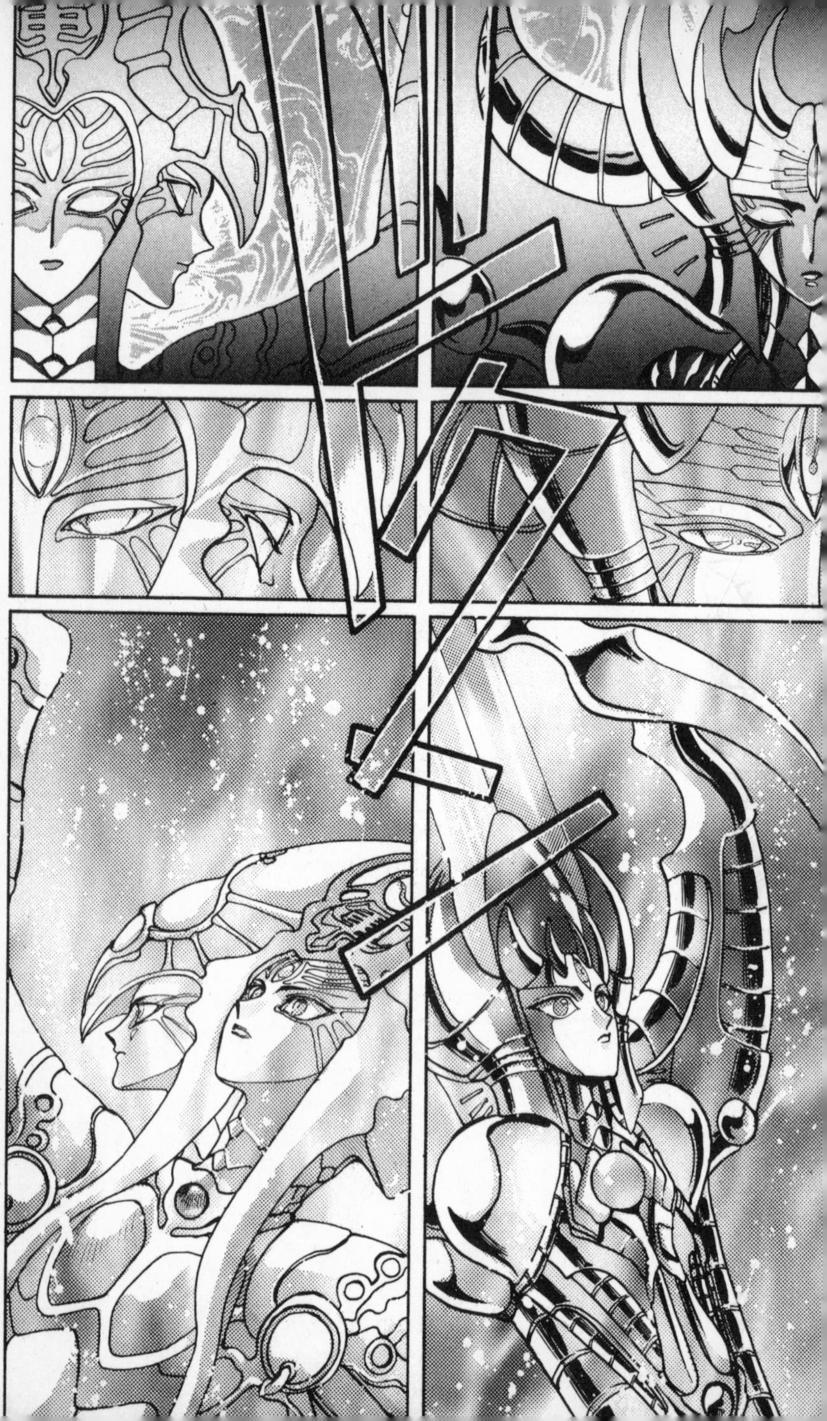

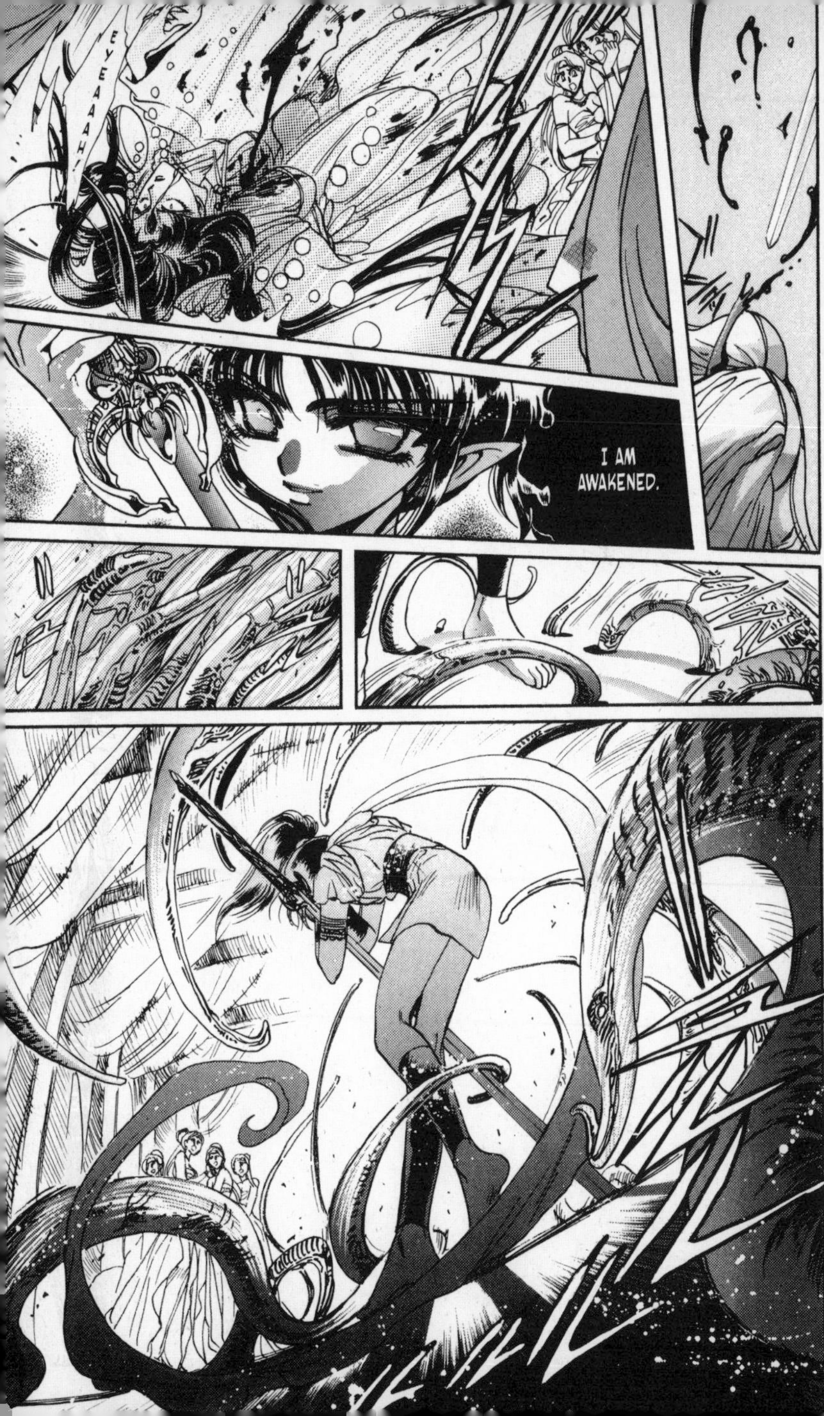
EYEAAAAH!!
I AM AWAKENED.

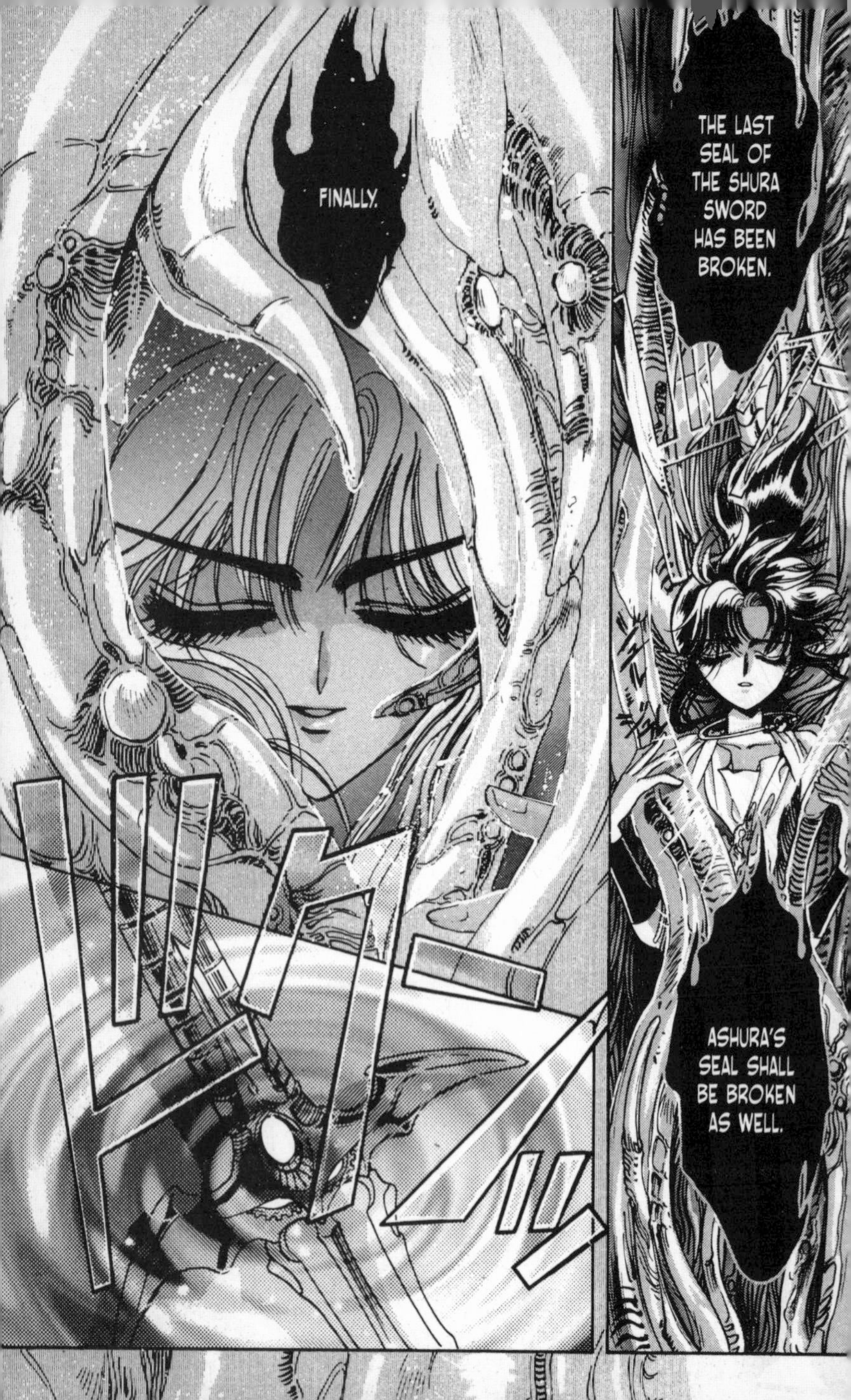
THE LAST SEAL OF THE SHURA SWORD HAS BEEN BROKEN.
ASHURA'S SEAL SHALL BE BROKEN AS WELL.
FINALLY.

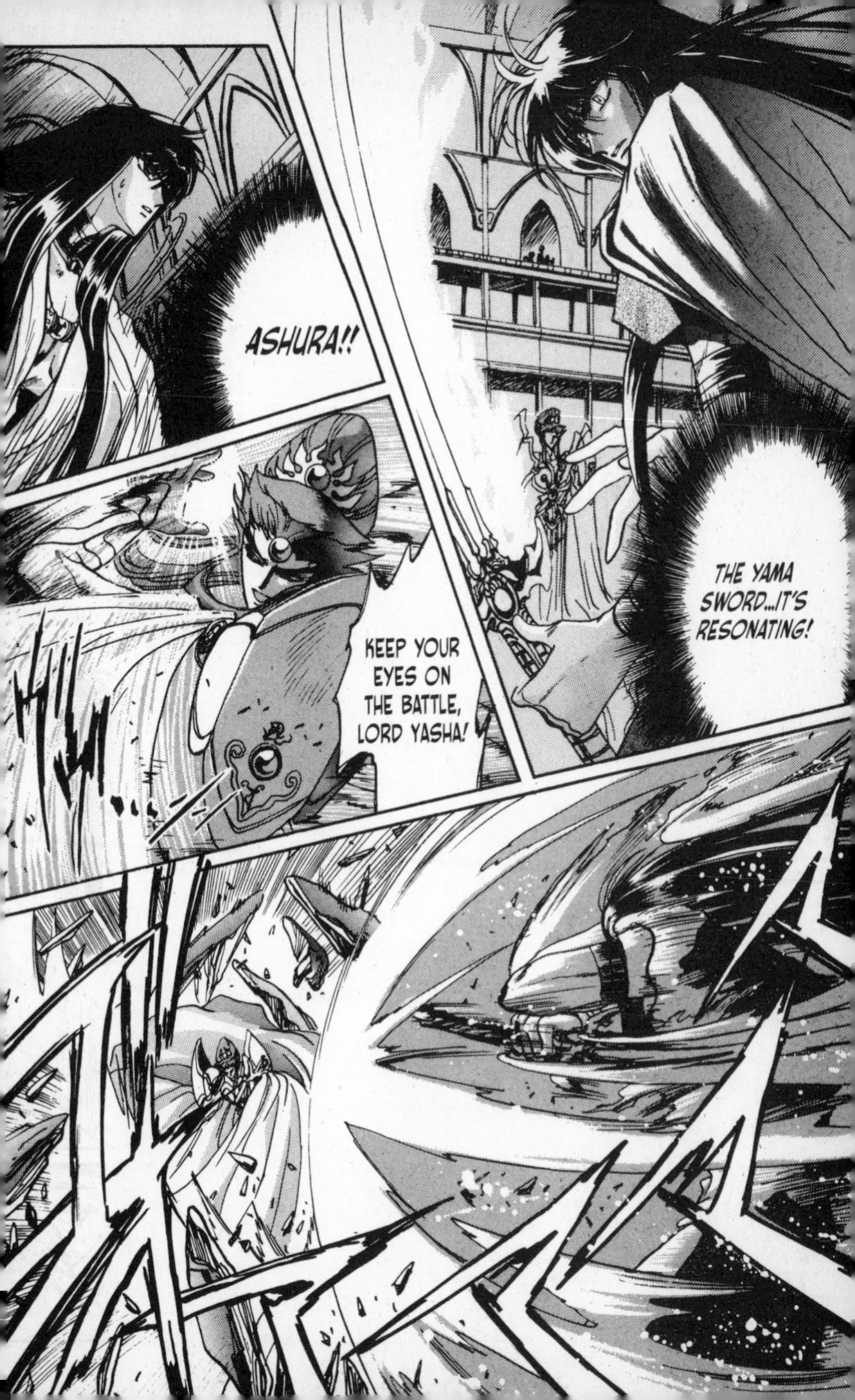
THE YAMA SWORD...IT'S RESONATING!
ASHURA!!
KEEP YOUR EYES ON THE BATTLE, LORD YASHA!

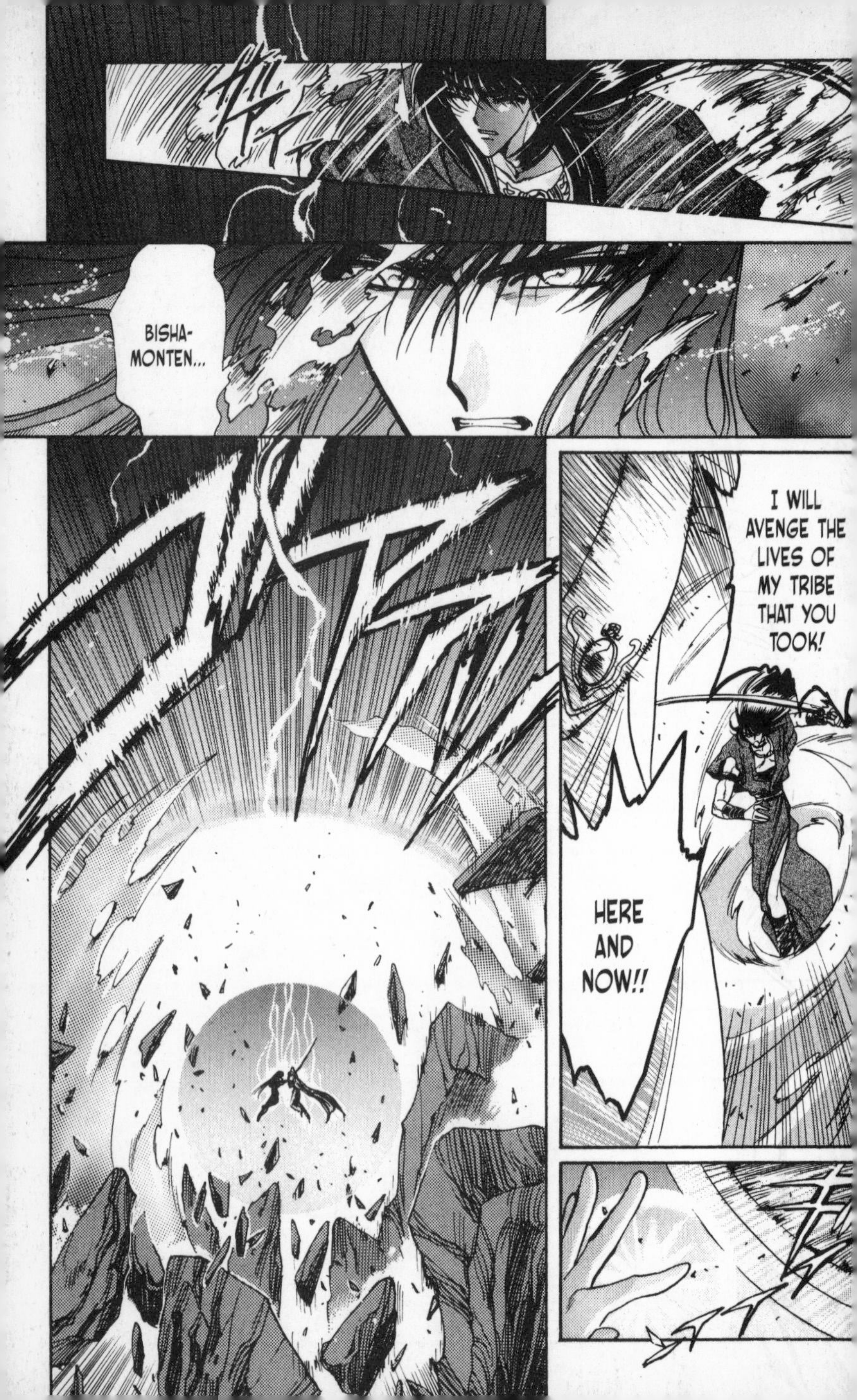
BISHA-MONTEN...
I WILL AVENGE THE LIVES OF MY TRIBE THAT YOU TOOK!
HERE AND NOW!!

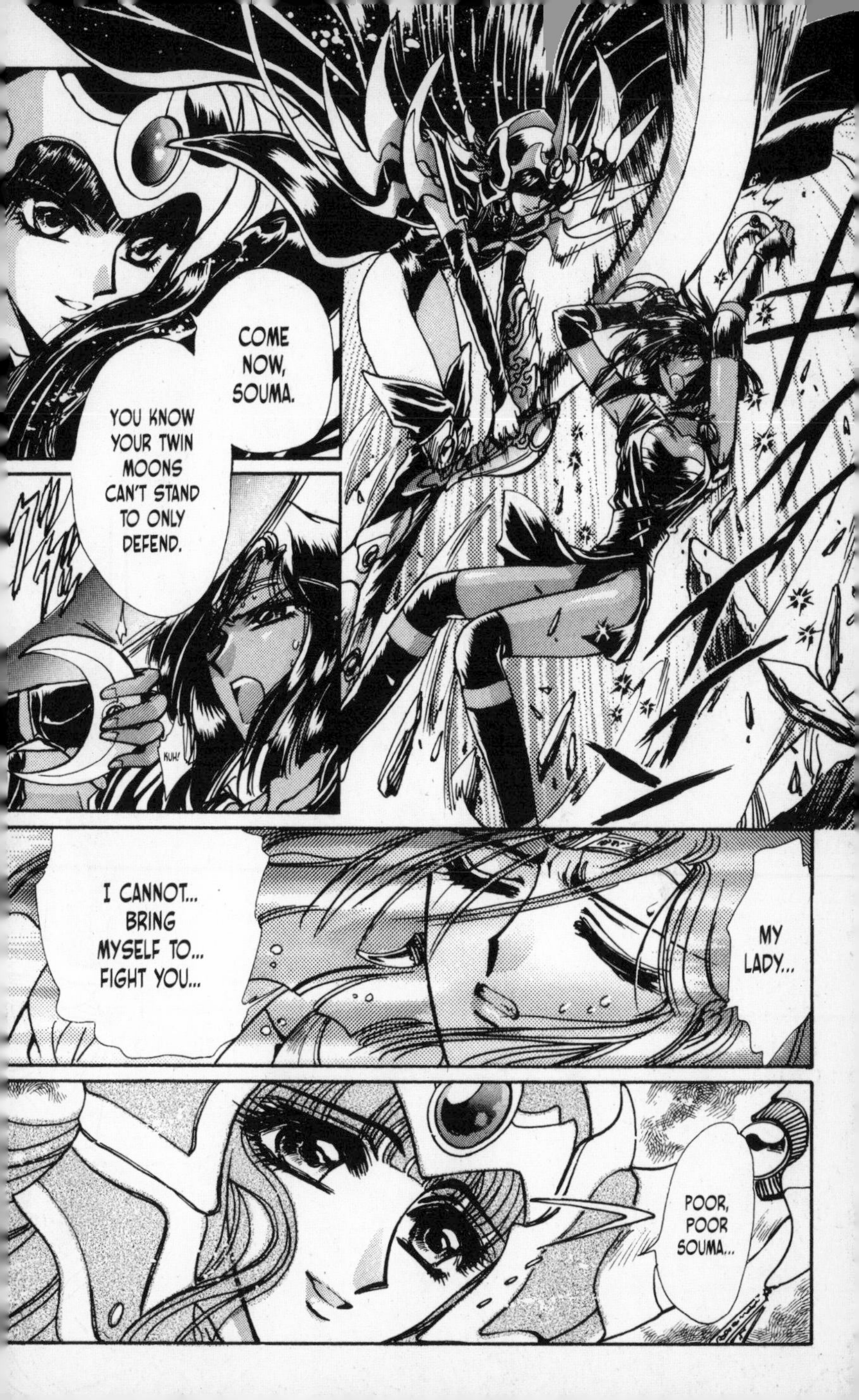
COME NOW, SOUMA.
YOU KNOW YOUR TWIN MOONS CAN'T STAND TO ONLY DEFEND.
KUH!
MY LADY...
I CANNOT... BRING MYSELF TO... FIGHT YOU...
POOR, POOR SOUMA...

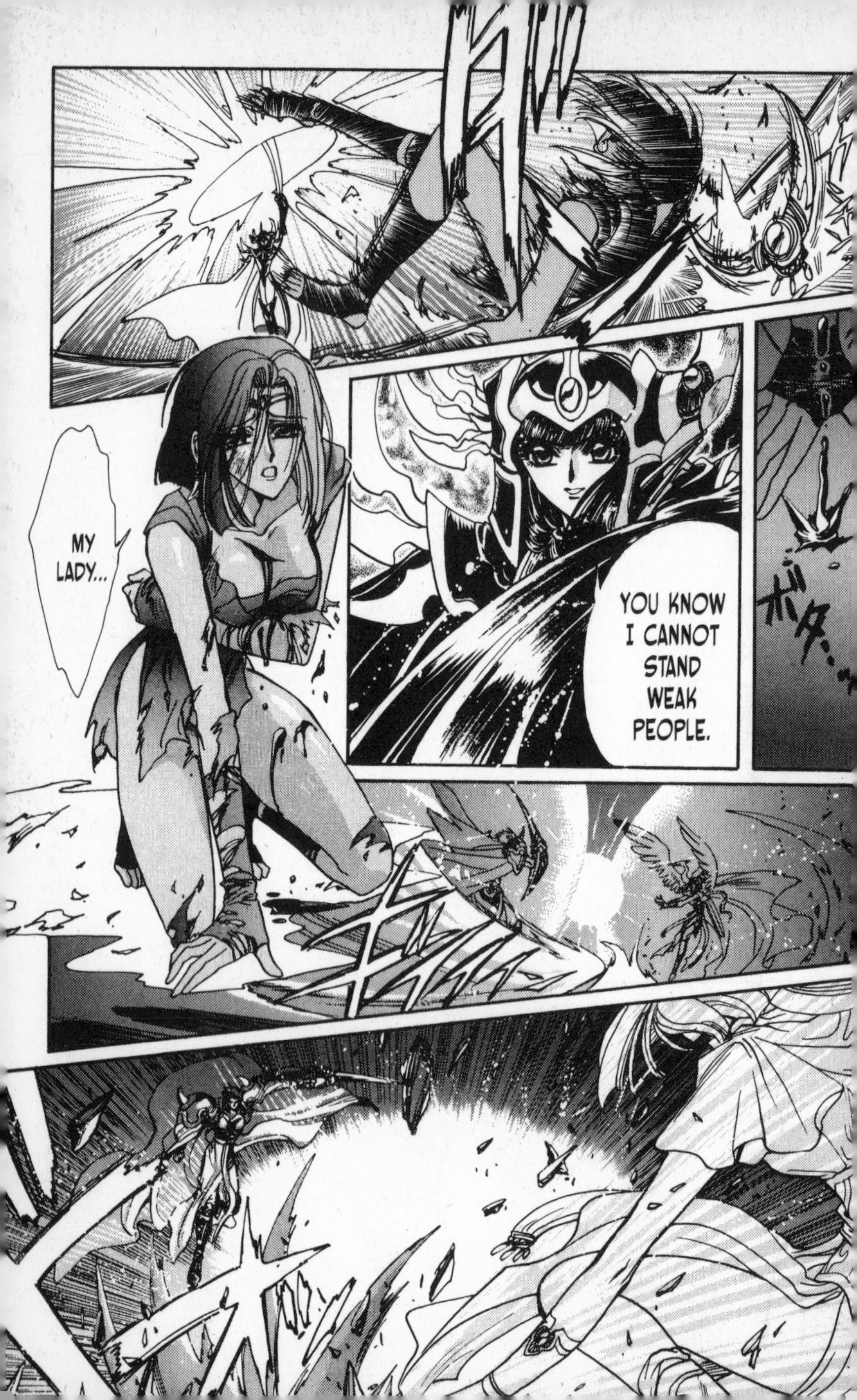
ボタ…
YOU KNOW I CANNOT STAND WEAK PEOPLE.
MY LADY...

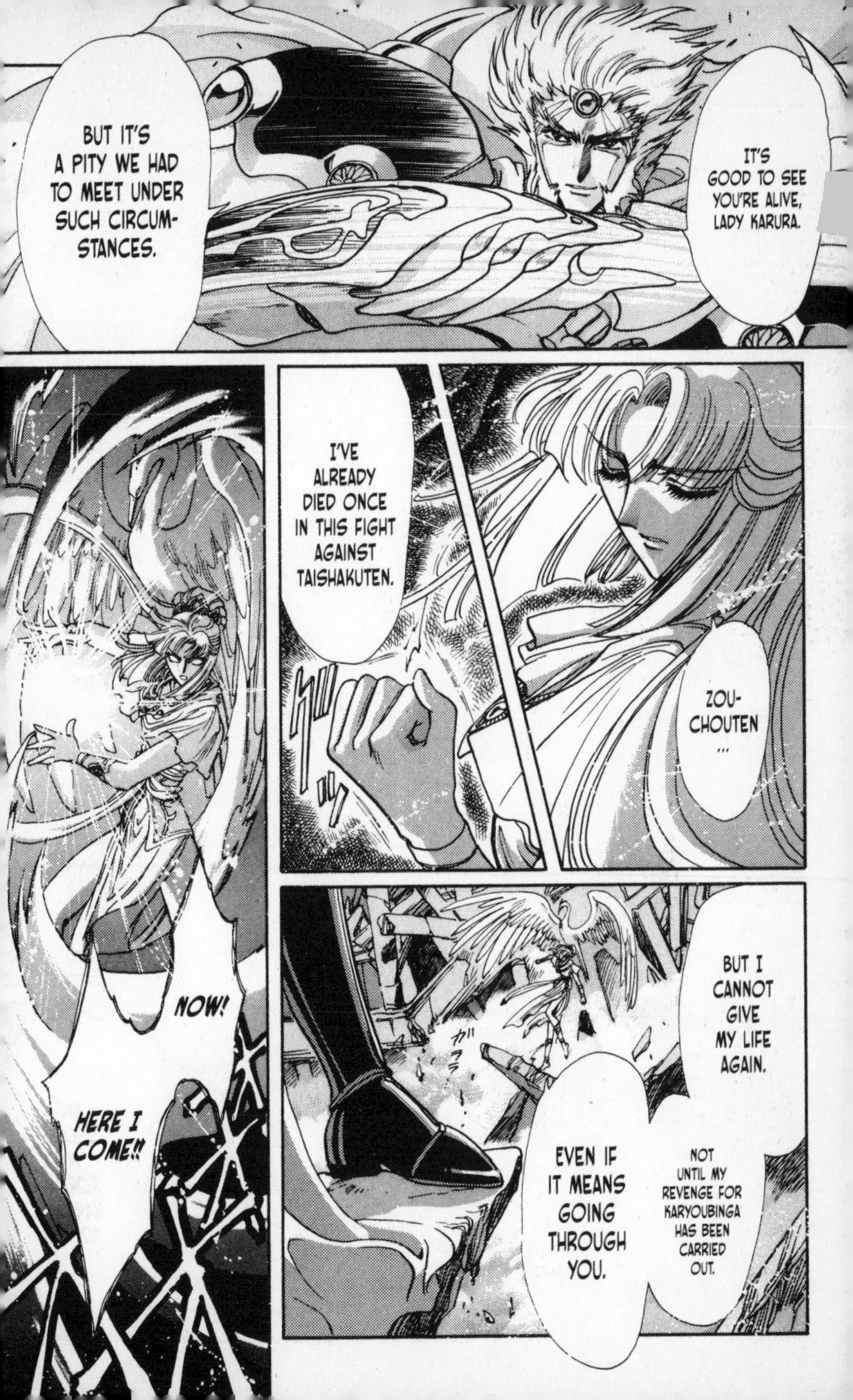
IT'S GOOD TO SEE YOU'RE ALIVE, LADY KARURA.
BUT IT'S A PITY WE HAD TO MEET UNDER SUCH CIRCUM-STANCES.
ZOU-CHOUTEN...
I'VE ALREADY DIED ONCE IN THIS FIGHT AGAINST TAISHAKUTEN.
BUT I CANNOT GIVE MY LIFE AGAIN.
NOT UNTIL MY REVENGE FOR KARYOUBINGA HAS BEEN CARRIED OUT.
EVEN IF IT MEANS GOING THROUGH YOU.
NOW!
HERE I COME!!

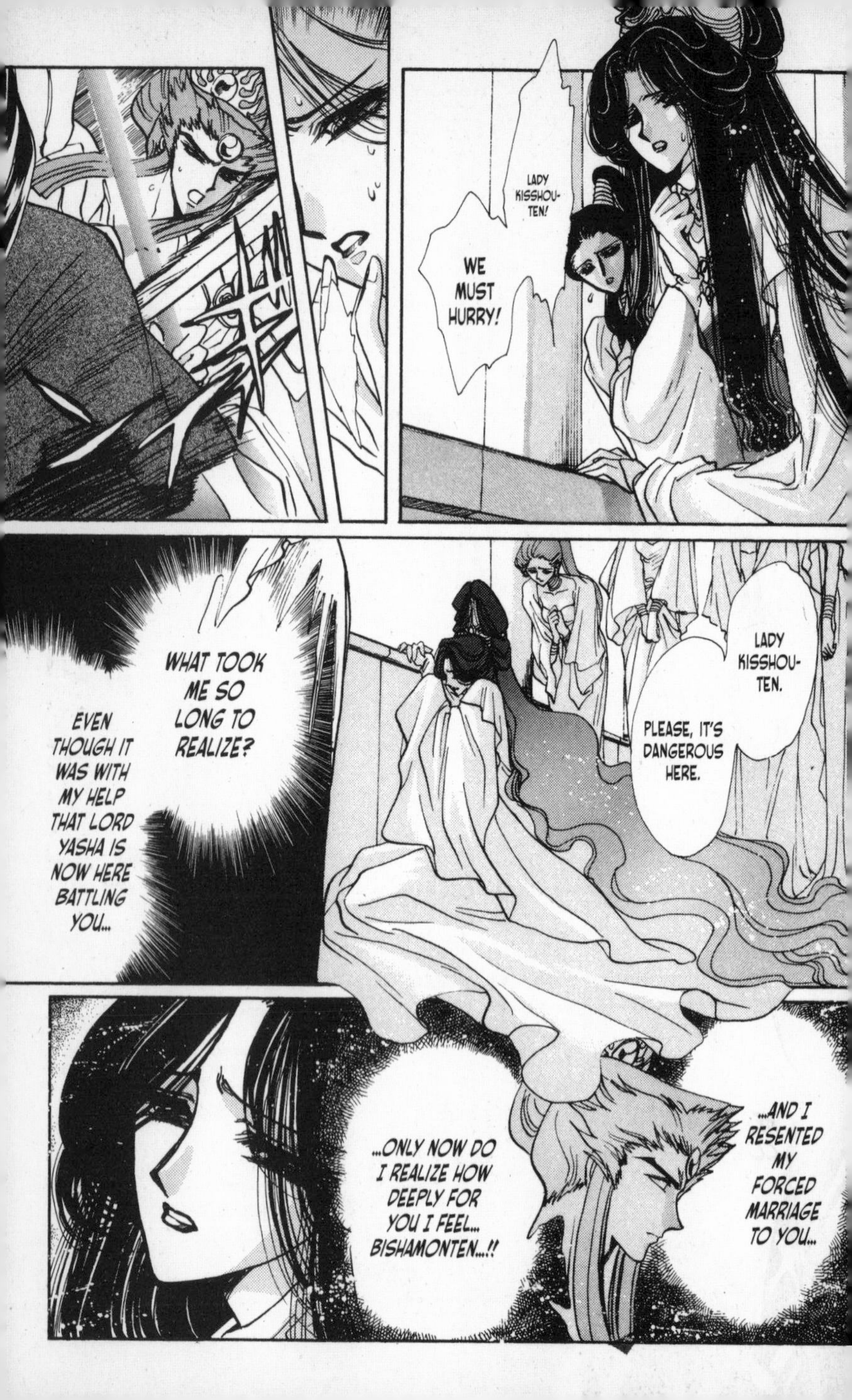
LADY KISSHOU-TEN!
WE MUST HURRY!
LADY KISSHOU-TEN.
PLEASE, IT'S DANGEROUS HERE.
WHAT TOOK ME SO LONG TO REALIZE?
EVEN THOUGH IT WAS WITH MY HELP THAT LORD YASHA IS NOW HERE BATTLING YOU...
...AND I RESENTED MY FORCED MARRIAGE TO YOU...
...ONLY NOW DO I REALIZE HOW DEEPLY FOR YOU I FEEL... BISHAMONTEN...!!

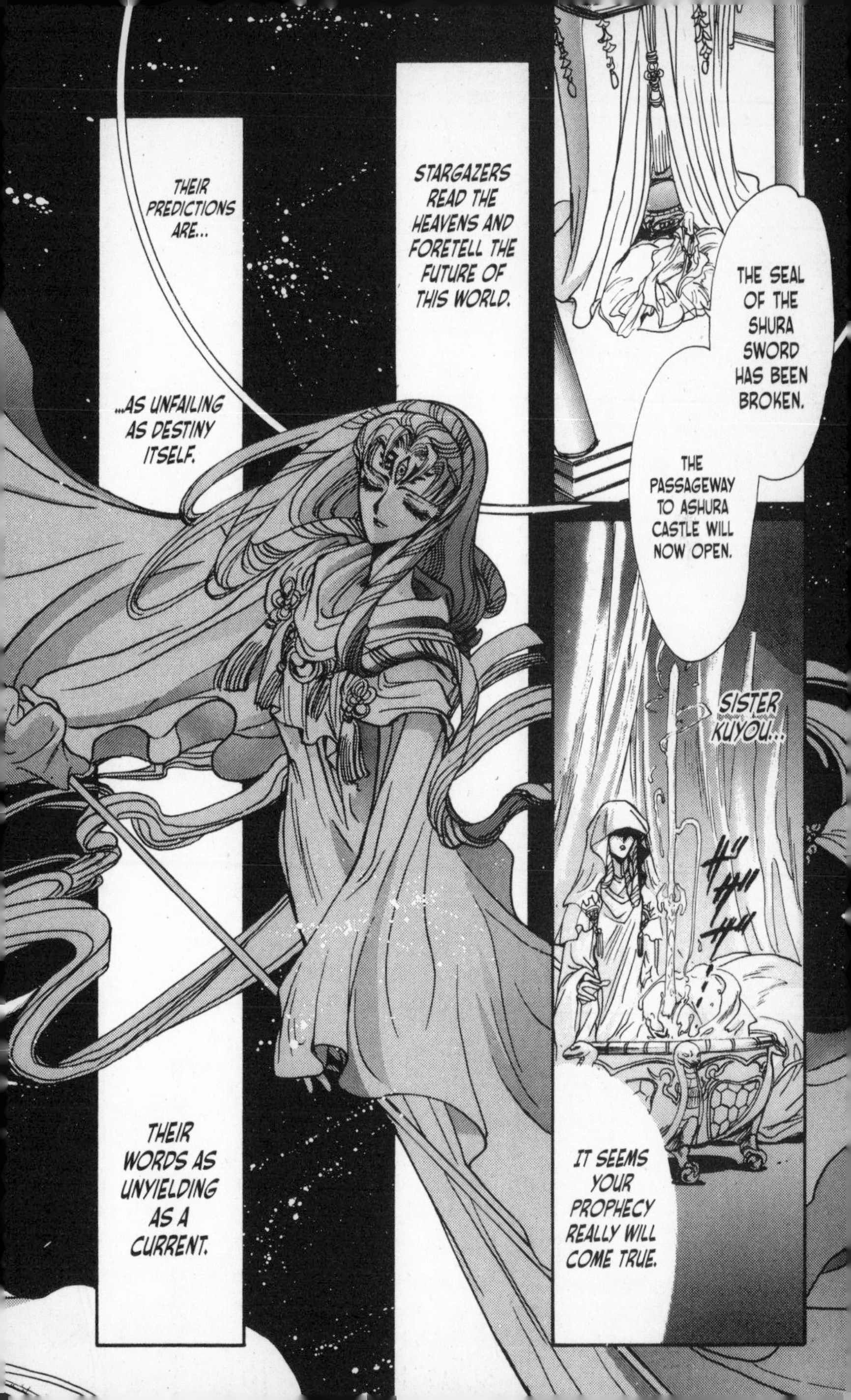
THE SEAL OF THE SHURA SWORD HAS BEEN BROKEN.
THE PASSAGEWAY TO ASHURA CASTLE WILL NOW OPEN.
SISTER KUYOU...
IT SEEMS YOUR PROPHECY REALLY WILL COME TRUE.
STARGAZERS READ THE HEAVENS AND FORETELL THE FUTURE OF THIS WORLD.
THEIR PREDICTIONS ARE...
...AS UNFAILING AS DESTINY ITSELF.
THEIR WORDS AS UNYIELDING AS A CURRENT.

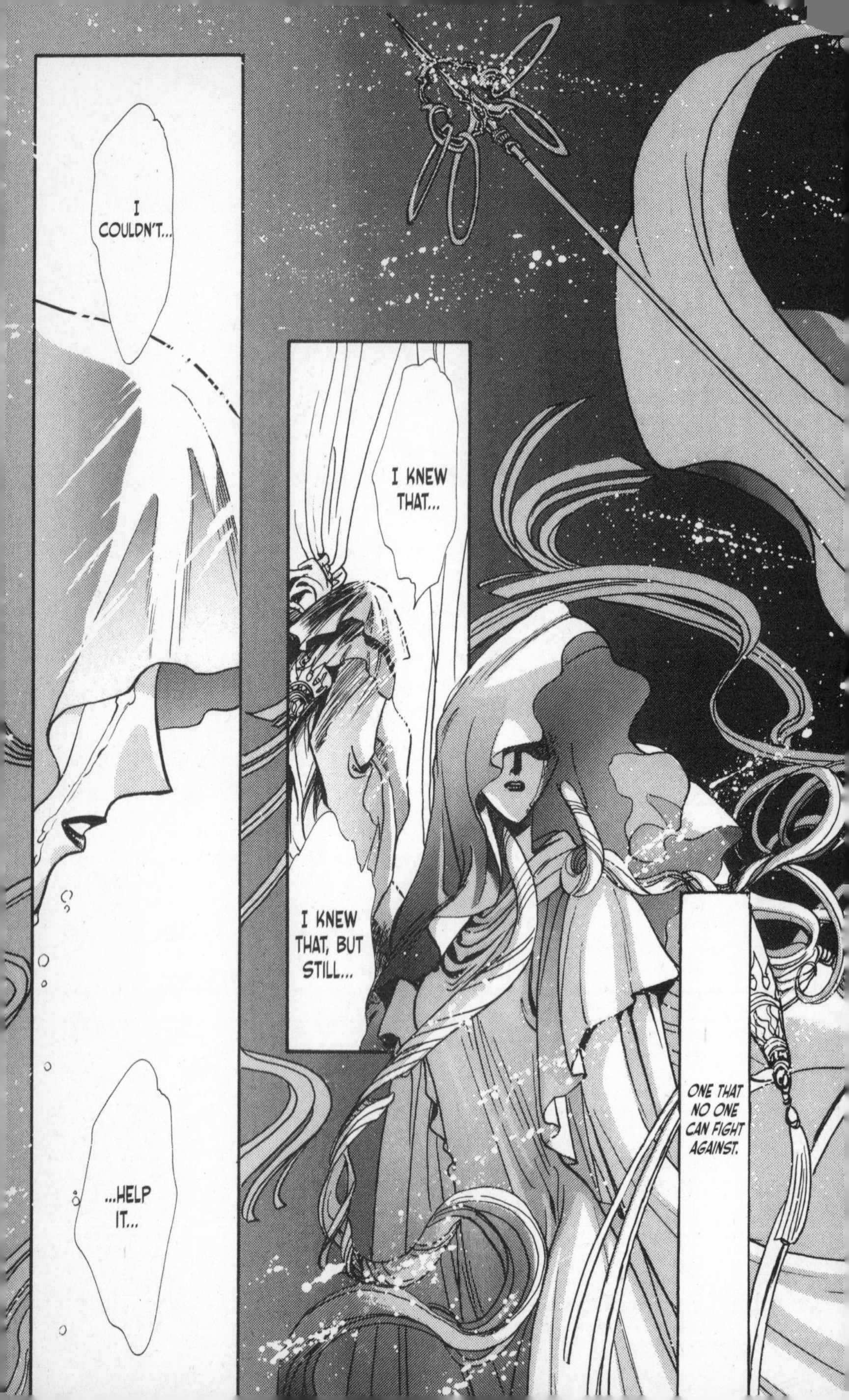
ONE THAT NO ONE CAN FIGHT AGAINST.
I KNEW THAT...
I KNEW THAT, BUT STILL...
I COULDN'T...
...HELP IT...

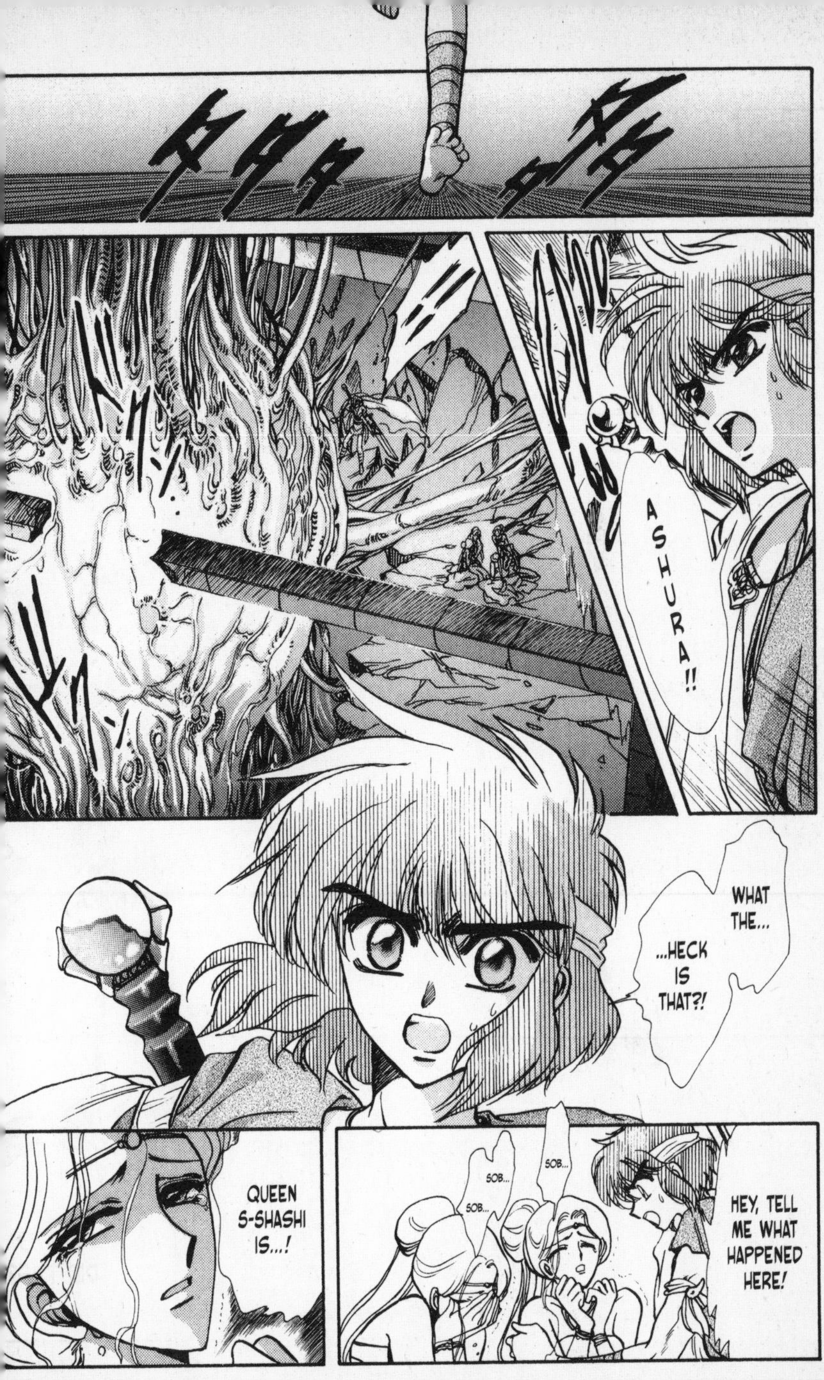
ASHURA!!
WHAT THE...
...HECK IS THAT?!
HEY, TELL ME WHAT HAPPENED HERE!
SOB...
SOB...
SOB...
QUEEN S-SHASHI IS...!

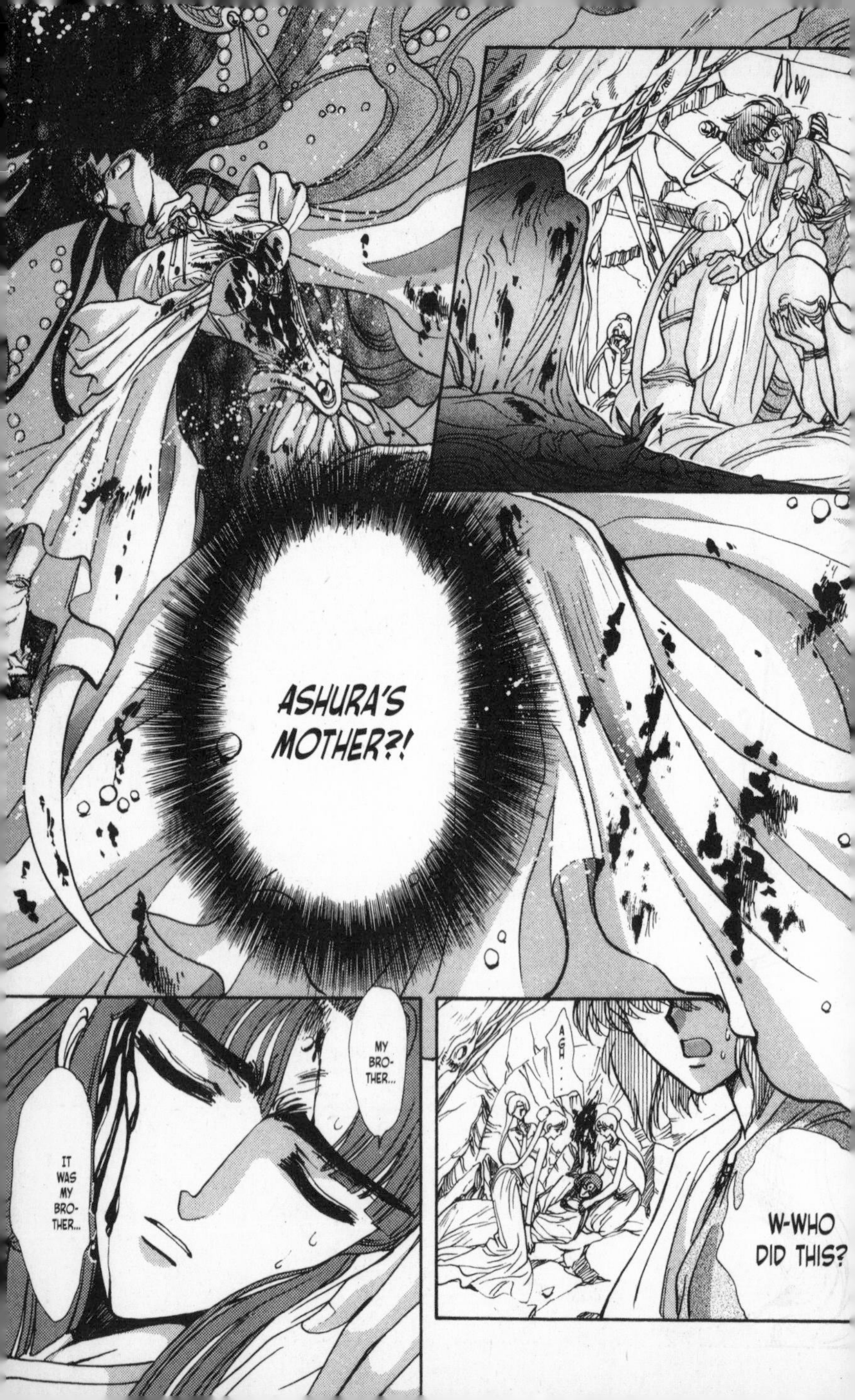
ASHURA'S MOTHER?!
AGH...
W-WHO DID THIS?
MY BRO-THER...
IT WAS MY BRO-THER...

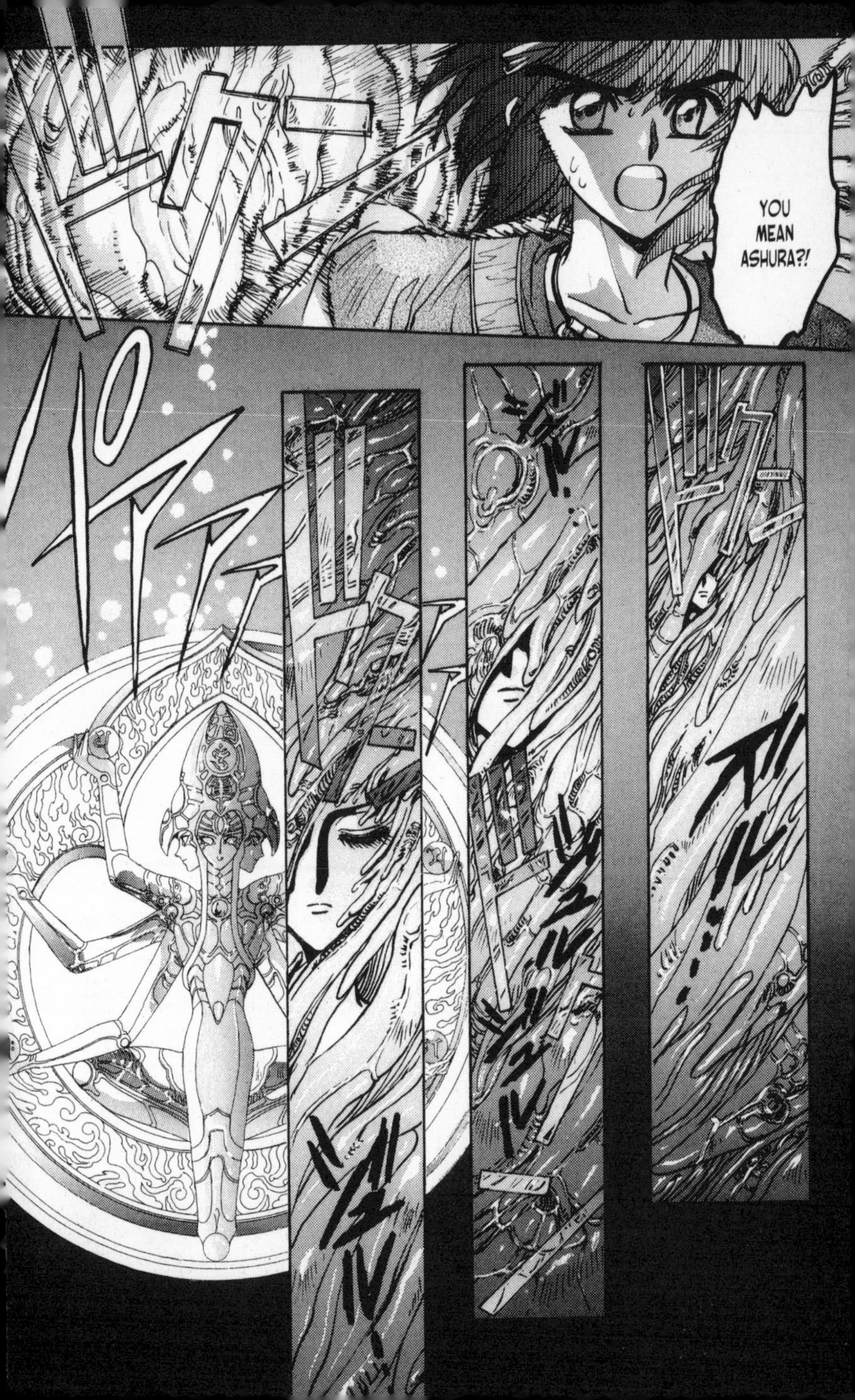
YOU MEAN ASHURA?!

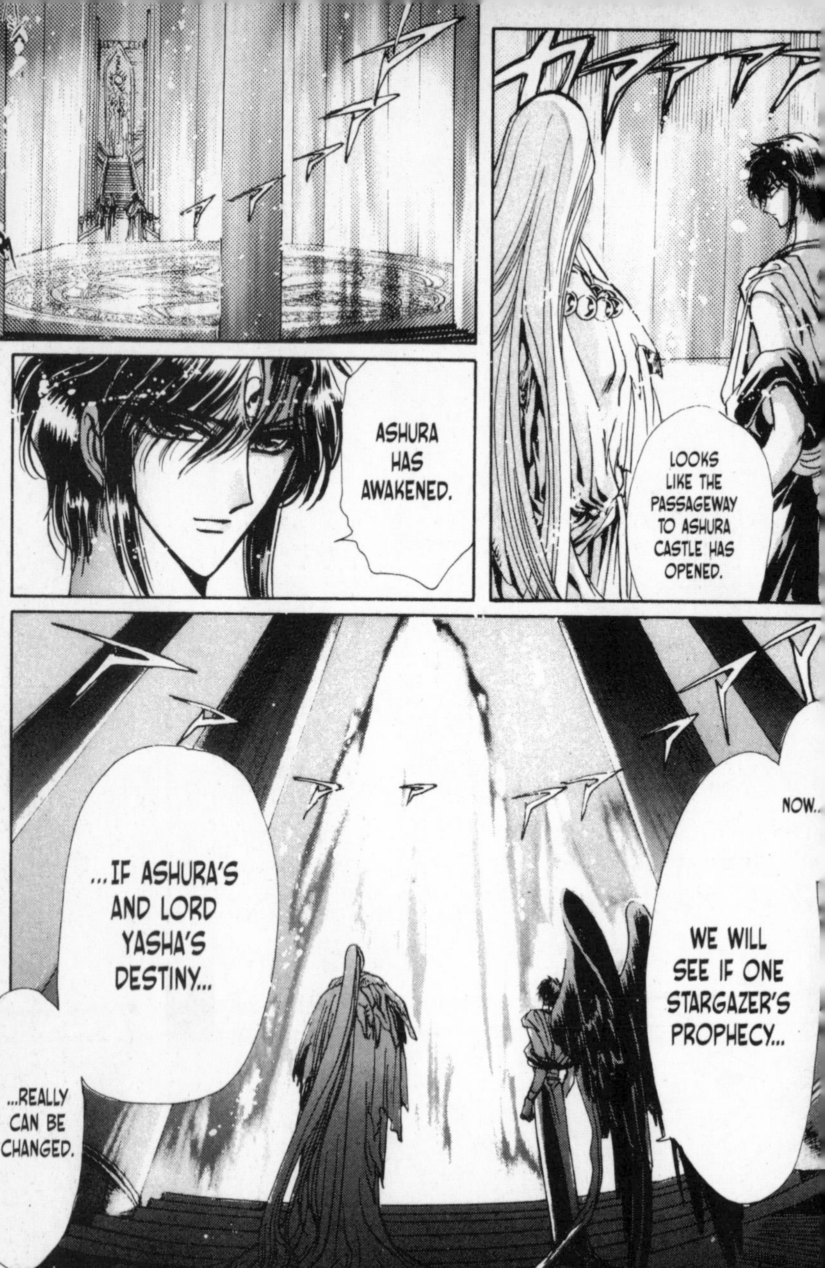
LOOKS LIKE THE PASSAGEWAY TO ASHURA CASTLE HAS OPENED.
ASHURA HAS AWAKENED.
NOW...
WE WILL SEE IF ONE STARGAZER'S PROPHECY...
...IF ASHURA'S AND LORD YASHA'S DESTINY...
...REALLY CAN BE CHANGED.

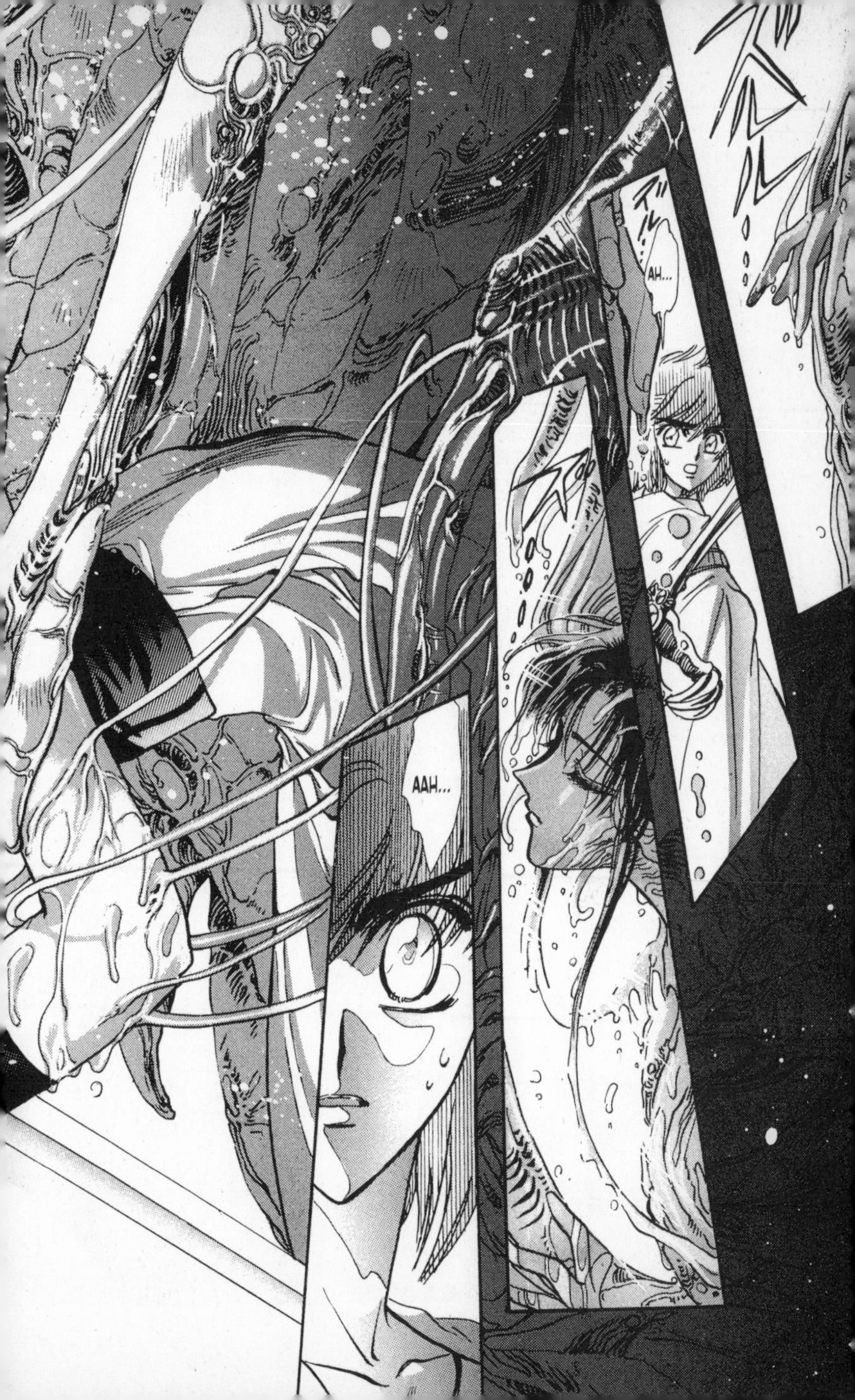
AH...
AAH...

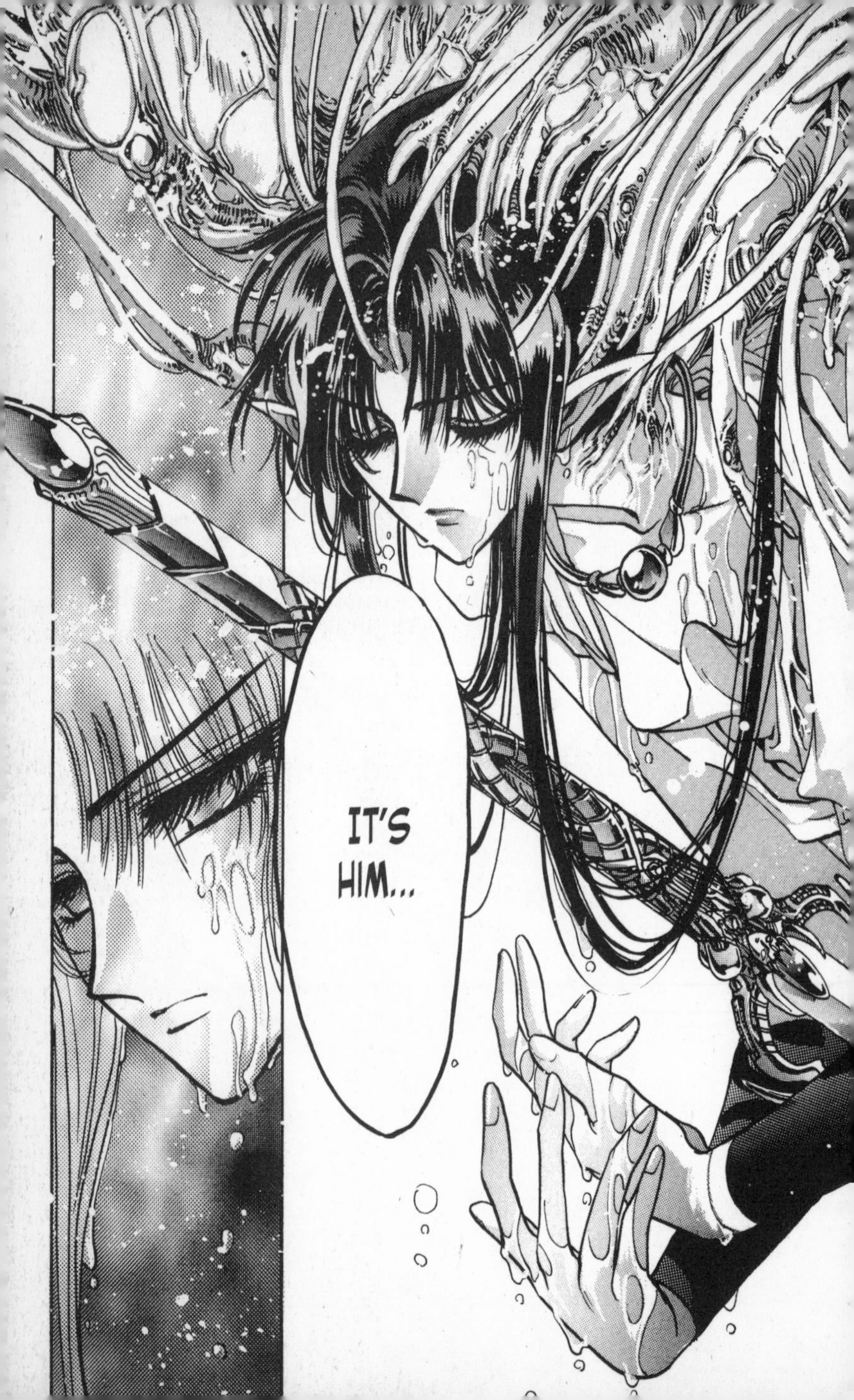
IT'S HIM...

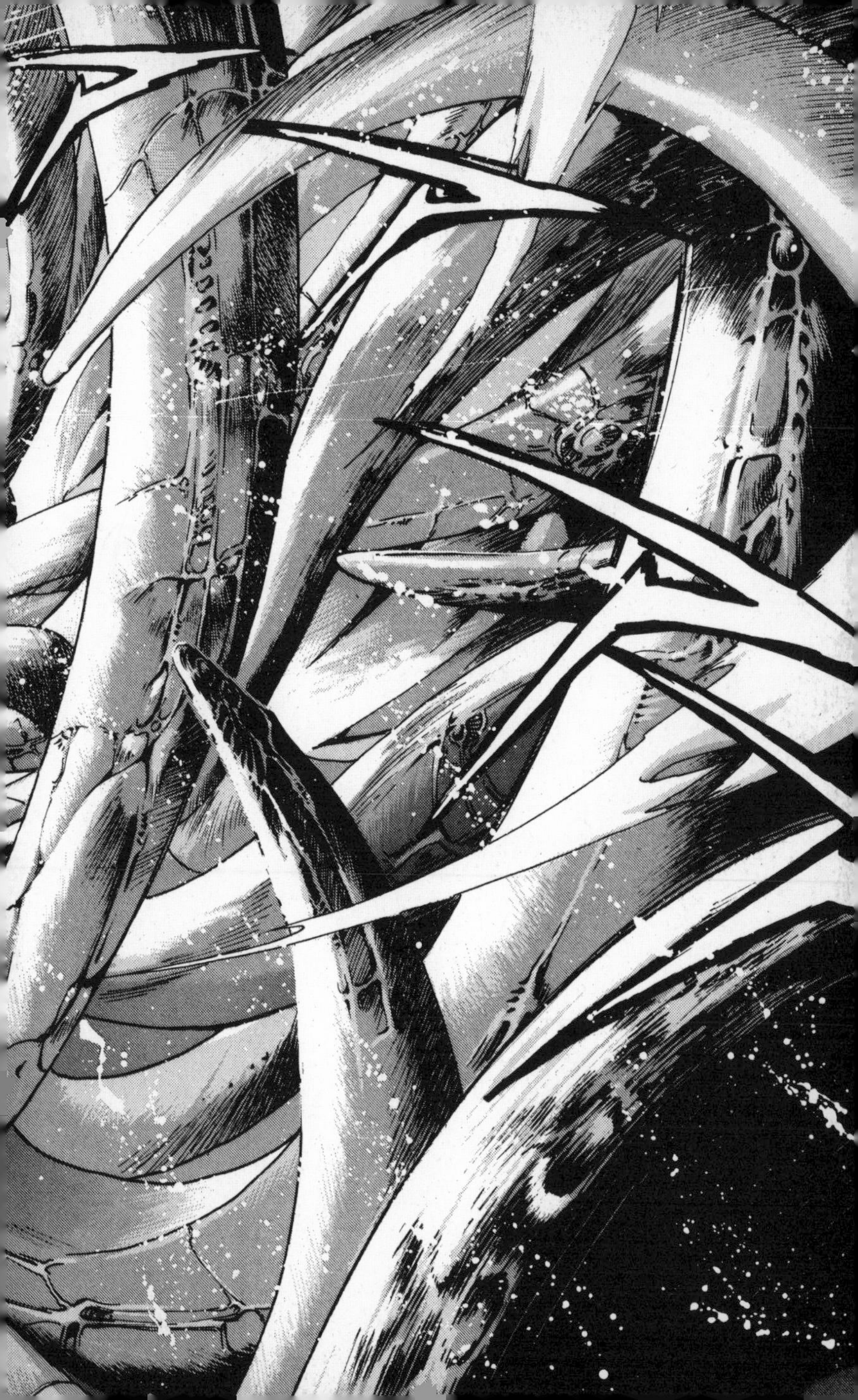

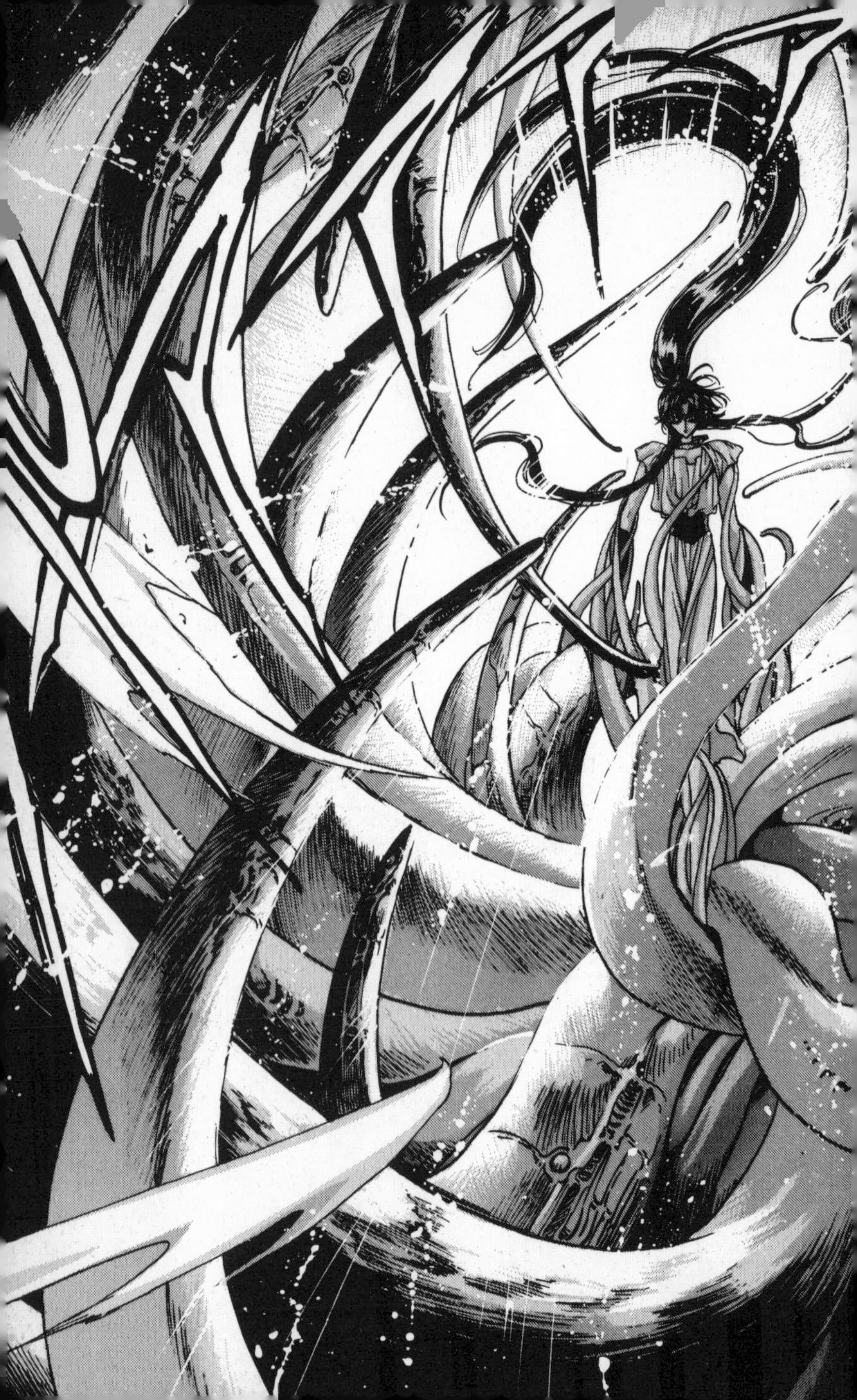

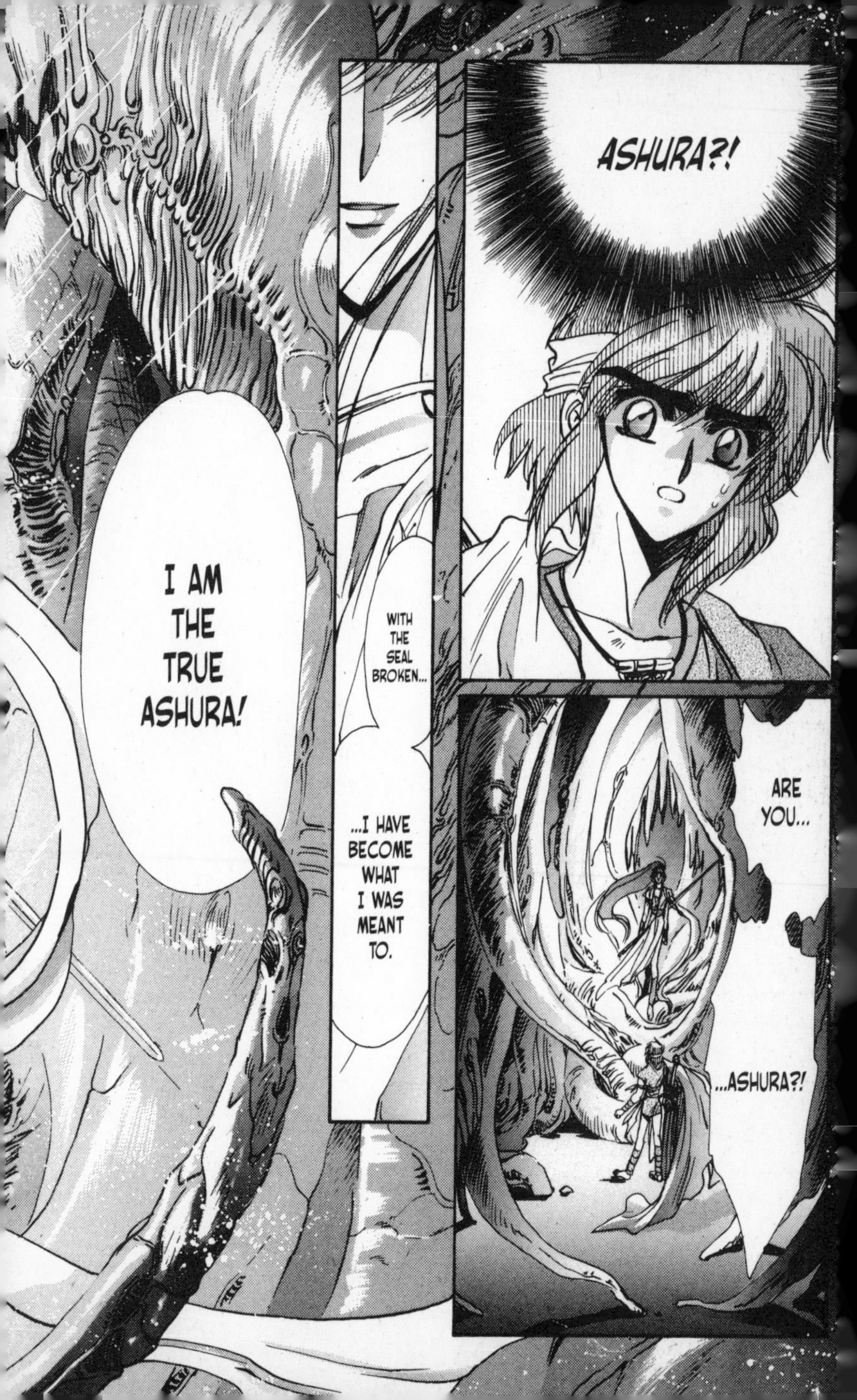
ASHURA?!
ARE YOU...
...ASHURA?!
WITH THE SEAL BROKEN...
...I HAVE BECOME WHAT I WAS MEANT TO.
I AM THE TRUE ASHURA!

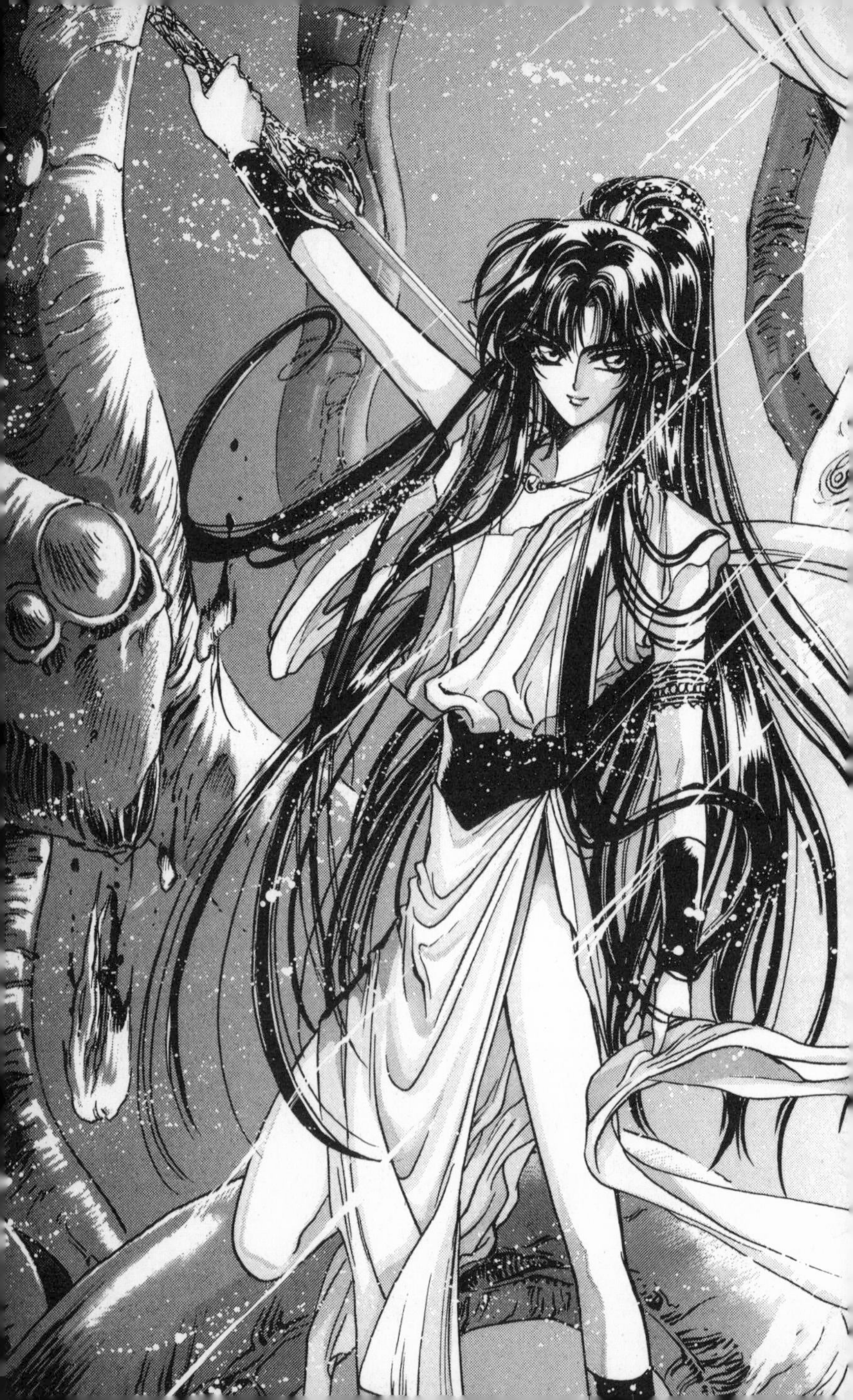

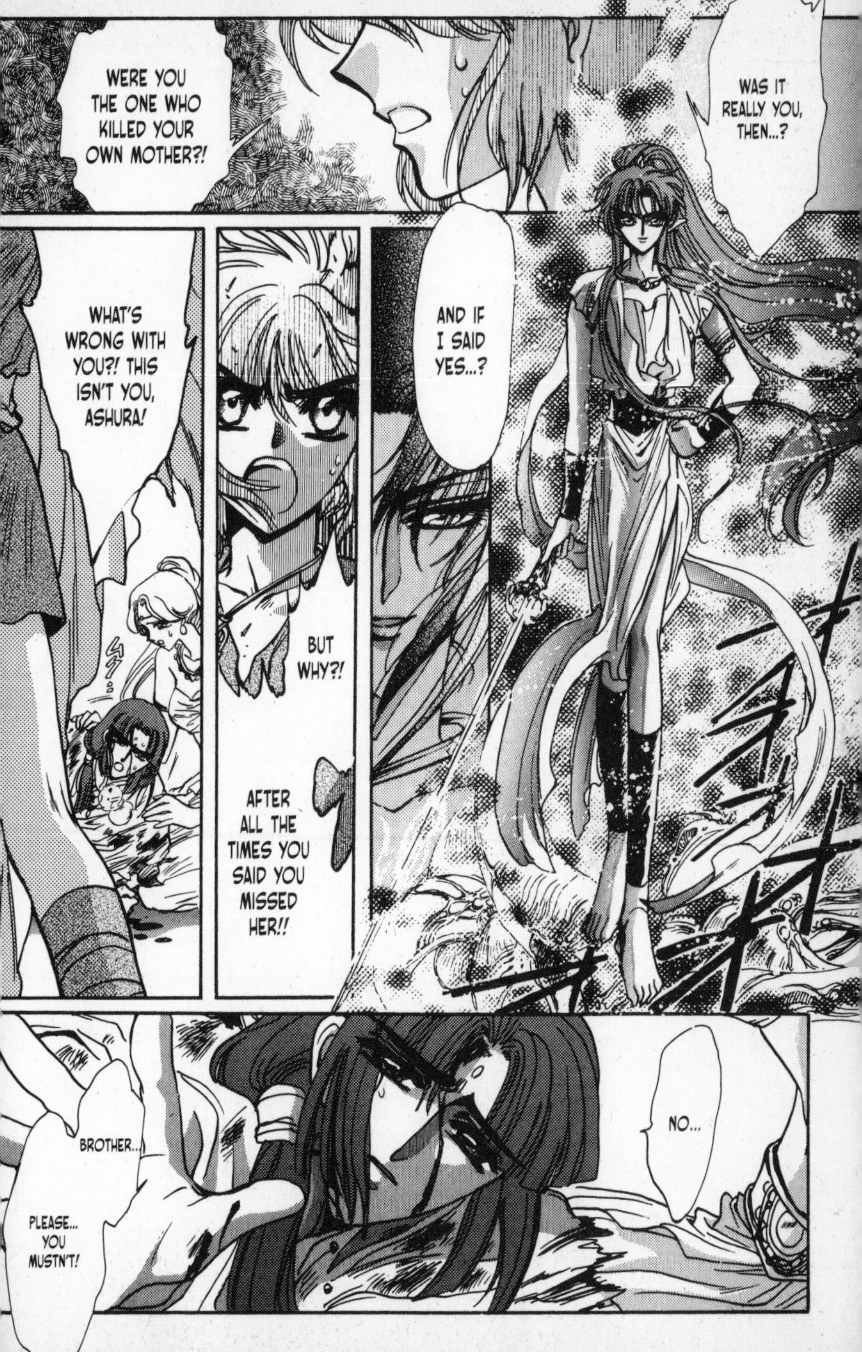
WAS IT REALLY YOU, THEN...?
WERE YOU THE ONE WHO KILLED YOUR OWN MOTHER?!
AND IF I SAID YES...?
BUT WHY?!
AFTER ALL THE TIMES YOU SAID YOU MISSED HER!!
WHAT'S WRONG WITH YOU?! THIS ISN'T YOU, ASHURA!
NO...
BROTHER...
PLEASE... YOU MUSTN'T!

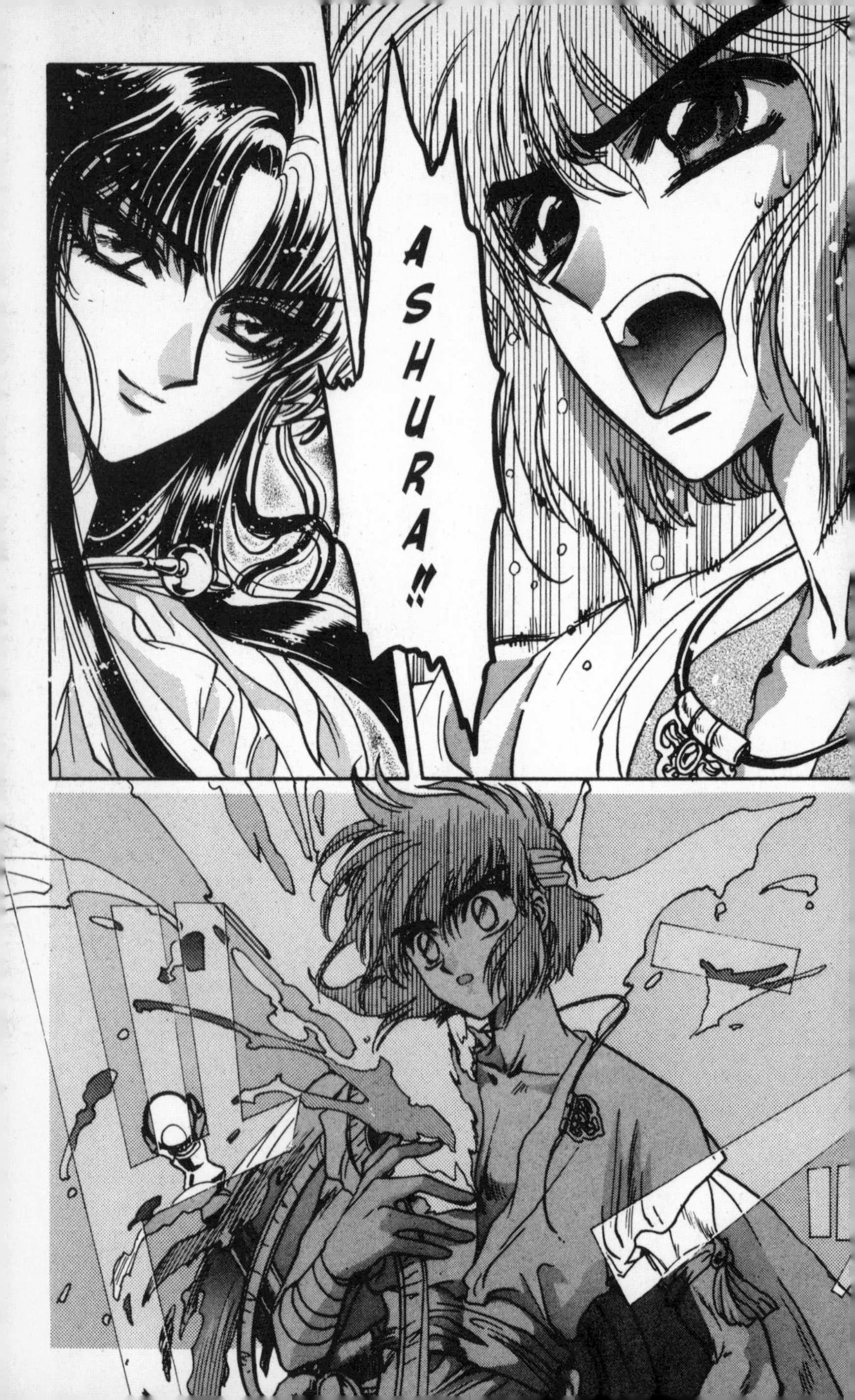
ASHURA!!

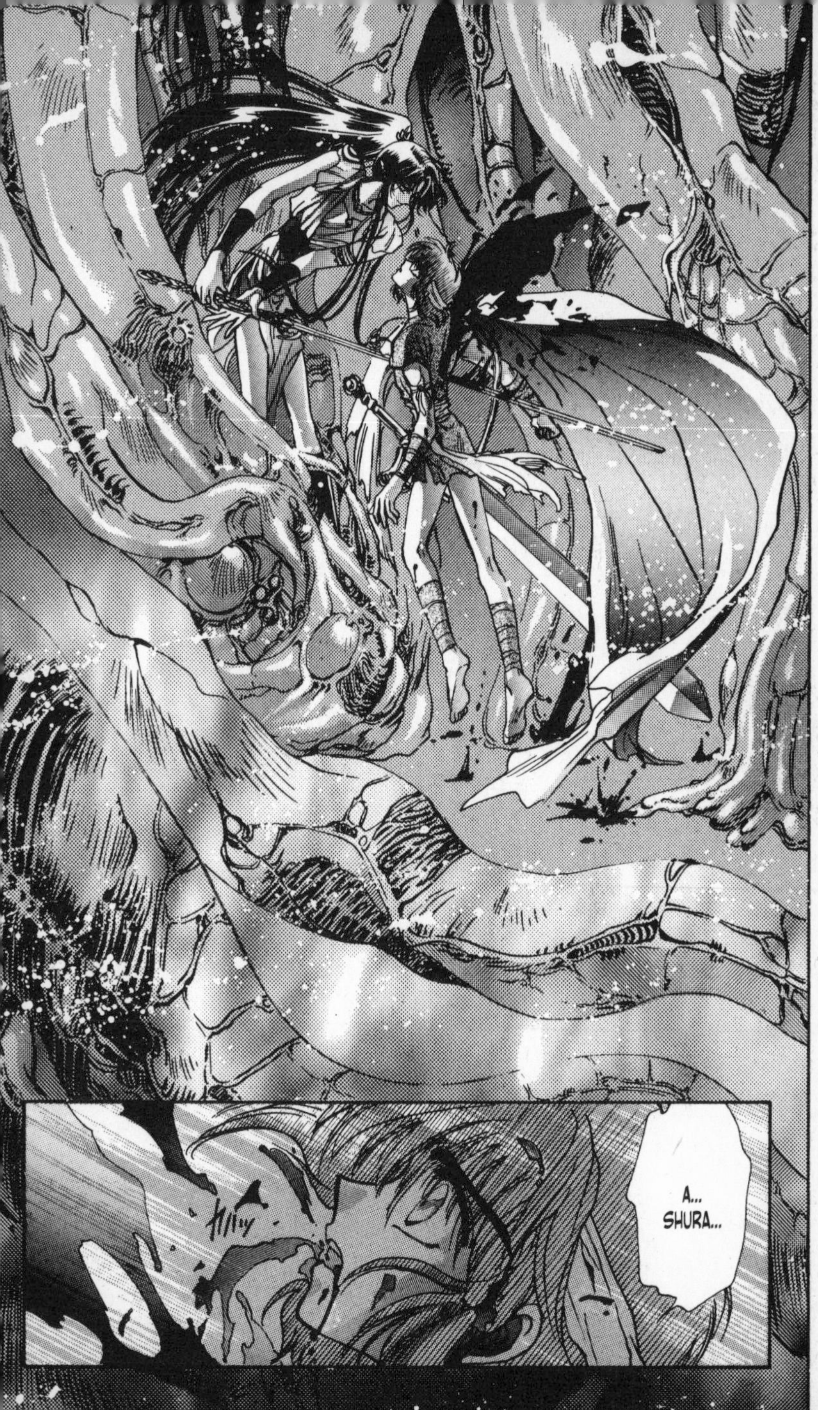
A... SHURA...

ASHURA.

I'M SORRY...

I'M...

I...

...BROKE MY... PROMISE...

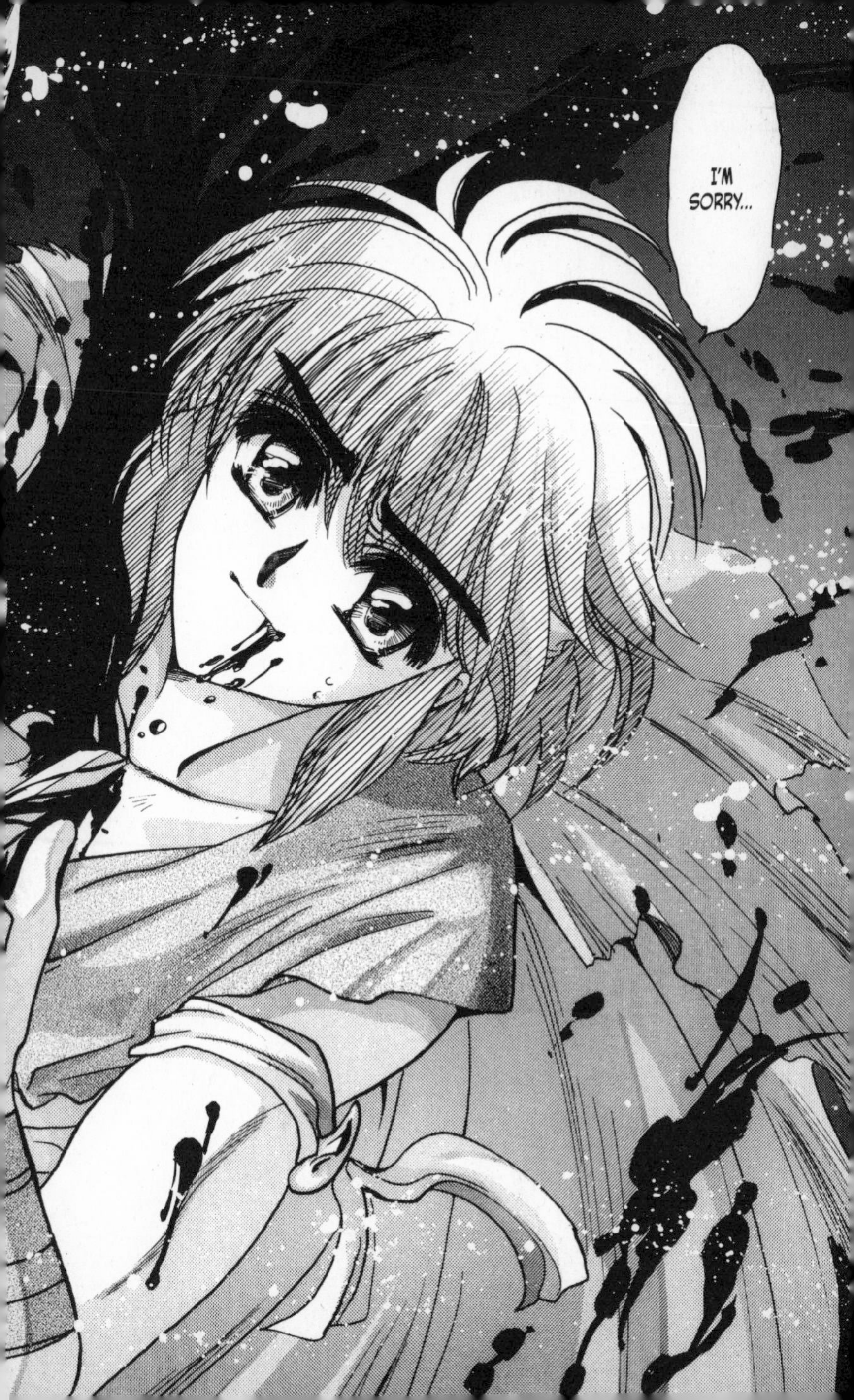
I'M SORRY...

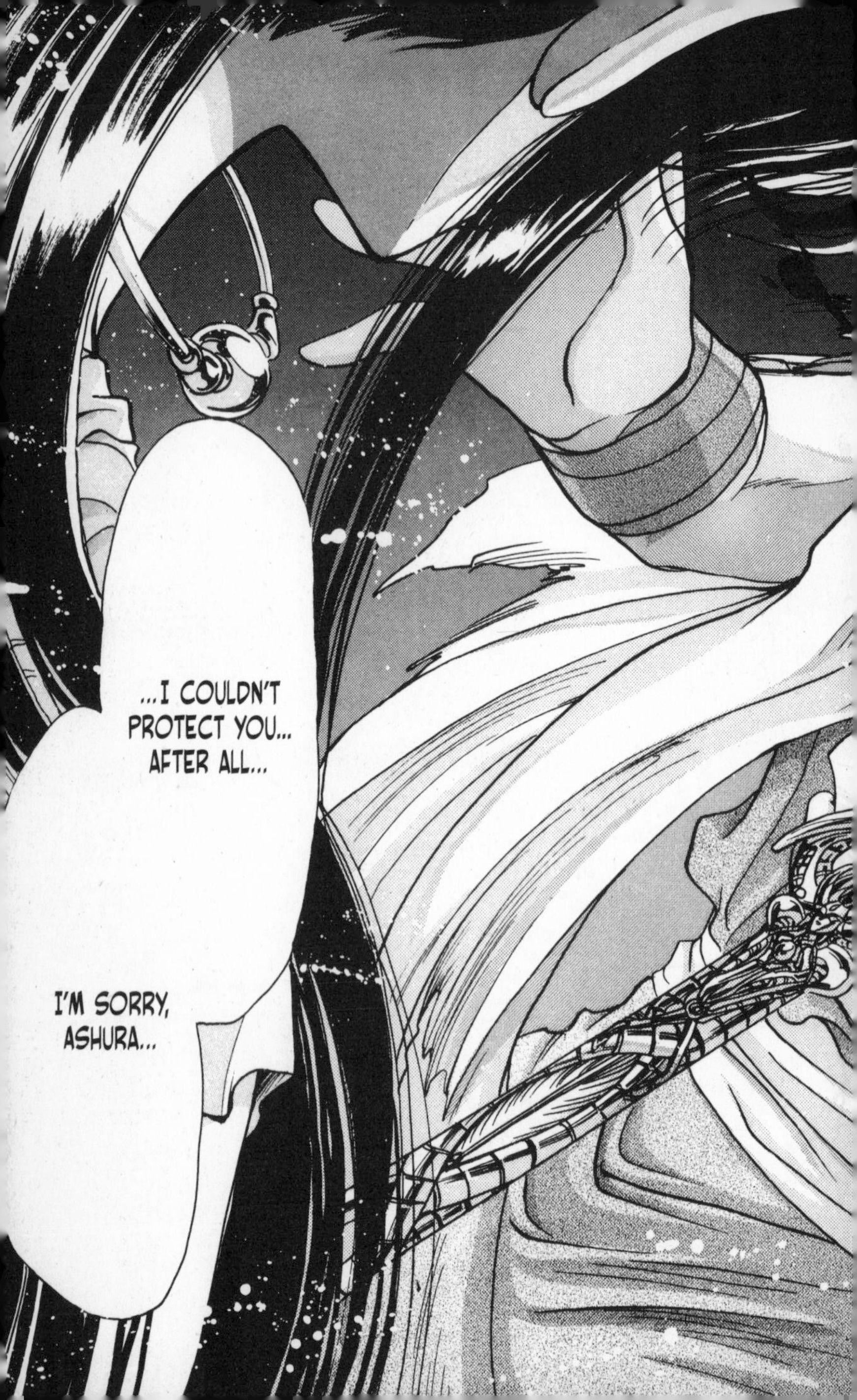
...I COULDN'T PROTECT YOU... AFTER ALL...
I'M SORRY, ASHURA...

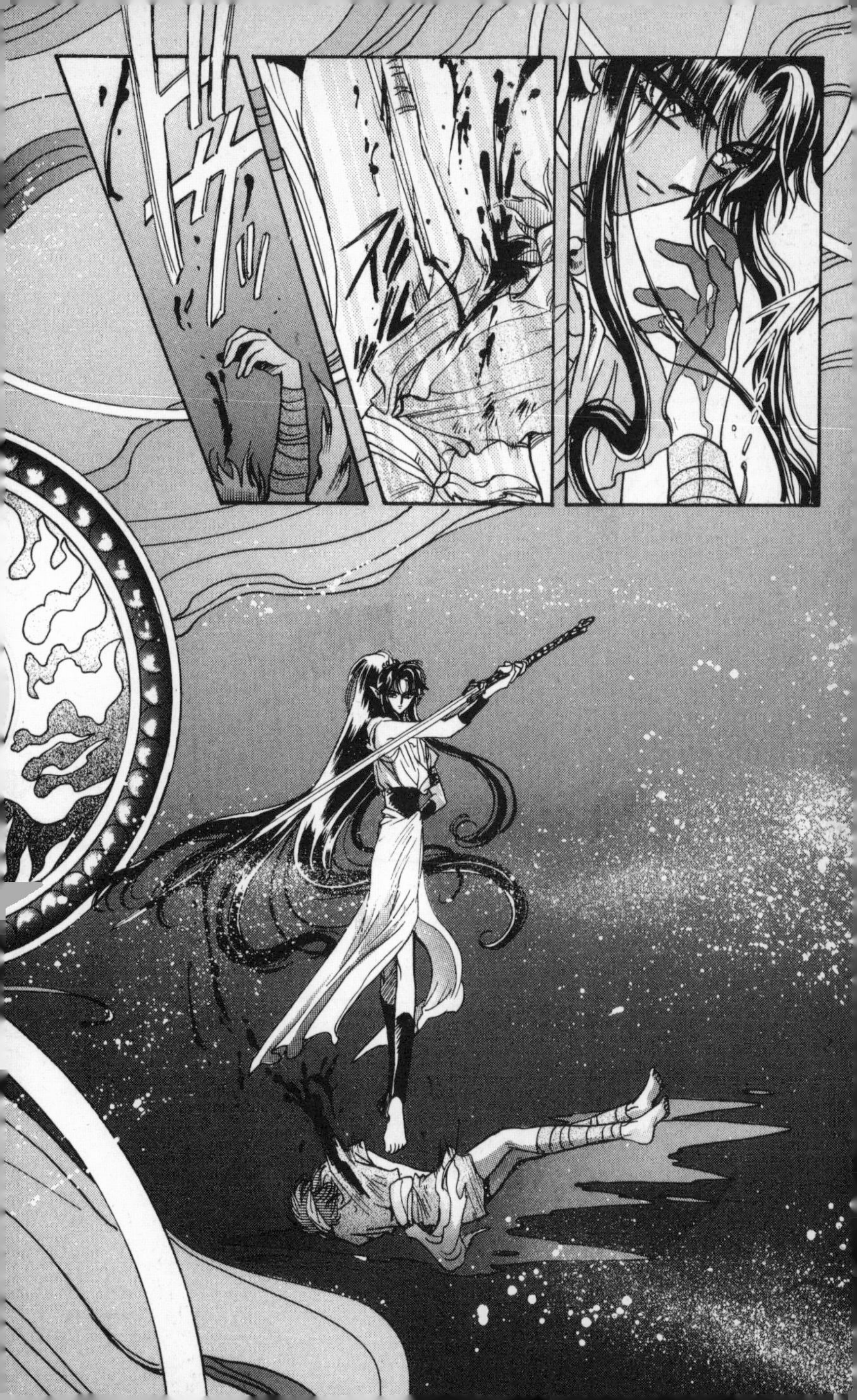
ドサッ

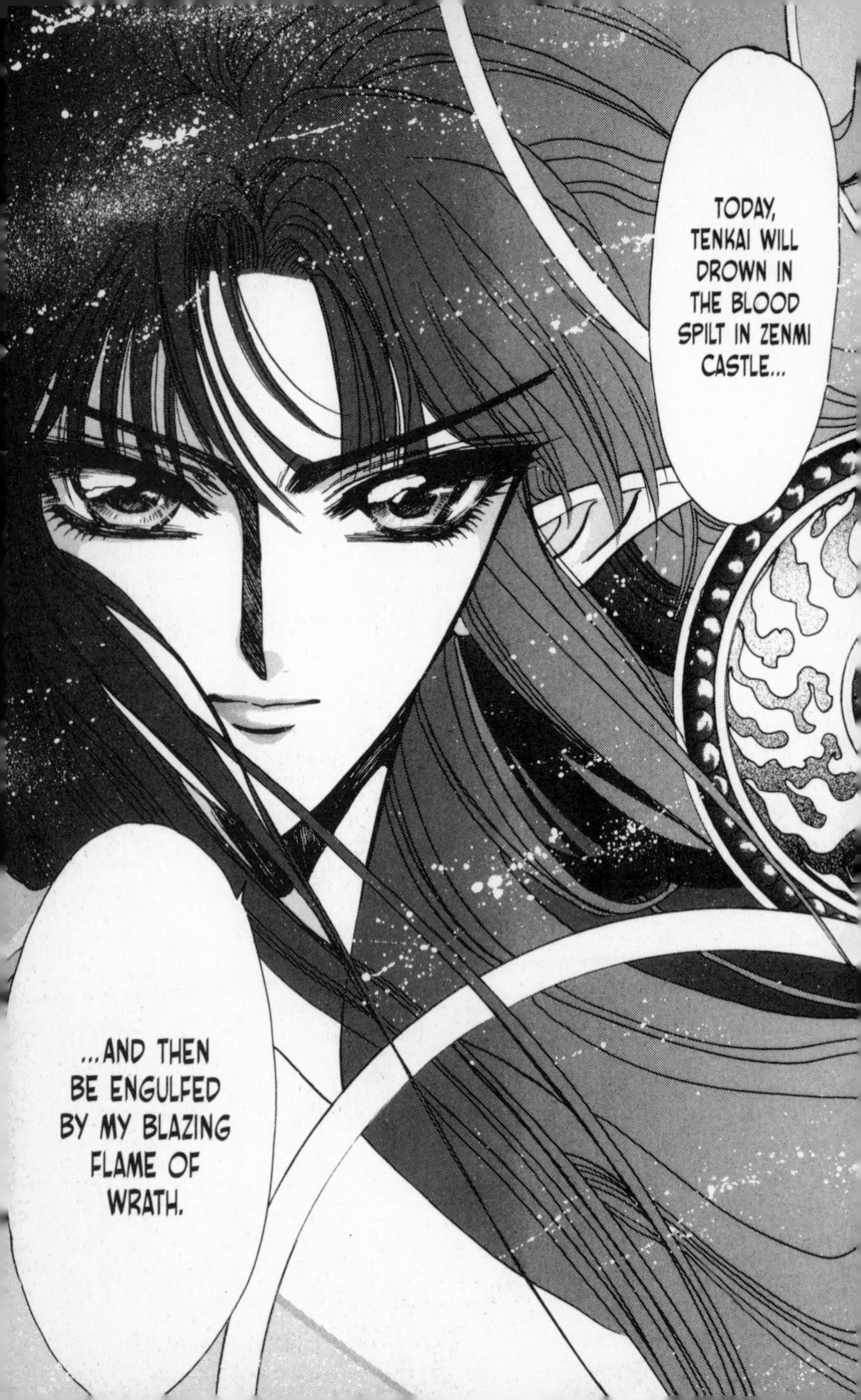
TODAY, TENKAI WILL DROWN IN THE BLOOD SPILT IN ZENMI CASTLE...
...AND THEN BE ENGULFED BY MY BLAZING FLAME OF WRATH.

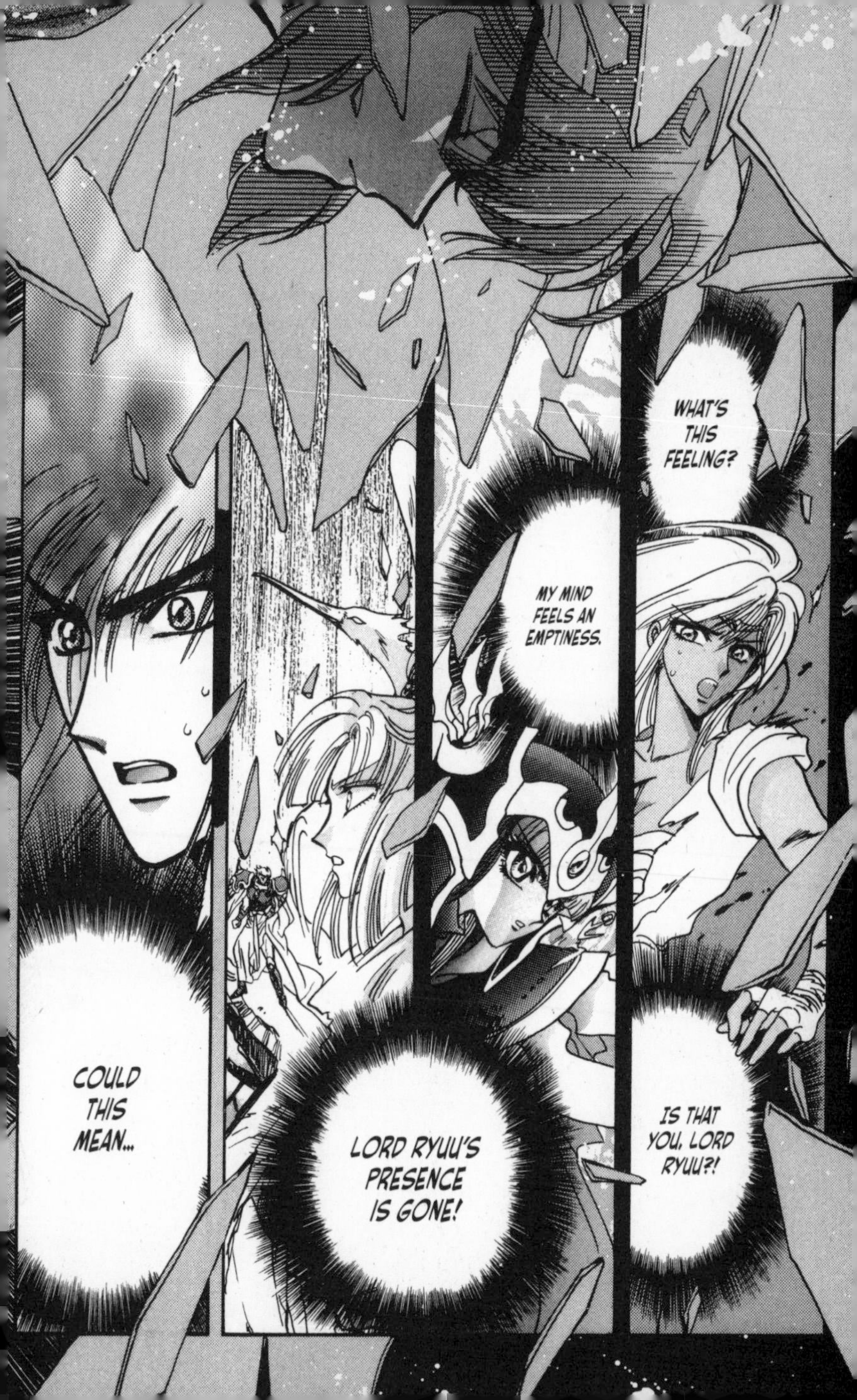
WHAT'S THIS FEELING?
IS THAT YOU, LORD RYUU?!
MY MIND FEELS AN EMPTINESS.
LORD RYUU'S PRESENCE IS GONE!
COULD THIS MEAN...

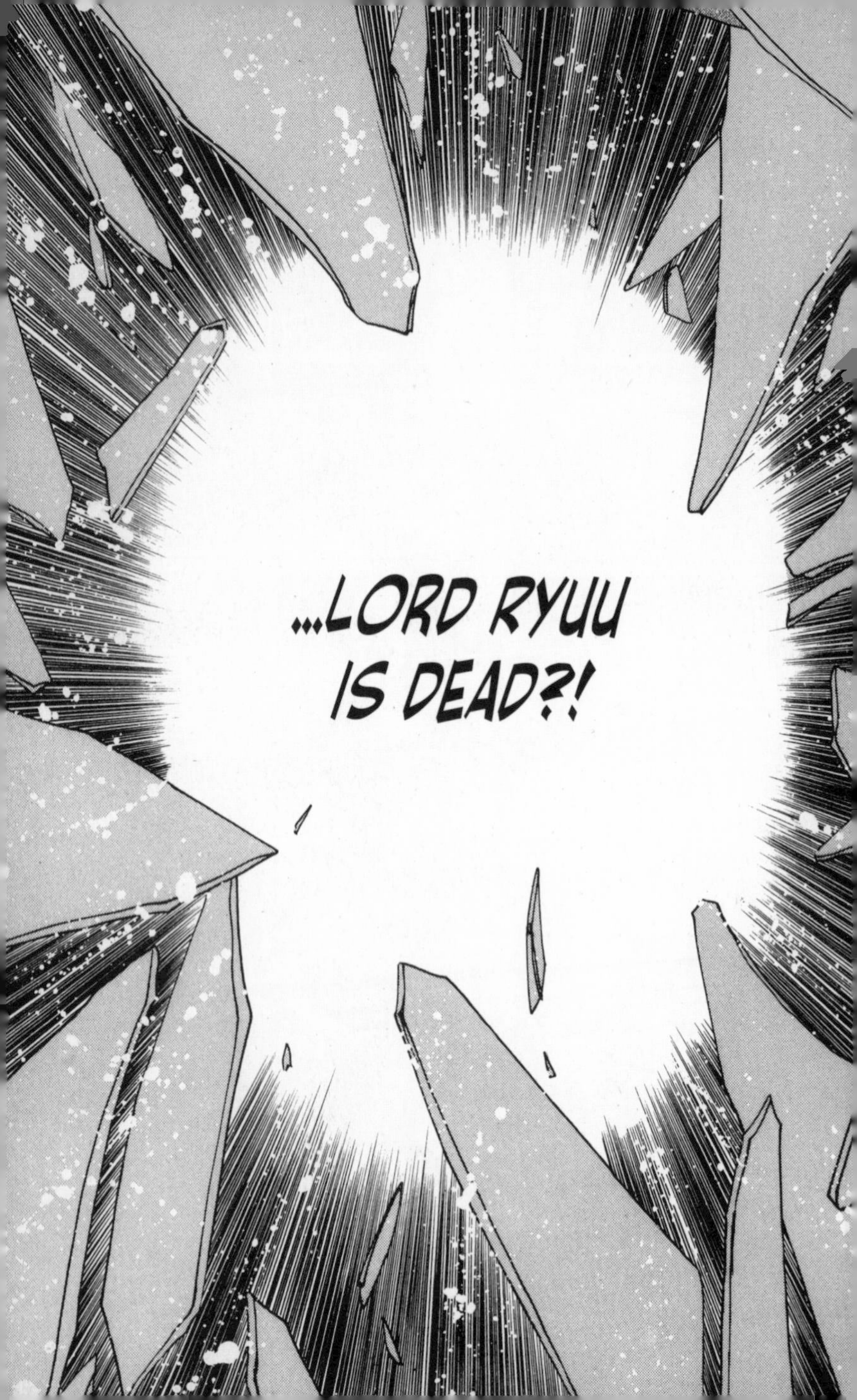
...LORD RYUU IS DEAD?!

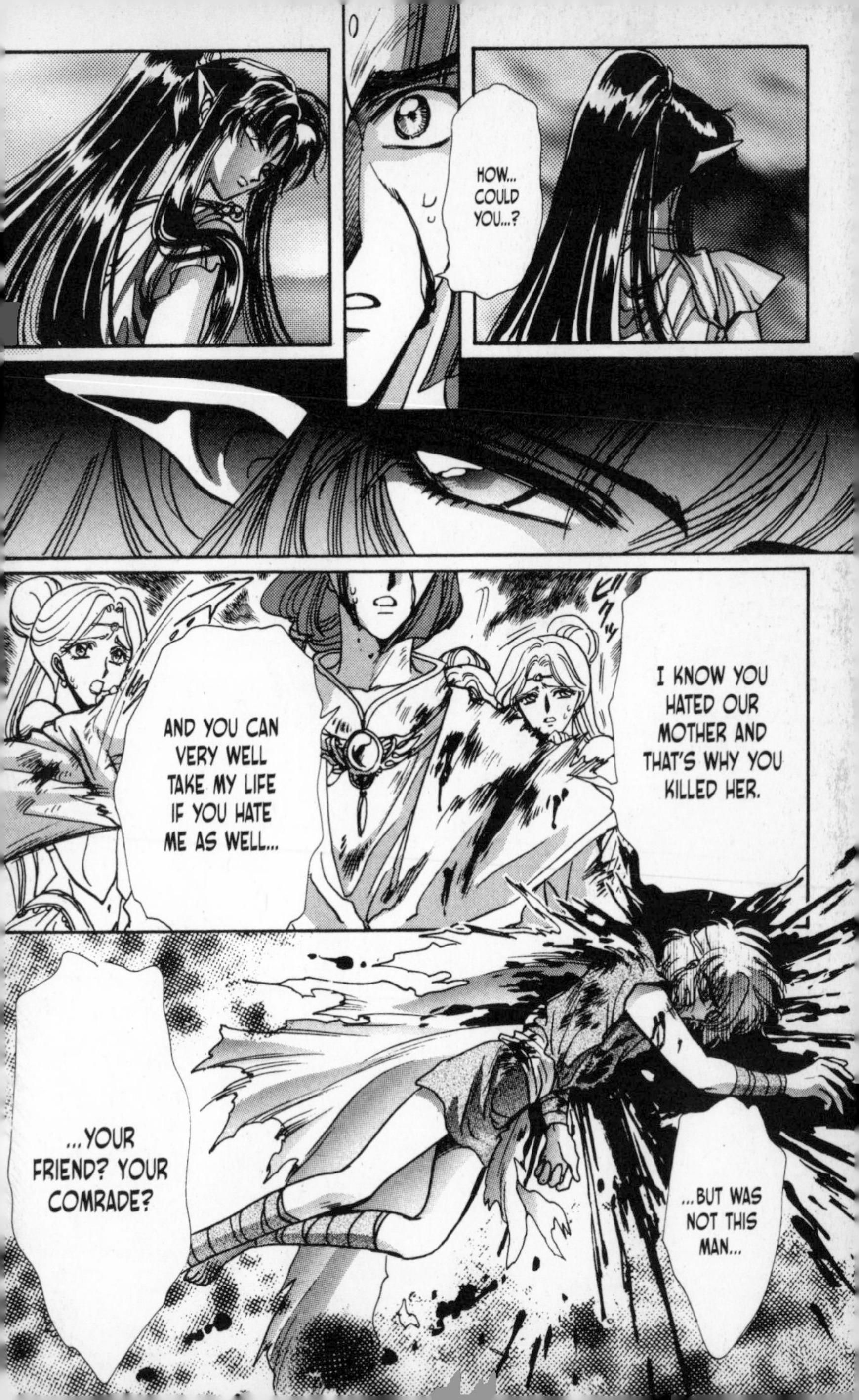
HOW... COULD YOU...?
I KNOW YOU HATED OUR MOTHER AND THAT'S WHY YOU KILLED HER.
AND YOU CAN VERY WELL TAKE MY LIFE IF YOU HATE ME AS WELL...
...BUT WAS NOT THIS MAN...
...YOUR FRIEND? YOUR COMRADE?

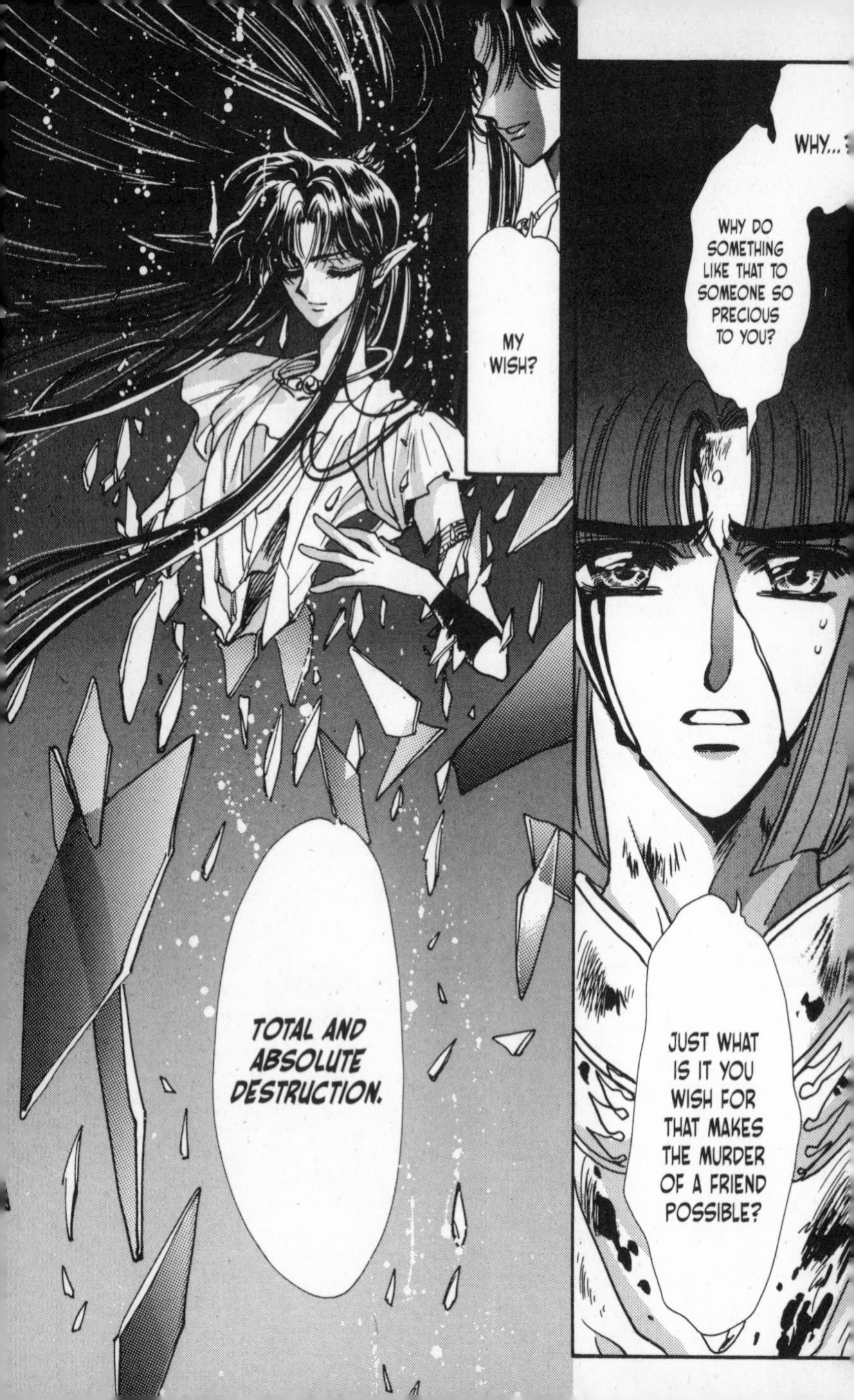
WHY...
WHY DO SOMETHING LIKE THAT TO SOMEONE SO PRECIOUS TO YOU?
JUST WHAT IS IT YOU WISH FOR THAT MAKES THE MURDER OF A FRIEND POSSIBLE?
MY WISH?
TOTAL AND ABSOLUTE DESTRUCTION.

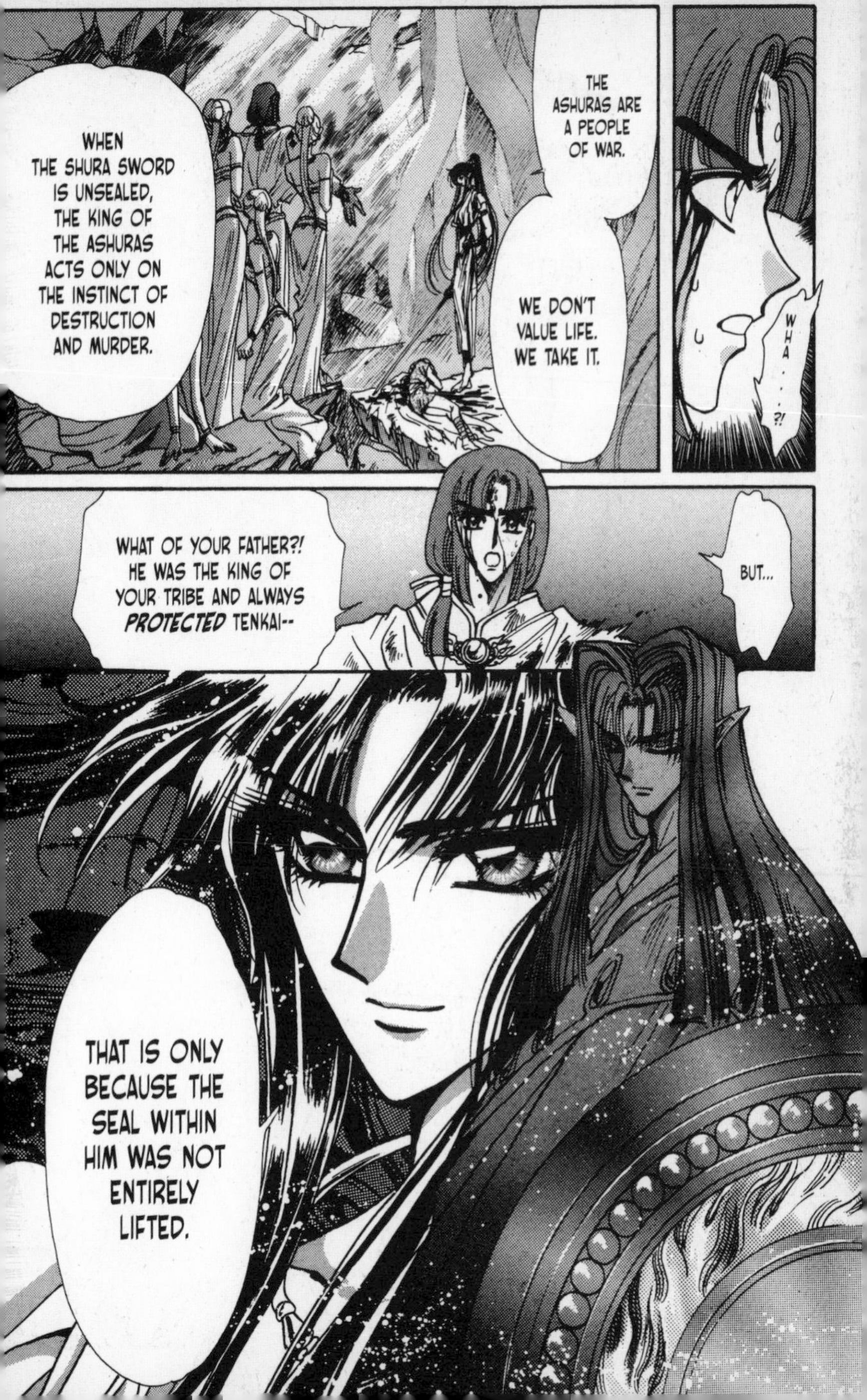
WHA...?!
THE ASHURAS ARE A PEOPLE OF WAR.
WE DON'T VALUE LIFE. WE TAKE IT.
WHEN THE SHURA SWORD IS UNSEALED, THE KING OF THE ASHURAS ACTS ONLY ON THE INSTINCT OF DESTRUCTION AND MURDER.
BUT...
WHAT OF YOUR FATHER?! HE WAS THE KING OF YOUR TRIBE AND ALWAYS *PROTECTED* TENKAI--
THAT IS ONLY BECAUSE THE SEAL WITHIN HIM WAS NOT ENTIRELY LIFTED.

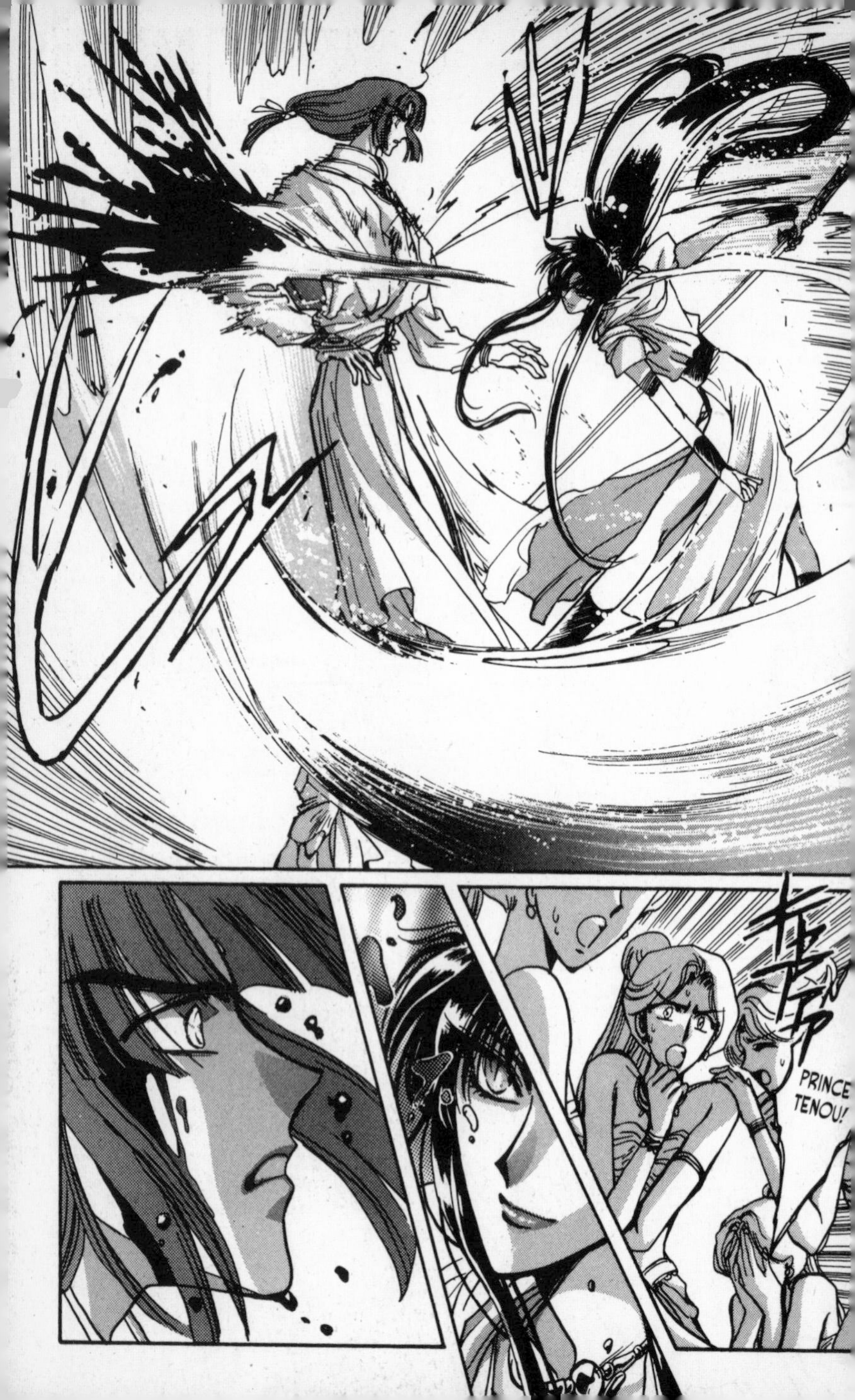
PRINCE TENOU!

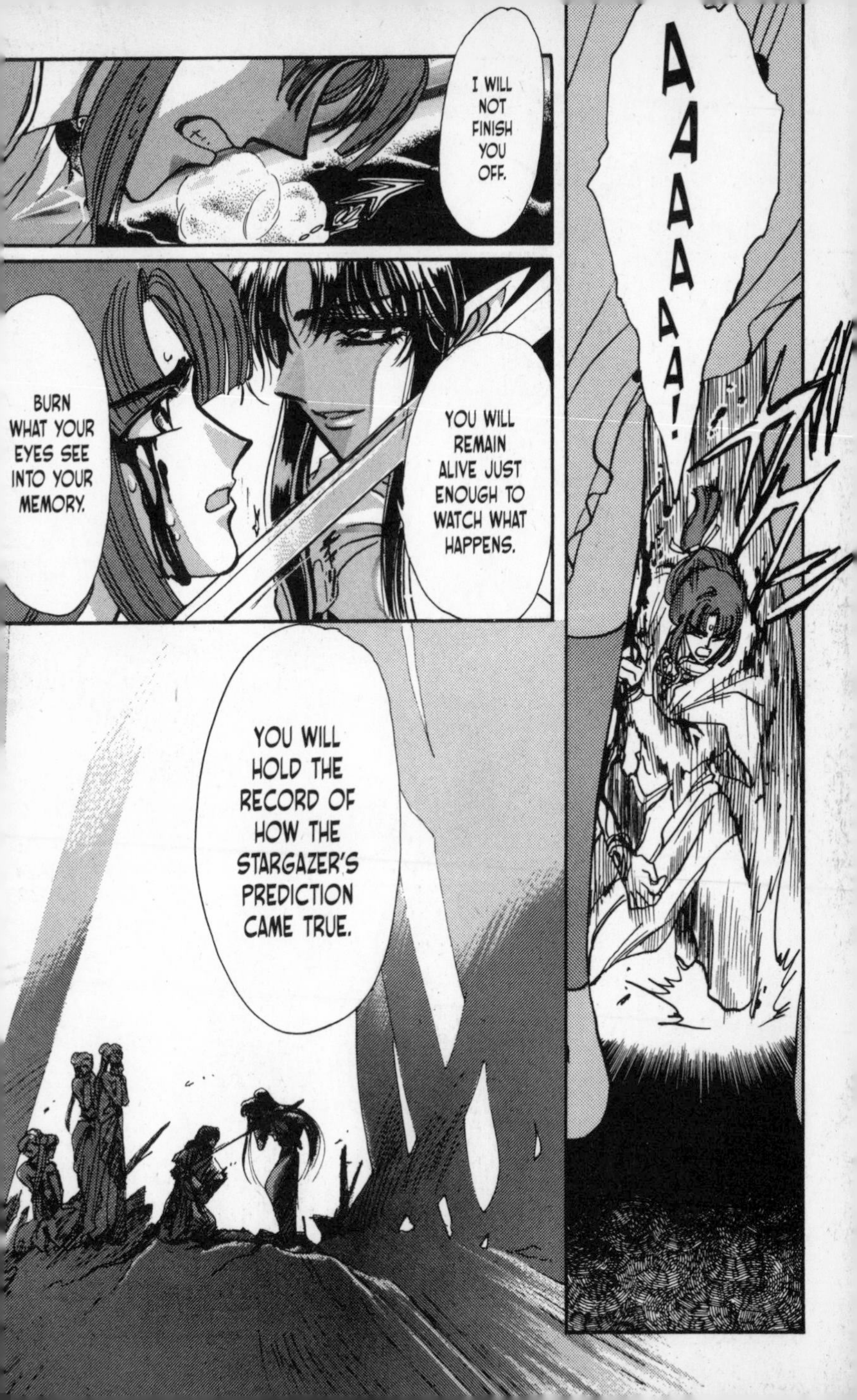
AAAAAA!
I WILL NOT FINISH YOU OFF.
YOU WILL REMAIN ALIVE JUST ENOUGH TO WATCH WHAT HAPPENS.
BURN WHAT YOUR EYES SEE INTO YOUR MEMORY.
YOU WILL HOLD THE RECORD OF HOW THE STARGAZER'S PREDICTION CAME TRUE.

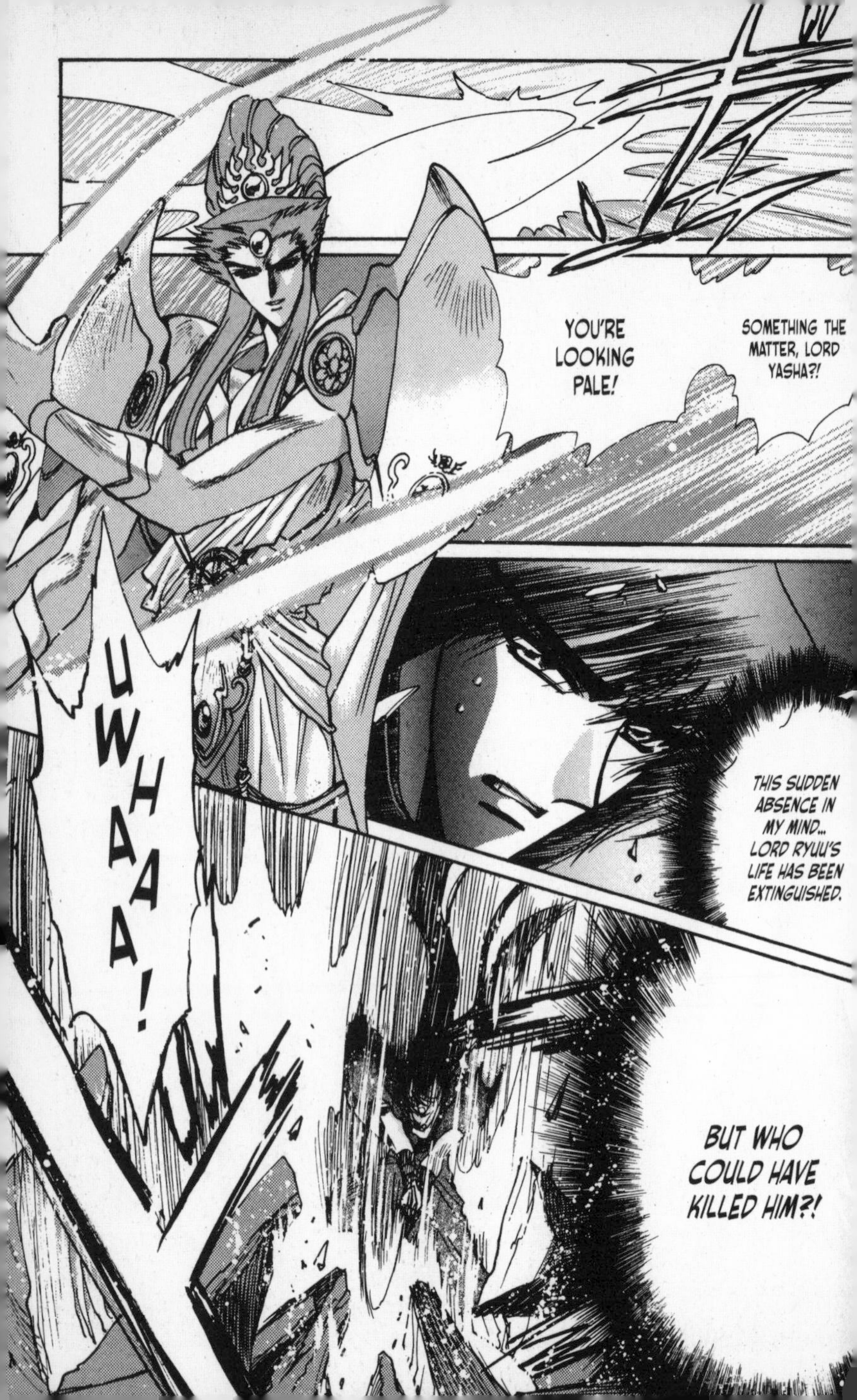
SOMETHING THE MATTER, LORD YASHA?!
YOU'RE LOOKING PALE!
THIS SUDDEN ABSENCE IN MY MIND... LORD RYUU'S LIFE HAS BEEN EXTINGUISHED.
BUT WHO COULD HAVE KILLED HIM?!
UWHAAA!

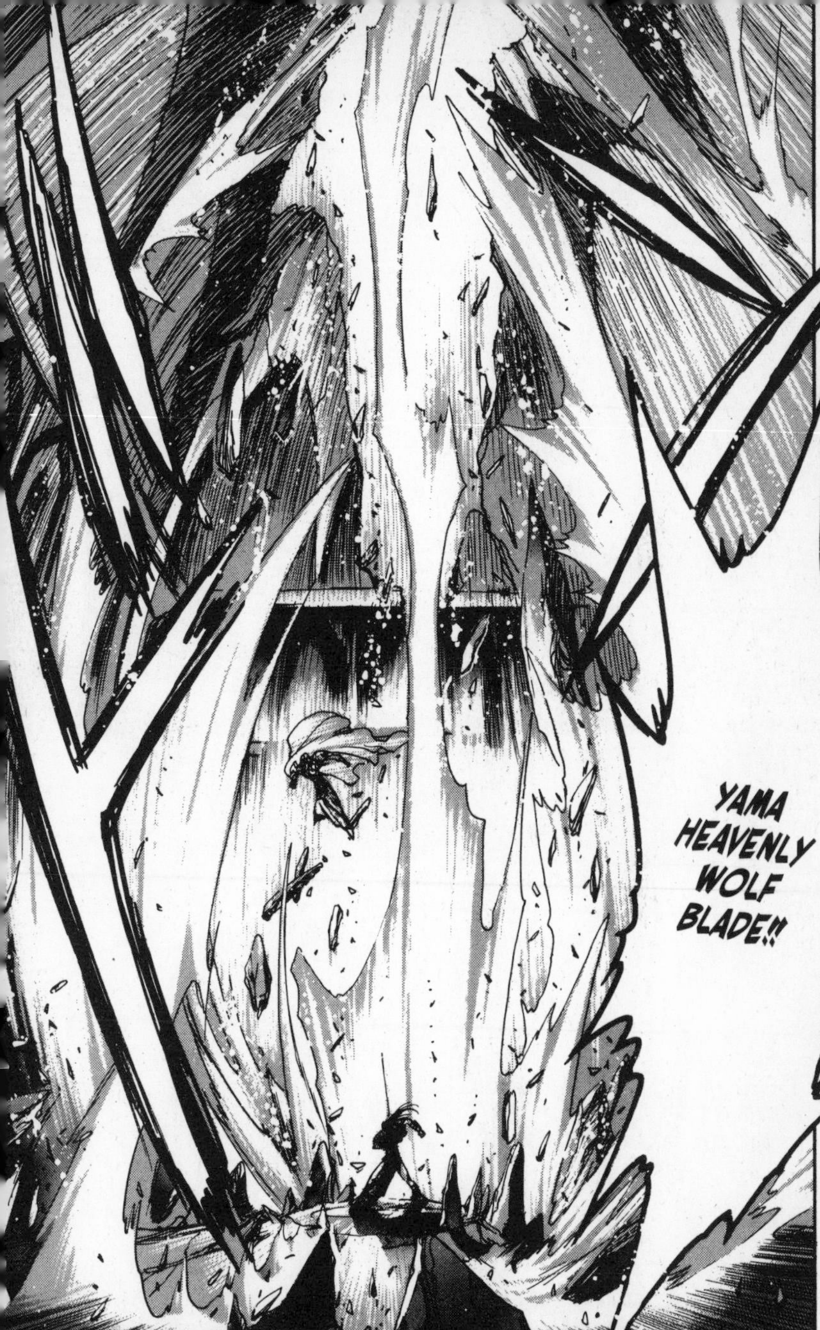
YAMA HEAVENLY WOLF BLADE!!

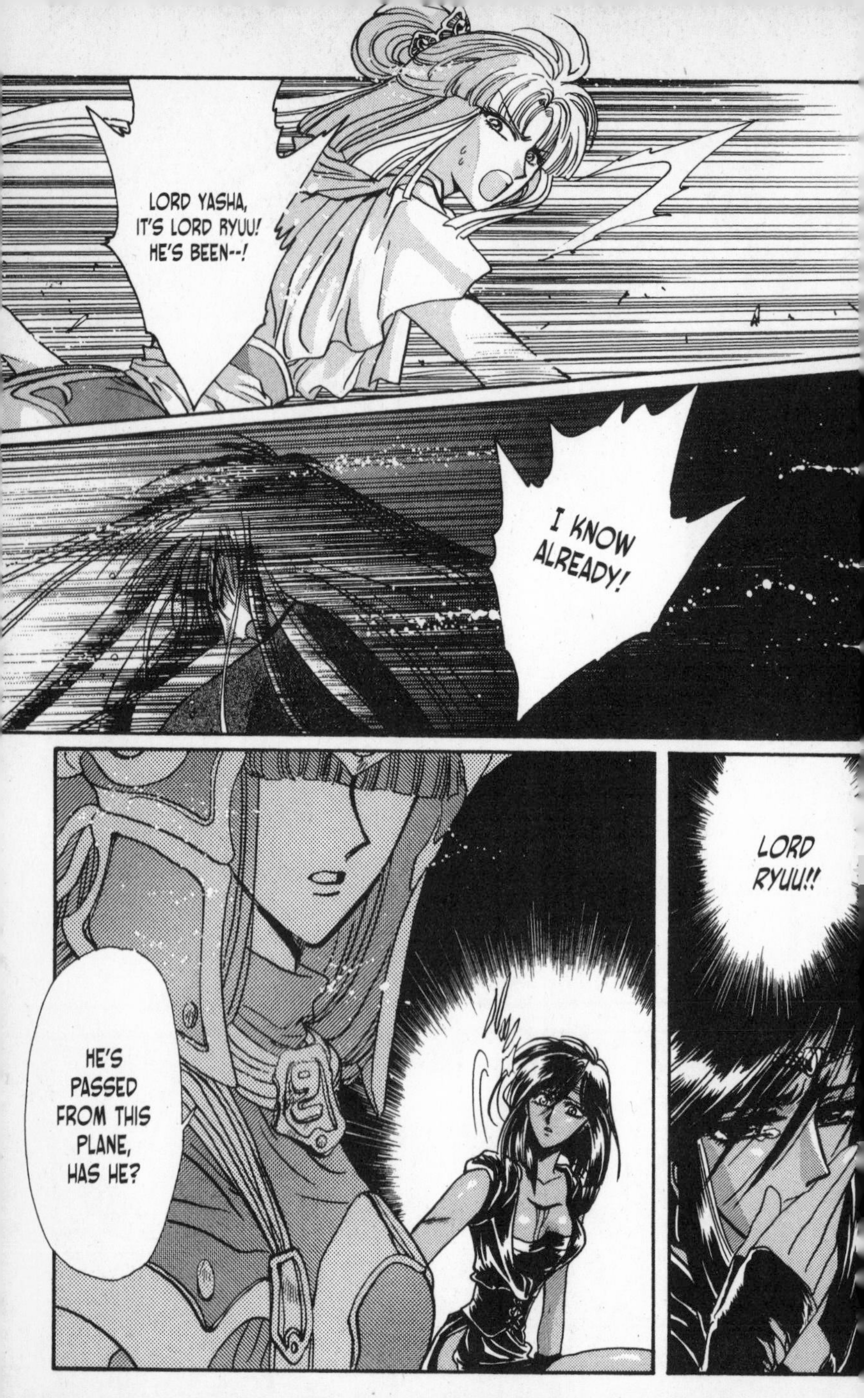
LORD YASHA, IT'S LORD RYUU! HE'S BEEN--!
I KNOW ALREADY!
LORD RYUU!!
HE'S PASSED FROM THIS PLANE, HAS HE?

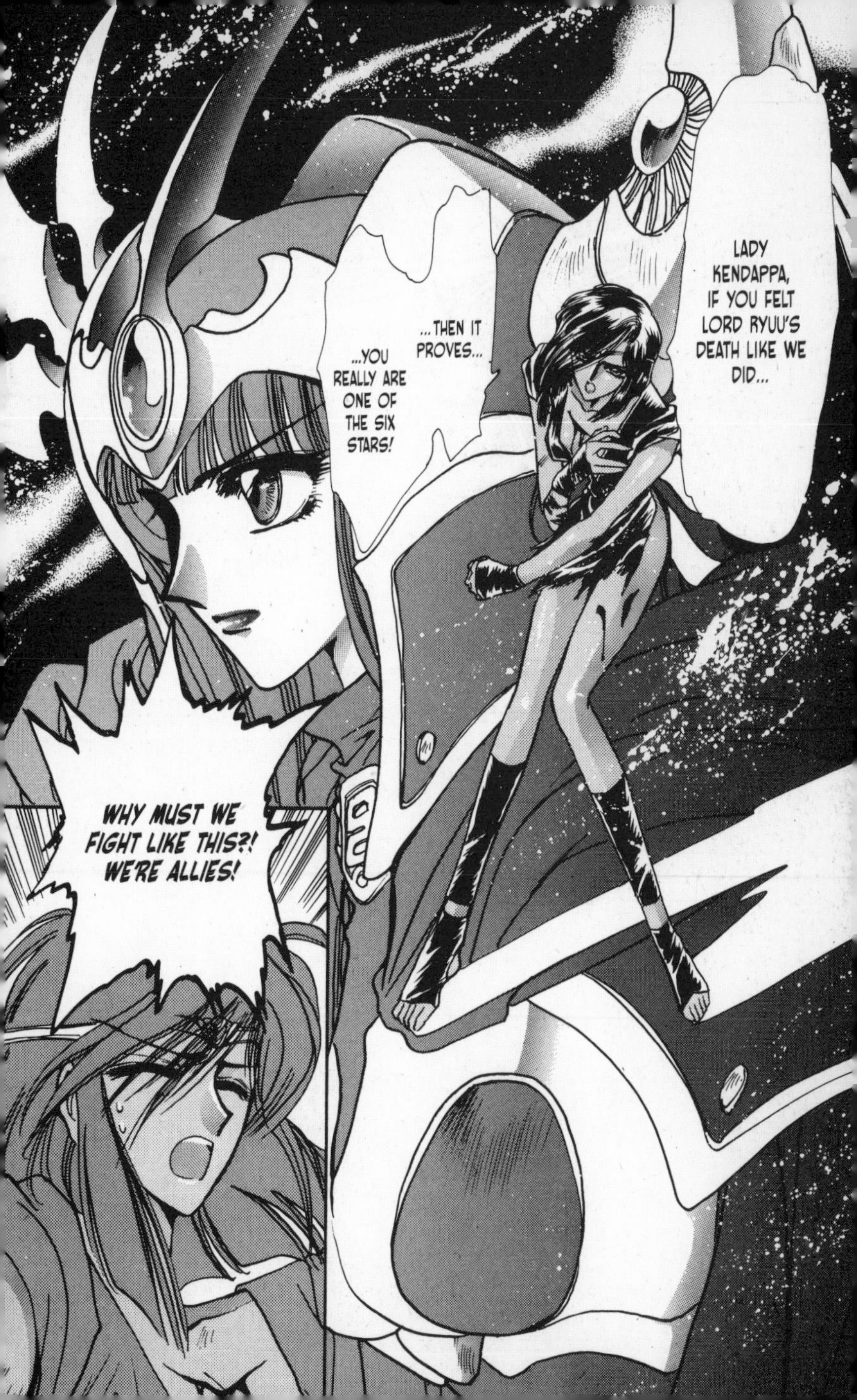
LADY KENDAPPA, IF YOU FELT LORD RYUU'S DEATH LIKE WE DID...
...THEN IT PROVES...
...YOU REALLY ARE ONE OF THE SIX STARS!
WHY MUST WE FIGHT LIKE THIS?! WE'RE ALLIES!

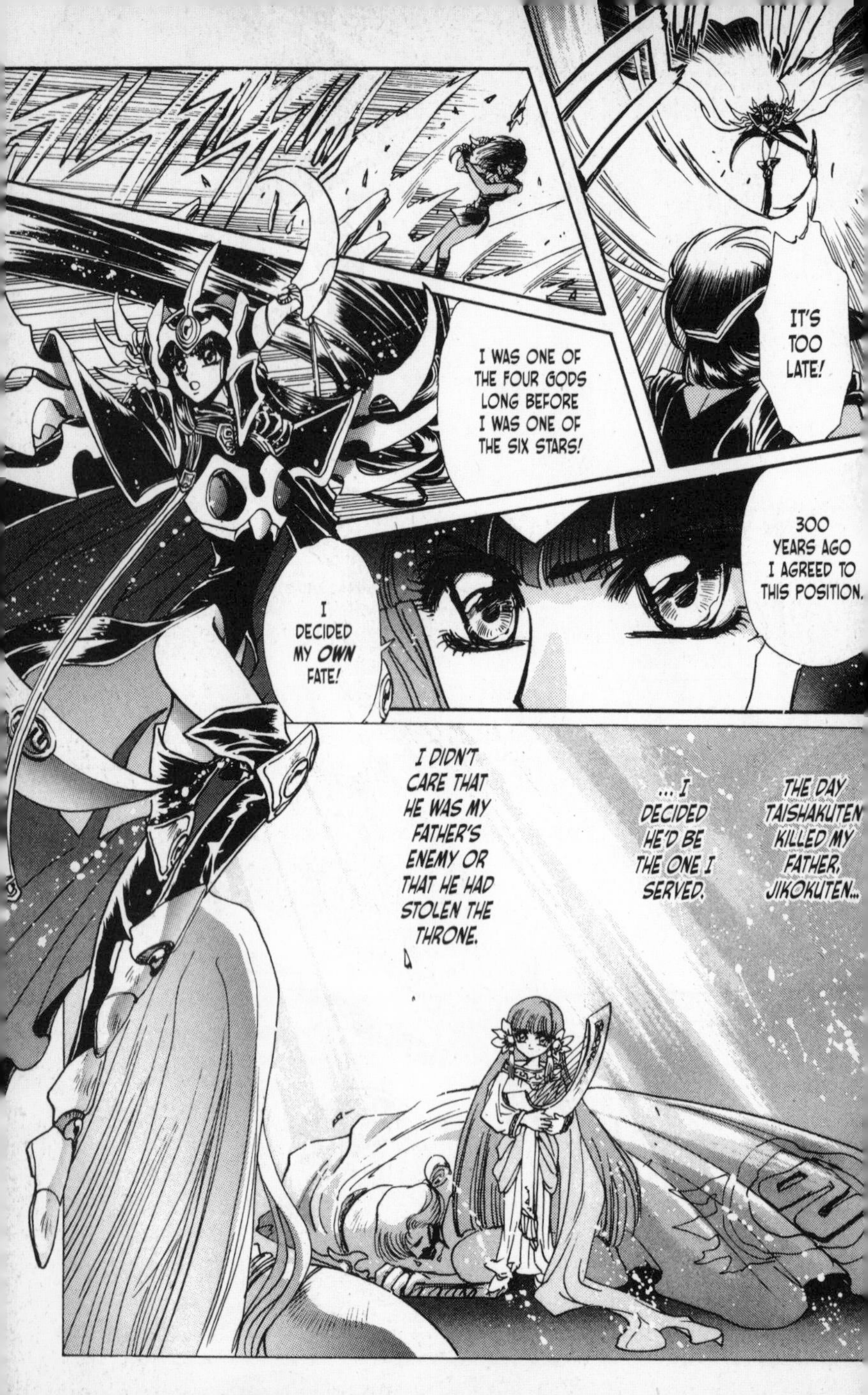
IT'S TOO LATE!
I WAS ONE OF THE FOUR GODS LONG BEFORE I WAS ONE OF THE SIX STARS!
300 YEARS AGO I AGREED TO THIS POSITION.
I DECIDED MY *OWN* FATE!
THE DAY TAISHAKUTEN KILLED MY FATHER, JIKOKUTEN...
... I DECIDED HE'D BE THE ONE I SERVED.
I DIDN'T CARE THAT HE WAS MY FATHER'S ENEMY OR THAT HE HAD STOLEN THE THRONE.

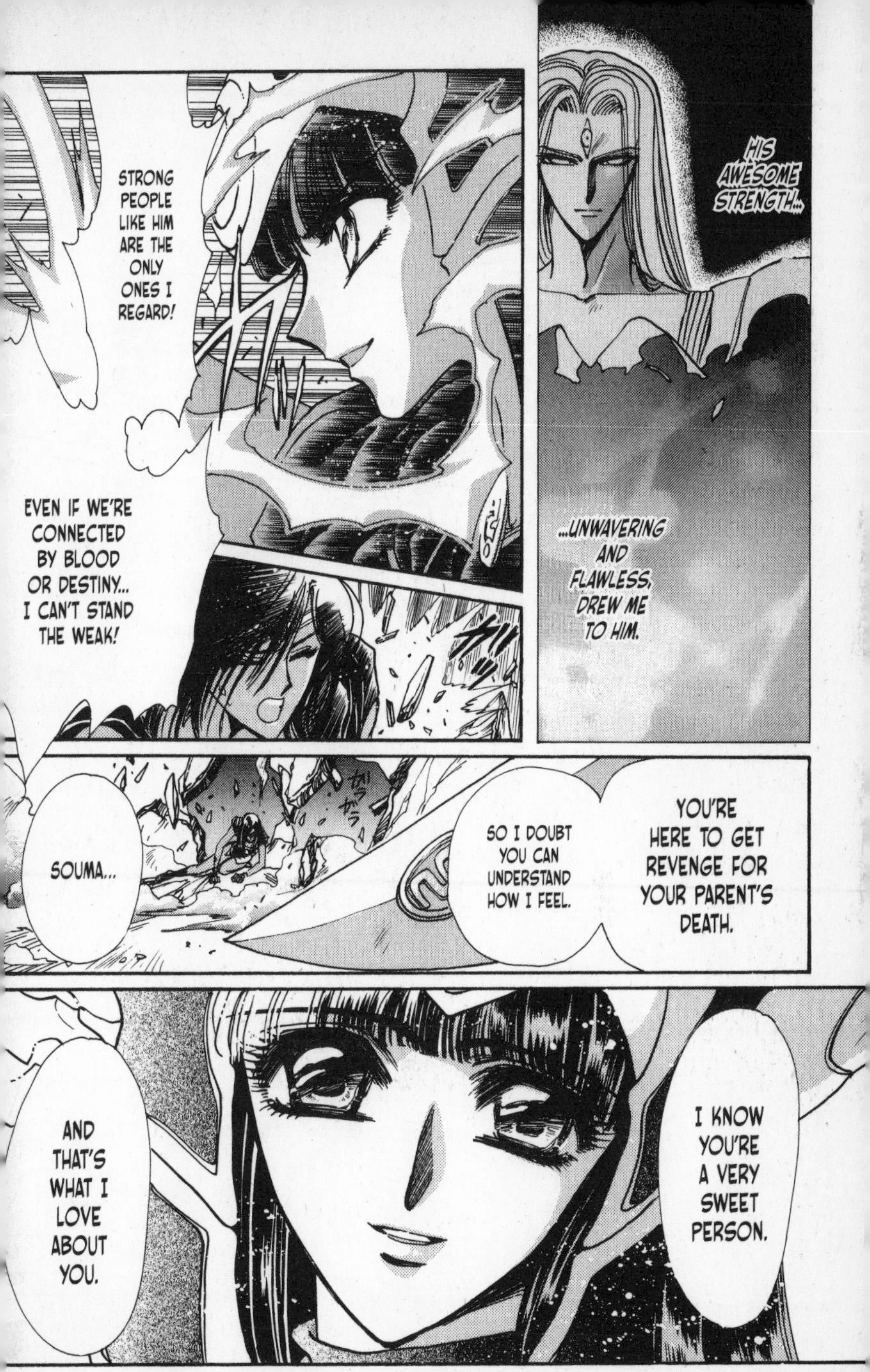
HIS AWESOME STRENGTH...
...UNWAVERING AND FLAWLESS, DREW ME TO HIM.
STRONG PEOPLE LIKE HIM ARE THE ONLY ONES I REGARD!
EVEN IF WE'RE CONNECTED BY BLOOD OR DESTINY... I CAN'T STAND THE WEAK!
YOU'RE HERE TO GET REVENGE FOR YOUR PARENT'S DEATH.
SO I DOUBT YOU CAN UNDERSTAND HOW I FEEL.
SOUMA...
I KNOW YOU'RE A VERY SWEET PERSON.
AND THAT'S WHAT I LOVE ABOUT YOU.

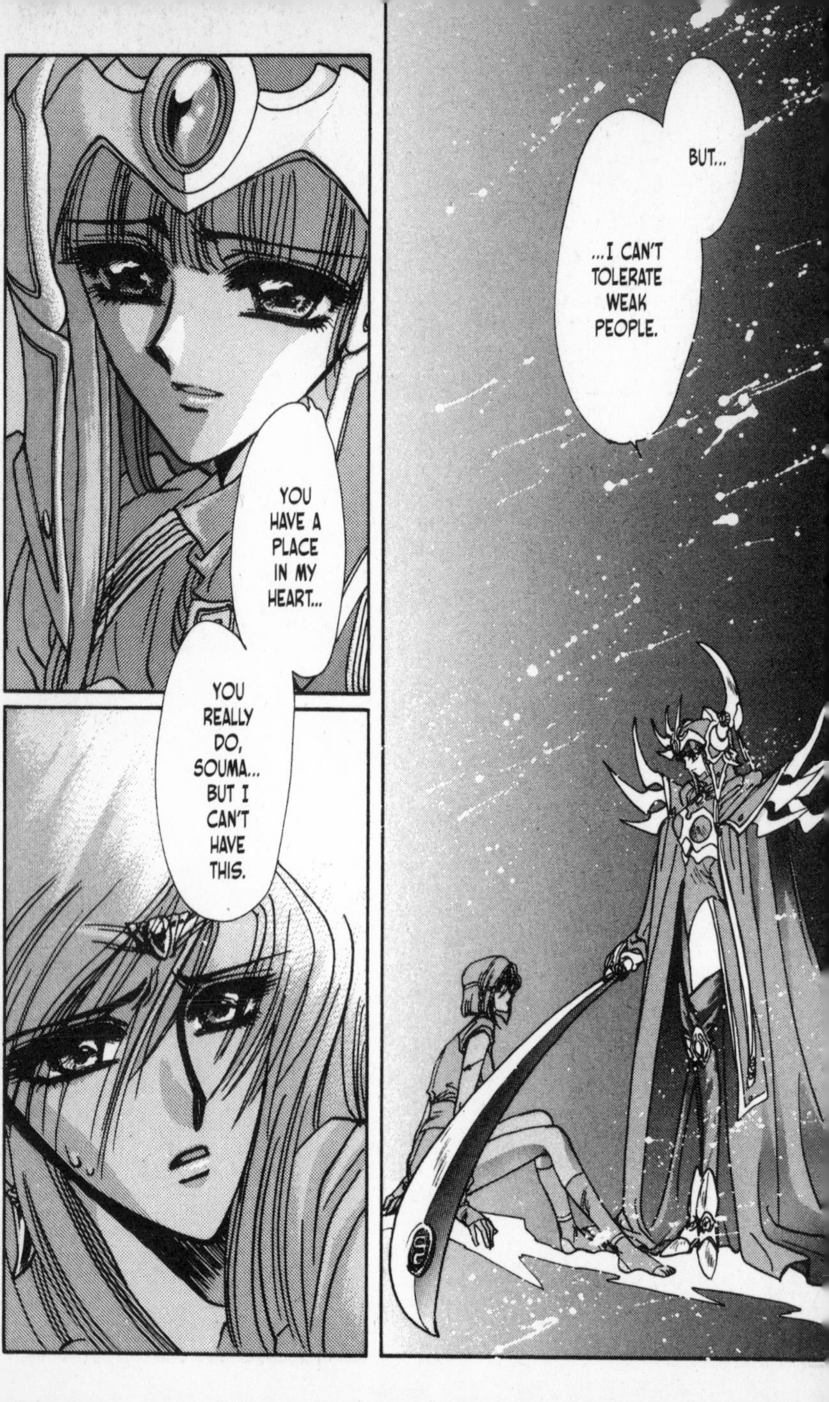
BUT...
...I CAN'T TOLERATE WEAK PEOPLE.
YOU HAVE A PLACE IN MY HEART...
YOU REALLY DO, SOUMA... BUT I CAN'T HAVE THIS.

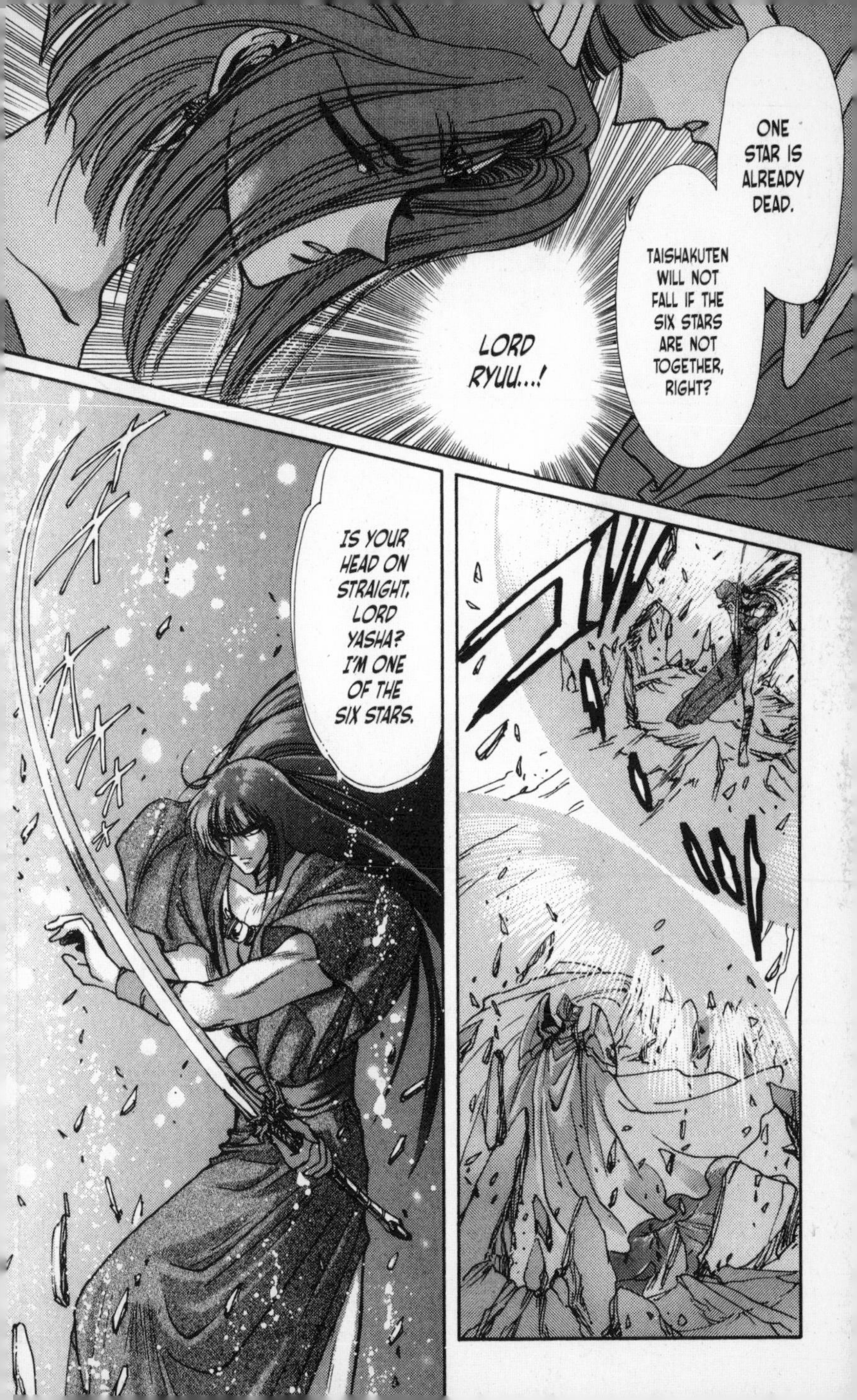
ONE STAR IS ALREADY DEAD.
TAISHAKUTEN WILL NOT FALL IF THE SIX STARS ARE NOT TOGETHER, RIGHT?
LORD RYUU...!
IS YOUR HEAD ON STRAIGHT, LORD YASHA? I'M ONE OF THE SIX STARS.

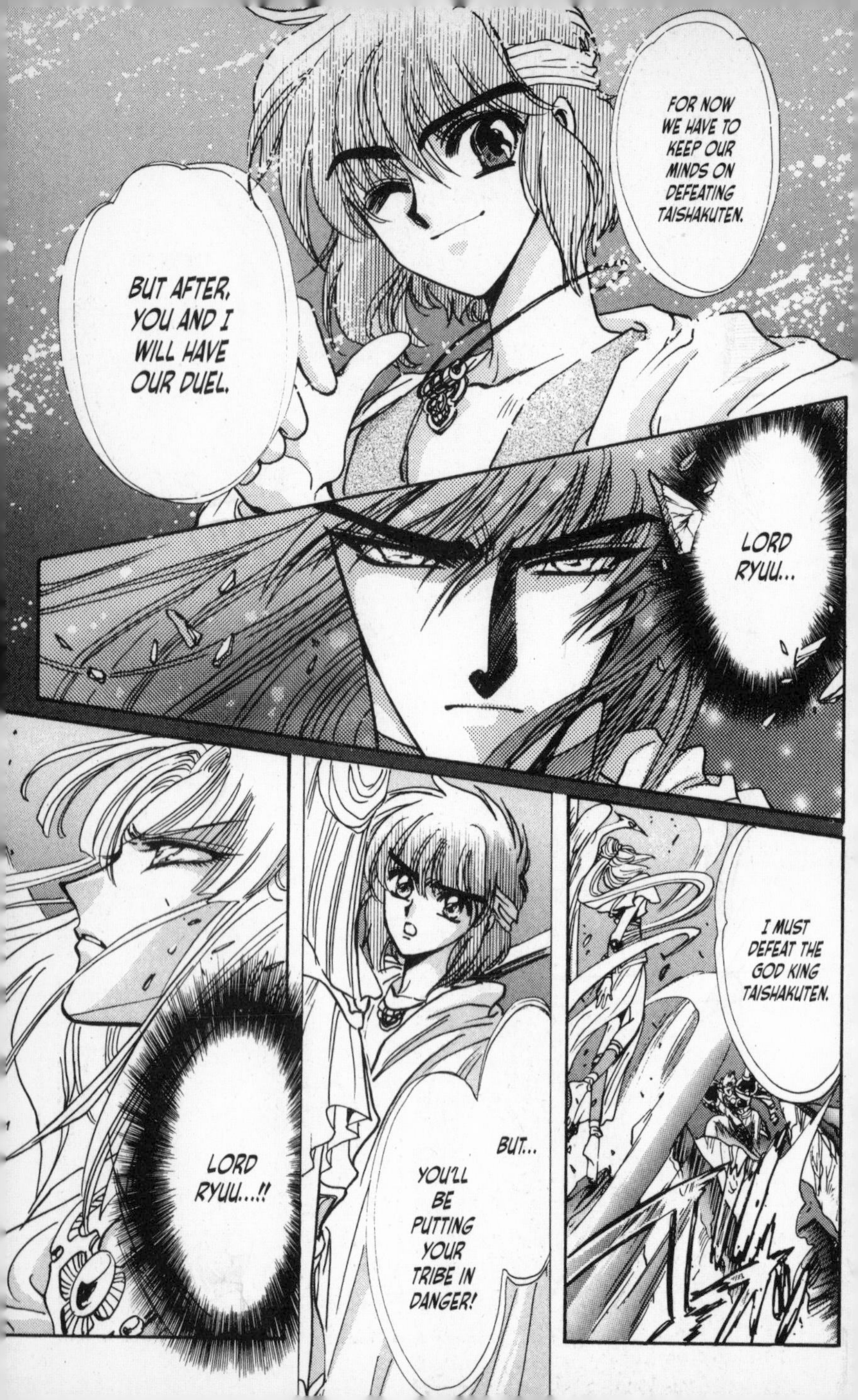
FOR NOW WE HAVE TO KEEP OUR MINDS ON DEFEATING TAISHAKUTEN.
BUT AFTER, YOU AND I WILL HAVE OUR DUEL.
LORD RYUU...
I MUST DEFEAT THE GOD KING TAISHAKUTEN.
BUT...
YOU'LL BE PUTTING YOUR TRIBE IN DANGER!
LORD RYUU...!!

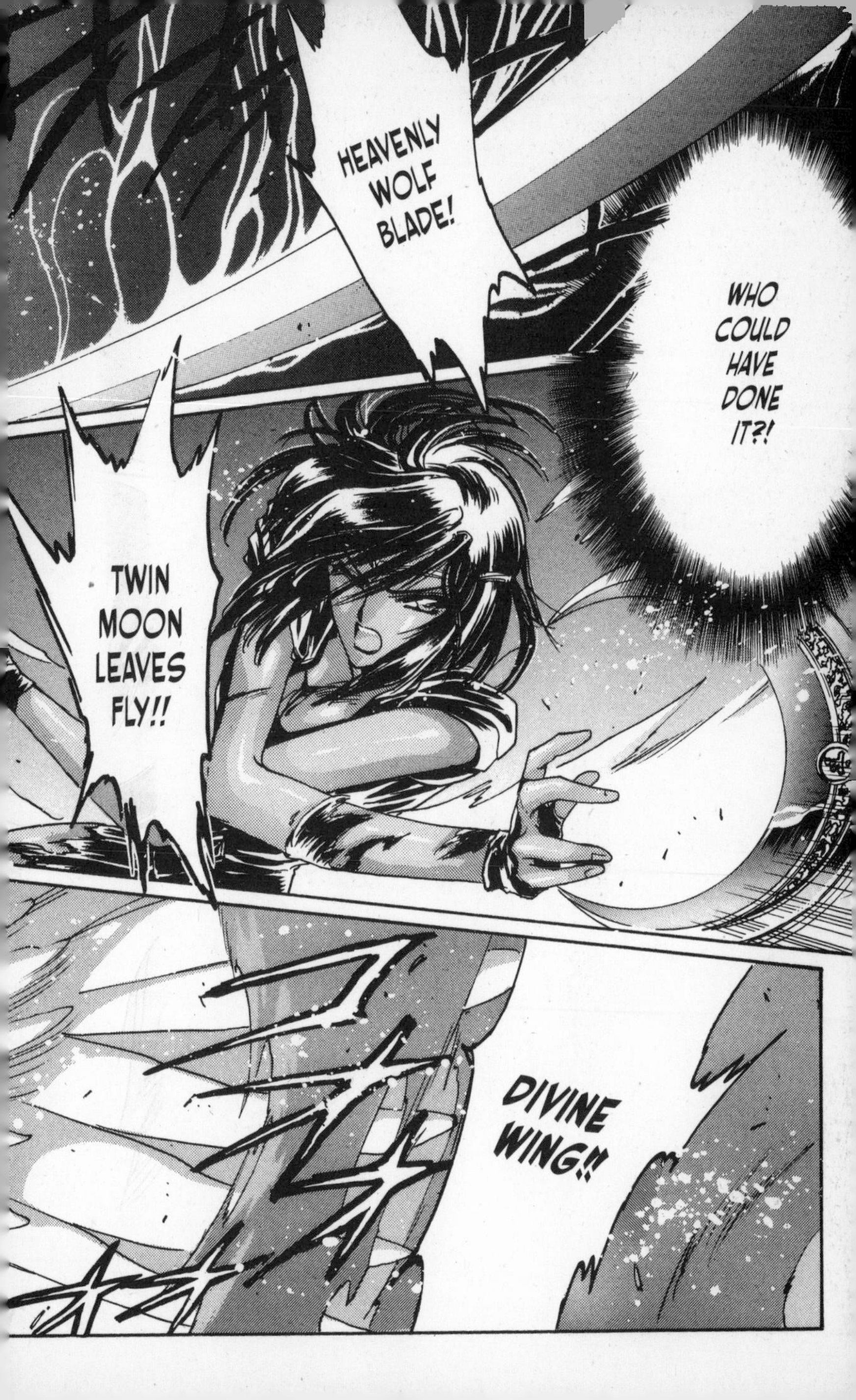
HEAVENLY WOLF BLADE!
WHO COULD HAVE DONE IT?!
TWIN MOON LEAVES FLY!!
DIVINE WING!!

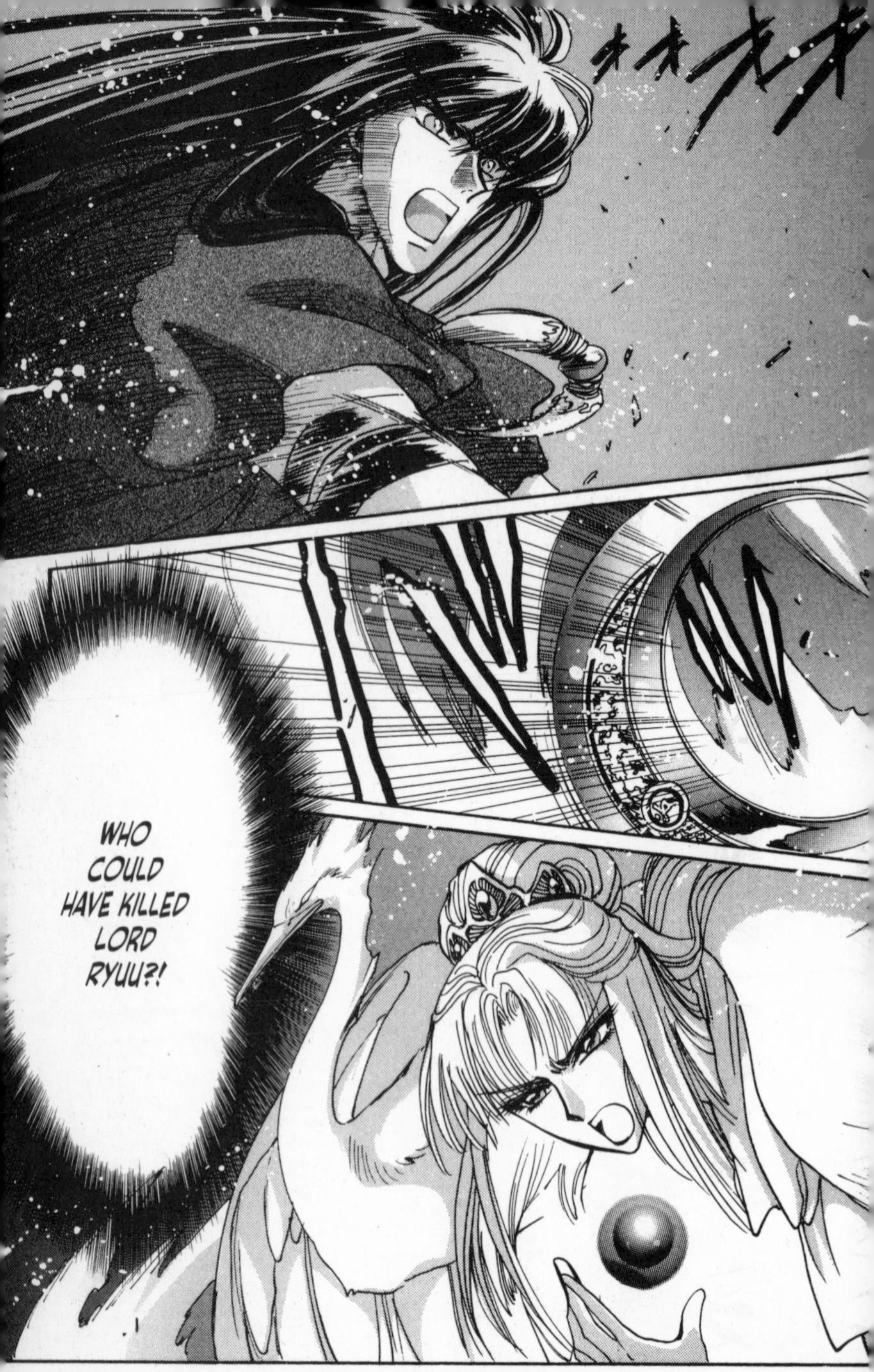
WHO COULD HAVE KILLED LORD RYUU?!

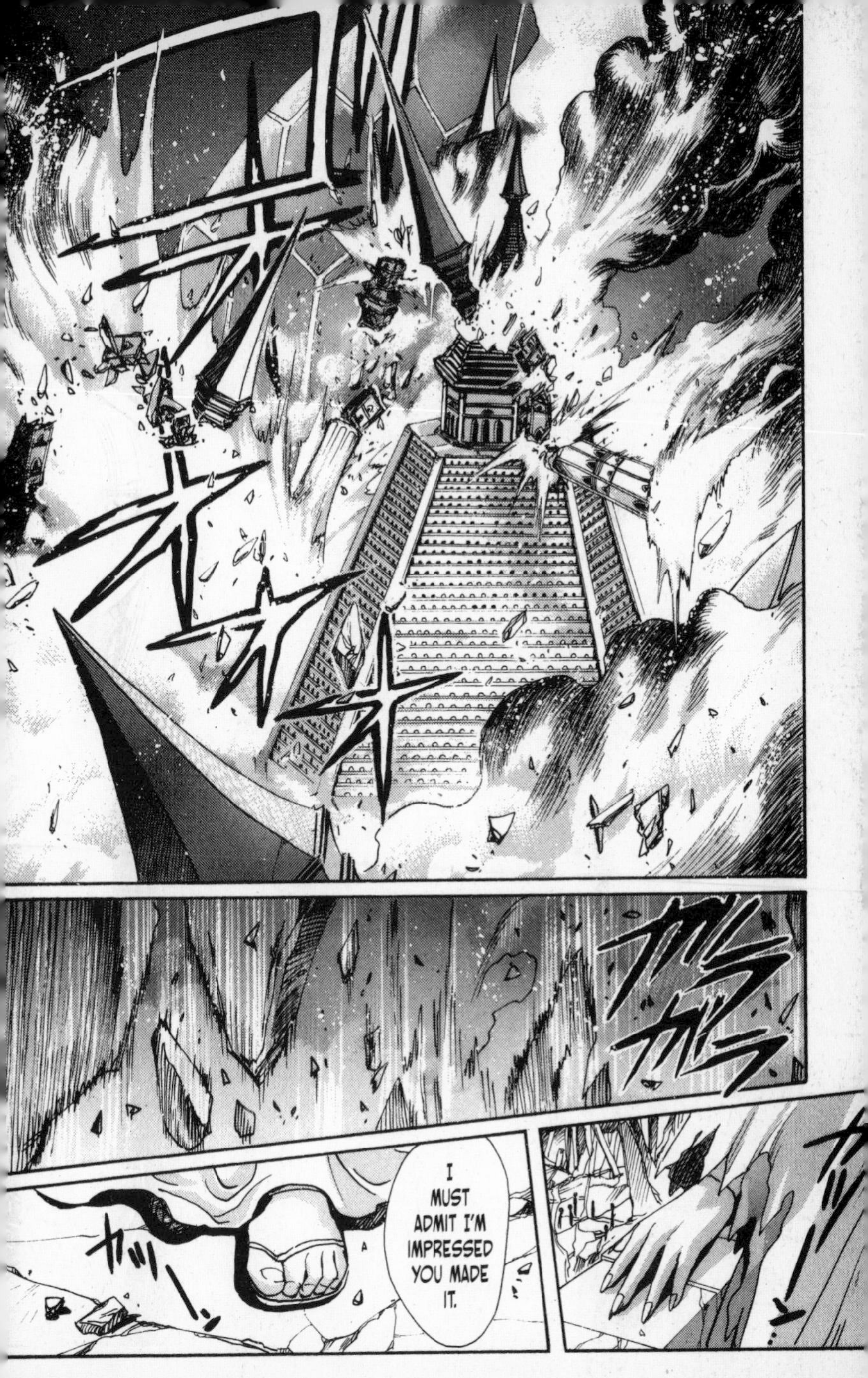
I MUST ADMIT I'M IMPRESSED YOU MADE IT.

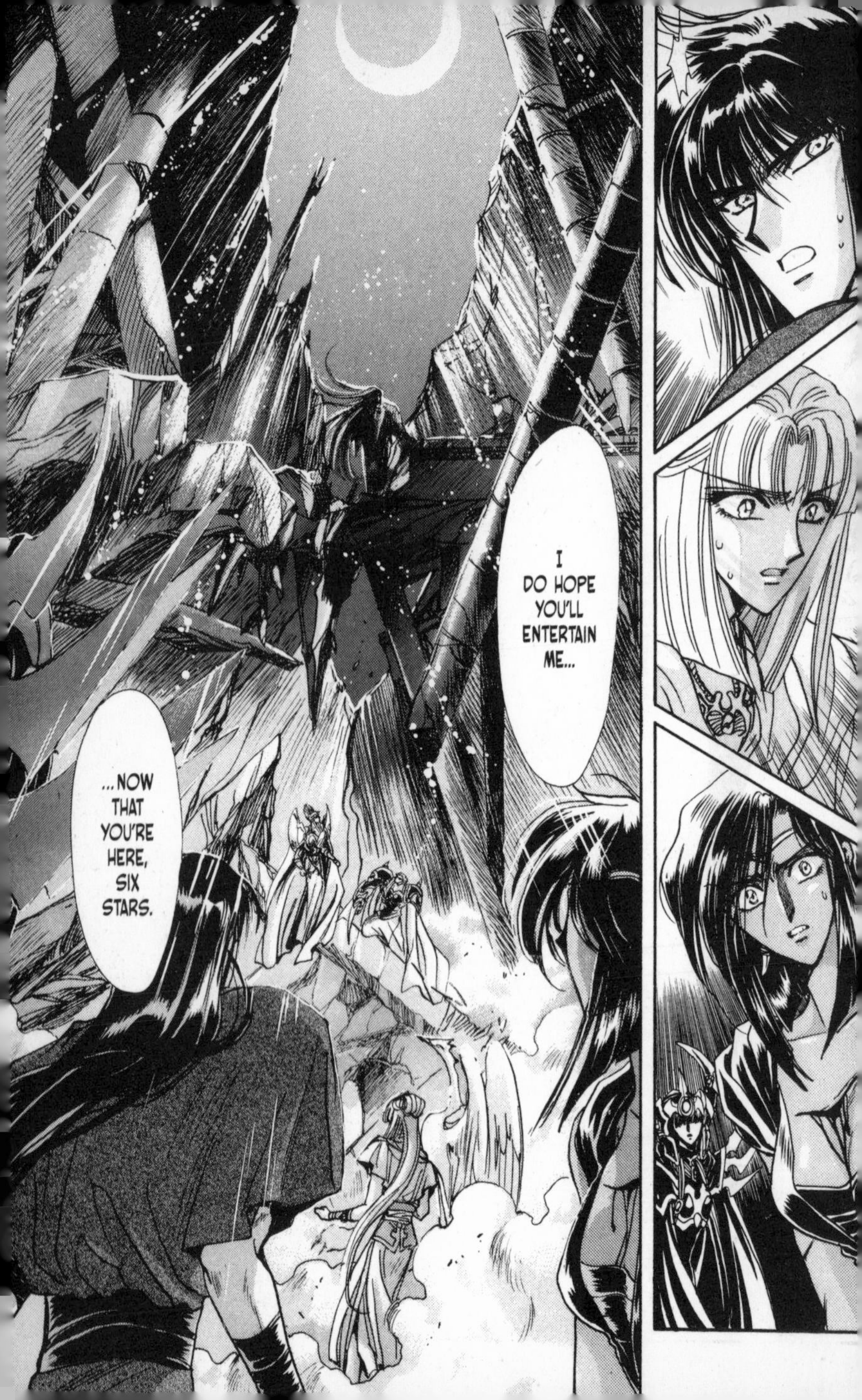
I DO HOPE YOU'LL ENTERTAIN ME...
...NOW THAT YOU'RE HERE, SIX STARS.

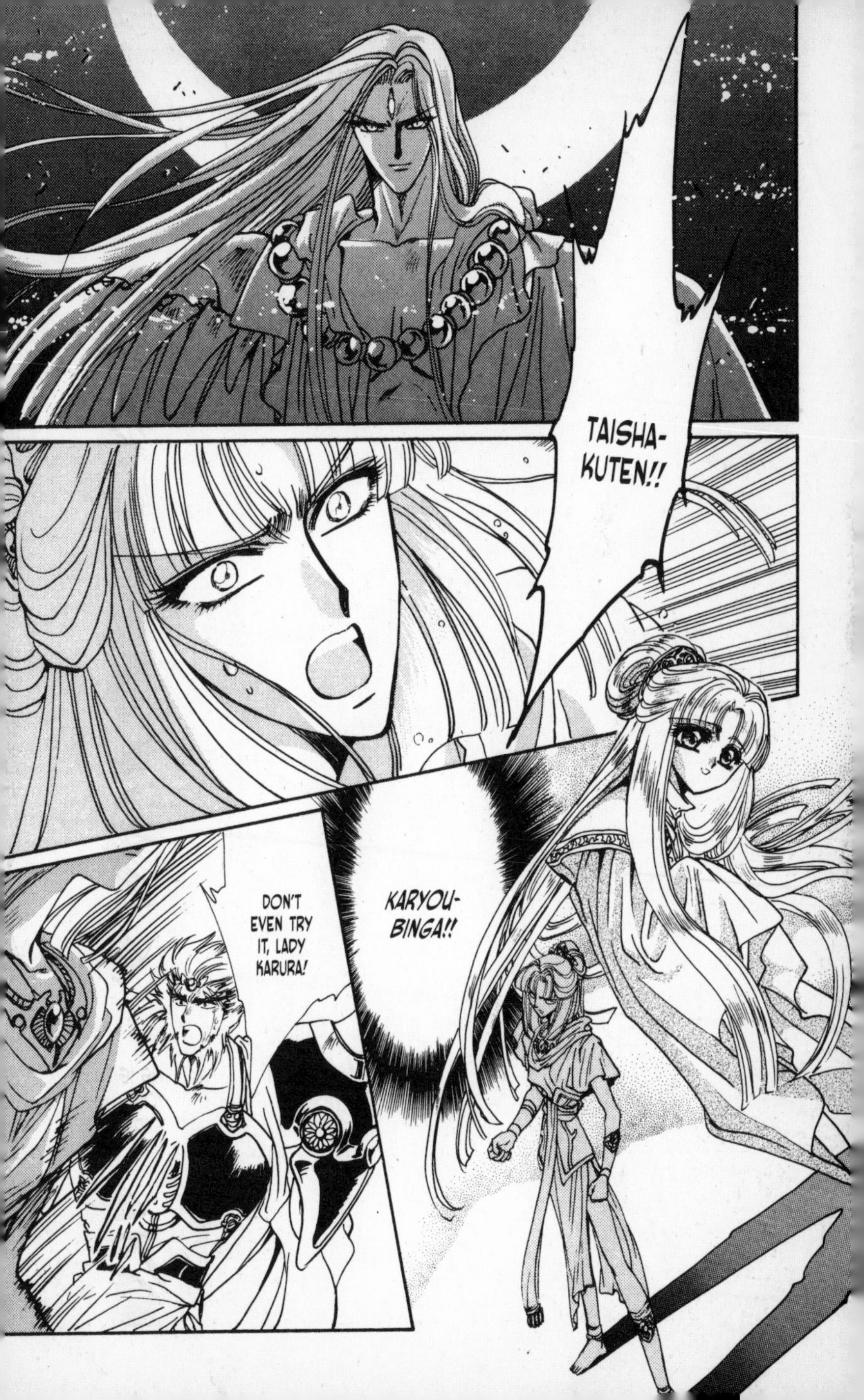
TAISHA-
KUTEN!!
KARYOU-
BINGA!!
DON'T EVEN TRY IT, LADY KARURA!

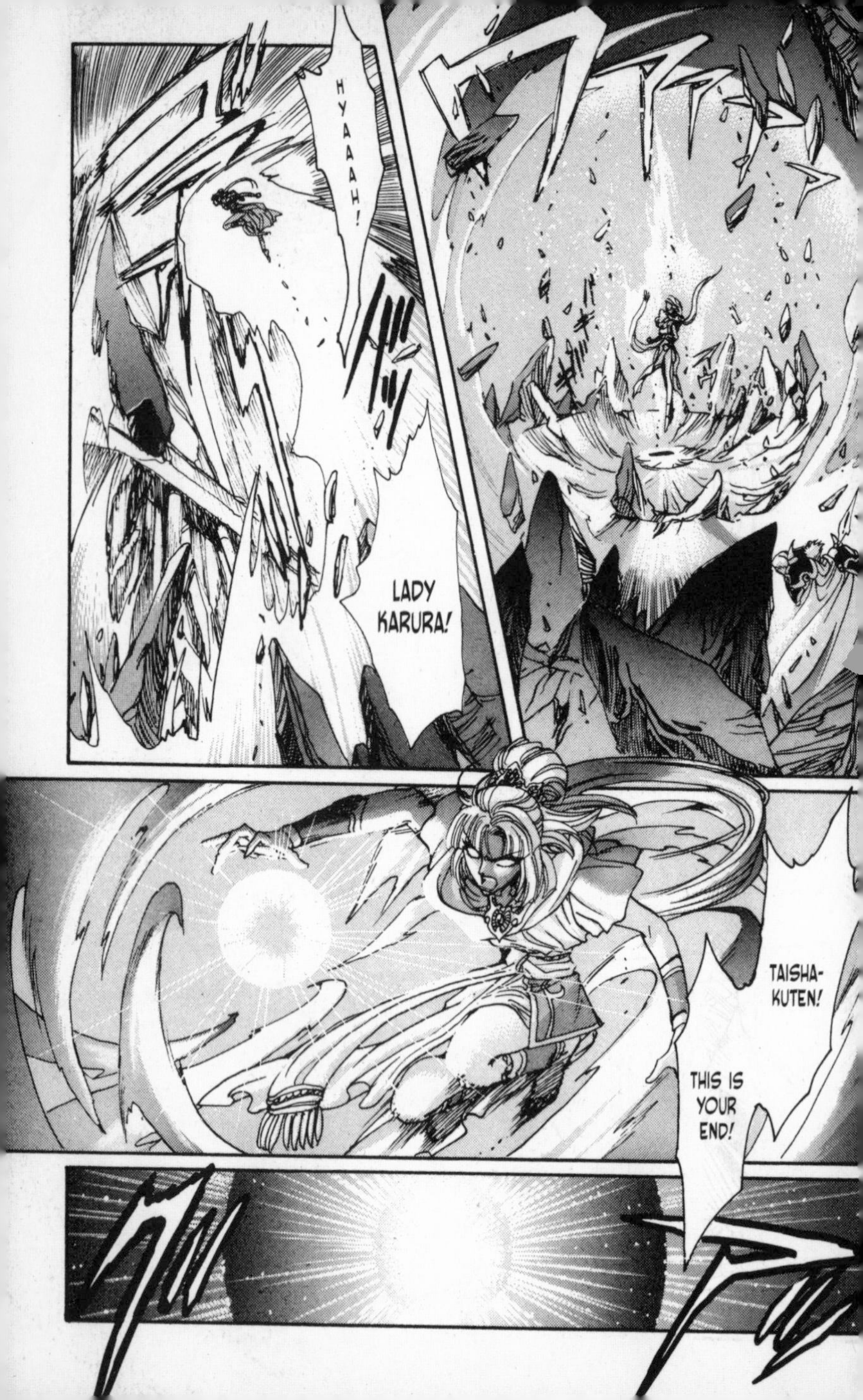
HYAAAH!
LADY KARURA!
TAISHA-KUTEN!
THIS IS YOUR END!

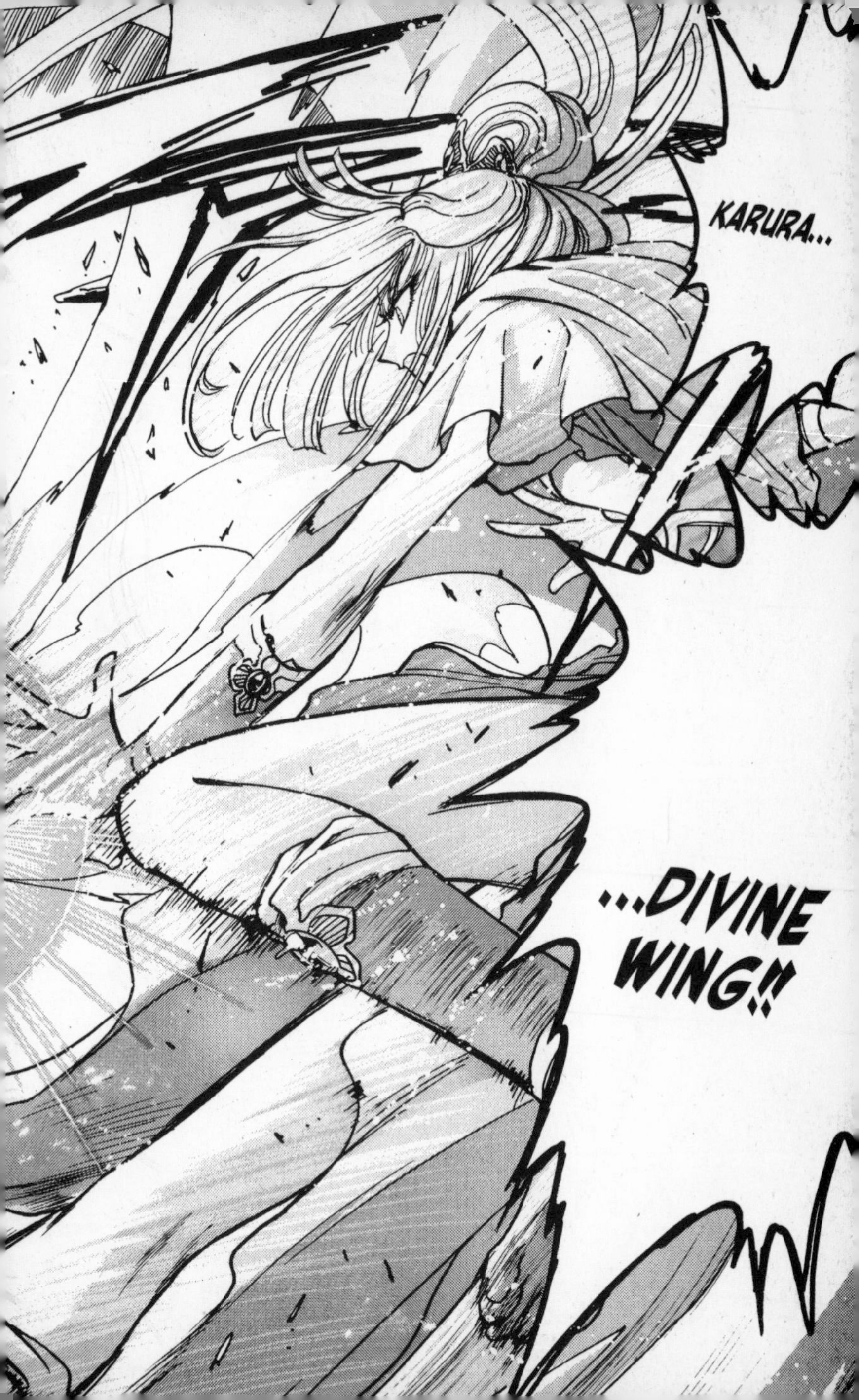
KARURA...
...DIVINE WING!!

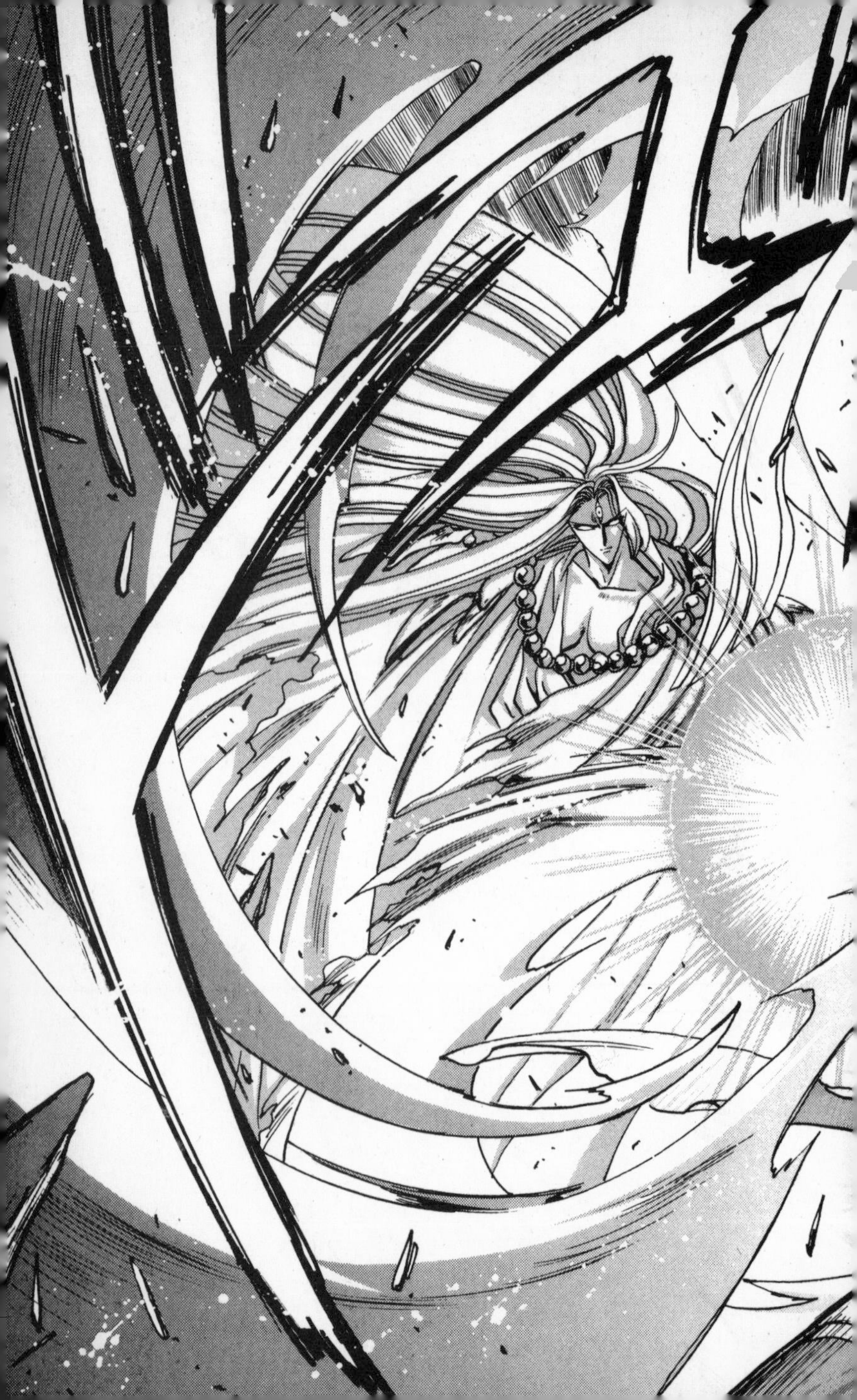

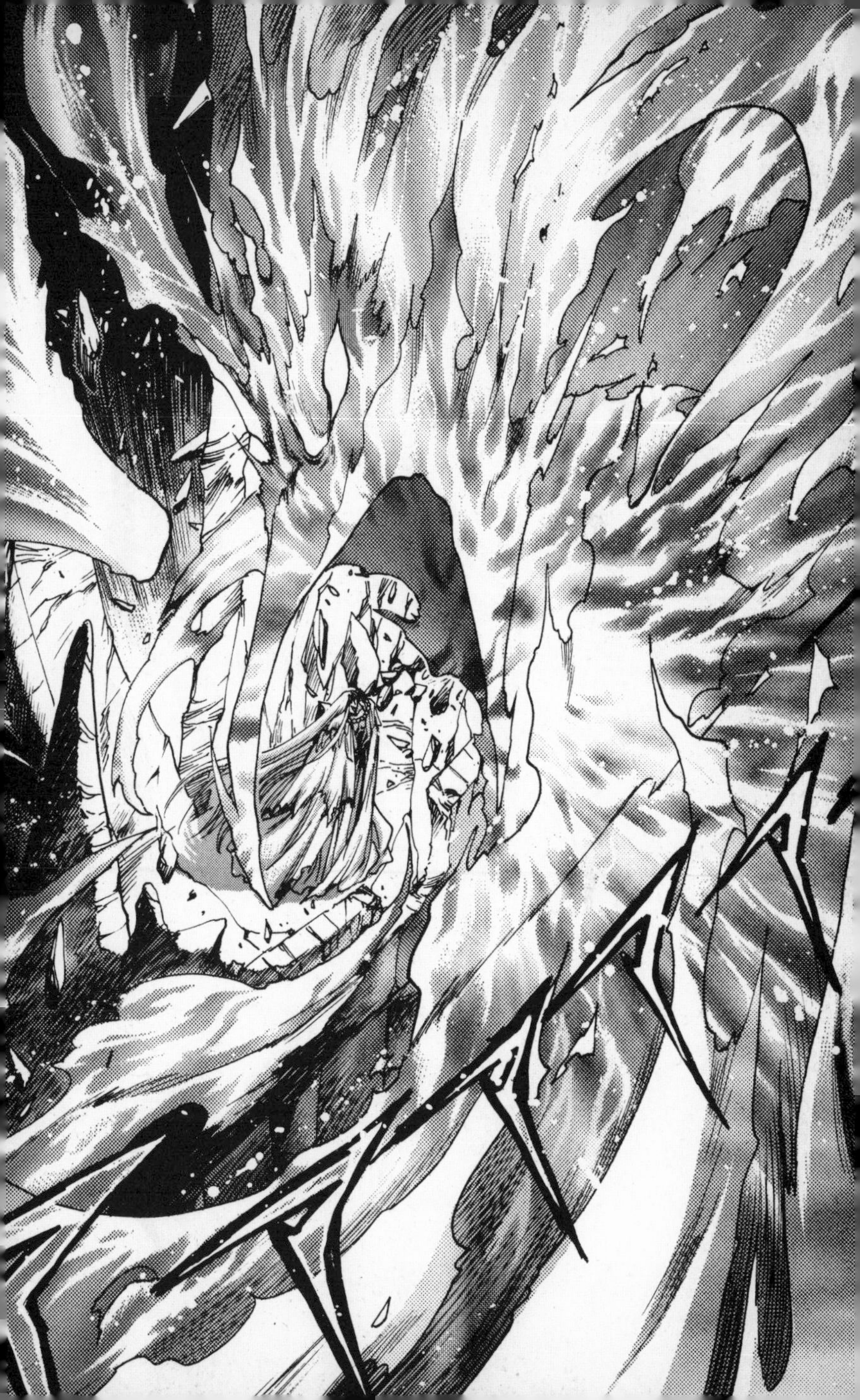

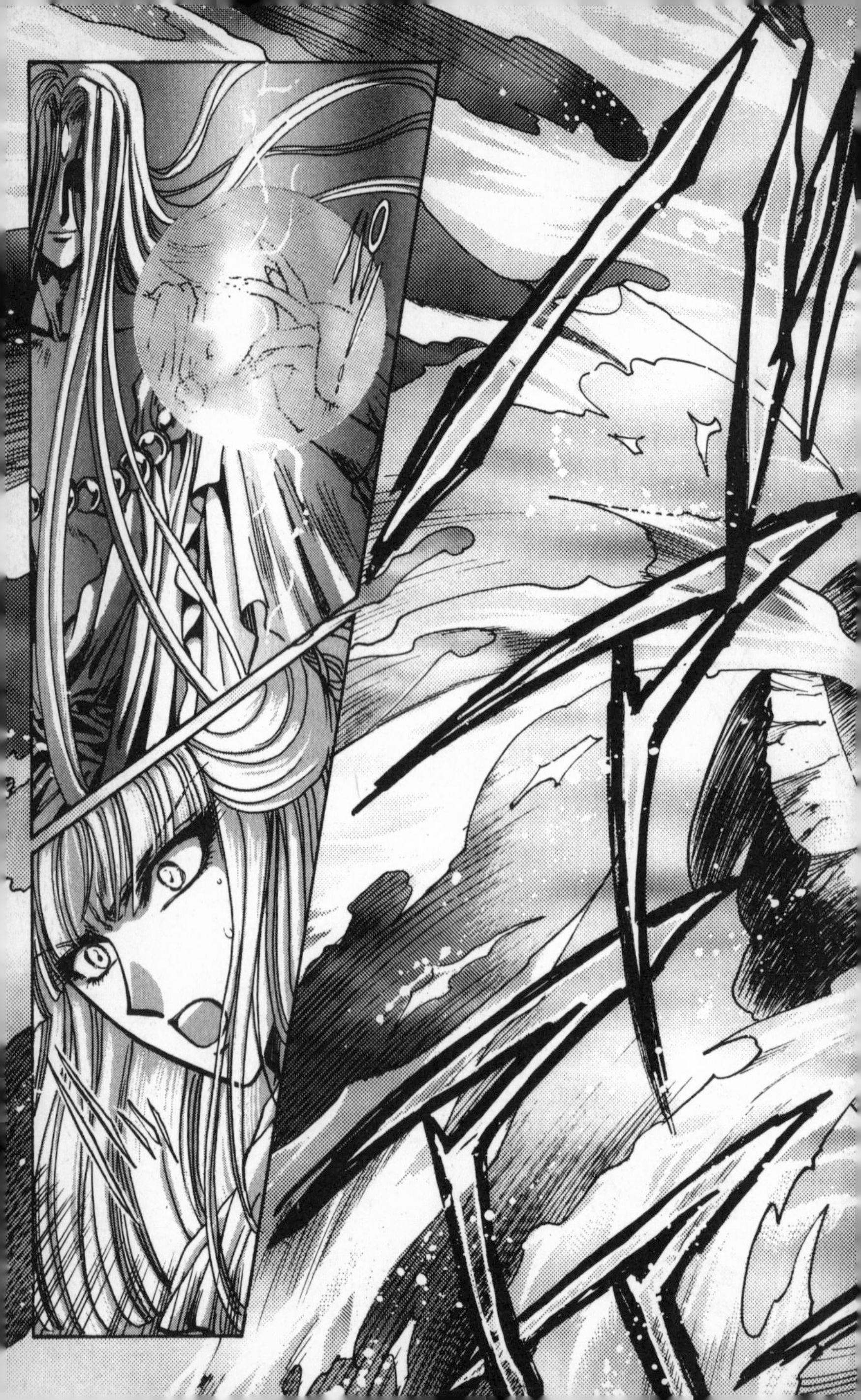

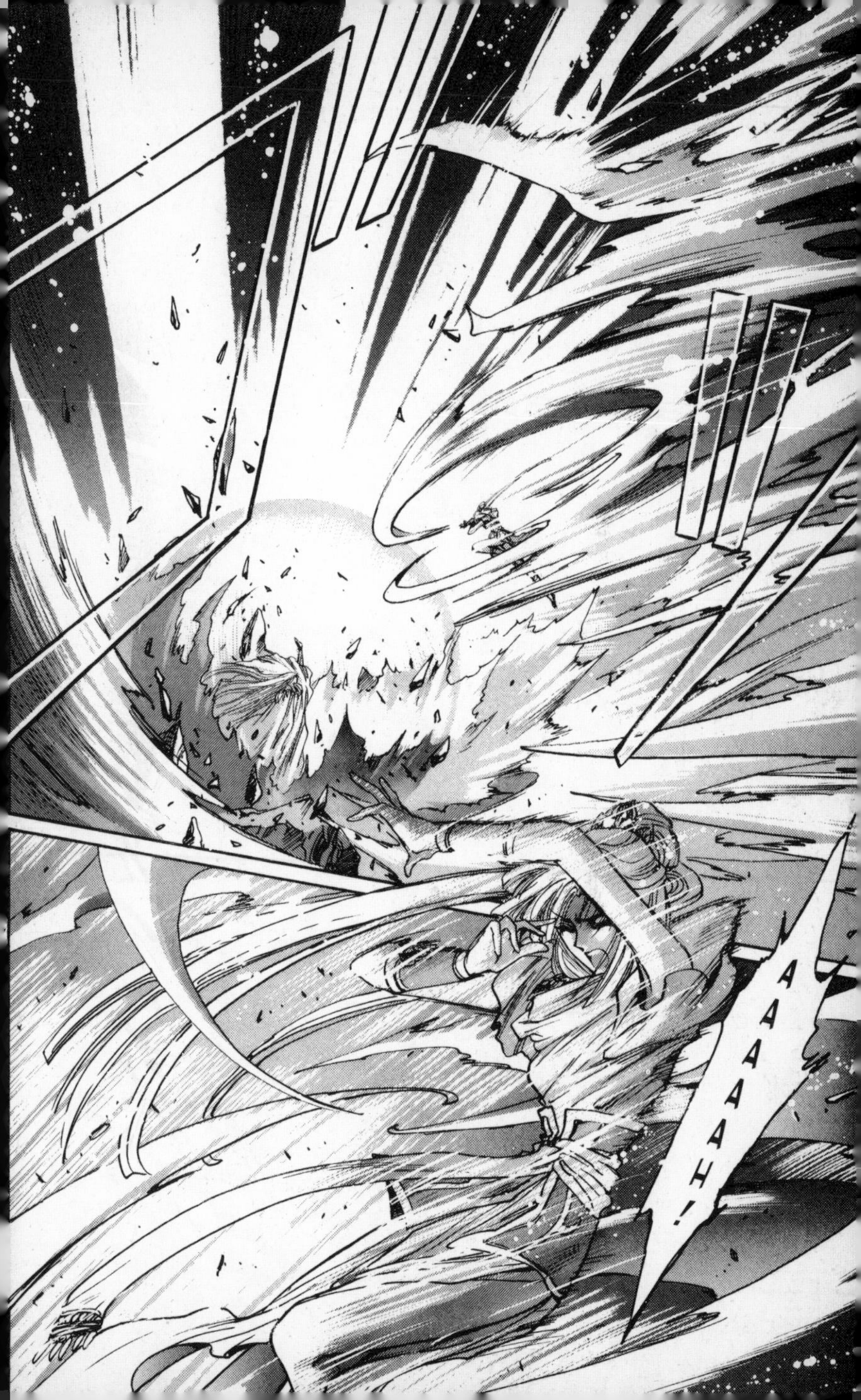
AAAAAAH!

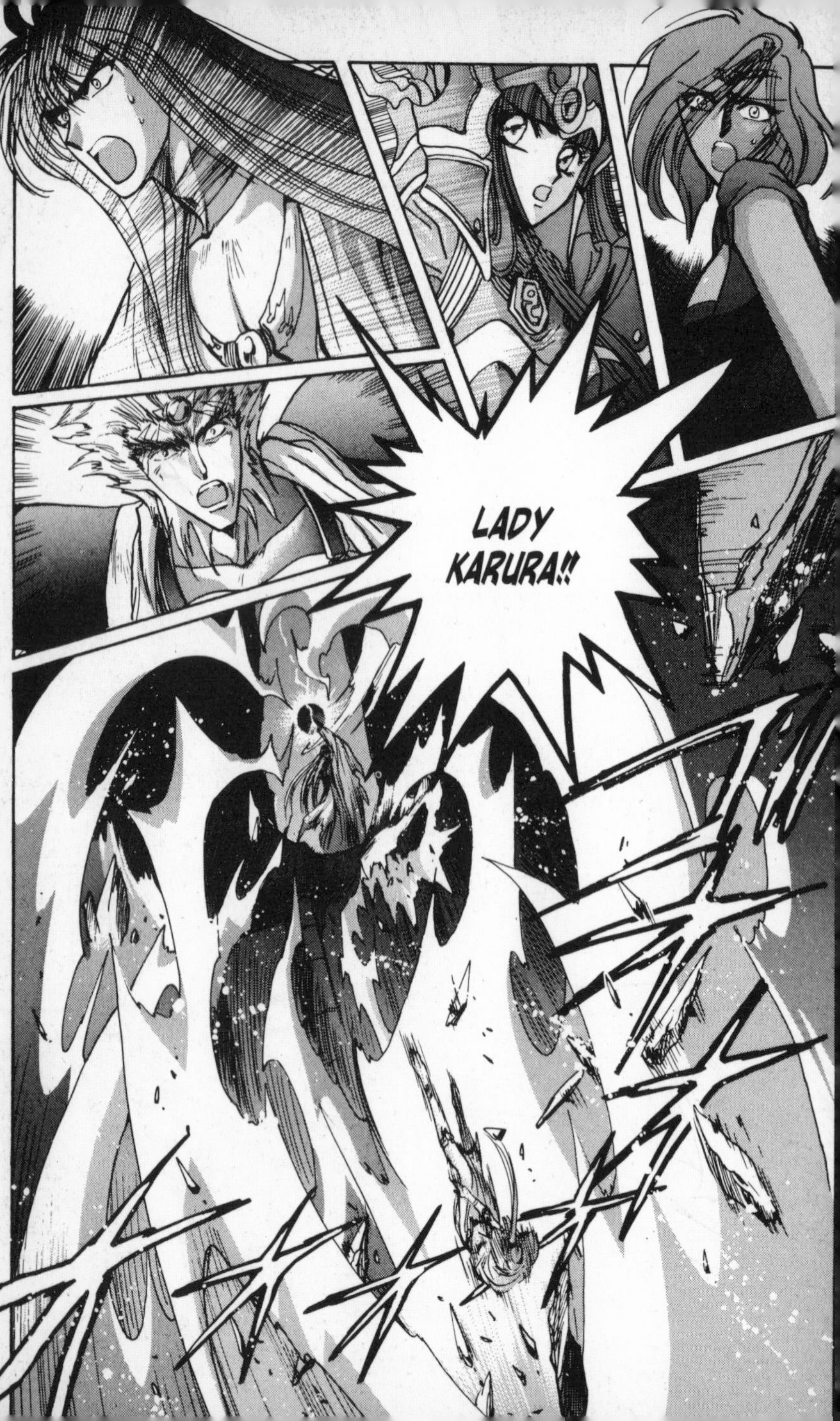
LADY KARURA!!

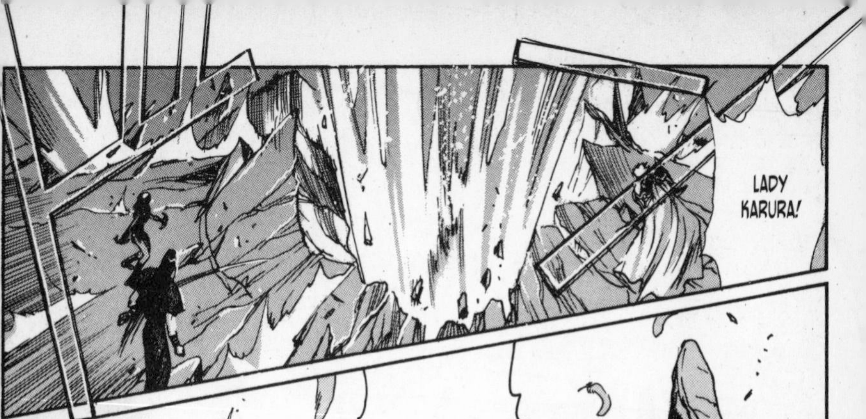
LADY KARURA!
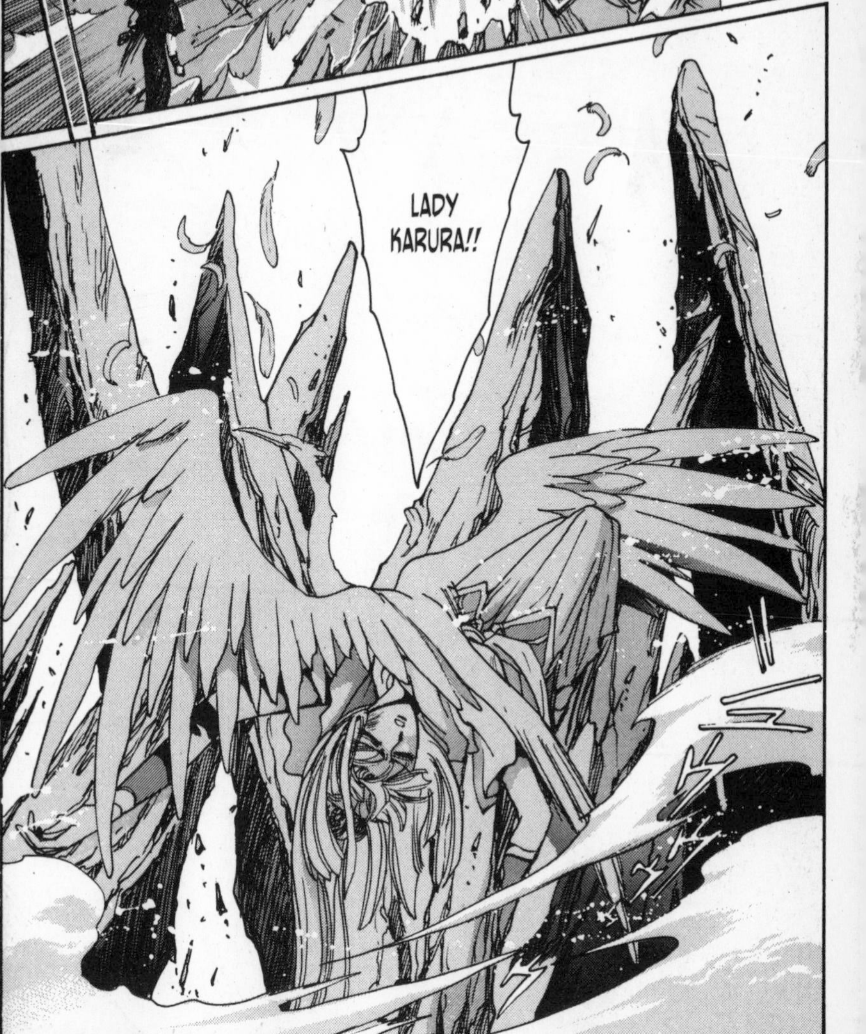
LADY KARURA!!

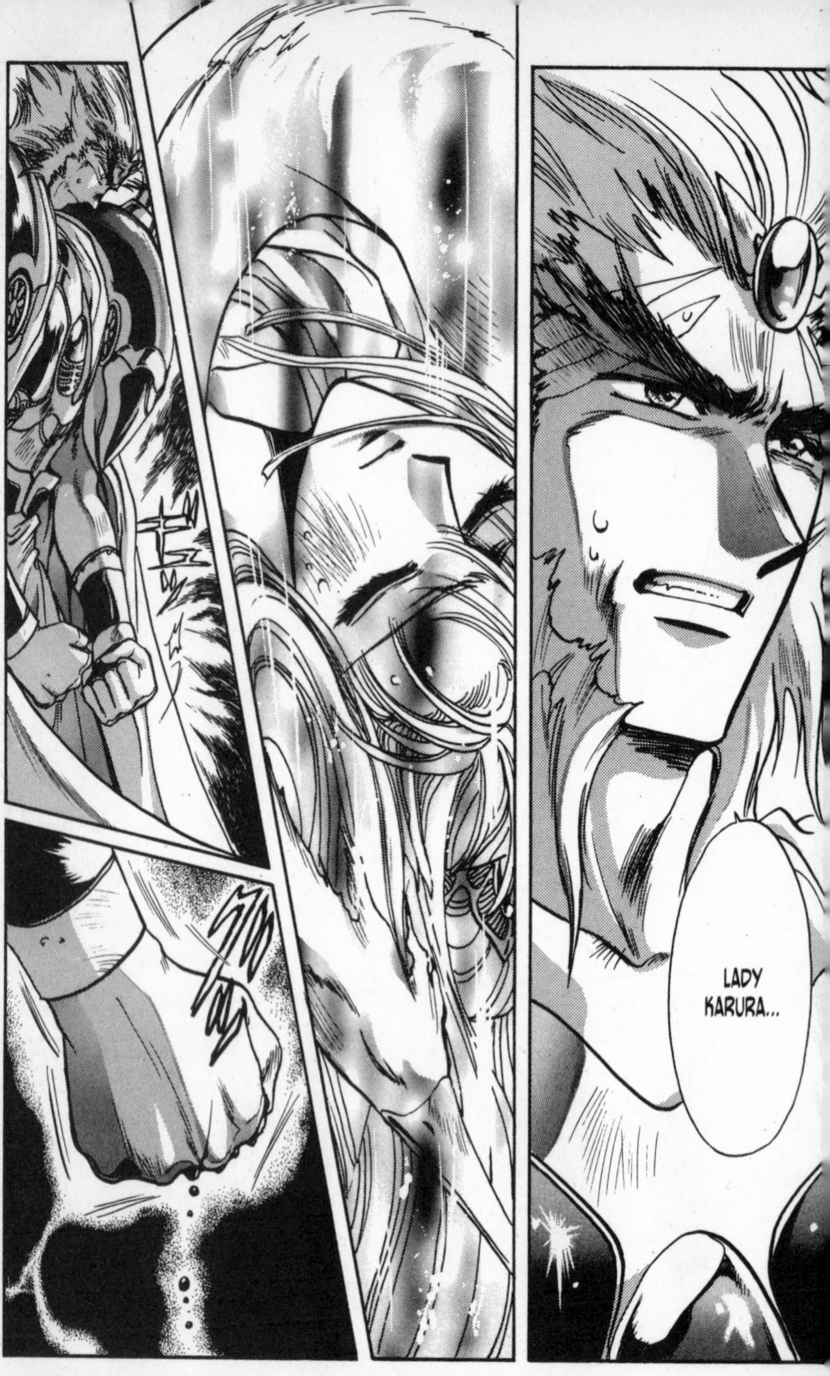
LADY KARURA...

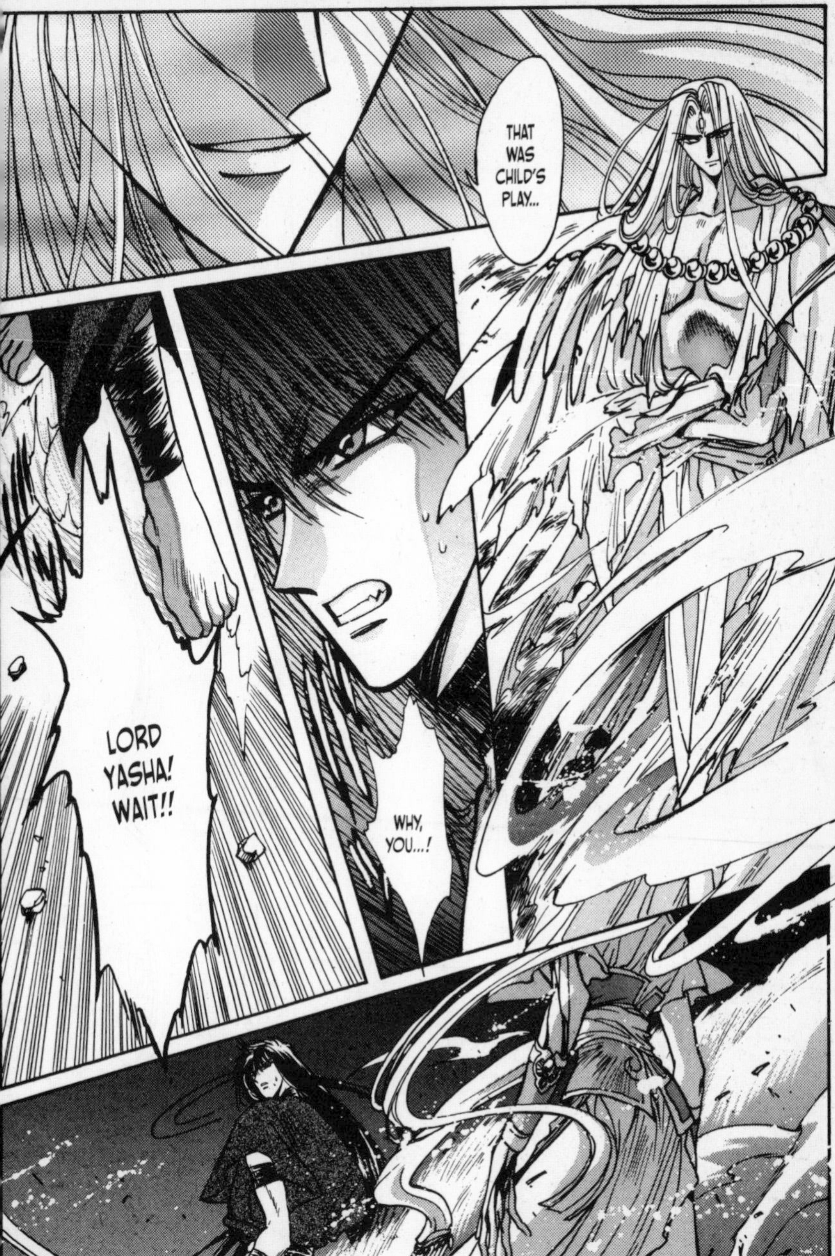
THAT WAS CHILD'S PLAY...
WHY, YOU...!
LORD YASHA! WAIT!!

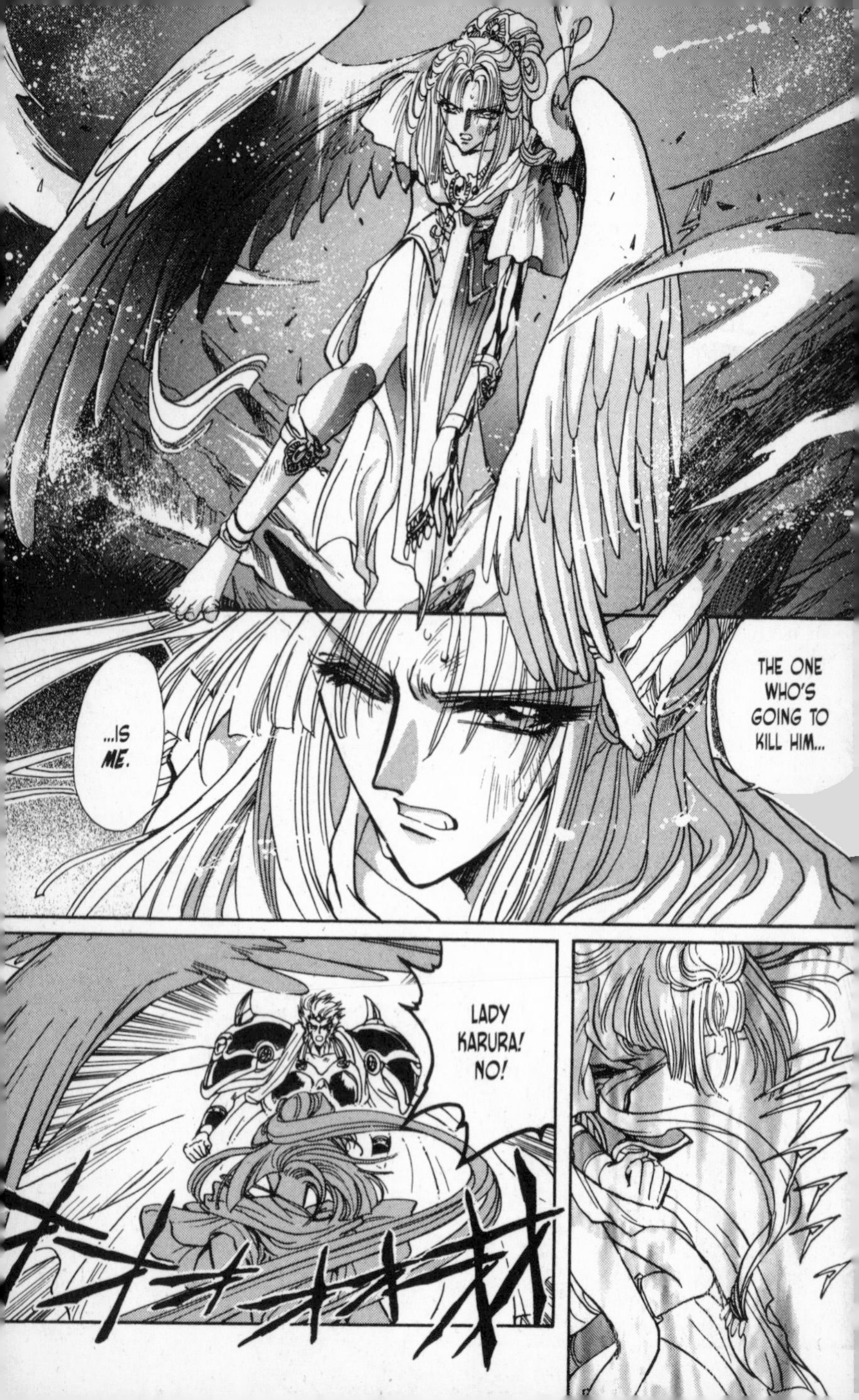
THE ONE WHO'S GOING TO KILL HIM...
...IS *ME*.
LADY KARURA! NO!

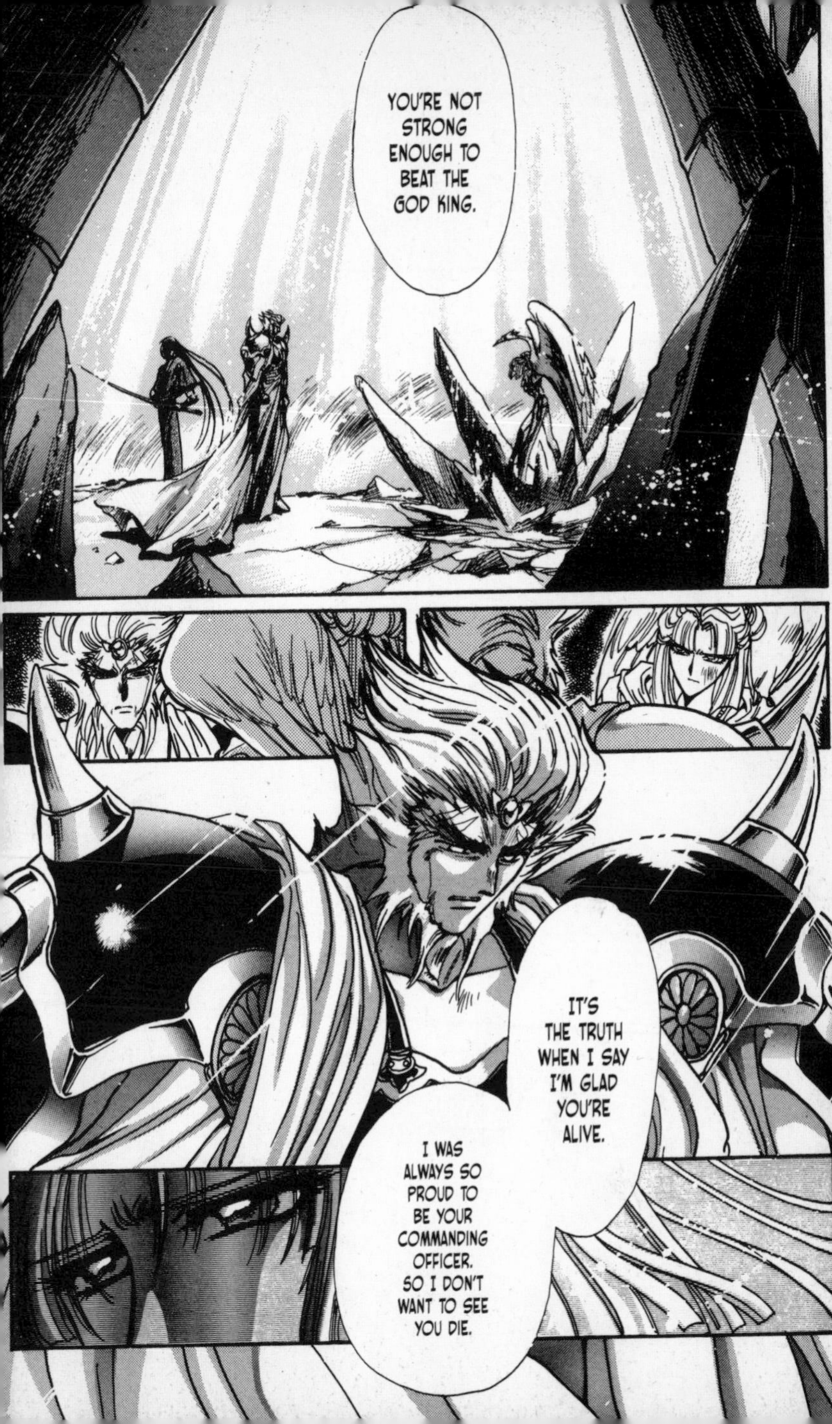
YOU'RE NOT STRONG ENOUGH TO BEAT THE GOD KING.
IT'S THE TRUTH WHEN I SAY I'M GLAD YOU'RE ALIVE.
I WAS ALWAYS SO PROUD TO BE YOUR COMMANDING OFFICER. SO I DON'T WANT TO SEE YOU DIE.

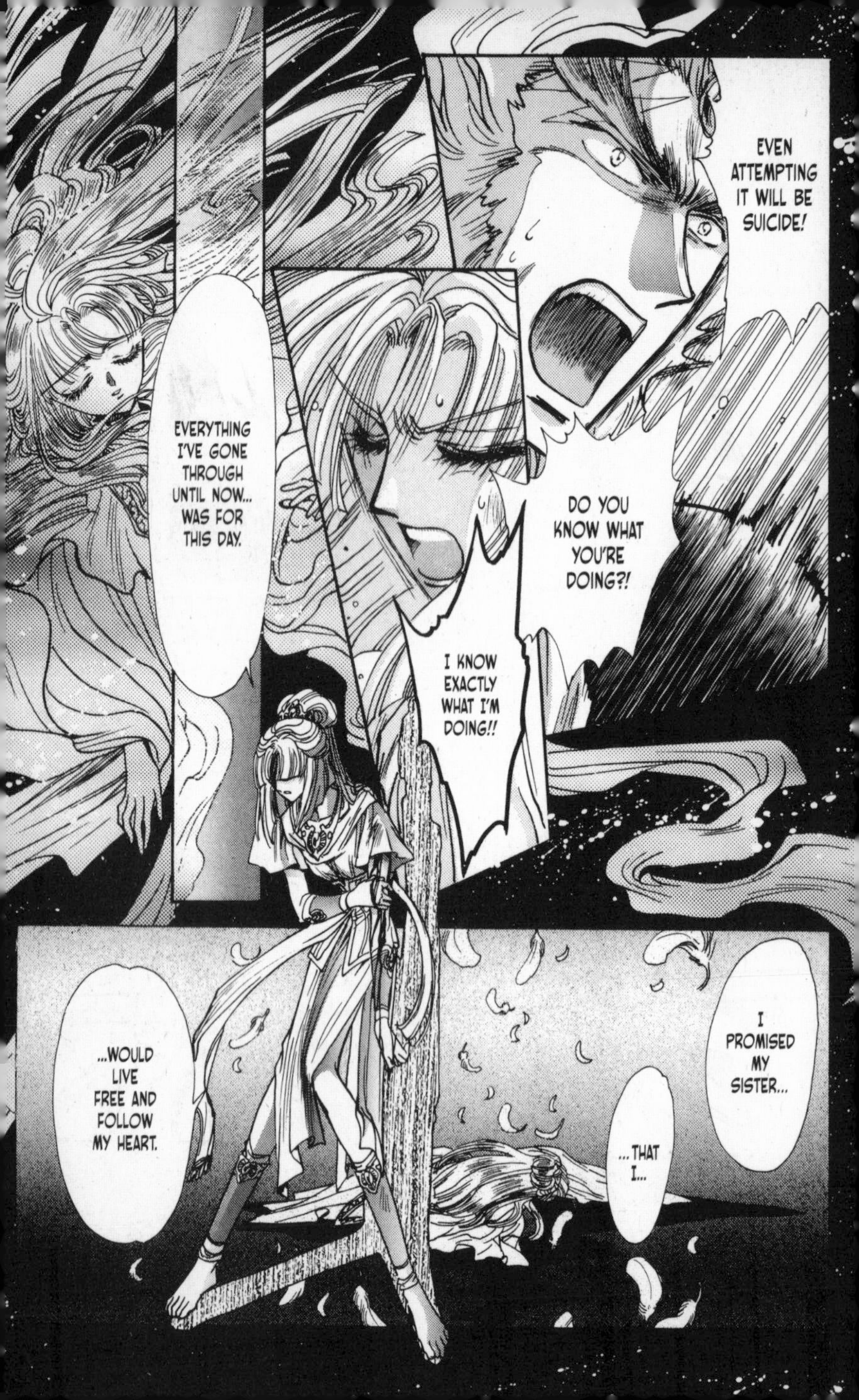
EVEN ATTEMPTING IT WILL BE SUICIDE!
DO YOU KNOW WHAT YOU'RE DOING?!
I KNOW EXACTLY WHAT I'M DOING!!
EVERYTHING I'VE GONE THROUGH UNTIL NOW...
WAS FOR THIS DAY.
I PROMISED MY SISTER...
...THAT I...
...WOULD LIVE FREE AND FOLLOW MY HEART.

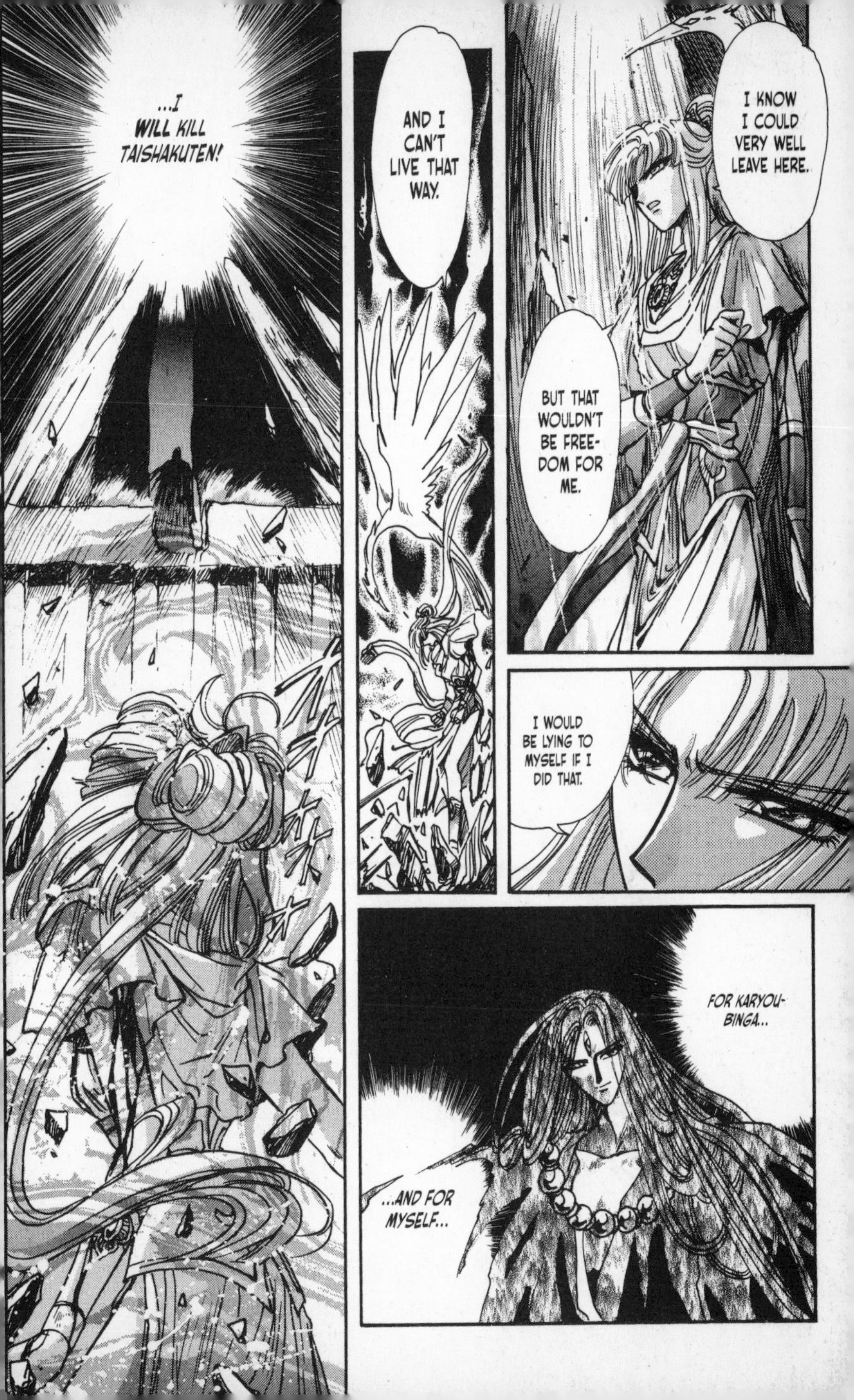
I KNOW I COULD VERY WELL LEAVE HERE.
BUT THAT WOULDN'T BE FREE-DOM FOR ME.
I WOULD BE LYING TO MYSELF IF I DID THAT.
AND I CAN'T LIVE THAT WAY.
FOR KARYOU-BINGA...
...AND FOR MYSELF...
...I WILL KILL TAISHAKUTEN!

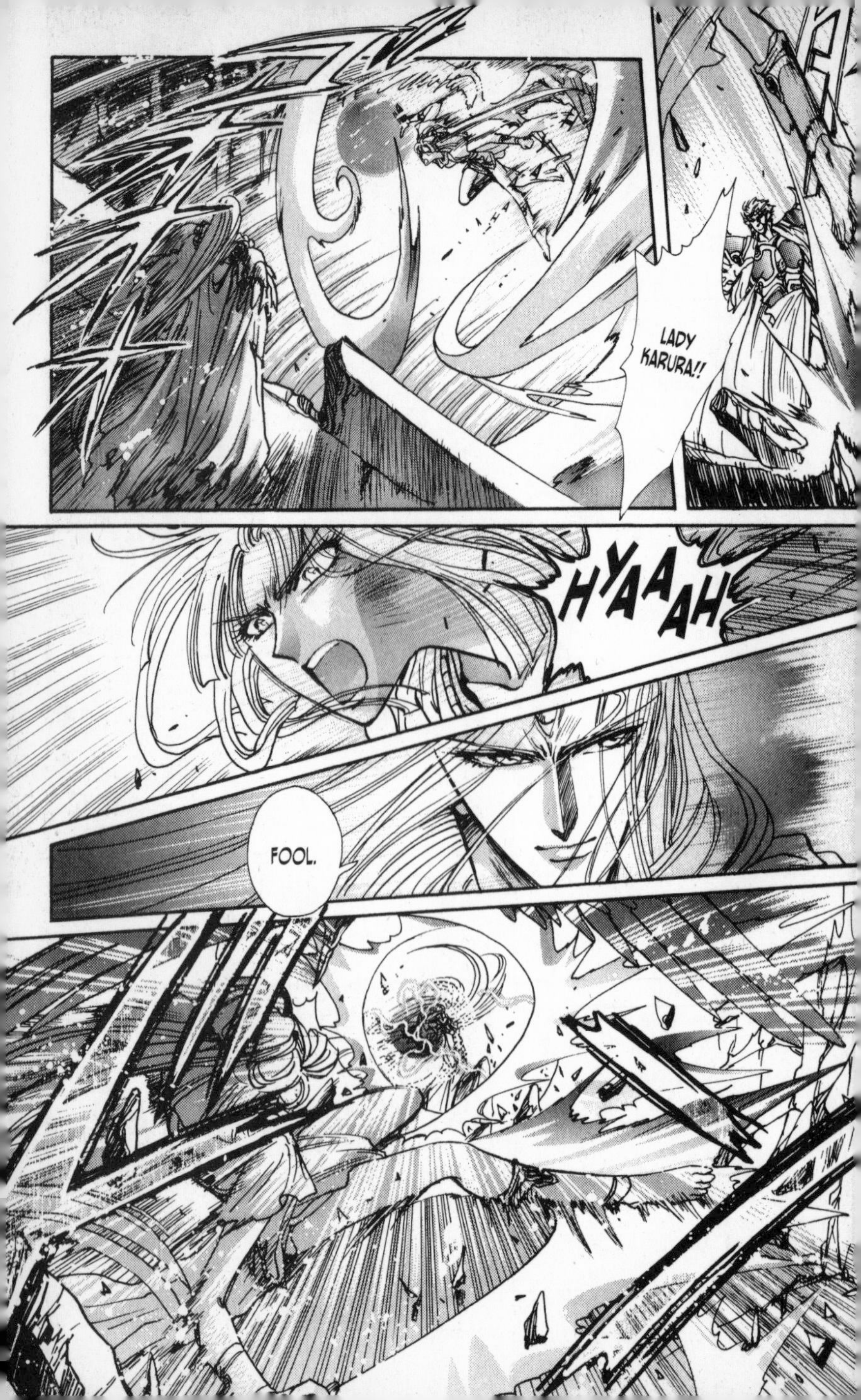
LADY KARURA!!
HYAAAH
FOOL.

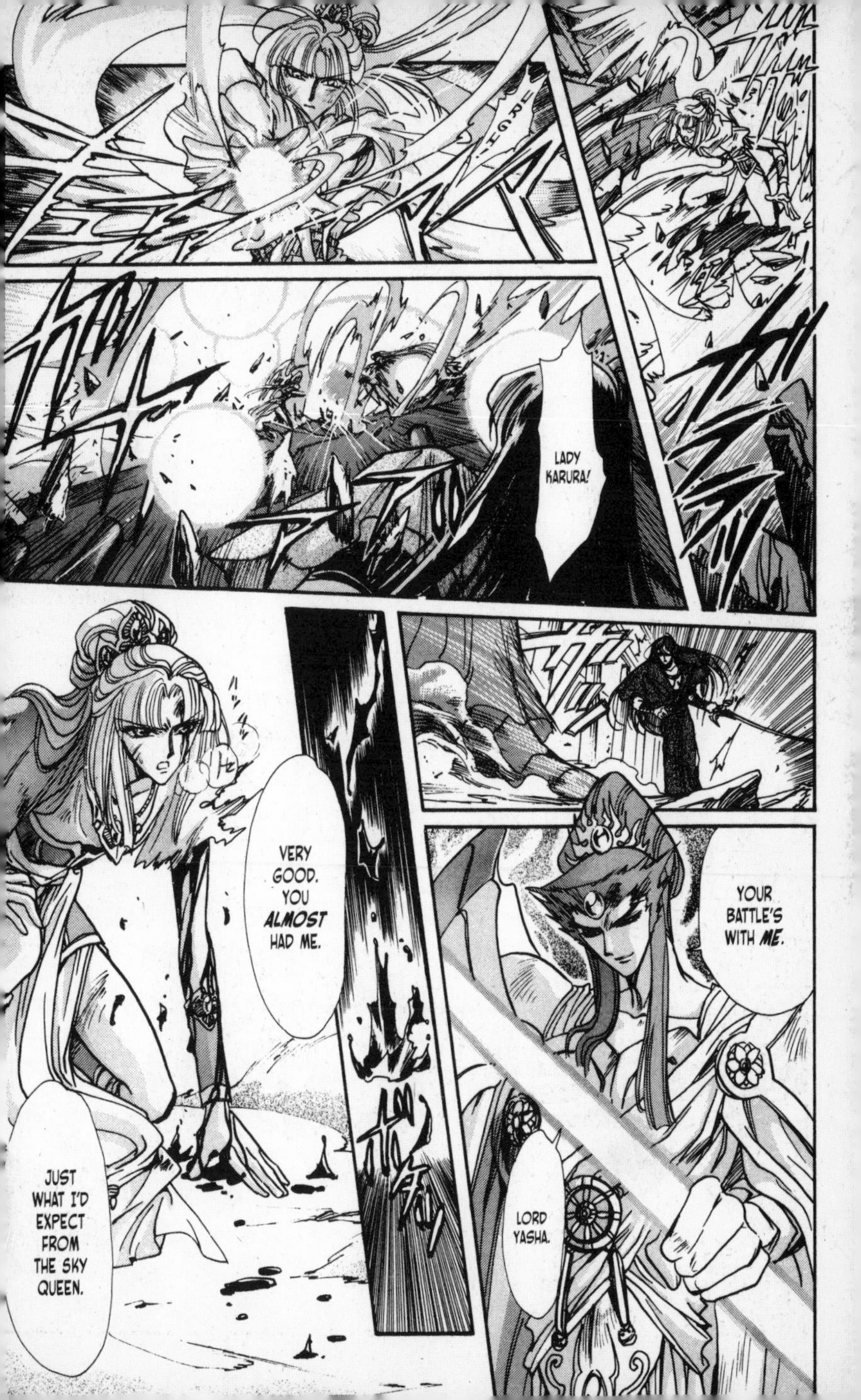
URGH!!
LADY KARURA!
YOUR BATTLE'S WITH *ME*.
LORD YASHA.
VERY GOOD. YOU *ALMOST* HAD ME.
JUST WHAT I'D EXPECT FROM THE SKY QUEEN.

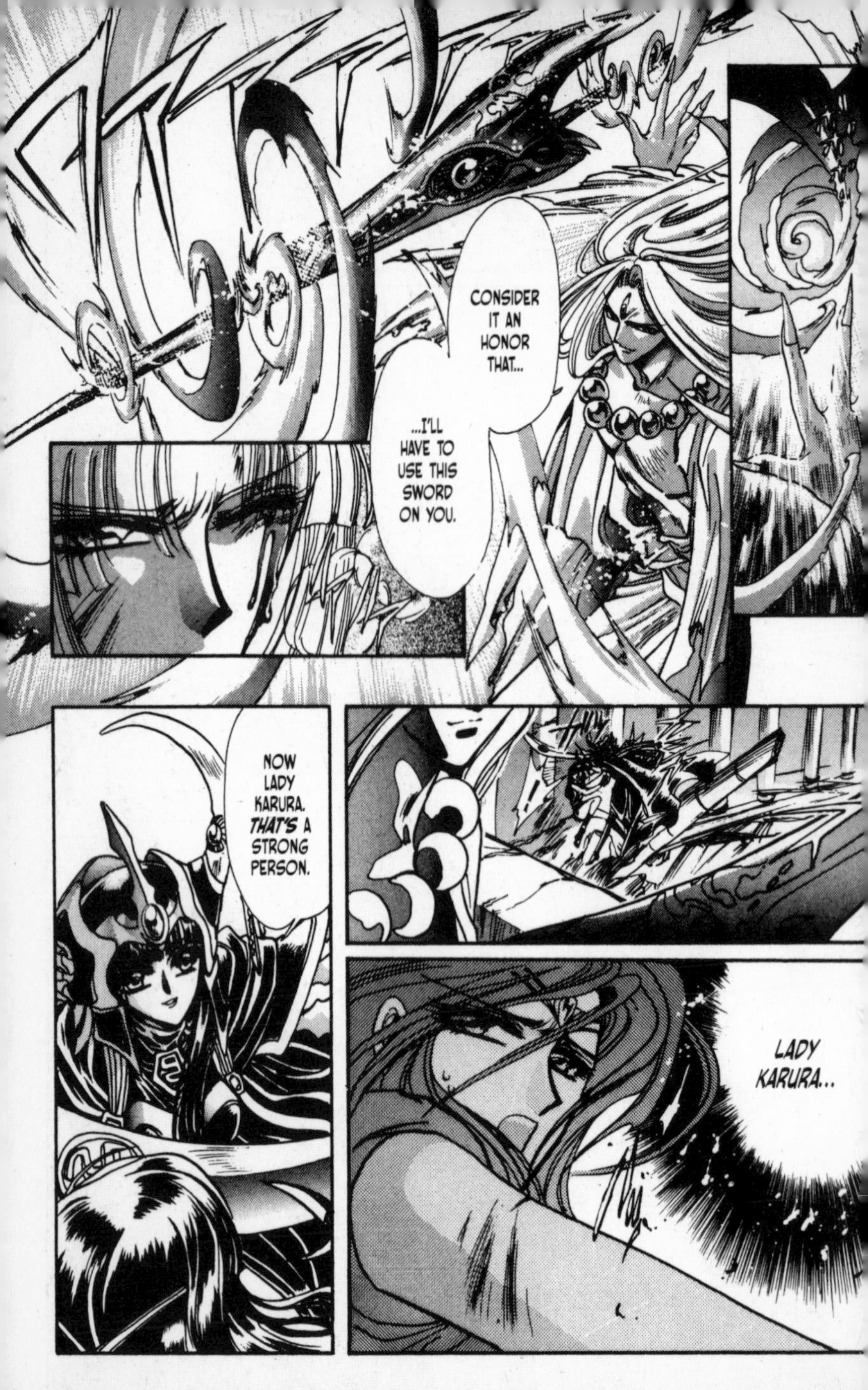
CONSIDER IT AN HONOR THAT...
...I'LL HAVE TO USE THIS SWORD ON YOU.
NOW LADY KARURA. *THAT'S* A STRONG PERSON.
LADY KARURA...

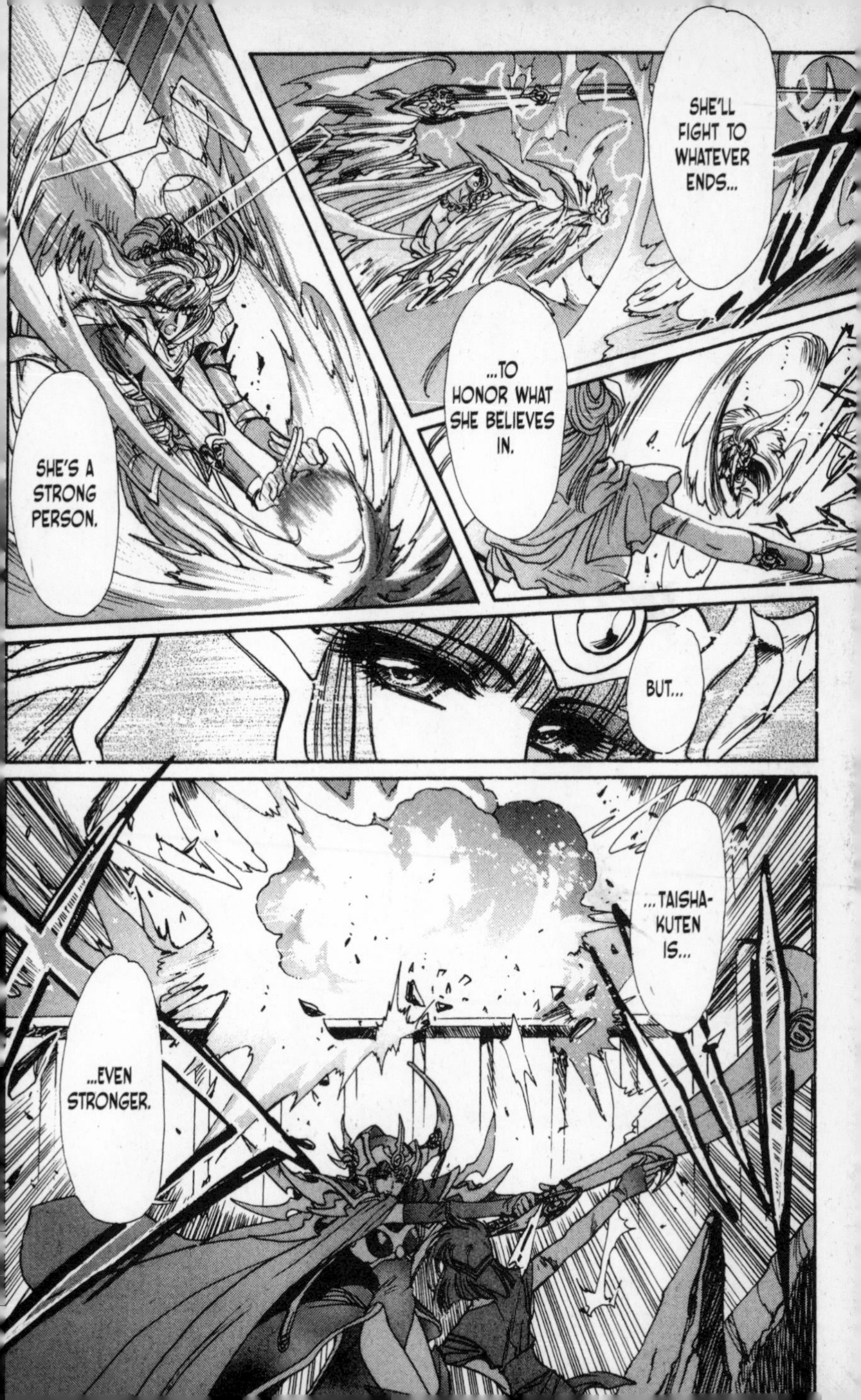
SHE'LL FIGHT TO WHATEVER ENDS...
...TO HONOR WHAT SHE BELIEVES IN.
SHE'S A STRONG PERSON.
BUT...
...TAISHA-KUTEN IS...
...EVEN STRONGER.

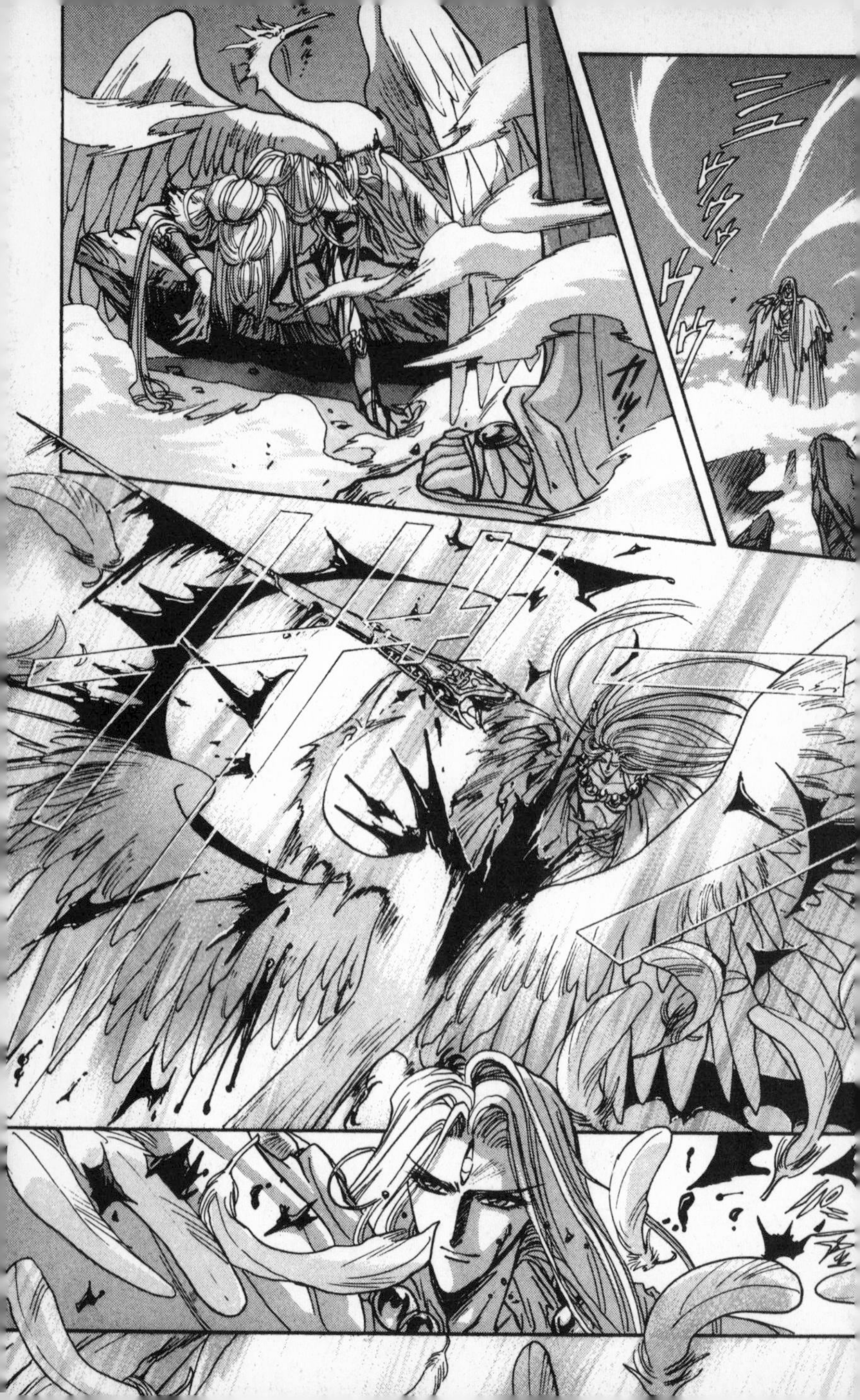
ミュウウゥウウ

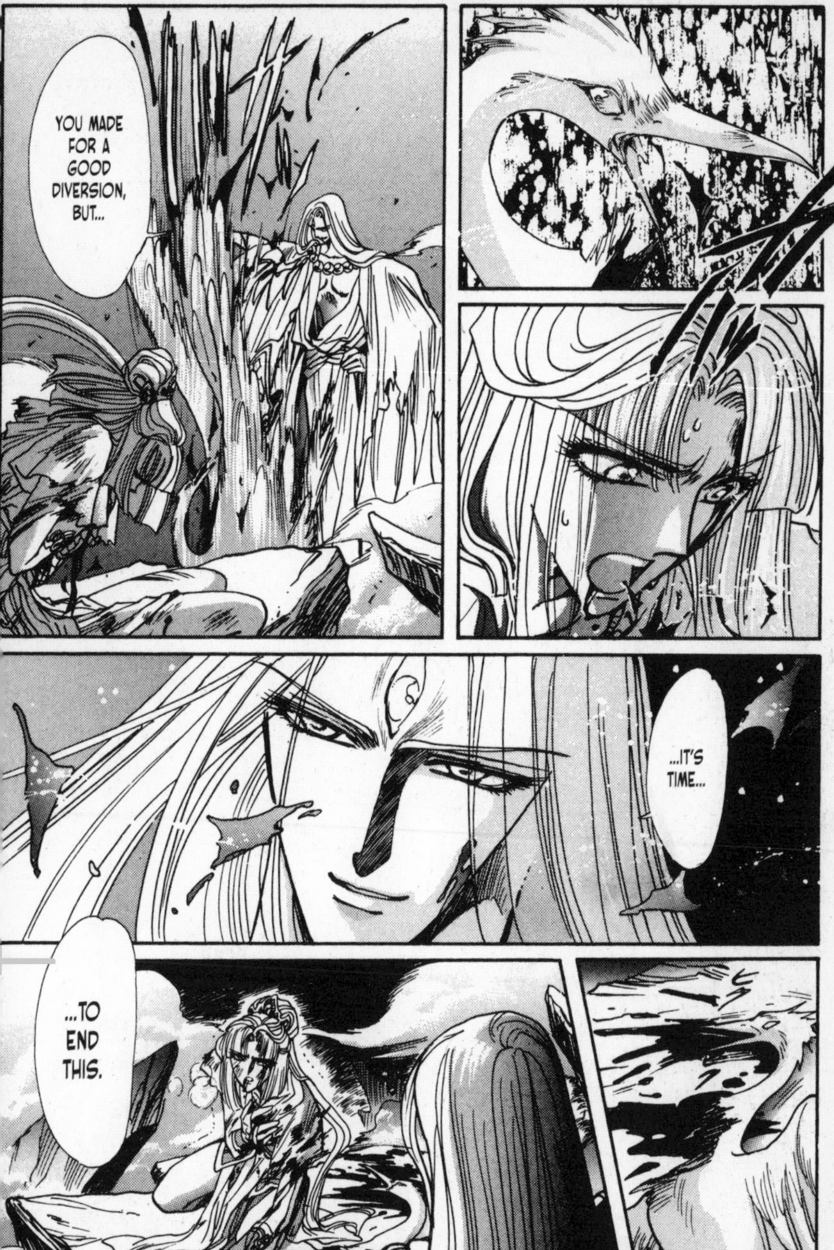
YOU MADE FOR A GOOD DIVERSION, BUT...
...IT'S TIME...
...TO END THIS.

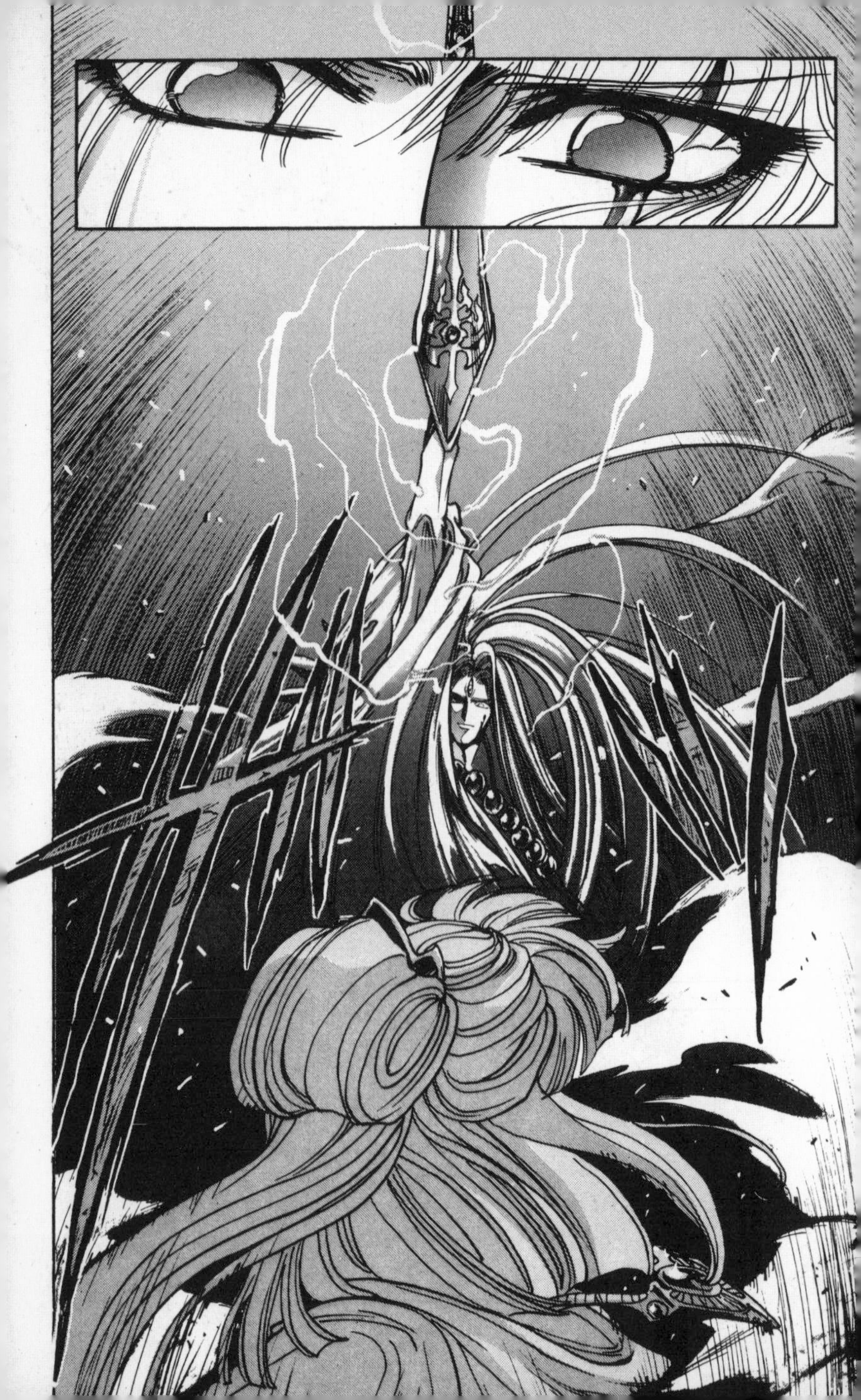

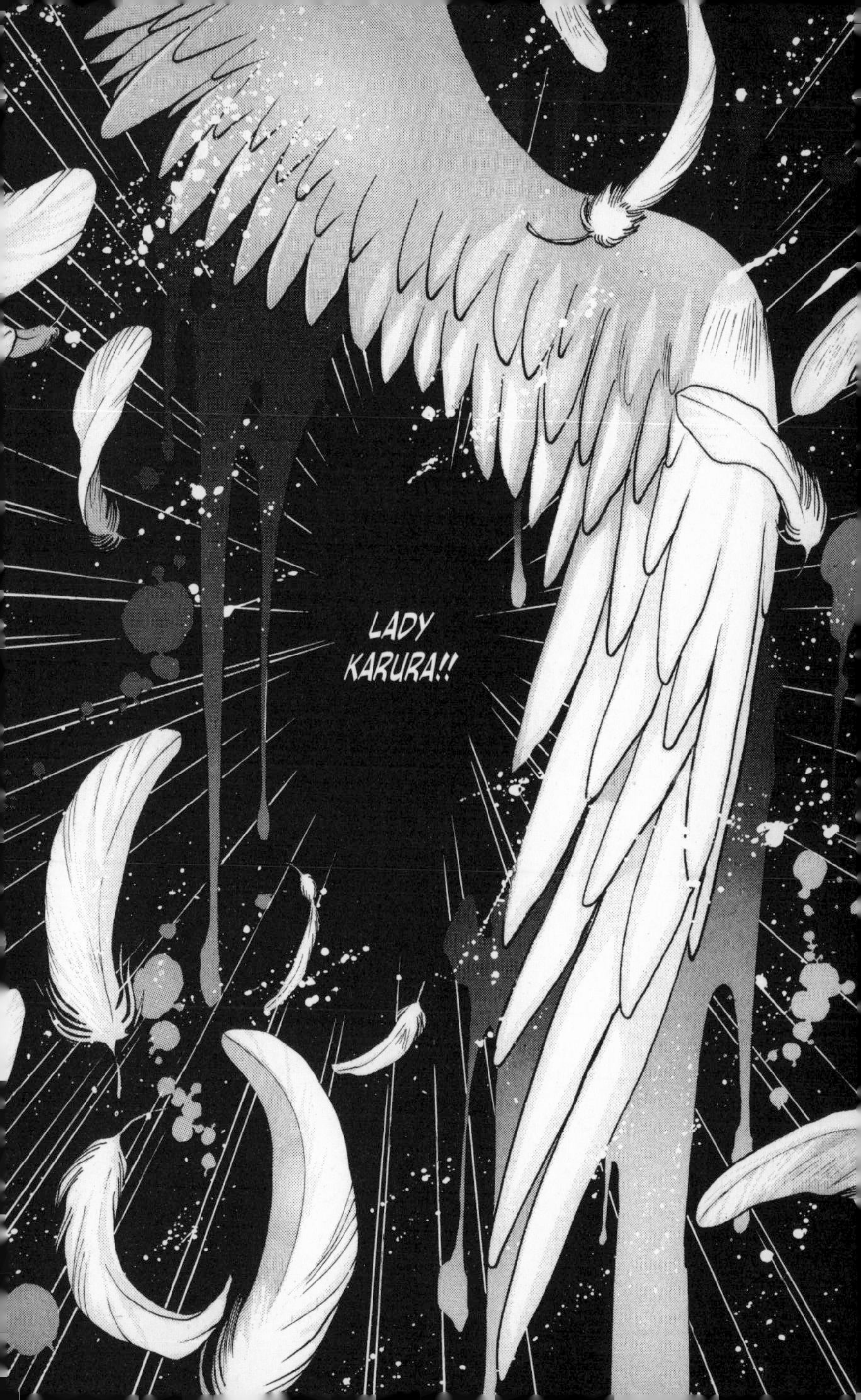
LADY KARURA!!

TWIN CASTLES IN FLAMES AND THUNDER I / END

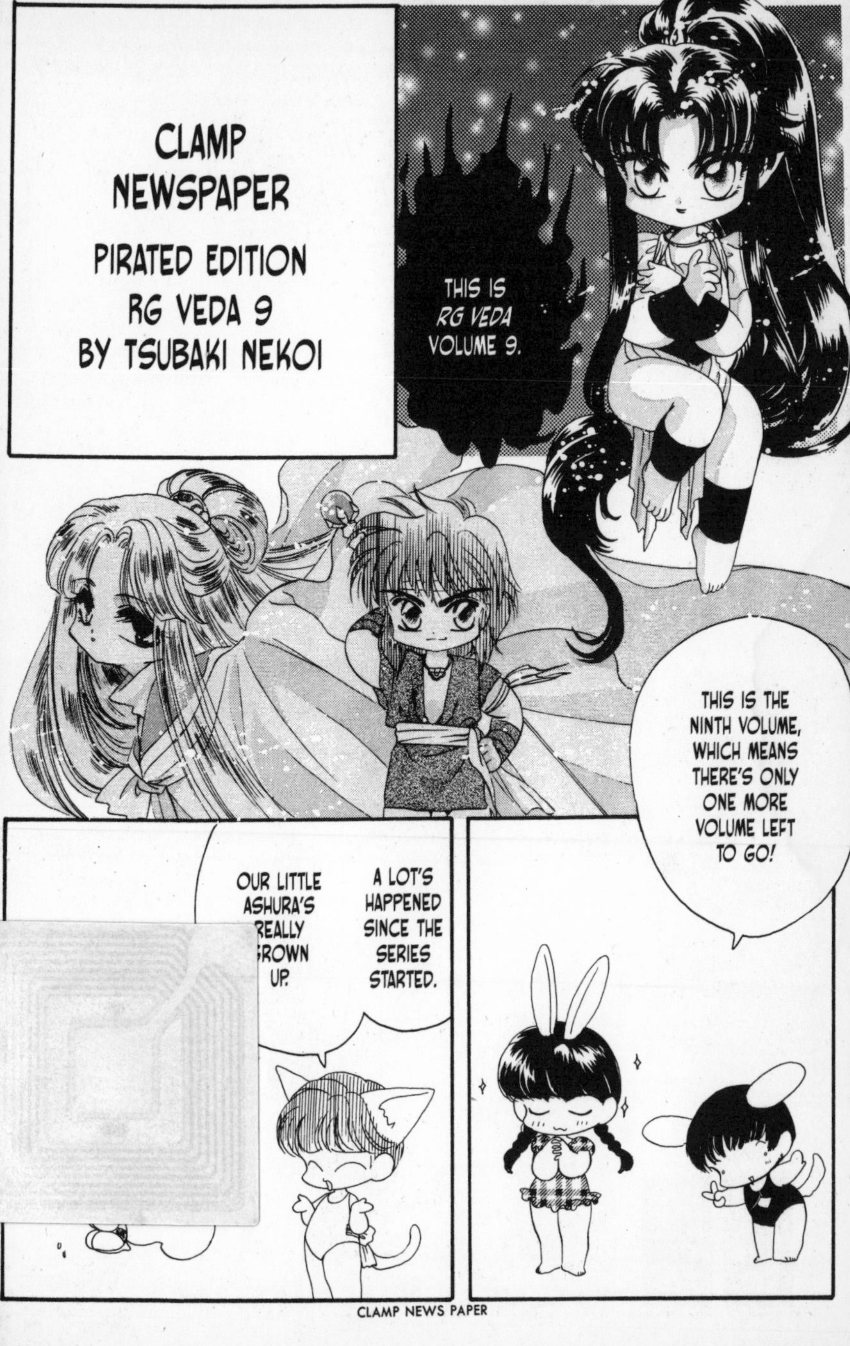
THIS IS RG VEDA VOLUME 9.
CLAMP NEWSPAPER
PIRATED EDITION RG VEDA 9 BY TSUBAKI NEKOI
THIS IS THE NINTH VOLUME, WHICH MEANS THERE'S ONLY ONE MORE VOLUME LEFT TO GO!
A LOT'S HAPPENED SINCE THE SERIES STARTED.
OUR LITTLE ASHURA'S REALLY GROWN UP.

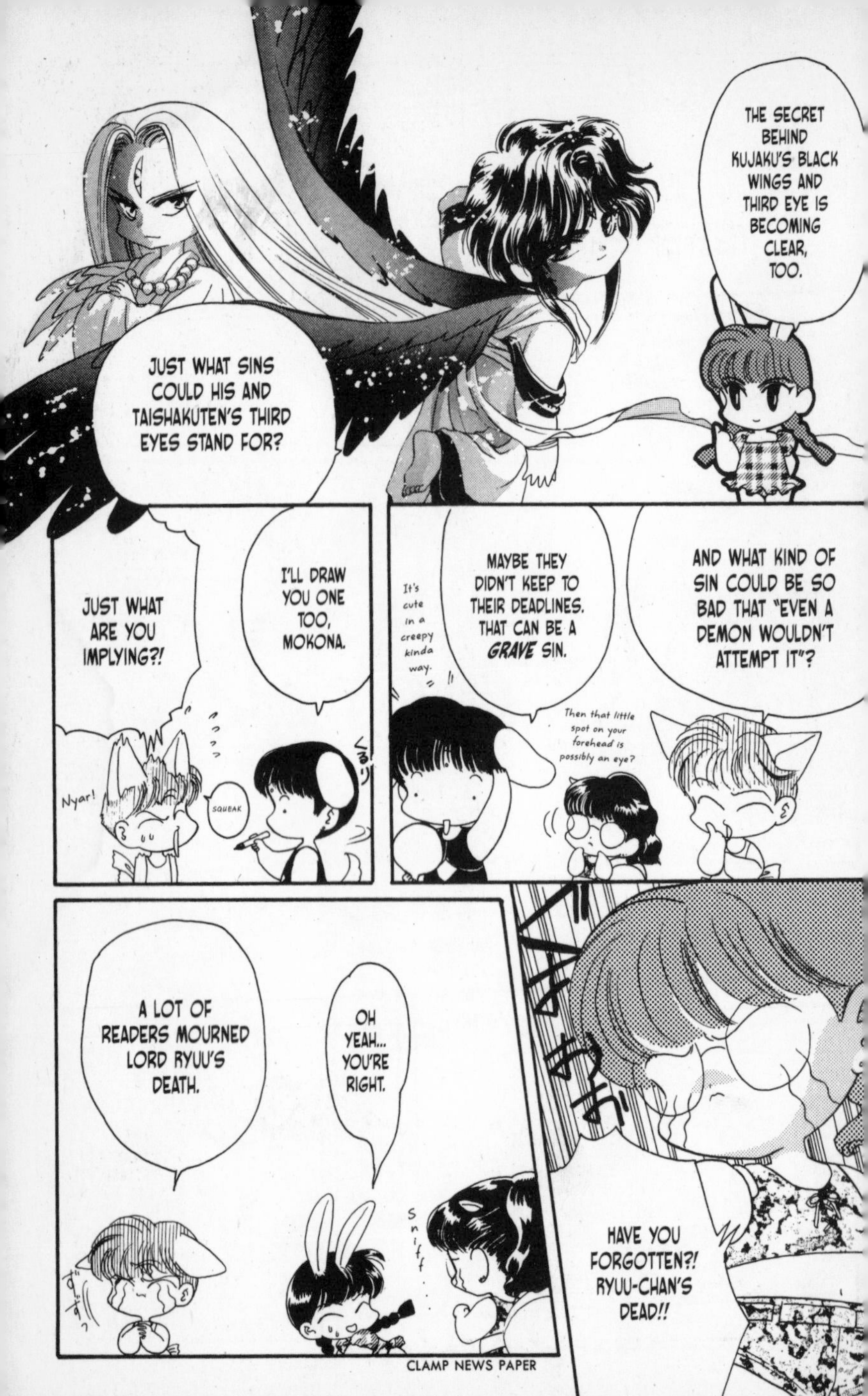
THE SECRET BEHIND KUJAKU'S BLACK WINGS AND THIRD EYE IS BECOMING CLEAR, TOO.
JUST WHAT SINS COULD HIS AND TAISHAKUTEN'S THIRD EYES STAND FOR?
AND WHAT KIND OF SIN COULD BE SO BAD THAT "EVEN A DEMON WOULDN'T ATTEMPT IT"?
Then that little spot on your forehead is possibly an eye?
MAYBE THEY DIDN'T KEEP TO THEIR DEADLINES. THAT CAN BE A *GRAVE* SIN.
It's cute in a creepy kinda way.
I'LL DRAW YOU ONE TOO, MOKONA.
SQUEAK
JUST WHAT ARE YOU IMPLYING?!
Nyar!
HAVE YOU FORGOTTEN?! RYUU-CHAN'S DEAD!!
OH YEAH... YOU'RE RIGHT.
Sniff...
A LOT OF READERS MOURNED LORD RYUU'S DEATH.

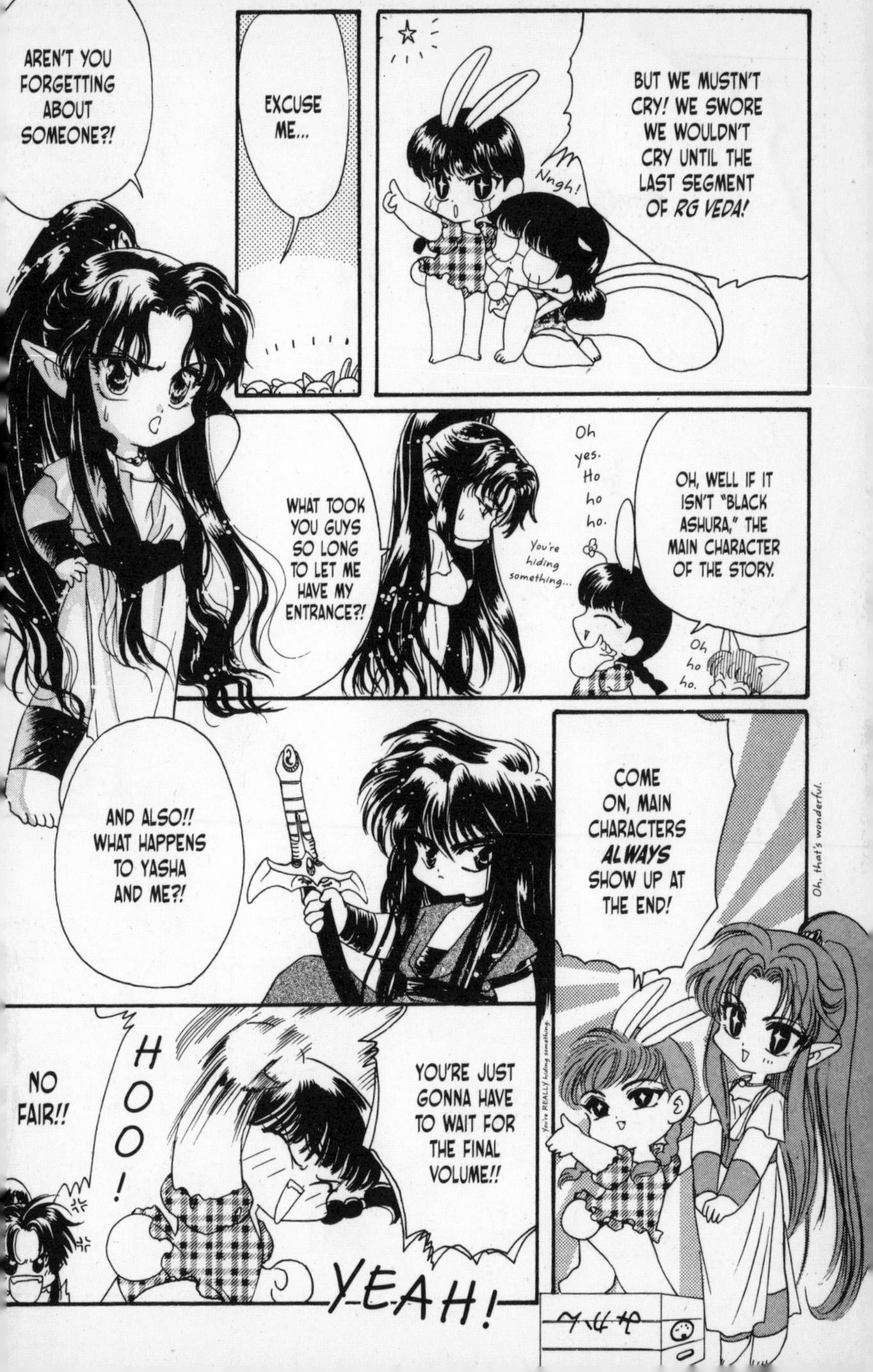
BUT WE MUSTN'T CRY! WE SWORE WE WOULDN'T CRY UNTIL THE LAST SEGMENT OF *RG VEDA!*
Nngh!
EXCUSE ME...
AREN'T YOU FORGETTING ABOUT SOMEONE?!
OH, WELL IF IT ISN'T "BLACK ASHURA," THE MAIN CHARACTER OF THE STORY.
Oh yes. Ho ho ho.
You're hiding something...
Oh ho ho.
WHAT TOOK YOU GUYS SO LONG TO LET ME HAVE MY ENTRANCE?!
Oh, that's wonderful.
COME ON, MAIN CHARACTERS ***ALWAYS*** SHOW UP AT THE END!
AND ALSO!! WHAT HAPPENS TO YASHA AND ME?!
You're REALLY hiding something.
YOU'RE JUST GONNA HAVE TO WAIT FOR THE FINAL VOLUME!!
HOOO!
NO FAIR!!
YEAH!

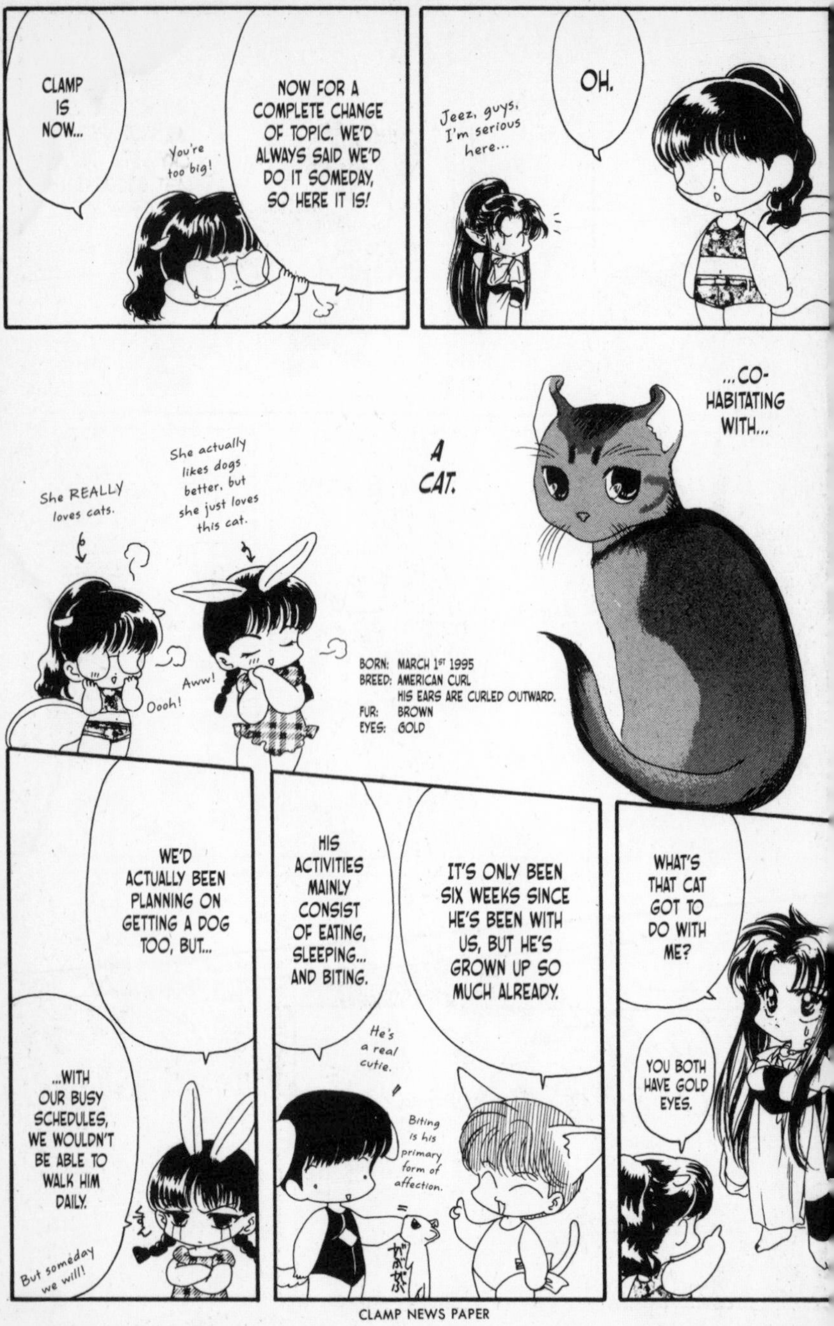
OH.
Jeez, guys, I'm serious here...
NOW FOR A COMPLETE CHANGE OF TOPIC. WE'D ALWAYS SAID WE'D DO IT SOMEDAY, SO HERE IT IS!
CLAMP IS NOW...
You're too big!
...CO-HABITATING WITH...
A CAT.
BORN: MARCH 1ST 1995
BREED: AMERICAN CURL
HIS EARS ARE CURLED OUTWARD.
FUR: BROWN
EYES: GOLD
She actually likes dogs better, but she just loves this cat.
Aww!
She REALLY loves cats.
Oooh!
WHAT'S THAT CAT GOT TO DO WITH ME?
YOU BOTH HAVE GOLD EYES.
IT'S ONLY BEEN SIX WEEKS SINCE HE'S BEEN WITH US, BUT HE'S GROWN UP SO MUCH ALREADY.
HIS ACTIVITIES MAINLY CONSIST OF EATING, SLEEPING... AND BITING.
He's a real cutie.
Biting is his primary form of affection.
WE'D ACTUALLY BEEN PLANNING ON GETTING A DOG TOO, BUT...
...WITH OUR BUSY SCHEDULES, WE WOULDN'T BE ABLE TO WALK HIM DAILY.
But someday we will!

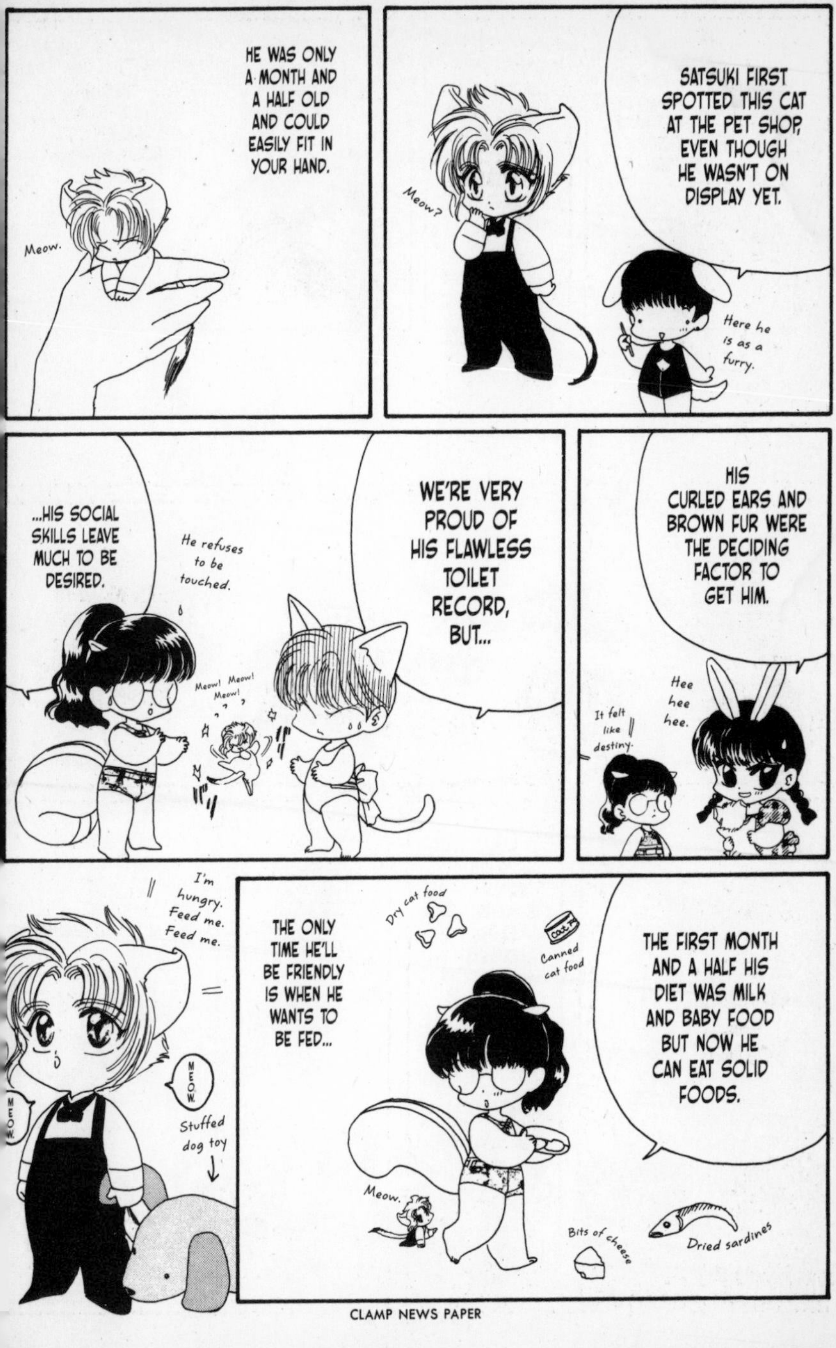
SATSUKI FIRST SPOTTED THIS CAT AT THE PET SHOP, EVEN THOUGH HE WASN'T ON DISPLAY YET.
Meow?
Here he is as a furry.
HE WAS ONLY A MONTH AND A HALF OLD AND COULD EASILY FIT IN YOUR HAND.
Meow.
HIS CURLED EARS AND BROWN FUR WERE THE DECIDING FACTOR TO GET HIM.
Hee hee hee.
It felt like destiny.
WE'RE VERY PROUD OF HIS FLAWLESS TOILET RECORD, BUT...
...HIS SOCIAL SKILLS LEAVE MUCH TO BE DESIRED.
He refuses to be touched.
Meow! Meow! Meow!
THE FIRST MONTH AND A HALF HIS DIET WAS MILK AND BABY FOOD BUT NOW HE CAN EAT SOLID FOODS.
Canned cat food
Dry cat food
THE ONLY TIME HE'LL BE FRIENDLY IS WHEN HE WANTS TO BE FED...
Meow.
Bits of cheese
Dried sardines
I'm hungry. Feed me. Feed me.
MEOW.
MEOW.
Stuffed dog toy

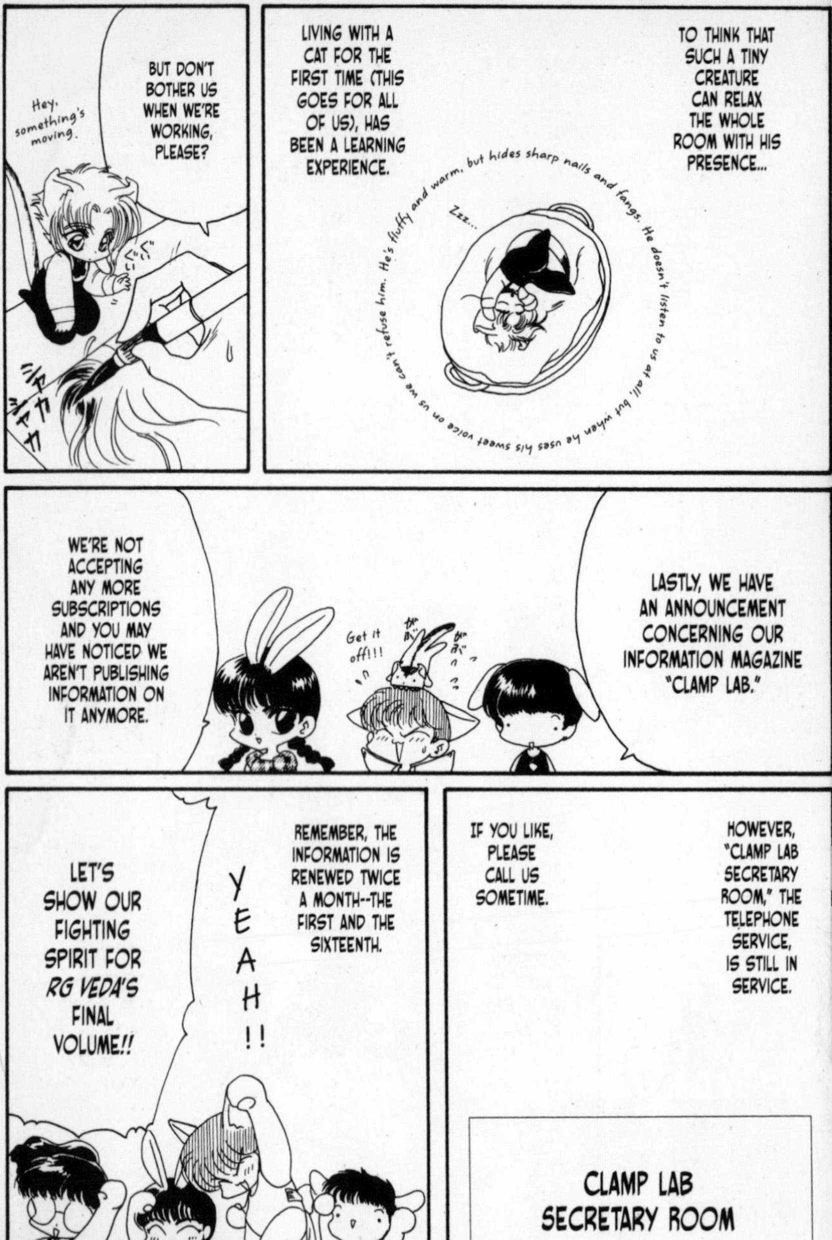
TO THINK THAT SUCH A TINY CREATURE CAN RELAX THE WHOLE ROOM WITH HIS PRESENCE...
LIVING WITH A CAT FOR THE FIRST TIME (THIS GOES FOR ALL OF US), HAS BEEN A LEARNING EXPERIENCE.
He's fluffy and warm, but hides sharp nails and fangs. He doesn't listen to us at all, but when he uses his sweet voice on us we can't refuse him.
Zzz...
BUT DON'T BOTHER US WHEN WE'RE WORKING, PLEASE?
Hey, something's moving.
LASTLY, WE HAVE AN ANNOUNCEMENT CONCERNING OUR INFORMATION MAGAZINE "CLAMP LAB."
Get it off!!!
WE'RE NOT ACCEPTING ANY MORE SUBSCRIPTIONS AND YOU MAY HAVE NOTICED WE AREN'T PUBLISHING INFORMATION ON IT ANYMORE.
HOWEVER, "CLAMP LAB SECRETARY ROOM," THE TELEPHONE SERVICE, IS STILL IN SERVICE.
IF YOU LIKE, PLEASE CALL US SOMETIME.
CLAMP LAB SECRETARY ROOM
REMEMBER, THE INFORMATION IS RENEWED TWICE A MONTH--THE FIRST AND THE SIXTEENTH.
YEAH!!
LET'S SHOW OUR FIGHTING SPIRIT FOR RG VEDA'S FINAL VOLUME!!
SEE YOU IN RG VEDA VOLUME 10...WE HOPE.

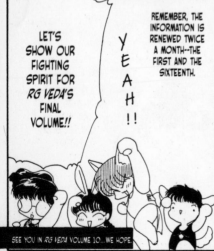

NEXT TIME IN RG VEDA

THE FINAL SHOWDOWN BETWEEN THE SIX STARS AND TAISHAKUTEN'S FORCES CONTINUES. AS LONG-KEPT SECRETS ARE FINALLY REVEALED AND DESTINY'S FABRIC UNFURLS, WILL THE BONDS FORGED BETWEEN FRIENDS AND LOVERS DEFY THE HEAVENS, OR IS THE FUTURE IMMUTABLE?

COMING SOON!

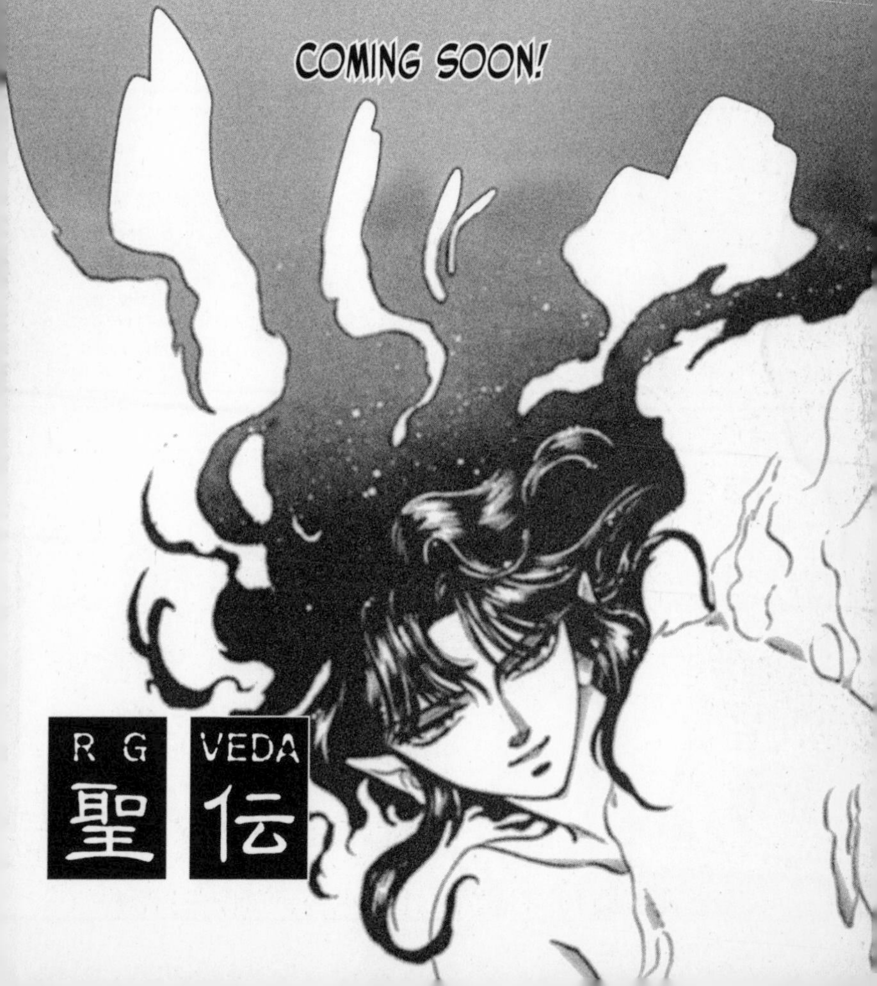
R G
聖
VEDA
伝

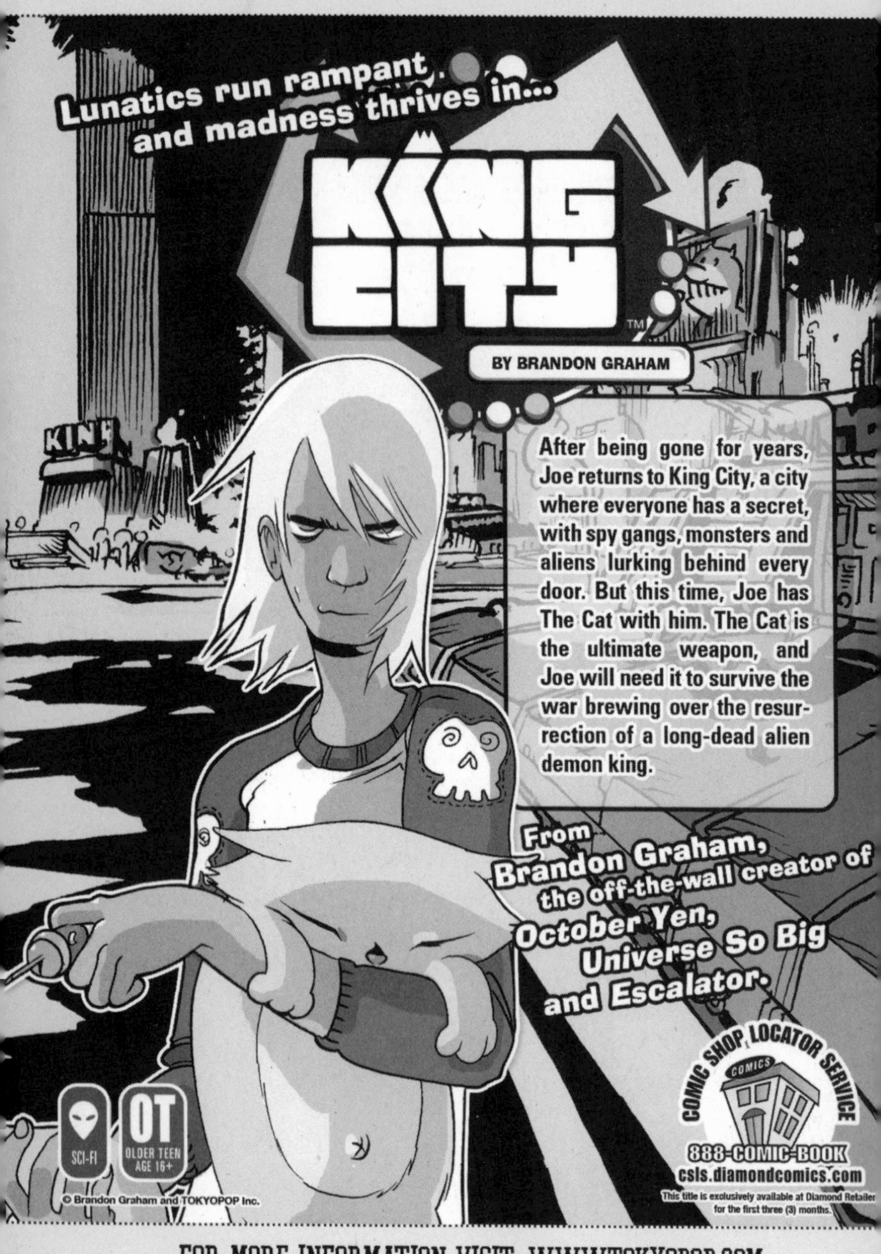
Lunatics run rampant... and madness thrives in...
KING CITY™
BY BRANDON GRAHAM
After being gone for years, Joe returns to King City, a city where everyone has a secret, with spy gangs, monsters and aliens lurking behind every door. But this time, Joe has The Cat with him. The Cat is the ultimate weapon, and Joe will need it to survive the war brewing over the resurrection of a long-dead alien demon king.
From Brandon Graham, the off-the-wall creator of October Yen, Universe So Big and Escalator.
SCI-FI
OT OLDER TEEN AGE 16+
© Brandon Graham and TOKYOPOP Inc.
COMIC SHOP LOCATOR SERVICE
COMICS
888-COMIC-BOOK
csls.diamondcomics.com
This title is exclusively available at Diamond Retailer for the first three (3) months.